Hoover Institution Publications 149

Herbert Hoover

HERBERT HOOVER

President of the United States

Edgar Eugene Robinson

and

Vaughn Davis Bornet

1975
Hoover Institution Press
Stanford University
Stanford, California

The Hoover Institution on War, Revolution and Peace, founded at Stanford University in 1919 by the late President Herbert Hoover, is a center for advanced study and research on public and international affairs in the twentieth century. The views expressed in its publications are entirely those of the authors and do not necessarily reflect the views of the staff, officers, or Board of Overseers of the Hoover Institution.

Hoover Institution Publications 149
International Standard Book Number 0–8179–1491–9
Library of Congress Catalog Card Number 75–18666
© 1975 by the Board of Trustees of the
     Leland Stanford Junior University
All rights reserved
Printed in the United States of America

You convey too great a compliment when you say that I have earned the right to the presidential nomination. No man can establish such an obligation upon any part of the American people. My country owes me no debt. It gave me, as it gives every boy and girl, a chance. It gave me schooling, independence of action, opportunity for service and honor. In no other land could a boy from a country village, without inheritance or influential friends, look forward with unbounded hope.

My whole life has taught me what America means. I am indebted to my country beyond any human power to repay. It conferred upon me the mission to administer America's response to the appeal of afflicted nations during the war. It has called me into the cabinets of two Presidents. By these experiences I have observed the burdens and responsibilities of the greatest office in the world. That office touches the happiness of every home. It deals with the peace of nations. No man could think of it except in terms of solemn consecration.

Secretary Hoover's statement to the
Republican Convention, 1928.

Books by Edgar Eugene Robinson

Powers of the President in Foreign Affairs, 1945–1965
    (Editor and Contributor)
The Memoirs of Ray Lyman Wilbur
    (Coeditor with Paul Carroll Edwards)
The Roosevelt Leadership, 1933–1945
They Voted For Roosevelt
The New United States
The Presidential Vote, 1936
American Democracy in Time of Crisis
The Presidential Vote, 1896–1932
Evolution of American Political Parties
The Foreign Policy of Woodrow Wilson
    (Coauthor with Victor J. West)

Books by Vaughn Davis Bornet

Labor Politics in a Democratic Republic
The Heart Future
    (For the Committee on Future Role, American
        Heart Association)
Welfare in America
California Social Welfare: Legislation, Financing, Services, Statistics
Ideas in Conflict
    (Contributor)

Contents

Preface		ix
Acknowledgments		xi
Photographs		xiii
Introduction		1
1.	A Crisis in American Politics	3
2.	Why Hoover Was Chosen	10
3.	A New Kind of President	25
4.	The Politics of the New Day	39
5.	Plans for the National Estate	52
6.	Hoover and the Farmer	68
7.	The Palsied Hand of Prohibition	82
8.	Legacy in Foreign Relations	97
9.	A Hostile Senate: The Tariff	110
10.	Financial Catastrophe: 1929–	123
11.	The President's Party Abdicates	134
12.	The Voters Turn Away	150
13.	A Political Impasse	168
14.	Hoover's Leadership in the World of 1931	179
15.	A Program for a New Congress	208
16.	The Politics of Distress: Bonus Marchers	228
17.	Hoover in the Campaign of 1932	239
18.	Hoover's Program for the Future	255
19.	Revolution by Election	267
20.	The United States at the Crossroads	279
	Epilogue	300
	The Historical Record	307
	Notes	333
	Index	389

Preface

In the long life of Herbert Hoover, the four years as president of the United States, 1929–1933, sometimes appear as only an interlude in a fruitful public career. Yet those years in the life of the nation were of crucial significance. The decades that have passed since then have revealed how the political and economic struggles in those presidential years shook the foundations of government in the United States. Action in the national interest was made exceedingly difficult as the special interests of states and sections, and the demands of local constituencies on their elected representatives in the nation's capital, inhibited action. That political conflict, which occurred at a crossroads in American history, is the primary concern of this book.

This book owes its origin to many conversations between Edgar Eugene Robinson and Herbert Hoover during the long period following his retirement from the presidency. These conversations took place on the Stanford University campus, where the Hoovers had a home, as well as at the Hoover residence of later years in New York City. Hoover's talk ranged over a wide variety of subjects, reflecting his extraordinary intellectual grasp of the economic and political problems confronting the world of his era.

The reader of history and biography must somehow divorce himself from the day and times of his reading and move back to an earlier era—in this case, to an old America of low (or no) income taxes, almost no social insurance programs in the federal government, and a very modest defense establishment maintained without a draft. The people of that time were engaged in a romance with radio loudspeakers and talking motion pictures. A new scientific age seemed to be dawning.

Research on the book extended over a period of two decades. Extensive use of the Hoover archival materials when the presidential papers were housed in the Hoover Library (later the Hoover Institution) was supplemented by use of manuscript collections in the Library of Congress. Account has been taken of recent publications on the Hoover theme and of such newly available resources as the 327 oral history reminis-

cences prepared under the auspices of the Herbert Hoover Presidential
Library Association, the lengthy diary of Henry L. Stimson, and other
materials. The vast holdings of the Herbert Hoover Presidential Library
at West Branch, Iowa, where the presidential archives were finally housed
together with related collections; manuscripts held in the Hoover Institution, Stanford, California; and the words of the president in conference,
speech, letter, and memoir are in the final analysis fundamental to this
book's story of the presidency of Herbert Hoover, 1929–1933.

EDGAR EUGENE ROBINSON

VAUGHN DAVIS BORNET

Acknowledgments

Innumerable friends and colleagues of Herbert Hoover contributed ideas and information during the preparation of this book. Ray Lyman Wilbur was especially helpful. His 3,500 pages of autobiographical material were particularly rewarding for insights into the inner life of the administration and the activities of the associates of President Hoover. Publications by an emerging generation of scholars on the life of Hoover offered factual and bibliographical assistance and new concepts. In the Manuscript Division of the Library of Congress we received valuable assistance from David C. Mearns, chief of the division, and from Katharine E. Brand, head of Recent Manuscripts Collections.

At Stanford University, the advice and counsel of President J. E. Wallace Sterling was greatly appreciated. Professor Thomas A. Bailey, who read the manuscript at several stages, made valuable suggestions. The directors of the Hoover Institution and the director and staff of the Stanford University Libraries were cooperative. Director W. Glenn Campbell made available to us all of the facilities of the Hoover Institution. At the Herbert Hoover Presidential Library in West Branch, Iowa, the work was greatly furthered by Library Director Thomas T. Thalken and his staff, especially Robert S. Wood, Dwight Miller, and Dale C. Mayer. Milorad Drachkovitch, Franz G. Lassner and Charles Palm, archivists of the Hoover Institution, and their staffs provided access to manuscript holdings and especially to the oral history reminiscences of Herbert Hoover prepared by Raymond Henle and others. At Southern Oregon State College, President James K. Sours, Library Director Norman Alexander, members of the library staff, the Research Committee, and Elizabeth Wilson eased many burdens.

A number of individuals gave permission to quote from their personal papers and from those of relatives. Special mention is especially warranted in the cases of Yale University, for permission to quote from the diary of Henry L. Stimson; the Herbert Hoover Presidential Library Association, Inc., for permission to quote from the oral history reminiscences; and Frank E. Mason who, on behalf of Allan Hoover and the

Hoover family, permitted quotation from the published writings of Herbert Hoover.

The editorial services of Marjorie Cutler were invaluable. Acknowledgment is made to many librarians, archivists, fellow researchers, and typists who need to be aware of the gratitude that is theirs. As always, the patience and encouragement of Beth W. Bornet were a comfort. At Hoover Institution Press, Brien Benson and Mickey G. Hamilton handled details of publication; Jean McIntosh read proof; and Sharon Willy compiled the index.

Finally, our thanks to Lisette Fast Robinson for her aid at each step in the preparation of this book.

Photographs

President and Mrs. Harding with Secretary of Commerce Hoover at a baseball game, Washington, D.C., April 13, 1922. *(Courtesy of Hoover Institution)*

President Coolidge with Secretary of Commerce Hoover, June 1928. *(Courtesy of Hoover Institution)*

The presidential candidate rides with California politicians: *center*, Burton R. Fitts, Lieutenant Governor; *right*, James Rolph, mayor of San Francisco, July 27, 1928. (*Wide World Photos*)

Charles A. Lindbergh discusses the future of commercial aviation with Secretary of Commerce Hoover, Washington, D.C., 1927, after lunch at the Hoover home. (*Courtesy of Hoover Library*)

The president-elect gives his daughter-in-law an American National Red Cross membership donation, November 16, 1928. *(Courtesy of Hoover Institution)*

The talking motion picture comes to the aid of American politics. *(Courtesy of Hoover Library)*

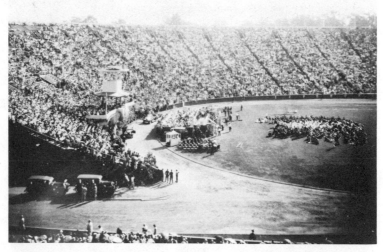

The scene in Stanford University football stadium during Hoover's acceptance speech, August 11, 1928. *(Courtesy of Hoover Institution)*

Herbert Hoover, Jr. *(left)*, age 23, candidate Hoover, and Allan Hoover *(right)*, age 20, at the S Street home in Washington, D.C., June 17, 1928. *(Underwood & Underwood)*

The candidate for
president at ease,
Palo Alto,
California, 1928.
*(Courtesy of
Hoover Institution)*

The candidate with his family, November 5, 1928, on the threshold of their home on
the Stanford campus. *Left to right:* Herbert Hoover, Jr., Mrs. Herbert Hoover, Jr.,
holding her son, Herbert III; Mrs. Hoover; Herbert Hoover holding Peggy, daughter of
his son Herbert; and Allan Hoover, younger son of the candidate. *(Wide World Photos)*

A Hoover doodle, apparently drawn at a budget meeting,
November 20, 1929. (*Courtesy of Hoover Library*)

Hoover with his friend Charles
Gates Dawes at the Dawes's
home in Evanston, Illinois,
July 17, 1928. (*International
Newsreel*—COMPIX)

The presidential
candidate with his
dog King Tut.
*(Underwood &
Underwood)*

Hoover cabinet members. *Sitting (left to right):* Patrick J. Hurley, secretary of war;
Charles Curtis, vice-president; President Hoover; Henry L. Stimson, secretary of state;
Andrew W. Mellon, secretary of the treasury. *Standing (left to right):* Robert P. Lamont,
secretary of commerce; Ray Lyman Wilbur, secretary of the interior; Walter F. Brown,
postmaster general; William D. Mitchell, attorney general; Arthur M. Hyde, secretary
of agriculture; Charles F. Adams, secretary of the navy; William N. Doak, secretary
of labor. *(Courtesy of Hoover Institution)*

The Haig Patigan green bronze bust commissioned by the Bohemian Club of San Francisco, 1929, as photographed by Gabriel Moulin. *(Gabriel Moulin Studios, San Francisco)*

The president and Prime Minister Ramsay MacDonald, October 1929. *(Harris & Ewing, Washington, D.C.)*

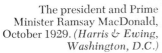

Hoover and grand-
daughter Peggy Ann,
leaving church after a
George Washington
memorial service,
February 22, 1931.
*(International
Newsreel*—COMPIX)

Hoover, dressed for relaxation, continues work
while aboard the U.S.S. *Arizona*, March 27,
1931. (*Acme*—COMPIX)

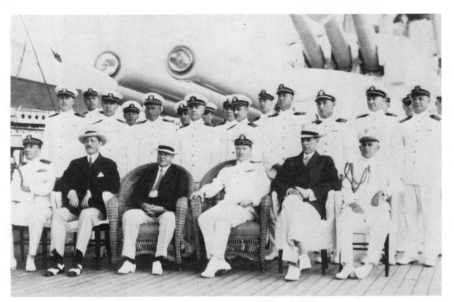

President Hoover en route to Puerto Rico and the Virgin Islands, March 1931, with *(left to right):* Captain Russell Train, the president's naval aide; Secretary of War Hurley; battleship *Arizona* Captain Charles S. Freeman; Secretary of the Interior Wilbur; and Colonel Blackshear Hodges, Hoover's military aide. *(Courtesy of Hoover Institution)*

The president rides "Billy" at Rapidan Camp, August 20, 1932. *(Underwood & Underwood)*

The president with members of the Republican National Committee, December 16, 1931 (J. Francis Burke is on Hoover's right and Senator Simeon D. Fess is on his left). *(International Newsreel*–COMPIX*)*

President Hoover and the Wickersham Commission. *(Courtesy of Signal Corps)*

German bank depositors assemble in response to the partial reopening of a bank in Berlin, July 16, 1931. *(Wide World Photos)*

A concerned president confers with two leaders charged with planning unemployment relief: *left*, Walter S. Gifford; *right*, Owen D. Young, September 18, 1931. *(Wide World Photos)*

A grim president leaving the Capitol after urging the Senate to act, May 31, 1932. *(Courtesy of Hoover Library)*

The Bonus Army and some dependents rest after a long day of pressuring Congress, July 5, 1932. *(Courtesy of Signal Corps)*

Walter H. Newton, secretary to President Hoover and coauthor of
The Hoover Administration, at his desk. *(Courtesy of Hoover Library)*

Theodore Joslin,
secretary to President
Hoover and author of
Hoover Off the Record,
at the White House,
1932. *(Courtesy of
Hoover Library)*

Hoover with members of the press. *(Courtesy of Hoover Institution)*

The candidate delivers a speech in San Francisco during the 1932 election campaign. *(Courtesy of Hoover Institution)*

Lou Henry Hoover
greets an Iowa
crowd from the
observation
platform, 1932.
*(Courtesy of James
A. Kent, Iowa City)*

A crowd greets candidate Hoover in San Francisco on election day, November 8, 1932.
(Courtesy of Hoover Institution)

The departing president bids farewell to the loyal "Little Cabinet," the hardworking secretaries of cabinet members, March 3, 1933. *(International Newsreel—COMPIX)*

The outgoing and incoming presidents talk pleasantly together on Inauguration Day, March 4, 1933. *(Courtesy of Hoover Library)*

The former president opens birthday greetings,
August 10, 1933. *(International Newsreel*—COMPIX*)*

Introduction

7:30–7:40, walking. Breakfast. No guests. 8:30–9:45,
to office. Beginning at 10:30 officials began to arrive
and were shown to the Blue Room.
White House *"Appointments Book,"* March 4, 1929

At eight minutes past one o'clock on March 4, 1929, Herbert Hoover came forward on the inaugural platform to take the oath of office as president of the United States. Hoover was well known to the thousands who had gathered before the Capitol on that rainy spring morning. As secretary of commerce he had served President Coolidge, with whom he had walked to the inaugural platform, and he had long been associated with Chief Justice Taft, who was to administer the oath of office.

The elaborate inaugural ceremony and the ensuing parade appeared (to many more Americans than ever before because of radio coverage by 117 stations) to be the launching of a new venture. In truth, of course, it was not a new innovation. Rather, it was a reaffirmation, by familiar and time-worn rites, of belief in presidential government.

The heart of the political situation in Washington was not in this ceremony, however, but in the preceding special session in the Senate, where Hoover and members of the Senate had witnessed the inauguration of Vice-President Charles Curtis. This was also the beginning of a new session for the ninety-five senators (there was one vacancy) who were to serve variously the next two, four, or six years. It symbolized the continuous element in the government of the United States, which had never experienced a break since the Senate first convened in New York City in 1789. It was then, after many days of waiting, that the Senate had arranged with the coordinating House of Representatives for the inauguration of President George Washington. The bicentennial of Washington's birth would be celebrated in the administration about to begin.

So, as they stood there together, senators and incoming president could take measure of each other. Half of the senators in this historic body had served in the capital for a quarter of a century. Five senators had actually been in office since the opening of the century. Fifty-four were older than the president, and five could have voted the year Herbert

1

Hoover was born. A Republican senator, Hiram W. Johnson, the most caustic critic of Hoover and his political rival in California throughout the preceding decade, would write to his son on the evening of this inauguration day in scathing terms of both outgoing President Calvin Coolidge and incoming President Herbert Hoover.

The lines were drawn: president and Congress, Republicans and Democrats. Soon other stress lines would be accentuated between wets and drys, high and low tariff advocates, foreign policy interpreters, and protagonists of programs in finance and in government assistance to citizens.

At the heart of President Hoover's program was his conception of mankind's adaptation to the new scientific age that had dawned with the opening of the twentieth century. As an engineer with scientific training and years of world-wide experience, as an administrator of sizable organizations, and as a notably successful cabinet officer under two presidents, he was keenly aware of the benefits that could flow from cooperation with nature in flight by air and communication by radio wave. The mechanical efficiencies that might flow from peacetime development of natural resources together with the ingenuity of men in creating powerful new technological tools were to Hoover familiar means to link man to a great new destiny. Herbert Hoover was at the time the prophet of a new age.

— 1 —

A Crisis in American Politics

There is no national party choice except that of President. No one else represents the people as a whole, exercising a national choice. . . . He can dominate his party by being spokesman for the real sentiment and purpose of the country, by giving direction to opinions, by giving the country at once the information and the statements of policy which will enable it to form its judgments alike of parties and men. . . . For he is also the political leader of the nation, or has it in his choice to be.

Woodrow Wilson, *Constitutional Government*

The Constitution of the United States provided for a "President of the United States." The task of assigning executive and legislative responsibility in the new government would have been easier, however, had the founding fathers provided for a king.

After all, at the time of the Constitutional Convention the accepted form of executive power known to Americans was monarchical. The idea of a hereditary monarch for the new nation was considered—and abandoned. But the powers soon delegated to the office of president were among the powers of a king. True, those powers were checked by the division of function with the Senate, by the span of elective term, and by the elaborate machinery of regular election. Yet the extent of presidential power was felt by those who were instrumental in creating this office. Washington himself, not long after taking the office, favored for a time the title "His High Mightiness, the President of the United States and Protector of their Liberties."

Washington as king might one day have died a popular monarch. The government might then have been in the hands of Hamilton (as

3

prime minister) while the leader of the opposition, Jefferson, might have
obtained and enjoyed a leadership role in the Congress without the necessity of aspiring to kingship.

To be elected president of the United States, even by indirect process,
has always required the support of an immense body of voters. It is they
who have chosen an executive. They have not found it an easy task, however, to choose a legislative program; nor has the choice of representatives
necessarily brought specific legislation into being.

American political parties would arrive, outside the government, to
deal with this problem. Operated by persons not always elected by the
people, parties have flourished as vehicles for the expression of public
opinion. As agencies for the selection and support of representatives holding public office, parties respond to public pressure through elections in
which party candidates appeal for support.

In precinct, county, state, and nation these party groups control politics. Individual members of the group aspire to office, and all members
exercise influence in achieving political results without holding elective
office. The parties in the dozen largest states have dominated national
elections, determining the outcome in considerable measure through the
national party organizations. The controlling members of these parties
have not been widely known. None has been a representative of the
people in government offices; almost all have worked behind the scenes.

Yet parties, as they aspire to achieve control of the national government, accept the leadership of those who somehow appear to fulfill the
desires of the people. So party managers have kept parties alive, but
presidents have given parties substance and meaning. The success of the
United States as a self-governing nation, indeed, may rest in a reassess-
ment of the presidency as the symbol of leadership. We would have a
much clearer understanding of the history of the United States since
1900, for example, if we knew exactly how each president dealt with the
groups who controlled party organization.

In any case, an understanding of the way in which Hoover presented
his program and in the end failed to attain many of his objectives in the
period 1929–1933 must begin with insight into party precedent and practice in the twentieth century.

With such an approach, we might understand why William McKinley,
at the beginning of the century, was on the whole thought of as a successful president, and why Theodore Roosevelt, in the important years to
1909, was thought to accomplish the popular will despite what those in
power in the Congress wished him to do. The administration of William
Howard Taft appears as the struggle of the president against a group of
"independents" within his own party who opposed him because of his

subservience to the great economic powers that dominated in the party organization. President Taft was unable to control the power inherent in the very party organization that had created him.

Woodrow Wilson was successful because he cooperated with his majorities in the Congress—although these majorities also represented a minority of the people of the United States. Wilson and his supporters in Congress were able, for a time, to provide a legislative and executive program because the Democratic party organization acquiesced in what Wilson proposed.

It was with the Harding nomination that the failure of direct self-government by a whole people was clearly revealed. Then it was that it came to be fully realized that the destinies of the people of the United States were controlled by party organizations, especially in regard to nominations for the highest office in the land.

It is an accepted fact that in our American practice the dissenter occupies a major place in the public eye. Born in the initial atmosphere of the early Republic and nurtured by the teachings of the Christian religion, this tradition of attention to minority views lives in the American attitude toward government. Criticism of prevailing practices and of those in office always has a hearing, even though specified change may be slow in coming. Much can be said for the right of individuals to protest, and to organize others in support of protest, and if sufficient public support is won during elections—to take over the government. Our present political parties have risen in this way (Jefferson as founder of the Democratic Republicans, later the Democrats, in 1800, and Lincoln as leader of the Republican party in 1860). Thus it is inevitable that parties not only protest and propose programs, but attack, abuse, and try to overwhelm those in power in the hope of their retreat from office. Still, change is not the whole story, by any means, and the party platforms over the years show much continuity.

The most powerful challenge to presidential leadership has been provided by those who controlled the party organizations. The party chairman and the national committee of the party are important even when negative in influence. They have been a constant influence in elections won or lost, and they have some role (or attempt to have one) in almost any action taken by the elected officers of the government. But famous senators or congressmen have often been "above" the national, state, or precinct committeemen who hoped to exert influence. At times, the chairman of the national committee of one or the other of the two national parties has won a national hearing, and, in fact, has been recognized as exercising a truly national influence. This was true of Senator Mark Hanna of Ohio, who, as chairman of the Republican National Committee in 1896,

secured and directed the nomination of Governor William McKinley of
Ohio for the presidency.

Characteristic of the American attitude toward political leadership
throughout the first third of the century was the people's enthusiasm for
political leaders who had been nominated for the presidency but had
failed of election. A half-dozen men in national politics in those years
achieved durable national recognition because they had tried and failed
to reach presidential office. Some of these might-have-beens—William
Jennings Bryan, Robert M. LaFollette, and Alfred E. Smith—swayed the
thinking and certainly the emotions of large groups within the electorate.

Another group whose leadership appealed to the public was composed of the sectional representatives in the Congress. A people interested
in regional needs clung to such leaders (who could somehow represent
"silver" or "corn" or mountains or prairies).

Sometimes in this period individuals in the Congress were thought of
as providing national leadership. A Speaker of the House of Representatives like Joseph Cannon was one who provided such leadership. Sometimes it was an outstanding congressman like George Norris of Nebraska,
later a senator, who in 1910 forced a change in the rules of the House
which greatly strengthened the power and opportunity of the individual
member.

Presidential leadership cannot be treated apart from the opposition
frequently expressed by influential newspaper publishers like William
Randolph Hearst, by nationally distributed columnists, and by influential
magazines. With each of these, criticism has been more meaningful than
support. Wilson found this notably true, as did Theodore Roosevelt before
him. It was of crucial importance to the Taft administration. This type of
critical opposition was of only minor influence during the Harding and
Coolidge administrations, but it was to become infinitely sharper during
the Hoover presidency.

When President McKinley was assassinated by an avowed anarchist
in September 1901, the American people had their first sharp intimation
of an intended world revolution through violence. At the time, however,
it seemed entirely alien to their purposes and hopes.

That McKinley catastrophe, the meaning of which was but dimly
understood at the time, was obscured by the stirring events of the seven
subsequent years of the affirmative, vigorous, and aggressive leadership of
Theodore Roosevelt. He came to be recognized as a peculiarly American
symbol, one who would bear the aspect of regular, insurgent, and rebel
in American politics. As president he took a road in domestic and foreign
affairs that all of his successors in that office have had to consider. He
left no doubt concerning his standard. As president he was leader of the

American people. Nevertheless, he was never able to dominate the Republican party organization.

Not until Roosevelt's defeat in 1912, as candidate of the most promising third party to appear in American politics since the Civil War, was it clear what he had done to American political practice. Representatives of the Middle and Far West had broken outworn party rules, but none had the opportunity, the audacity, and the vision of Roosevelt in both domestic and foreign policy. He did not accept the doctrines of the ruling elements in the Republican party. In his middle course and his pragmatic approach, he never betrayed the basic meaning of earlier American political experience. Builders of a free society must be free. Participants in a free society must be informed.

Perhaps nothing was so characteristic of the "politics" of the period 1901–1929 as the slogan "restore the government to the people." This appealed to many of the electorate who felt that party organizations had become subservient to special interests. (Yet calls for fundamental change in the basis of American economic life came only from Socialists and the "independents" who felt as they did.) The average citizen was quite content to believe that the managers of the great political enterprise they called the United States were the practical men known as "politicians."

The presidents who met the desires of the majority in those years were men who held the view that party organization was essential. McKinley, Taft, Harding, and Coolidge upheld the basic principle of party as it had developed in the United States—that is, that the president is the coordinating power, rather than a single superior leader.

Theodore Roosevelt and Woodrow Wilson held no such view. The high place they occupy in any roster prepared by experts is explained by the fact that they were leaders.[1] They used the presidential office to push programs of their own. Saying that they represented the people as a whole, they certainly did not represent the party organizations. When these presidents are called leaders in the American tradition, it is not because of their daily, routine use of constitutional power; rather, they were enabled by events to exercise, for a time, powers that bordered on the absolute. While Roosevelt and Wilson were not absolutists, of course, they were, even so, thought of by millions of the electorate as "saviors," especially in times of extraordinary crisis.

Throughout the twenties, the great private economic interests of the nation continued to build a structure in finance, in production, and, to a lesser extent, in distribution, quite apart from governmental support. The war period had witnessed a growth of power in labor organizations. The farming population was a declining factor in an industrial nation, and had a diminishing influence on national thought. The farmer made up for it—indeed it was a reflection of his condition—by insistent calls for government action to aid him in his plight.

Basically, government and business cooperated. Economy in government and business methods applied to government expenditure fitted well into this picture. Two developments showed clearly the direction of Republican planning. One was the passage in 1922 of the Fordney-McCumber Tariff Bill, which provided the highest protection for American products to that point in American history. The other was tax reduction legislation, which released profits for speculative use by American business. By the end of the decade the results of these governmental policies were evident not only in the reduction of the public debt by one-half, but in the tremendous sums released for investment and in the resultant stock market inflation.

There was an official Republican position upon the issue of government ownership with reference to such wartime-launched projects as Muscle Shoals on the Tennessee River (the future TVA): maintain government apart from the traditional field of private enterprise. But within the ranks of Republican representation in the Senate and the House were vigorous opponents of such a view. Still, the railroads were returned to private ownership after the war.

It is doubtful whether the basic issue of government ownership and control was apparent to any large number of citizens. There was no great debate at the time. Those of "liberal" view spent much effort in comment on the scandals of the Harding administration and condemnation of the complacencies of the Coolidge administration.[2] In general, these years were filled with minor struggles in American politics despite the Progressive candidacy of Robert M. LaFollette in 1924.

As the Coolidge administration approached an end, signs appeared that the close cooperation of government and business had produced decided benefits for the industrialist, the financier, those who had money to invest, and millions of wage earning Americans. Yet some who labored in factory or farm did not profit fully (despite the general increase in real wages), so that prosperity was unevenly distributed.

The events of the Harding-Coolidge era, 1921–1929, produced a group of senior leaders in the Republican party who secured and then held national attention. Senator Robert M. LaFollette aspired to the presidency, only to be defeated as the candidate of the Progressive party in 1924. But there remained in the Senate, untouched by LaFollette's defeat, a formidable element of insurgency. William E. Borah had won his national reputation long before the fight over the League of Nations Covenant. George Norris had won national attention in his fight against Speaker of the House Cannon in 1910. Hiram W. Johnson was everywhere known as the running mate of Theodore Roosevelt in the disastrous campaign of the Progressive party in 1912. These Republican senators could claim national attention equal to that held by the presidents of those years.

The Republican party organization had never enjoyed so complete a unity of purpose and direction with party office-holders in executive and legislative branches as it did during the twenties. It appeared that there might be achieved in time a union of power in the presidency and in the Congress capable of working with party organization.

During the later years of the Coolidge administration, renewed interest in the possible selection of a member of the Senate as the Republican presidential nominee grew from memory of the elevation of Senator Harding to the presidency. Thus, as the nation approached the election of 1928, the typical Republican party organization member favored neither "independent" Herbert Hoover, nor "outsider" Frank Lowden, ex-governor of Illinois. But many citizens were seeking a new type of leader in the modern world, and a few Americans saw that the provincialism of most nineteenth century chief executives was no longer possible. A state leader, a war hero, a party chieftan—none of these could now meet the need. A new president was to be a spokesman for a continental nation, a figure in all international discussions. He would be called upon to represent a financial and industrial giant preparing to take first place in the new age of science.

Thus, the crisis in American politics which had been in the making since the beginning of the century was at the breaking point in the late twenties. The crisis was inevitable, not merely because of profound changes in the social and economic structure of a nation entering a new age, but because growing awareness of the difficulties and perils of self-government made many people see that a naïve view of party organization and of party allegiance was no longer possible in the United States.

— 2 —

Why Hoover Was Chosen

✓ *It is a complete answer to those Republicans who ask anxiously what will become of the party organization under Mr. Hoover. Let them study his record, let them realize that organization and collective effort are his mainstays, and they will appreciate that after four years of Hoover as President, the Republican party will be better organized, more effective, and more vigorous than in many a long year. He will inspire it with a new life and spirit, and will make a particularly strong appeal to men and women of the younger generation who do not seem fully to appreciate how important a part of the machinery of government our parties are.*

Ogden Mills, March 16, 1928,
Mills Papers, Library of Congress

The belief and the faith of many who brought Herbert Hoover to the presidency rests in the impression made upon the public mind long before he became an active participant in the cabinets of two Republican presidents.

American missionary workers overseas had been considered for more than a century to be part of the American contribution to the welfare of mankind. As American goods and methods and businessmen expanded into all parts of the world, it was still the American missionary who seemed—to those who considered the matter of international relations— the person most representative of American idealism.[1] Inasmuch as America had been throughout its history the land of opportunity for those seeking a better life, any American overseas whose career combined individual success with a desire to help those in need was certain to appear characteristically American. After 1914 it was easy for many to see Hoover the engineer in this symbolic role. This would prove important.

Hoover's approach to government and politics was unusual. To him, politics was not the basic concern of Americans; government was. He believed that only as the problems of government were comprehended by the people could there be any functioning of democracy. Such a belief grew out of his own diversified experiences.

He had dealt with governments in various parts of the world, yet it was not until his service in London in 1914–1917 in organizing the relief of Belgium that he had given much thought to the relationship which he himself might bear to government. He entered upon that vast project of relief as a volunteer; as such, he organized volunteers. He created an organization to carry on what was in a very real sense a public enterprise, although it was in private hands.

His experience in Europe and his relations with the governments of Great Britain, France, and Germany, as well as of Belgium, left him with convictions about how government might best be carried on. But his was not the view of one participating overseas as a representative of the people nor was it the view of the scholar studiously and minutely analyzing government. Rather, it was the view of an observer who watched what governments were doing, viewed problems officials were called upon to solve, and sensed how those placed in public office related what they were doing to what their constituents expected them to do (or judged them for not doing).

Hoover's early contacts with the government of the United States were essentially those of a volunteer.[2] He was appointed United States Food Administrator by President Wilson on May 5, 1917, and served until the Food Administration was dissolved in late 1918. This appointment was a natural outgrowth of the voluntary activity he had given Belgian Relief. In his work in the Food Administration he came into direct contact with the citizens of the United States. His role was as the leader of a great voluntary undertaking to save food, especially wheat and sugar, for the benefit of the allies.

At the same time, this work brought him into direct contact with a president, in this case Wilson, who was carrying on the manifold duties of the head of government. Hoover soon discovered a political part of life: that the president is bound to a considerable degree by the views of leaders of his own party in the Congress. It was from Congress that Wilson needed to obtain not only official approval but appropriations to carry on the work of the new food conservation program in his administration.

Hoover was aware that, whereas the government (represented in either the person of the president or in the membership of the Congress) was the force with which he had to reckon directly, the vast population

of the United States was always there. What information they had, and
what propaganda they came to believe, were primary concerns. Hoover's
knowledge of how politicians operated grew greatly as he appeared
before committees of the Congress to explain and defend policies he had
adopted.

In the preliminaries of the campaign of 1920 Hoover had been thought
of by a great many citizens as a presidential candidate. In January, February, and March of 1920, the *New York Times* carried a number of stories
describing spontaneous and widespread movements in each of the parties,
notably in Georgia, Michigan and California, which revealed that Hoover
was considered a presidential possibility in both Republican and Democratic parties. Some prominent Democrats were publicly committed to his
candidacy. Franklin D. Roosevelt then referred to Herbert Hoover, in a
letter to a friend, as "certainly a wonder" and remarked, "I wish we could
make him President of the United States. There could not be a better
one."[3]

Hoover let it be known, however, that he had long been registered as
a Republican and considered himself a Republican. While some of his
adherents felt that this might lead to his nomination by the Republican
convention, it did not. The campaign to make him the Republican candidate was not supported by accepted leaders of the party. They nominated
instead Senator Harding, who was not well known to the public. They
won an overwhelming victory. Hoover's adherents were pushed aside by
practical politicians, and those who had seen in Hoover the promise of
efficient government in an era of problems now gave grudging support
to the party in the hope that success would crown a subsequent effort.

Soon, a considerable number of party organization members looked
with doubt upon the appointment of Hoover to the cabinet of President
Harding. Despite the fact that Hoover served throughout the period of
Harding's presidency and in the Coolidge years, the recollection persisted
that Hoover had been thought of by many as a man without strong party
ties. Moreover, he was considered to be an "old Progressive" and more
forward looking than most. Earlier in the year Harding had casually
written a constituent in precisely such a vein:

> You can get no dispute from me about the high qualifications of Mr.
> Hoover. I think he is really a very wonderful fellow. I think he is so really
> wonderful that he would probably be a candidate above the party which
> undertook to honor him, and of course that does not appeal to me, because
> I am abidingly a Party man. I believe ours is a Government to be operated
> through political parties and I think parties ought to make platforms, enum-

erate policies, and then choose candidates who best represent the policies enunciated.[4]

• During his eight years as a cabinet member, Hoover became familiar not only with the problems of the Congress, but with the trials and tribulations of the president himself. At the same time he came to be better known to the members of the Republican party in the Congress. He was visible also to leaders in the party organization who exercised great influence. As secretary of commerce, Hoover centered his attention upon the development of cooperation between business and government. Nor was this all. An economist judges:

> By focusing on Hoover as a "Depression President," historians have neglected too often those highly significant years in which he stimulated and directed American enterprise at home and abroad. His influence on such major problems as war debts, reparations, the tariff question, branch factories, and new foreign loans, has been underestimated. Likewise, historical analysts have given insufficient attention to Hoover's campaign against foreign monopolization of essential raw materials, even though much international controversy was aroused over this issue.[5]

Hoover's work in commerce brought him into close relationship with Andrew Mellon, secretary of the treasury, and from the outset he had a friendly association with Charles Evans Hughes, secretary of state.

At the close of his period of service as a cabinet officer he appeared to the voters as a devoted public servant, divorced from active politics almost as much as he had been during his long period of humanitarian service abroad and at home.

Still, the picture of Hoover in the minds of both the members of Congress and leading members of the Republican party organization was not the sketch that appeared to the people of the country as a whole.

Perhaps the most notable feature of Hoover's period of government service was his development of a program. He was not, while secretary of commerce, engaged in determining how far his program would appeal to great masses of people at election time, but in visualizing how far a program could be developed in many areas for the advancement of the people of the United States.[6]

It was often said of Hoover that he knew the world. He knew it in — depth as well as in its contemporary surface appearances. He knew the economic history of the nineteenth and twentieth centuries, a period during which the whole habitat of mankind had been subjected to profound changes wrought by industrialization and the mechanization of transpor-

⌐—tation. Hoover had entered upon his profession in the final decade of the nineteenth century, when Americans realized that a nation stretching across a continent, rich in natural resources, one that stood between the industrial population of western Europe and the awakening rural population of Asia, was bound to play a leading role in the new century.

There would be great services rendered by this atypical cabinet member (who was offered posts in the Departments of Agriculture and the Interior, as well as the one he occupied). It was clearly Hoover's determination, techniques, knowledge, and reliance on investigation into the facts that made it possible for the Harding administration to force reduction of the twelve-hour day in the steel industry to an eight-hour day. The famous Harding letter that put unbearable pressure on Judge Gary was written by Hoover.[7] Moreover, the pioneering President's Conference on Unemployment in the Harding years was strictly a Hoover enterprise, aided, as was often the case in the 1920s, by Edward Eyre Hunt.[8]

———Hoover envisaged the future as an outgrowth of the free enterprise system that had enabled the American people to achieve a higher degree of success in demonstrating the possibilities of a new economic era than had any other people in the world. He foresaw that mechanization of agriculture and the further development of continental transportation would in time remove much of the conflict between urban and rural economic interest. Increased use of natural resources was the basis of the new age, for it meant bulk processing of metals, refinement of oil for fuel, mass production of durable goods, and wider use of gas and electricity by a mounting population. Natural wealth harnessed to inventive processes confirmed his belief that in this new age the common man would surely advance. Ceaseless experimentation by experts was, Hoover thought, a necessary preliminary to continuous and needed change.

Friends of Hoover throughout the nation would in time enter upon a second movement to make him a nominee for the presidency. He himself had entertained the idea, even prior to this time, but it was only following the Coolidge statement in August 1927 that he "did not choose to run," that Hoover undertook an active campaign. In the course of the preliminary canvass for delegates to the Republican National Convention, it was at once apparent that the body of public leaders and politicians in the Republican party did not favor Hoover's candidacy, although there were exceptions. It was evident that there were several potential candidates in the Senate of the United States. Governor Lowden of Illinois, who had for years been accepted as a member of the Republican party organization, received widespread support.

Nevertheless, early in March 1928, 110 of the 237 Republican members of the House of Representatives declared themselves in favor of

Hoover. These were influenced in part by the claim of Secretary Hoover's supporters on January 16 that they had at least 300 future delegates virtually pledged to his candidacy. In early 1928 a staff poll of New York State names in a who's-who-type directory showed that of those replying from the 5,500 polled, 1,010 favored Hoover, 149 favored Coolidge, 21 Hughes, 19 Dawes, 16 Butler, and 11 Lowden.[9]

A considerable number of western Republican congressmen and senators were then determined to take over the Republican national organization on behalf of the farmer. Some party elements were sufficiently sympathetic with organized labor to hope to win its support.

Despite its long record of appealing to the voters, the Socialist party was not the vehicle for the degree of national protest that existed. Its doctrinaire approach and its obvious bias toward public ownership made it unacceptable to both farm groups and most of organized labor. The unreality in the appeal of third parties indicated that they would have little quantitative importance in 1928.

The Democratic party, defeated ignominiously in 1920, had done little better in 1924, and had revealed deep schisms on social questions and on international relations.[10]

A hope that the Republican party might provide an effective and efficient national government might be realized with support for Herbert Hoover. This hope could be realized if a political group—a powerful one—could gather strength as the president's party.

Despite his declarations of allegiance to the Republican party, Hoover might well be thought of as an "independent" candidate for the presidency in 1928. For reasons that were only in part personal he had a great following, particularly among liberal groups and among college men and women. They saw in his absence of usual political experience an opportunity to form, around his programs, his principles, and his outlook upon problems, a political party to meet new needs in a new age. This party would have as its primary concern the citizen rather than the party member, the industrial worker, or the farmer.

It was said in later years that politicians destroyed Herbert Hoover because he did not understand "politics." It was, however, *traditional party practice* that destroyed much that the Hoover administration could have accomplished. Had Hoover had working with him a political party to match his own politics, the result might have been quite otherwise. But this was at the time quite out of the question. Never had a party organization favored any leader so experienced in "government," yet so removed from "politics." If Hoover could win under such circumstances, the traditional form of party organization might be changed. Forms and rules would remain, of course, but practices would be greatly altered.

——By the time the campaign of 1928 opened, the Republican party could no longer conceal its divergent elements. It had always been an amalgamation of diverse economic interests. In the period between 1900 and 1920 two well-recognized divisions had developed: eastern and western, urban and rural. In the days of Theodore Roosevelt these diverse elements were termed "progressive" and "conservative."

—— The conservatives dominated administrative procedures, in general, while the progressives furnished the greatest amount of key legislation. In the presidencies of Harding and Coolidge the conservatives had dominated the party organization, even though the progressives, after revolt within the Republican Party in 1912, had for the most part remained within the party.

Thus party allegiance had become a many-colored thing, with the House and Senate seating representatives of many different types of Republicanism. Voters in different sections of the country responded to the kind of Republicanism in which they believed, irrespective of organization, platform, or president.

——In truth, the Republican national organization that had functioned during the first three decades of the century was dying at the top. The national leadership by party bosses that had been displayed in 1896 and again in 1920 no longer existed. The convention proceedings of 1928 clearly showed this. The titular party organization had become a shell. It had been succeeded by a much larger group of politicians (including powerful leaders from sections like the Middle and Far West), and by groups representative of certain economic interests which usually looked to Republicans in the executive branch and in the Congress to further their objectives in national government.

—— Now there would be an increasing influence of organized labor and of various national and sectional organizations representative of agricultural interests. There was a particular rise in power by industrial and financial interests concentrated for the most part in twelve states of the East and older Middle West. Moreover, the state party organizations in four of the most populous states (Ohio, New York, Pennsylvania, and Illinois) were more powerful than they had ever been.

—— The patronage system, inherent in the national administration, which had been of tremendous help to presidents (who had the power to appoint), had been largely displaced by the growth of the civil service. Old-time political organization was weakened further by the extension of mass education, the rapid increase in the use of radio in the twenties, and the emphasis upon opinions of commentators both on the radio and in every newspaper or journal of wide circulation. Boss control through party machines became less effective. The day was at hand when an able president could, if he wished, deal more directly with the people.

Day by day, the gulf between two kinds of public servant was deepening. The elected public servants made public service in office a basic career. Their fundamental concern was the satisfaction of the voter. They were experts in public relations (to use a phrase not yet generally in circulation). The civil servants, who were increasing in number as the need for expert training in government rather than in politics increased, were concerned primarily with effectiveness of administration. Their goal and task was the satisfactory solution of public problems.

At such a time as this it was clear that a president would find himself — torn between two elements in political power: the demands of a party organization—weaker in fact than at any time since its birth, yet insistent upon its rights of patronage—would be contested by a body of advisers representing various economic interests in the nation that were traditionally symbolic of the basic appeal of the Republican party.

Professional politicians saw in Hoover little that was familiar and much that was difficult to understand. Those who had been associated with him in his early adventures and who took the trouble to seek what lay behind his efficiency, his public shyness, and his love of life found a most unusual man. The image was that of a scholar and statesman. There had been authorship of a textbook, *Principles of Mining* (1909), translation with his wife of a Latin folio, *De Re Metallica* (1912), and the writing of a book of social interpretation.[11] Constant living and preaching of the simple life of the American family did not, however, reveal the whole man.

Hoover could idealize David Starr Jordan and believe in the ideals of Woodrow Wilson, yet differ with both of them on questions of government and business. He could read into American history not the story of politics that had made so many men arrogant and ruthless, but the story of builders in state and church, in school and industry, who believed that being an American provided a unique opportunity to serve mankind.[12]

During the 1928 Republican National Convention in Kansas City, the Senate membership reestablished a party leadership that was noticeably absent during the convention of 1924. Senator Simeon D. Fess of Ohio was temporary chairman. Senator George H. Moses of New Hampshire permanent chairman. Senator Reed Smoot of Utah was chairman of the Resolutions Committee. Senators James E. Watson of Indiana, Charles Curtis of Kansas, Guy D. Goff of West Virginia, and George W. Norris of Nebraska were all offered for the presidential nomination. A stellar role was played by Senator William E. Borah of Idaho in formulating the platform and defending it.

The convention revealed that a considerable number of Republicans

of long service would not support Hoover—either for personal reasons or
because of convictions on particular policy questions. Most of these
Republicans of independent view came from western states. Several had
long records of opposition to President Coolidge and his policies, and to
President Harding as well.

The true engineer of the nomination was William H. Hill, New York
State chairman of the Hoover campaign forces and a former congressman.
He prevented the Hoover enthusiasts from arousing more antagonism
from party regulars than they already had. (The regulars were very
apprehensive about parallel or rival work.)[13]

There was an attempt at the convention to defeat the Hoover supporters by uniting the elements representing the existent party organization. Because this attempt failed, Hoover won the nomination. An observer
explained this well:

> The nomination of Herbert Hoover as the Republican standard bearer
> did not take place at Kansas City; it was merely ratified there. Months, even
> years before, a small army of men and women dotted all over the United
> States formed a group of missionaries whose work had been accomplished
> before June 12. These were the men and women who had served with Mr.
> Hoover during the past in one or more of his gigantic enterprises. A momen-
> tary personal touch with the Secretary of Commerce had implanted in these
> people the spark which no politician could extinguish, a spark which de-
> veloped a quiet, irresistible, expansive quality that spread steadily from the
> thousands to the millions. It was translated politically at Kansas City, not
> only by delegation after delegation pledged by popular mandate to support
> Secretary Hoover, but by large numbers of men who, since the time of their
> association with Mr. Hoover, had entered the field of practical politics and
> become powerful leaders.[14]

It can be said that Charles Curtis, who became the vice-presidential
candidate, represented the party organization view.[15]

As the convention was not unified in the nomination of Hoover,
neither was it unified on the platform that emerged. This was contrary
to the desires of those who hoped that the selection of Hoover as the
Republican nominee would strengthen the Republican party. One editorial thought the nomination "bids fair to go a long way in the direction
of uniting a party which for a number of years has been torn by internal
dissension, and to bring back into its ranks many, if not all of those, who,
while naturally Republicans, have, in fact, been Republicans only in
name."[16]

The Republican party organization had been in danger of splintering
many times in the preceding thirty years. Now, after three decades of

uncertainty, it would have to show conclusively that it could continue to live half eastern, half western; half conservative, half progressive. The internal struggle, although real in the convention of 1928, was inconclusive in outcome, and the nomination of Herbert Hoover was a symbol of that fact. He was fully satisfactory to no political bloc in the convention. Of western leaders, Borah was for him, but Norris of Nebraska and John J. Blaine of Wisconsin were not. Senator Hiram Johnson of California was an avowed enemy. Among eastern leaders, Ogden Mills was an early supporter; Andrew Mellon (to an extent) joined the ranks of supporters later. The dominant powers in the East were not solidly for Hoover. He probably did get the bulk of the progressive Republican vote in the Middle and Far West.[17]

On the whole, the Hoover supporters in the convention envisaged a campaign based on Hoover's personal appeal to independent voters (of whom all politicians are more than willing to make use). But such a campaign was also to include party assurance to Republican voters and leaders that, with Hoover as president, the general policies of the two preceding administrations would continue. This was an odd assumption.

On July 14, 1928 Hoover resigned his post as secretary of commerce in order to participate in the campaign. In the stadium at Stanford University near his home, he formally accepted the nomination on August 11 before a crowd of 70,000 people and a nationwide radio audience.[18]

In the course of the campaign, the various elements in the party did not come into open conflict. Had the Democrats not nominated Al Smith, who could be attacked, and was attacked, as a machine politician, an advocate of repeal of Prohibition, and a follower of the Catholic faith, the divergent elements in the Republican party doubtless could not have held together during the campaign as well as they did.

The first appeal which all Republican orators made to the voters was the promise to maintain prosperity. A second appeal was the promise to retain the Eighteenth Amendment and the separation of church and state, and to do away with Democratic machine politics.

Hoover's own campaign was a reflection of the man himself. There would be no attack from the candidate against Governor Smith. A writer remarked that "the Chief liked our policy of never attacking Smith. In fact, it was our policy to mention him very seldom—only when we couldn't avoid it—but we never attacked him."[19] In his acceptance speech, Hoover —— pointed out that in the recent past there had been increases in national production, consumption, and home ownership. The purchasing power of wages had risen while hours of work had gone down. Job security had increased and "unemployment in the sense of distress" was widely disappearing. Gifts to charity had also increased. This prosperous situation led Hoover to remark that "we in America today are nearer to the final triumph over poverty than ever before in the history of any land."[20]

Throughout the campaign, but particularly in an address delivered in Newark, New Jersey on September 17, Hoover stressed the fact that there was identity of interest in America between employer and employee. Each group had come to accept high wage theories, saw virtues in efficiency and mechanization, and believed in "full personal effort." Such things would bring labor the reward of higher wages. Both groups rejected socialism, he said.

In the campaign, Hoover emphasized his belief that Americans were not bound by any class system. He insisted that maintaining the decency and dignity of family life, providing free and universal education, and preserving equality of opportunity would constantly refresh the stream of leadership in the nation. The *New York Times* commented on September 18 that perhaps he was just the man needed "to head the greatest business government in the world." His comments were "sound and just." After all, ever since the campaign of 1896 there had been recurring discussion of the need of engaging businessmen in active politics. The time seemed to have come.

Candidate Hoover followed, on the whole, the precedent of helping to elect Republicans in the House and Senate. His experience in Washington had clearly shown him that under the American form of government it was possible to accomplish results in the field of public affairs only by using a political party. As early as 1920 Hoover had indicated his view of the importance of the American system of party government:

> Nothing could be more disastrous than the development of several party organizations representing the complexion of every group in the country. With the legislative and executive function more widely separated than in any other democracy, the whole process of constructive government will come to an end if we have more than two dominant parties. If we should come to this position there will be no possibility of the American people securing the will of the majority and we shall be entirely ruled by log-rolling minorities or sterile political coalitions.[21]

Unlike his immediate predecessors, Coolidge and Harding, Hoover had not been a worker in precinct, state, and national party councils, nor had he been a member of Congress. He did not know from personal experience the intricacies of the American party system.

Hoover parted company with those who, in dealing with public policies, sought first to find out what it was that the people themselves believed at any given moment was their desire. More than this, he did not at any time indicate that he gave special weight to the convictions of individual members of the party on what ought to be done—although he did consider their ideas. His primary concern was to have a plan. If the plan was to be put to use, it must be explained not only to the party leaders but to the voters. Then the party leader would presumably help the president, or the candidate for president, to educate the people to approve the plan.

Candidate Hoover conferred, of course, with those who held public office. He interacted with those who held high positions in private enterprise. He conferred with representatives of the press. But in no way did he indicate in any of these discussions that, should he become president, he would represent their views. A careful reading of what he said and a careful survey of his relations with the representatives of the Republican organization in the course of the campaign must lead to the important conclusion that Herbert Hoover would place the intentions of a great mass of voters in the United States ahead of the desires of party officials in or out of public office. Hoover would serve the purposes of the electorate, not party officials.

It was the firm belief of his long-time friends and his closest adherents that, as President, Hoover would provide a "New Day" in American national development. Many thoughtful citizens, and particularly those devoted to public service on behalf of the less privileged and less fortunate, were eager and ready for this development in every field.[22] For them it was to be a "Hoover Era," in which government rather than politics was emphasized—a point of view that gave first place to constructive action by the national government in fields hitherto little touched.

Of course, this point of view did not appeal to professional politicians. They dominated the atmosphere of Washington. Their chief interest was in the game of politics, a game played within a framework of action and thought familiar to every citizen. Americans had themselves developed it with all its terminology and its rules. They had lived with it for more than a century. Every time political party organizations had engaged the thoughts of voters and office-holders, their confidence in the game was renewed. Although lives were seldom lost, it was a deadly game. Such leaders as McKinley and Lincoln fell to the assassin, and Theodore Roosevelt had a close call. The stakes were office, place, influence, and especially residence in Washington, D.C.

In their platform of 1928, the Socialists opened with the following statement: "We Americans are told that we live in the most prosperous country in the world." A little later they added: "Yet poverty abounds." They maintained that prosperity was only in the stock market. Farm tenancy and unemployment were, it was declared, widespread. A tiny band of Communists supported a Workers Party.

The American Federation of Labor executive council endorsed neither Hoover nor Alfred E. Smith. The Brotherhood of Railway Engineers supported neither. State federations and unions sometimes endorsed Smith. But some distinguished labor leaders did support Hoover and it was known that they did. A Wage Earners Protective Conference headed by AFL vice president Matthew Woll supported higher tariffs.[23]

The campaign of 1928 was marked by a bitterness on the part of thousands of party workers that clearly indicated an uneasy state of mind about such questions as racial tolerance, social position, invasion of privacy, and membership in powerful church organizations.[24]

——Hoover's own campaign had been marked by continual emphasis upon his view of the social philosophy of individual freedom that had made the United States of America great. Underlying this was his belief that prosperity could be assured to an increasing body of men and women through private enterprise—fostered, aided, and, at all times, regulated by a powerful government. In a campaign speech delivered on November 5, 1928, candidate Hoover spoke thus:

> We are a nation of progressives; we differ as to what is the road to progress.
>
> This election is of more momentous order than for many years because we have entered into a new era of economic and moral action, not only in our own country but in the world at large. Our national task is to meet our many new problems, and in meeting them to courageously preserve our rugged individualism, together with the principles of ordered liberty and freedom, equality of opportunity with that of idealism to which our nation has been consecrated and which has brought us to the leadership of the world.[25]

Such a view was not reflected in the press and other public comment of the late twenties. In fact, it is still something of a mystery how this determined figure, whose own life in profession, public service, and government was so reminiscent of traditional America at its most vigorous, could win the huge support given him in November of 1928. For he appeared before a public that was confused in a new world of invention, technology, and science. The American people at the time were lacking in realism, inclined to isolationism and scares about radicalism, and were absorbed by the question of Prohibition. (The Smith candidacy unfortunately provided its own detours from consideration of justifiable issues.) One can now in retrospect think of public figures of the twenties who might have symbolized in the presidency the irrationality and the frustration so frequently pronounced in the press, radio, and literature, but Herbert Hoover was not such a man.

Hoover's activities as secretary of commerce and his discussion of the American economy seemed to produce orderly results that fitted into a general picture of optimism and of boundless hope in America's future. He had used the Department of Commerce to increase the dependence of business upon investigations made by government bureaus. Business itself became interested in agreements designed to increase the American market both at home and abroad, and looked with favor upon the progress made by the Commerce and State Departments through their overseas representatives. New governmental units came into being to foster cooperation in the new world of radio, to build the merchant marine, and to develop aviation.

The vote was great and the victory for the Republican party throughout the nation not only for the presidency but for the House and Senate was overwhelming. In considering why Hoover was chosen in 1928, it should be recalled that there were many Hoovers in the minds of various groups in the population. There was, undoubtedly, Hoover the war hero in civilian clothes; there was, as well, the Hoover who had eluded the politicians in 1920; there was the man who had reorganized with great success and initiative the Department of Commerce; and there was the candidate who seemed on the face of his declarations to be sufficiently compatible with the Republican administrations of the eight years from 1921 to 1929. But there was also the Hoover who seemed to have something of the outlook and many of the purposes of Woodrow Wilson in world affairs. Perhaps it was this very conflict of images that raised questions about his capacity for clear-eyed and predictable leadership. Would he succeed?

Professional political scientists saw in Hoover a man engaged in carrying on large enterprises without any direct concern for the political implications that underlay large-scale economic activity in the modern world. This naturally bothered them. A comment of Jesse H. Jones summed up a view widely held at the time: "While strictly a partisan candidate and running as a partisan, Herbert Hoover has been elected President of the United States by a non-partisan vote ... on one issue.... In all parts of the country there is a feeling that business will be safer with Herbert Hoover." Norman Thomas, who viewed the overwhelming victory for Hoover as a "long step" toward disintegration of the Democratic party, and the rise of the Socialists "as the principal party of opposition," claimed, "During the campaign we furnished the only intellectual opposition to Hoover's capitalism."[26]

In a private letter of October 13, 1928, Harlan Fiske Stone wrote: "The next ten years in this country will see the development of great economic problems and likewise social problems, having their sources in the economic development of the country. I have never met any man who had such a grasp on these problems as Mr. Hoover. That, to my mind, is the big and conclusive reason for his election."[27] A few voters saw in Hoover what a trained journalist expressed much later: "Here's a man probably more internationally minded than anyone in my lifetime, if not in the country's history."[28]

Such thoughts were common.[29] Journalist William Allen White believed after the election that Hoover would measure up as President along with "the big ones": Lincoln, Washington, Roosevelt, and Wilson.[30] The time would soon be at hand for testing this commonly held expectation.

— 3 —

A New Kind of President

In our form of democracy the expression of the popular will can be effected only through the instrumentality of political parties. We maintain party government not to promote intolerant partisanship but because opportunity must be given for expression of the popular will, and organization provided for the execution of its mandates and for accountability of government to the people. It follows that the Government both in the executive and the legislative branches must carry out in good faith the platforms upon which the party was intrusted with power. But the government is that of the whole people; the party is the instrument through which policies are determined and men chosen to bring them into being. The animosities of election should have no place in our Government, for government must concern itself alone with the common weal.
Herbert Hoover, Inaugural Address, March 4, 1929

On the evening of November 6, 1928, John Philip Sousa was leading his band in a concert at Stanford University. As the program was concluded, it was announced to an expectant audience that Democratic candidate Alfred E. Smith had wired Herbert Hoover congratulations upon his election as president of the United States. Hoover, an alumnus of the university and a member of its Board of Trustees, was at his home on the university campus when he received the first word of his victory through the Associated Press. The band and the audience and a large gathering of students and townspeople proceeded up San Juan Hill to the home of the president-elect where an impromptu serenade continued for some time. Within the hour, friends and neighbors had gathered at the house. As the crowd outside increased, Mr. and Mrs. Hoover appeared, and he said: "I thank you all for coming here tonight and greeting me. I appreciate it from the bottom of my heart." The evening concluded with a singing of the Stanford Hymn.[1]

Three days after the election it was announced that the president-elect would return from his home on the Stanford University campus to Washington, D.C. by way of Latin America. The plan was widely acclaimed as a good will tour. President Coolidge placed the battleship *Maryland* at the disposal of the president-elect, who, along with Mrs. Hoover and a party of twenty-five, sailed from Los Angeles on November 19. Such a tour of a president-elect was unprecedented, but quite in keeping with Hoover's desire to visit leaders in countries with whom the United States had close relations. He visited eleven countries, returning to Washington on January 6.

At his house on S Street, Hoover began a series of conferences. For two weeks in January, from headquarters in the Mayflower Hotel, Hoover engaged in political activity. On the seventh he made a formal call on the president. On the eighth, Vice-President-elect Charles E. Curtis called at the Hoover home; on the same day Senator Borah was a breakfast guest. Later in the day Mr. Hoover conferred as well with Senators Brookhart, Jones, and McNary. Notable among guests at the house during the first week were Elihu Root and William J. Donovan. The stream of visitors continued; during that first week Hoover received twenty senators and eighty representatives, and as many more friends and political associates, including Edgar Rickard and Henry M. Robinson.

While these meetings were taking place, Charles Michelson, who was later to become a violent critic of the Hoover administration, predicted that Hoover would lose his battles for farm relief and for enforcement of Prohibition, and that a split in the Republican party would result. On December 3, 1928 Michelson had written in the *New York World*: "To begin with, Mr. Hoover starts without a single friend in the Senate."[2]

Charles E. Hughes breakfasted with Hoover on January 13. The president-elect on the same day held a conference with Speaker of the House Longworth, Senator Edge, and Ogden Mills. On the eighteenth Senator Borah spent two hours with him, and the following evening Mr. and Mrs. Hoover were the dinner guests of President and Mrs. Coolidge.

Of the relations between the president and the president-elect, Mark Sullivan wrote that they broke tradition by their close relationship in the period of interregnum. "The time he [Hoover] has spent with Mr. Coolidge has been greater than the time he has spent with any other person except members of his family and his staff."[3]

On January 21 Mr. and Mrs. Hoover left for Florida. The month spent by Hoover in Florida was devoted in large part to fishing. Guests were at a minimum and were preponderantly friends rather than politicians. Senator Smoot of Utah made a trip to see the president-elect.

On January 29 former Governor Alfred E. Smith, who was visiting in Florida, made a formal call upon President-elect Hoover. They had met eight years before, but were not well acquainted. A half hour was spent discussing the experiences of the recent campaign. This friendly visit was in marked contrast to the statement made by the recently elected Democratic governor of New York, Franklin D. Roosevelt. In a lengthy interview Roosevelt discussed the recent campaign and summarized the replies made to him in letters he had sought from three thousand county leaders throughout the United States.[1] He was quoted as saying of the reactions of his correspondents:

> Bigotry; ignorance of democratic principles; spread by unspeakable and un-American methods of the most atrocious falsehoods; unfair and improper pressure brought to bear upon workers in specially favored Republican industries; false claims for the prosperity of the country and kindred propaganda, cheated, so my correspondents feel, our party out of the Presidency.[5]

Senator Thomas J. Walsh of Montana had sent to Roosevelt on November 27, 1928 an analysis of the Democratic defeat:

> It seems to me that nothing is to be gained by overlooking the fact that the result was a rout, the most serious feature of which is that we were in disfavor in every section of the country, except in Massachusetts and Rhode Island. Senator Caraway expresses to me the view that the bitterness engendered in the southern states will keep the party divided factionally in many of them for years, with the probability that each group will be courting the negro vote, assuring repeated Republican victories in that section. I do not accept unreservedly his prognosis. . . . The country is overwhelmingly dry, as has again been demonstrated, and our party must bear the consequences of having conducted at least a near-wet campaign. The Houston platform is a clear abandonment of our time-honored tariff policy, as expressed in previous authoritative declarations of the party, though it may be in harmony with the course actually taken by the party in framing tariff legislation. Moreover, the country appears to be as strong for a high tariff as it is for prohibition. The Republican managers are openly proclaiming their purpose to raise the rates. . . . However such a purpose may have been entertained within the last half century, no responsible leader has ever dared openly to advocate it. The worst of it is that the farming sections will be in harmony with such a purpose. . . . Millions of our people have become investors in stocks and bonds, most of them with a perfectly settled conviction that their investments will suffer by Democratic

success. . . . It has happened before, and is sure to happen again, that some turn in events quite unexpected will overthrow a ministry or a government, and we must hope something of the kind will transpire as we proceed.[6]

On the way to Florida, Hoover was accompanied by Hubert Work, chairman of the Republican National Committee, and James Francis Burke, counsel of that committee. In 1928 Burke was a close political adviser of the president-elect in charge of his personal headquarters. He was a man of wide acquaintance and had served with the national committee for more than twenty years. He had been a member of Congress and for some time was party whip in the House of Representatives. At this time Burke revealed to an inquiring reporter his view of the necessary and essential processes involved in forming a sound cabinet. These were, he said, the selection of men of unquestioned integrity and intellectual qualification, with wide knowledge of economics and national affairs, and sympathy with party policies and decisions of the government. Geographic location and the representation of labor, agriculture, and finance were also important considerations. When Mr. and Mrs. Hoover returned to Washington on February 19, political conferences were resumed. It was obvious that selection of the cabinet was now the important task.

The kind of cabinet chosen by a president-elect is always of keen interest to political managers, contemporary commentators, and the public. The men chosen are presumed to reflect the purposes of the recently elected leader, who is, however, strongly influenced by the pressing need of appeasing conflicting aspirations, and by a sense of indebtedness to a party organization that made his election possible. Lincoln and many another president found this to be so.

President-elect Hoover brought to the task of choosing his aides experience as an administrator and wide knowledge of men in public life. To lead had been his role; he was accustomed to depend heavily and continuously upon the advice, information, and recommendations of the men he chose to aid him. It is apparent that Hoover asked Harlan F. Stone for advice in the formation of the cabinet. It is clear also that Hoover offered Stone a place in the cabinet and that Stone refused. This did not lessen, however, the warmth of their friendship.

There were ten cabinet posts to be filled. The president asked Andrew W. Mellon of Pittsburgh to continue as secretary of the treasury. It had been Hoover's wish to have Henry L. Stimson of New York, currently governor general of the Philippines, become attorney general. Stimson did not wish to do this and said so. It was then, apparently, that Hoover

learned of Stimson's willingness to serve as secretary of state, and on
January 30 Stimson received word that the president-elect had decided
to appoint him in that capacity.[7] After Hoover received Stimson's acceptance, he asked Frank W. Kellogg to act until Stimson could return to
America and take the oath of office.

For the Department of War, Hoover chose James W. Good of Iowa,
long a member of the House of Representatives. For the Navy, he asked
Charles Francis Adams of Massachusetts, hitherto unknown in Washington public life. Secretary of Labor James J. Davis of Pennsylvania continued in the cabinet. He and Hoover had been appointees of President
Harding. Robert P. Lamont of Illinois became secretary of commerce.
Ray Lyman Wilbur, president of Stanford University, became secretary
of interior, and Arthur M. Hyde of Missouri, secretary of agriculture.
The postmaster general was to be Walter F. Brown of Ohio, and for
attorney general, Mr. Hoover chose William DeWitt Mitchell of Minnesota, the solicitor general, a Democrat and a "dry." Thus, two members
of the cabinet had served under President Coolidge. Two members were
thought of as Democrats.

No member of the new cabinet had served in the Senate. No one was
closely identified with the official Republican party organization. Two
members came from Pennsylvania and one each from New York, Massachusetts, Ohio, Illinois, Iowa, Minnesota, and California. One only could
be thought of as a personal friend—Wilbur of California. But as events
were to show, he was a man uniquely equipped to fulfill the manifold
duties of the secretary of the interior.

The president-elect had gathered about him a group of advisers in
whom he had great confidence. Several of them knew Washington almost
as well as he did. Others brought at once to the council table the fresh
vision of men either unaccustomed to public office, or long concerned
that particular tasks should be undertaken by the national government.
Stimson had disagreed with Hoover in 1917 when Hoover was director
of the Food Administration. But the Hoover style in administration rested
squarely on such men. As Hoover remarked, "The essence of all good
administration is to select a man in whom you have confidence, tell him
what you want done, and give him a desk or a ticket as the case may be."[8]
But the vast Hoover storehouse of knowledge made this difficult to carry
out in practice.

Hoover was younger than most of these future associates in the
government. Davis, Mitchell, Wilbur, and Hyde were close to him in age;
Good, Adams, Lamont, and Brown were older, as were Stimson, Dawes,
Hughes, Borah, Johnson, and Norris. Mellon was almost twenty years
older. Mills and Gibson were about ten years younger.

On the Saturday evening before the inauguration, Mr. and Mrs. Hoover held a reception at their home on S Street for the 500 members of organizations of which Mr. Hoover had been "chief."

The inauguration was a reflection of the man himself. Hoover had come to that high moment in his life quietly and in such a matter-of-fact manner that even the fixed routine of this significant day had been followed by him as a matter of course. He had taken his usual brief walk before breakfast. The day gave high place to old friends and it gave first place to his family. He was not to be on display, except as it was necessary to fulfill an essential part of his gigantic task.

When the clerk of the Supreme Court returned the Bible used in the inaugural ceremony to George Akerson, the president's secretary, he wrote: "In accordance with the President's expressed direction, I held this Bible open (at page 693, the same being Proverbs, Chapter 29) during the administration of the oath by the Chief Justice. At the conclusion of which I proffered the page which the President kissed at the 18th verse: 'When there is no vision the people perish; but he that keepeth the law happy is he.' "[9] After the ceremony at the Capitol and the return to the White House, President and Mrs. Hoover lunched with the Inaugural Committee and then went to the reviewing stand.

Between five and six forty-five that afternoon, they received 353 guests at a reception. It was not until 7:30 P.M. that they dined with the family and only four guests, Secretary and Mrs. Good and Secretary and Mrs. Wilbur. Later in the evening the President received a call from James Francis Burke, and a telegram from Governor-elect Franklin D. Roosevelt, who had barely carried New York:

> Please let me extend to you the felicitations and good wishes of the people of the State of New York on your inauguration. Mrs. Roosevelt and I also send you and Mrs. Hoover our personal congratulations and good wishes.[10]

Of his inaugural address, which was in truth a clarion call to service of the nation, Hoover later wrote, "I was somewhat hampered by the fact that I was succeeding a President of my own party, a man for whom I had the warmest of personal feeling, for whose integrity I had the highest respect, and to whom I was indebted for many kindnesses. I paid tribute to Mr. Coolidge in my address, and I could not in good taste say anything that indicated certain differences in our points of view."[11]

To millions who had followed his campaign utterances, it was not a surprise that the President in his inaugural address gave great place to promises of law enforcement.[12] Nor was it a surprise to those who had reason to be apprehensive, or to those in the population—and they were numerous in the twenties—who looked upon all public declarations with cynicism and were frankly skeptical of the ability of government to deal with moral laxness. To them, doubtless, the president directed these words: "If citizens do not like a law, their duty as honest men and women is to discourage its violation; their right is openly to work for its repeal."[13] The key to the Hoover idea lies in the following statement:

> Our people have in recent years developed a new found capacity for cooperation among themselves to effect high purposes in public welfare. It is an advance toward the highest conception of self-government. Self-government does not and should not imply the use of political agencies alone. Progress is born of cooperation in the community—not from governmental restraints. The Government should assist and encourage these movements of collective self-help by itself cooperating with them.[14]

Altogether, the long inaugural address dealt with twenty-two objectives. There was the expected call for a limited revision of the tariff and long-promised legislation to aid the agricultural interests of the nation. Upon each of these issues, the well-informed knew what Hoover had favored, not only in the recent campaign, but in earlier pronouncements and earlier activities.

Known too was his view of the needed revision of government action on "enforcement of prohibition," as part of a larger law enforcement program. On the enlargement of American action in foreign relations, it was known that Hoover favored naval reduction and American adherence to the World Court.

When Hoover became president of the United States, a new political situation confronted the American people, whether they fully realized it or not. The president had not come to his high office as the leader of an opposing party. He did not at the time appear to face any crisis, domestic or foreign, that required prompt declaration of an unfamiliar program. His proposed actions had to do with familiar domestic issues. It was not expected that either of the major questions (the revision of the tariff and the readjusted farm program) would excite successful Senate opposition, however long the actual legislative battle might last.

A close look at the Republican party organization, however, would have shown at the time that the state, local, and, to an extent, the national government of the United States was under the ultimate control of the type of party organization fully accepted by the American people since the opening of the twentieth century. This party organization was highly conservative. It had been repeatedly impervious, in the decade following the end of World War I, to calls for change or for modification in its role and function. "For the most part stiff-minded, tightly wedded to provincial ideas, and sticklers for precedent, they [party leaders] are unable to comprehend the Hoover type of President, because it is so completely different. . . . This new and amateurish politician in the White House knows more real politics than the professionals. . . ," wrote a respected commentator.[15]

Herbert Hoover was fully aware of this cleavage between himself and his party organization. He was not by character, interest, or intention disposed to be either conservative or party minded. Many leaders knew this. Neither was he a politician in the long-accepted sense of that term (candidate, legislator, party manager). Arthur Krock, then of the *New York Times* Washington bureau, recalls that "party politics did not interest Hoover as such; he was surely no professional."[16] A man of lengthy administrative experience but of no legislative experience, he was now charged with the first administrative office in the United States.

It was the man himself, in character, experience, interest, and intention, who created the new situation in the American government that should have promised much for efficiency and steady advance. In the realm of politics, as understood in practice, the new situation was, however, fraught with peril. For unlike his immediate predecessors, Hoover was not a comfortable man to follow. He had too many ideas! Wrote a commentator:

> He is going to be a different and more dynamic President than the United States is prepared for. Business men are going to come in for their share of jolting. The business world is going to approach the new President in the fond belief that he is primarily a business man. . . . But they are going to discover that first of all Hoover is a Humanitarian and an economist. . . . Herbert Hoover is going to be a hard President for business to get along with, a hard President for agriculture to get along with, a hard President for Congress to get along with—until each of these groups learns one simple fact: that in every decision he makes and in every action he initiates, Hoover will always be controlled by the welfare of *all* the people. . . ." [17]

At the outset there was no question that the man, Herbert Hoover, dominated the scene. Those with whom he had worked already had an image of him, of course; members of the press who had followed him as secretary of commerce or earlier as food administrator needed to see him in this new capacity. Every gesture, every word and, in particular, every expression of opinion or policy or possible direction was now seized upon as an indication of the "real" meaning of this forthcoming leadership. Only in time did the familiar Hoover figure merge with the figure of "the president." Hoover's own appreciation of this change of position is seen clearly in his first press conference on March 7, 1929. Needless to say, the figure of Hoover as president would change with the passing years and become a greatly altered image when he left office four years later.

Hoover's experience in public affairs and his apparently inexhaustible mental energies greatly impressed all commentators. There were some, however, who thought that his energies assumed even greater importance because they were accompanied by a high code of moral conduct. In his daily life and in his public activities he had already convinced great numbers of men and women (many of whom had worked with him) that personal relationships were predictable and for the most part to be taken for granted.

It was as a builder of vast and spectacular enterprises before and during World War I that Hoover had come to be known to the American people. In addition, he was known for his humanitarianism, tremendous physical endurance, unusual ability to work under high pressure, and, certainly in the minds of those who were closely associated with him, his breadth of vision and depth of understanding of contemporary society.

A group of men who by ability, education, talent, and interest had become influential in public life and who saw in the president such qualities as theirs, existed in Washington in 1929. Its most potent members, both Republican and Democratic, were either from the East or from the Old South. They had never fully accepted Hoover during his period of service prior to 1929. But not since the days of Theodore Roosevelt had they had a president who knew and understood them. Wilson had been to them an outsider, and, for the most part, he scorned them. Neither Coolidge nor Harding knew in full measure that they existed. But Hoover had drawn heavily upon them as secretary of commerce, and particularly in his service as a humanitarian worker. They came to trust him, and even if the passage of time did not bring personal association with them, he did not cease to influence them. Who were these individuals?

Depicting the life of such a group in society is one of the most difficult of analytical tasks. Reticence and habitual recourse to privacy are at a premium among such individuals. It is clear that the man aware of the world who is the core of this portion of American society lives in a world of achievement where little is claimed for personal achievement. It is simply assumed.

Few presidents have been part of such a world; many of them have not known that it existed and would have scorned it had they known. Washington as president—and on the path to that office—was such a man. John Quincy Adams had many of the qualities so needed by a president of this type. Not until Theodore Roosevelt's administration, however, was it clear that in the national government such a man was in a position of real power.

—— Like so many of his predecessors who had risen from humble beginnings, Hoover was by no means born to this elite group. His world experiences, however, and his deep understanding of the makeup of society entitled him to a definite place in it. Certainly those who worked with him realized that as president Hoover would accept the elite group and use it in the work he planned to carry forward. This gave him an inner strength, and oftentimes access to very valuable advice. But his acceptance of the existence of such a group weakened him in the eyes of all who distrusted the elite, particularly those who had risen to place in public life asserting that there was in the United States a government of the people (meaning thereby that all policies were at bottom "politics," and that everything must be explained to the voter in terms that he would understand).

The presidency, as it appeared to Hoover, was the one office in which a single leader, removed from the pressures that rest upon legislators and routine administrators, might be able to determine directions not only by decision but by the association he had with others in conference. Moreover, by public utterance to appear in the press or through platform speech and the radio, the President could influence and advance the thinking of the people upon public questions of complexity and great moment.

Better than any president before him, he knew from experience the powers exercised by large-scale economic and social units in modern industrial society. He knew what it was to deal with men of great power around the council table; for a period of fifteen years he had dealt with leaders not only of the United States but of the nations of the world.

Not since the early days of the Republic had a president brought such years of previous experience in dealing with foreign relations. John Adams and John Quincy Adams, as well as Thomas Jefferson, saw no such far-flung world as did Herbert Hoover, but they had developed an American point of view in a world of conflicting philosophies. To an extent unequalled by any of his contemporaries, Hoover had for three decades seen the United States as a nation in a world of great nations. He had viewed the United States in Asia, and in Europe, and in Africa before he had seen it so closely in America. As one close to the powers that were building modern civilization, he had known the world that was emerging in the decade and one-half before the outbreak of World War I in 1914. For seven years he had been concerned, as no other public official had been, with the basic problems of this new, emerging world of the twentieth century: security, food, development, and opportunity.

The incoming secretary of state was not long in discovering these characteristics in his new chief. Spending his first ten days in Washington as a guest at the White House, he soon recorded the following in his diary:

> Of course he was thoroughly acquainted with foreign affairs, with a knowledge of Europe, also of the Far East from his early mining experience, and finally with Latin American affairs from his recent trip. I, on the other hand, had been out of the Caucasian world for a year and had paid very little attention to European affairs since the war . . . . This ten days was, therefore, extremely valuable to me.[18]

The fact that Hoover had spent the preceding eight years in Washington had made him aware of the weaknesses of the vast bureaucracy that had come to be the United States government. In those years he had sensed the gulf developing between the great business, industrial, financial, and labor interests in the day-to-day operation of the national government of tradition.

He had come to believe that the work of the world was done by men who had programs based upon *facts*; men who were accustomed to disagree, perhaps to compromise when necessary, and to unite in executing a decision when it was made. He believed in efficiency as an ultimate goal, one not always easily attained but always kept in mind. He knew from his experience how wasteful, inefficient, and indirect the governmental process had become, compared with its potential. If ever a man in the presidency knew, when he came to power, the extent of human frailty, the depth of human suffering, and the possibilities of human greatness, Hoover was that man. As so many had commented, he had few illusions. He habitually saw obstacles, but he never lost sight of ultimate objectives.

Here was a man who apparently gave no thought to the importance of winning friends or political allies as an identifiable goal. He simply pursued his way with the deep conviction that there certainly were many who felt as he did and who, seeing facts, would do as he would do. It was this retirement from many of the usual amenities that would blind almost all commentators to the fact that Hoover was, in reality, one of the most gregarious of presidents.

Despite his reputation for the making of quick decisions and despite the somewhat brusque manner in which he proceeded, the man was deeply humble. There was an unusual candor in his approach, not only to what others said and believed, but to what he himself was moved to say and to what he believed. Of course, many have stressed the compassion he felt for mankind in distress, but there were few who realized how a sense of the weaknesses and needs of humanity guided him in his daily life.

Hoover was uniquely equipped to function as president in the way in which George Washington might have proceeded if a latter-day president. This marked him out at once as one who would not proceed as did Lincoln or Theodore Roosevelt. Hoover's natural grasp of the problems of public policy, his belief that these policies were to be dealt with by men of good intention, and his conviction that in due time great masses of interested, intelligent people would come to approve of such policies, gave him the unique power which he was to exercise again and again as leader in time of crisis. It is only as it is clearly seen that he functioned in this way and not as a leader in the popular understanding of political leadership that one may measure fairly his accomplishments.

The administrative "style" was well established by the White House years. It brought results—and it also brought life-long loyalties. Recalls his under secretary of state, "Mr. Hoover never short-circuited his Cabinet secretaries by consulting their subordinates. I did not even discuss the Japanese situation with him until afterwards except that I sometimes had to see him about details in the absence of Mr. Stimson. I have never known a man who so completely and honorably played the game with his subordinates as did Mr. Hoover."[19]

Despite his early identification with the work of Stanford University and his early interests in the learning of scholars and scientists, Hoover did not come to the office of president with the active support of the bulk of college and university men, as had Woodrow Wilson.

Throughout the period of his preparation for the presidency and during his presidency, Hoover did not share the approach of the professional scholar to public questions. Many were misled to believe that he did. This was because he had early interested himself in documentation, and was fully aware of the importance of the written record of the activities of mankind. He believed that a man of learning was to be listened to—so far as he devoted himself to examination of the record or to study of a problem in laboratory or library. Hoover's view was that such an individual, whatever his capacities and contributions, was not an individual whose opinion in a matter of practical programming was to be considered of final importance. Still, Hoover had a high regard for the capacity of the specialist operating within his own special field, whatever it might be. He had less regard for viewpoints expressed by professional men in the field of practical (or partisan) politics or economics.

Hoover on the one side and his later critics on the other maintained, in effect, that neither really dealt effectively with the major problems of government. It is only thus that we see that Hoover, the practical man—despite his great interest in all that makes for learning and for advancement in accumulation of knowledge—was much nearer than he appeared to be, both in his immediate reactions and in his personal comments, to the thoughtful men of action. It is only as we see this aspect of Herbert Hoover that we fully understand why it was that in the campaign of 1928 there was widespread acceptance of him as a man of *action*.

Hoover was a man of pronounced reading habit, consuming quantities of volumes in a very brief time.[20] It was his imaginative power, and what might be termed his original point of view, that characterized the basic exploration that went into the plan of any new venture. He did not draw his power from analysis and synthesis of already existing data, and this kept him from being confined in the conclusions he reached. He was continuously curious about the way society operated, and he met new problems with what might be thought of as a new method.[21]

Despite the loyalty Hoover rendered to the presidents he served, he was known by each of these men for the objectivity of his judgments. In fact, it is probable that it was this quality of independence which he exhibited in such striking degree during his tenure as president that kept him from easy association with any of his three predecessors. Hoover never surrendered his independence of view to any one of them. This was, in truth, a factor of great importance and an element of great strength.

Thus there was no doubt in the minds of those who watched the activities of the president immediately following his election that he would be a new kind of president. A decade later, a coworker and subordinate of many years summarized what he perceived to be the core of the Hoover approach in those years. Turning from a discussion of unemployment after World War I, Edward Eyre Hunt wrote the following to Hoover:

> Your chief instrumentalities were private. Even when you were Secretary of Commerce and President you used unofficial committees and private research bodies for the bulk of the work. When government officials were included in the committees they were a minority; when government agencies contributed to the technical studies they acted as subordinates and not directing bodies.[22]

This president would present his programs to the Congress and to the people and would push them actively and aggressively until they were enacted into laws. If this failed then President Hoover, on the basis of the record, would take the position that there should be repeated public presentation of the program, a repetition of arguments in favor of it, and an expectation that there would be a long process of education and discussion before it was enacted into law. Here was dependence upon the slow formation of public opinion. Here was conviction that only as matters were thrashed out in public discussion could there possibly be a decisive choice among many opposing points of view and a choice that would be comprehensible and acceptable to the people as a whole.

— 4 —

The Politics of the New Day

We are steadily building a new race—a new civilization √
great in its own attainments, . . . the American people
are engrossed in the building for themselves of a new
economic system, a new social system, a new political
system. . . .
  Herbert Hoover, Inaugural Address, March 4, 1929.

Although the new president's inaugural address included a great deal of
generalization about the meaning of the Republican party victory at the
polls, he had a program of his own. There was nothing novel in this
program to those who had followed closely the thinking of Hoover in the
past. He was now in a position to initiate his program by radio and newspaper presentation to the people, by argument with the Senate, and by
persuasion in the House. At least this seemed the prospect.

The president envisaged an advance for American interests, not merely
an adherence to American practice. There was much in the program for
the New Day that inspired Hoover's early supporters to believe (and say)
that in truth a new epoch had opened in American political life. Nearing
the end of the third decade of the twentieth century, alert Americans had
for a generation been preparing for the opportunities offered by a new
age of new devices for communication—an intercontinental radio and air
age, limitless in possibilities for good or ill.

As Hoover had envisioned it, the American people would continue to
build a new economic, social, and political system on the basis of equality
of opportunity. There must be maintenance of initiative, he said, as well
as reliance upon the creativeness of the individual citizen. This had been
a central theme in much he had been saying since the publication of his
book *American Individualism*. Drawing upon his own experience of "the

spread of revolution over one-third of the world," he had written there in 1922:

√   Seven years of contending with economic degeneration, with social disintegration, with incessant political dislocation, with all of its seething and ferment of individual and class conflict, could but impress me with the primary motivation of social forces. . . . And from it all I emerge . . . an unashamed individualist. But let me say also that I am an American individualist. For America has been steadily developing the ideals that constitute progressive individualism.

    Our individualism differs from all others because it embraces these great ideals: *that while we build our society upon the attainment of the individual, we shall safeguard to every individual an equality of opportunity to take that position in the community to which his intelligence, character, ability, and ambition entitle him; that we keep the social solution free from frozen strata of classes; that we shall stimulate effort of each individual to achievement. . . .*[1]

Hoover's economic philosophy was expressed by the need, as he saw it:

√   To curb the forces in business which would destroy equality of opportunity and yet to maintain the initiative and creative faculties of our people. . . . The government must keep out of production and distribution of commodities and services. This is the deadline between our system and socialism. Regulation to prevent domination and unfair practice yet preserving rightful initiative are in keeping with our social foundations. Nationalization of industry or business is their negation. . . .[2]

With prophetic intuition of the spread of communism over the world, he stated:

    There is never danger from the radical himself until the structure and confidence of society has been undermined by the enthronement of destructive criticism. Destructive criticism can certainly lead to revolution. . . . It has been well said that revolution is no summer thunderstorm clearing the atmosphere. In modern society it is a tornado leaving in its path the destroyed homes of millions with their dead women and children. . . .[3]

He found in American institutions a substitute for revolution:

    The primary safeguard of American individualism is an understanding of it, of faith that it is the most precious possession of American civilization, and the willingness, courageously, to test every process of national life upon the touchstone of this basic social premise. Development of the human institutions and of science and of industry have been long chains of trial and error. Our public relations to them, and to other phases of our national life, can be advanced in no other way than by a willingness to experiment in the remedy of our social faults. The failures and unsolved problems of economic and social life can be corrected. They can be solved within our social scene and under no other system. . . .[4]

In the first weeks following Hoover's inauguration, the main outline of his procedure for the four years to come was clearly indicated. He conferred continuously with a stream of advisers. To those close at hand in and about the White House, Hoover seemed to be pursuing a course familiar and basic throughout his preceding years in Washington. This personal life of contact with the world of leadership is a key to understanding of the man. He and Mrs. Hoover were entertaining at lunch and dinner and often had as overnight guests the friends of earlier years. Also to the White House came Cabinet members, members of Congress, and representatives of the Republican party organization. There was continuous discussion. In the first weeks Congress was not in session, although for a brief period the Senate had an executive session. A number of the leaders were in Washington, however, and the number of Congressmen increased as the day of the special session approached. This had been called by President Hoover to meet on April 15.

Justice Stone was a member of the pre-breakfast medicine ball exercise sessions which were an early development of the administration. Of these Stone wrote: "Mr. Hoover is a man peculiarly dependent on his friends, and I think perhaps the gathering of them every morning and the exercise do him good, as they do me."[5]

It was characteristic of Hoover to rearrange the formalities of the White House that would not be directly useful to him. On March 25, he sent seven horses quartered in the White House stables to the War Department to be used at Fort Myer. The presidential yacht *Mayflower* was sent to the Philadelphia Navy Yard to be decommissioned. "The Secretary of the Navy reports that it costs over $300,000 a year to maintain the yacht and that it requires a complement of nine officers and 148 enlisted men . . . I have considered that this expenditure and the use of the men on the *Mayflower* is no longer warranted. . . . Therefore," he added whimsically, "I have concluded to do without that boat."[6]

He took over the press conference and made it his own, speaking to the newsmen and women directly, simply, often whimsically. In time, however, he came to insist on written questions, submitted in advance. The first conference, attended by one hundred newsmen, was held on

March 5, 1929. The president said, "I am anxious to clear up the twilight zone, as far as we can, between authoritative and quotable material, on the one hand, and such material as I am able to give from time to time for purely background purposes on the other."

There was general rejoicing among the newsmen. Even those who were usually hostile were won over. It was felt that the president would do the talking for the new administration, and "with a greater degree of frankness in relations between President and Press than ever seen in America."[7] The succession of presidential conferences from March to July, 1929 were packed with information and elicited thanks and rejoicing and general approval from the newsmen. They had little apprehension in those months, and there was no talk of dictation.

The President was proceeding as he had usually done. He presented a multitude of facts; he gave free reign to his great capacity for formulating programs; he drew up patterns of procedure; and he asked his aides, and on occasion newsmen, to perform the task as he had outlined it.

Hoover discussed the situation of the administration, as he saw it, before the Gridiron Club on April 13, 1929. On this occasion he talked frankly of his relations with the press. His words were sharp and they were subtle. The soft irony with which the public was to become so familiar in the years following his presidency was characteristic of the entire address.

It was to this body of newsmen that the chief executive revealed his thinking on the problem of cooperation with Congress. "One of the primary difficulties of a new administration is the over-expectation which is aroused in political combat. . . . The mere process of election does not mean achievement. . . . I have no feeling that my position is . . . 'A king for a day.'"

And then, of what was in his mind and in the minds of his audience because of the impending meeting of the special session of Congress, Hoover said: "One of the important problems of every President is the relationship between the Executive and Congress. . . . I know of no more able and devoted legislative body in the world than our Congress." If the president had chosen to talk to the public in this way more often, it would have been clearer what this new President's program meant.[8]

—— The basic assumption of Hoover's critics, then as now, was that the world he saw and knew and wished to improve or save had collapsed.[9] Dedicated to saving lives, Hoover wanted to saves ideas also. He believed that in the United States it could be done. In using the term *New Day* Hoover believed that old American ideas would be useful.

——Nothing so clearly indicated, as this expression, that Hoover would move beyond the conceptions of his immediate predecessors in his plan for using the natural resources of the nation—and all of the hitherto little used facilities for research—to bring about such a New Day.

Hoover often revealed to the press that he wished above all else government reorganization in the interest of efficiency as well as economy. He would eliminate overlapping functions and bring about "a single-handed direction under which policies can be formulated and where they will be much more under public inspection." He emphasized this when he talked of conservation of water, oil, and land, and when he discussed plans for flood control.

A careful reading of his earlier writings, as well as his campaign speeches, reveals that Hoover was preparing for the opening of a new epoch in conservation. This new epoch must be called into being not only by a president, but by a Congress and, finally, by a vast constituency prepared to follow leadership in action. There were no indications in the vote cast—and little indication in the widespread acclaim given to Hoover—that there was public realization of his program.[10]

Hoover moved at once to review oil leases and curtail abuse of public lands; he presented a plan for the development of inland waterways; he would scrutinize the national forests; he initiated a plan for the limitation of armament; he called for a new declaration of freedom of the seas. As was expected, he called on the nation to consider needed law enforcement and appointed a commission to investigate this field. He asked the Congress to legislate on farm relief and on the tariff. He asked for a cut in income taxes and government expenditures.

As Hoover faced the new task, he recognized its familiar aspects: the directing of a great enterprise; explaining it to the public; utilizing his wide acquaintance among men in the industrial and financial world for advice and aid; and framing the international problems with which the national government had to deal. To all of these activities he was accustomed.

There were of course other aspects of his presidential duties. He must now deal with the Congress as a coordinate power. In particular, he must deal with representatives who were in majority control in each House of Congress. Hoover had hitherto dealt with the Congress in the capacity of cabinet officer. Now he must meet the demands of representatives of the Republican party organization interested in political patronage and face the press, for he not only continued to be a source of information (as before), but now he could give the final word.

To assist him in his efforts, the new president had as assistant in charge of press relations George Akerson (to 1931); Larry Richey was in charge of appointments; Walter Newton acted as congressional liaison; and French Strother was assistant to the president. It was an able and loyal (and sometimes overly loyal and protective) team, which could make it difficult for strangers—important ones—to get the president's ear. Here was human nature at work.

President Hoover took charge of his new office with an assurance that belied the diffidence, mild manner of speech, and apparent shyness which had misled some observers. Following the intense activities of the campaign and inauguration, he entered upon a routine of daily activity that was to remain unaltered until the summer months brought repeated breaks in journeys to the Virginia mountains, where he and Mrs. Hoover established a summer camp on the Rapidan River. To the country at large, the president appeared to be engaged in presenting his views to the press in preparation for the meeting of Congress in special session. He seemed also to be taking steps to further law enforcement. He and Mrs. Hoover desired to avoid publicity on the details of a delightful family life with their children and grandchildren.

By the middle of June 1929 Hoover reached a high point in his assertion of leadership. Against great odds in a struggle with the Senate, he won his way on Farm Relief. The victory was won at great cost, however. To most political observers in the United States, it appeared as a victory of the executive branch in a field which was of primary concern to agricultural interests and therefore to a majority of western Republican supporters. The struggle revealed that the basic conflict within the Republican party was now centered on the tariff, and here Hoover had an old problem, many more antagonists, and a bewildered constituency.

The political organization which had helped, however reluctantly, to place Herbert Hoover in office had not continued to aid him. This was clearly indicated by mid-summer. For the most part, this political organization was actuated by many of the purposes of the preceding eight years, if not of the preceding twenty-five years. Indeed, some of the members of the Republican organization were distinctly hostile to the new procedures that would be required of them by the new president. A struggle between the president and the representatives of political power was thus brewing even during the first three months of the administration. On the whole, however, Hoover maintained control.

The new president was fully aware, as we have seen, of the role that party organization had always played in the government of the nation. He had been in close association with several of the officials of the Republican party organization just prior to inauguration and in particular with his old friend James Francis Burke, counsel of the Republican National Committee. This close, personal friendship continued until Judge Burke's sudden death on August 8, 1932.[11] It was evident that party patronage was not the only matter discussed between Hoover and the organization, for at the outset both faced the necessity of reorganizing the Republican National Committee. Dr. Hubert Work resigned from the chairmanship of the committee on June 4, 1929. The president interested himself in the choice of a new party chairman, but it was not until late in the autumn that the actual choice was made.

Despite Hoover's hope that in the work of the committee efficiency would be a guide during the period of the administration, inexplicable confusion was now revealed. Party records of the meetings were lost and not found. (The minutes of the national committee were later announced as lost, possibly in the White House fire of 1930.) There was delay in organizing the new committee. On August 22, 1929, prior to appointment of a new chairman, Vice-Chairman Ralph Williams suggested that no meeting be called until December and that he, as vice-chairman, be permitted to act until then.[13]

`Meanwhile, Hoover had not been inactive. On March 4, late in the evening, he had conferred with Judge Burke, who was considered by many to be a "secretary without portfolio." On March 16 and 17, Claudius Huston, who had earlier served as assistant secretary of commerce and who had been active in the campaign, began a systematic collection of political materials. On occasion he made suggestions on appointments to White House appointments secretary Lawrence Richey and to the president.[13] But a weakening factor for the new president was his succession from a previous Republican; vacancies due to resignation were scarce. This was politically unfortunate.

Throughout the summer of 1929 there was speculation about the choice of the new national committee chairman. Appeals from Ripon, Wisconsin, and Jackson, Michigan calling for a presidential statement on this for the seventy-fifth anniversary of the Republican party were unsuccessful. Hoover said he did not wish to go into this "moot" question.

Early in September, Claudius Huston was chosen chairman. Much was made of his earlier relationships with the president, and of his knowledge of the South. It seems clear that in fact he had been carrying on business for the committee and the president for some weeks.[14] Huston had become Hoover's choice for the job, a task that Hoover considered a public service. It was only through organization of political parties that the will of the people could be expressed at the polls. Hoover told Jeremiah Milbank that Huston, by retiring from private business to undertake this work, was placing the chairmanship upon the plane it deserved.[15] There was evidence of Hoover's appreciation of the power of the committee in his choice of a former member of the Congress, Walter H. Newton, as an administrative assistant. Newton had been chairman of the Speakers' Bureau of the Republican National Committee in 1928.

Huston's occupancy of the chairmanship was not to be for long, however. He was not the choice of the powerful leaders in the party and, following a request of twenty Republican senators that he resign, the president requested Huston's resignation. Huston submitted it on August 6, 1930. Here was renewed evidence of the schism in the party. Huston was succeeded by Senator Simeon D. Fess of Ohio, who had been leader of the draft-Coolidge movement in 1927 and 1928. Senator Fess was an outspoken "dry," a standpatter, and a believer in a high protective tariff. His past attitude toward the president was shown in his opposition toward Hoover's administration of postwar relief funds and his inclusion in the Harding cabinet. He once termed Hoover one "whose Americanism is . . . in question. . . ."[16] But Fess was a loyal party man above all else.

All through the early months of the administration there was public discussion of the attitude the president would take toward patronage in the South. Considerable attention was paid by members of the national committee to the plans made by those who spoke for the organization of the party in several of the southern states.[17] The president came to be highly aware of congressional love of patronage.[18]

One of the most trying political problems developed in the president's own state of California, where an early effort had been made to place the party organization under the control of Hoover's personal followers.[19] This was a difficult matter, in that the guiding powers in the Republican organization of the state of California were friends of the senior senator from California.

Ever since the election of Hiram Johnson as governor in 1910, the Republican party organization in California had been seriously divided, and it furnished a battlefield for some of the most violent intraparty battles of two decades. On the whole, the Johnson adherents had the upper hand, but often they failed to win in conflicts with the old guard that had ruled the state prior to Johnson's gubernatorial election. The resulting divisions had provided the basis for the defeat of Charles Evans Hughes in 1916, although that was far from the purpose of either group.

Johnson had gone to the Senate in 1917, and for the most part his adherents continued to rule in the state. C. C. Young, governor in 1928, belonged to the Johnson wing. Samuel Shortridge, Johnson's colleague in the Senate, spoke for the old guard. The distribution of patronage during the Harding and Coolidge administrations had shown the continued success of the old guard in representing republicanism in Washington, although the Johnson forces in California and Washington were able, on occasion, to rule or at least prevent action. And there were times when Johnson worked actively with the old guard in Washington as it was represented in the Senate and in the national committee. Hoover had no part in this conflict but some of his closest friends were in the midst of it. Most of them were of course definitely anti-Johnson. Chester Rowell, a conspicuous supporter of the early Progressive movement, was by 1928 clearly anti-Johnson and now a close friend of Hoover.

It is true that the California delegation to the Republican National Convention in 1928 had identified itself with the candidacy of Hoover. Outwardly at Kansas City the Hoover demonstrations before as well as after the nomination were led by Californians. But Hoover had not been the first choice of the state organization, and no one of his personal representatives at the time of the convention was identified with leadership in California politics.

When Hoover was elevated to the presidency, his friends of course desired to take over the party organization in the state. The powerful southern California influence, spearheaded by Harry Chandler, publisher of the *Los Angeles Times*, constantly attacked Johnson and his followers and supported Hoover. In the elections of 1930, the Hoover forces in California strengthened their control over the state organization. Mark Requa, for example, was made national committeeman in the autumn of 1931.

Hoover's personal friends were the core of the loyal support for the administration in California. This was particularly true of Mark L. Requa, Henry M. Robinson, Leland W. Cutler, and Ray Lyman Wilbur, who were in constant consultation with Hoover.[20]

Early in the administration, Senator Johnson made it clear that he not only persisted in his personal opposition to Hoover, but was unsympathetic with the recommendations of the Republican president on tariff legislation, on the proposed "national origins" bases for legislation on immigration, and on the conservation of such national resources as oil. Consequently, all through the first year of the administration, the struggle for control of the state organization of California affected Hoover's influence over the national committee itself.

In the battle for control, the administration had in its favor a widespread western interest in the development of Hoover's policies.[21] These included oil conservation, continued development of natural resources by private interests, and, particularly, the improvement of waterways and the building of such projects as the San Francisco Bay Bridge.

The weakness of the administration in seeking continued support in California lay in part in its commitment to the enforcement of Prohibition. In the western group California was the leading "wet" state, despite considerable "dry" support in rural areas. As administration policy developed, notably in the appointment of the Wickersham Commission, the opposi-

tion to Hoover among the "wet" interests in California became more
pronounced.

The interest of the western states, particularly Washington and
Oregon, in a "western" president, and in much that was associated with
the West in the program formulated by Hoover, decreased with the
emergence of local issues; it was most favorable in Arizona, New Mexico
and Nevada. Borah of Idaho, considered a "western" senator with a
general following throughout the West, was a vigorous supporter of
Hoover in 1928; only later did he develop so violent an opposition to
Hoover that he did not support him in 1932.

It was also evident that a problem involving the party organization
leaders in the state of New York gave Hoover much concern. He was
more disposed to confer with certain outstanding national figures, that is,
Republicans from the state of New York, than with the New York organization itself. This situation was complicated by the fact that the "wet"
advocates in the New York Republican party were at variance with the
widespread "dry" sentiment among Republicans in the state.

In the art of party manipulation Hoover did not succeed, either in
the nation or in his own state of California. At no time after Huston's
resignation did Hoover have a chairman of the Republican National
Committee who represented his view or his program.

Moreover, the committee, as the year 1930 opened, was functioning
under the disadvantage of constant appeals for help in the unemployment crisis. That the party's committee deteriorated in efficiency was due,
perhaps, not only to inadequate staffing, but to the fact that it was seriously divided, as was the Congress, on the pressing questions of prohibition and tariff revision.[22] Personal antagonisms among Republicans in
New York, Pennsylvania, and California over the party program compounded the difficulties under which it functioned.

When the president came to the crucial test of his political leadership
in the congressional campaign of 1930, his disadvantage did not stem
from his own failure in dealing with the committee or in dealing with the
titular party leaders in both houses of Congress. This should be stressed.

The party committee was simply not responsive to *presidential* leadership. A fundamental weakness in American party practice was here
revealed. Republican leaders in the House and Senate did not identify
their brand of republicanism with the program of their Republican president. Hoover did not practice politics in the traditional manner. In any
case, the failure of party organization to function effectively in these very
difficult years brought catastrophe. Discussion in the Senate gave the

interested public a complete picture of the disruption of the incumbent party now over a decade in "power."

Hoover had gathered together during his activities of the previous fifteen years a devoted band of admirers. To them he emphasized that in his appointments he was interested in the record of the individual and in the individual's willingness to serve a *cause* rather than himself. He often praised appointees for their record of devoting time to public service, to activities on behalf of some national or community interest.

This often led him to undervalue those job recommendations that rested solely or primarily on political considerations. It caused him to be suspicious of congressional recommendations if they were based, or seemed to be based, on some party or partisan interest. Politicians, in turn, were suspicious of him.

There was logic on both sides, in his record and in their practice. Eventually a modus vivendi was worked out, but it was never very stable. Finding "the right man" was not always easy.[23]

Senator Borah, while he was still supporting Hoover, wrote:

> I feel that the President, the appointing power, ought to be entirely free to choose those upon whom he must rely in the administration of the government—free from organization or senatorial influence, other than such as is provided for in the Constitution. The President should, particularly in selecting judges and officers of the court, be wholly disembarrassed from the insistence of political influence. We cannot, and I do not think we would want to, do away with the confirming power of the Senate. But the Senate, acting as a body, is wholly different from two Senators presuming to dictate before the appointment reaches the Senate *as a body*.

This gratuitous statement, from one who had long experience in the Senate (but who was admittedly not much of a party man) was capped by another:

> I believe the people would overwhelmingly support you in an announced policy that you would feel free to select men purely upon their fitness and regardless of organization or senatorial recommendations. I feel furthermore that if such a policy were announced, a goodly majority of the Senate would support the practice. Of course, if the matter came up as a test upon particular appointment, the situation would be different.[24]

The last sentence was underlined by the President, who wryly commented, "just where it would come up."

The devotion of his personal followers and the growing support of his appointees by the citizenry revealed that Hoover at the time was regarded not as a politician but as a representative of the people in whom they had faith. Yet under the American political system as it had always functioned, this did not increase his strength.

Hoover made it clear from the outset that he intended to use both party organization and expert public servants to carry forward his program. To do so successfully meant displaying to the vast army of voters what his program actually was; he also had to convince the average voter that he was using both old and new types of organization to attain his ends.

The separation of powers provided for in the Constitution had long since gone far beyond the division laid down in theory. The president of the United States lives apart from the eyes of the public, from the Congress, and of course from the Supreme Court. Yet most emphatically, because he shares in legislative power—in suggestion, in recommendation, in portrayal, and in veto—he must in activity always be in a sense a "member" of the forum, that is, of the Congress. The Court can be his refuge, because he shares nothing with the justices; they and he, as well as the people, know that.

The daily history of the Congress, particularly the Senate, is most revealing of the culture and interests and intent of the American people. With striking exceptions, no member of the Congress really represents the nation, and few indeed live in a milieu that suggests a national outlook. Both senators and members of the House remain local members of local communities in their conception, in their outlook, and in their choice of pathways to effective political action.

As the situation appeared in late summer of 1929, the new president had already made enemies among high tariff advocates, big navy supporters, Prohibition fanatics, and patronage seekers.[25] Added to these might be all those who dreaded change. Hoover had pushed the idea of actual disarmament by slashing army costs and cutting navy construction. He had insisted on farm relief without debentures, on limited tariff revision, and on genuine economy in government with emphasis upon reorganization of bureaus. A Child Health Conference was planned, and a research committee on social trends would be created. Furthermore, the president had insisted on publicity for income tax refunds. He had started discussion of the conservation of oil lands, while the study of water conservation and of the utilization of power was already under way. Judges an historian, "Certainly no earlier president had done so much so quickly."[26] His world "was aggressively modern: his ideas and programs for society arose from experience in engineering and international business."[27]

As he looked over the vast continental estate of the nation in these early months, Hoover did see a promising future for Americans. Plainly, his imagination was challenged as he contemplated Charles Lindbergh's flight from Mineola, New York to Jacksonville and Miami, Florida, and from Mexico City to Brownsville, Texas; the coast-to-coast record flight (eighteen hours, twenty-one minutes) of Frank Hawks; the flight of the dirigible *Graf Zeppelin* across the Atlantic to Lakehurst, New Jersey; and the tour of the Russian plane *Land of the Soviets* from Moscow to Vancouver, Washington, and New York.

Hoover plainly believed that orderly, careful, precise, and scientific planning would make a difference in such an age. He would act on that belief.

— 5 —

Plans for the National Estate

We are but started as a Nation. We have feverishly garnered the harvests of the ages in minerals, oil, gas and timber. We have often ruthlessly destroyed the plants and animals that have fought the fight of the ages. We have successfully replaced the buffalo with our domestic herd animals; but when we divided the continent into States, counties, townships, quarter sections and lots, and developed private ownership and fences, we often lost sight of the stern dictates of Nature and of the inter-relation of mountains and valleys, trees and farms, plants and floods. We have been tolerant of fires, overgrazing, reckless lumbering, and suddenly find undue spring floods, autumn drought and rapidly silting reservoirs as our penalty. Now we must bring back where we can that proper balance upon which fundamental success depends. Regardless of sovereignty, each tree and plant plays its part in that scheme of Nature of which we are the almost helpless pawns. We need new vision for a new West. We need to accept wise guidance if we are not to lose much of our heritage.

Ray Lyman Wilbur, September 17, 1930,
The Memoirs of Ray Lyman Wilbur

As Hoover looked at the possibilities that were before him as president of the United States, it was natural that he saw them with the eyes of one who had been brought up in the West and who was trained and experienced in engineering. He was thoroughly familiar with the problems of conservation; in his youth he had served upon geological and other government surveys in western states. As secretary of commerce he had worked toward the conservation of fisheries and of oil resources. He considered what he saw against the background of his experience in developing pioneering projects in mining in Australia, China, Russia, and

in other countries. He knew from his experience in government the problems that had arisen thus far in the unlimited use of the natural resources
of the United States.

In emphasizing the importance of science in the development of the
natural resources of the nation, President Hoover was in the tradition of
Washington and Madison, Jefferson and Lincoln, and especially Theodore
Roosevelt.[1]

Hoover, as a young man, had been an enthusiastic admirer of Theodore
Roosevelt. This admiration was directed not only at the aggressive position taken by Roosevelt in foreign affairs, but at the vision with which he
related national power to the continuing existence of the great natural
resources of the United States. Roosevelt's plans for the conservation of
natural resources seemed to Hoover to provide a sound approach to their
future use by the American people.

As secretary of commerce, Hoover had had much to do with the
problems involved in the distribution of American products and the
organization of American business for an ever expanding market. None
of this had interested him more than the possibility that within the United
States natural resources could be used in building up more productive
bases for the future of the people of the United States in the world.

In his proposals dealing with such subjects as oil reserves, land still in
the possession of states, the use of water power, bridge building, improvement of waterways, provision for proper drainage, and the construction
of great dams, Hoover revealed his desire to use the national heritage in
the interests of all of the people. His proposals led to extensive discussion
and debate in the Congress and in the nation. During his first six months
as president he made ten major statements on his plans for use of the
public domain. He saw these problems not only as problems of practical
conservation, but as problems in the development of a political opinion
on the most efficient and productive uses of resources.

Hoover chose as his secretary of the interior neither an engineer nor
a politically minded conservationist, but President Ray Lyman Wilbur of
Stanford University, who had had wide experience in the medical profession prior to his work in university education. The critical, creative
mind of this scientist was, in the thinking of the president, the best aid
he could have.

The problems that confronted an engineer, and a scientist endowed
with all of the power that the United States government could provide,
were not simply the problems of development of water power, limitation
upon the use of oil reserves, or the long-term preservation of the vast
wealth of the national forests. The immediate problem lay in the use that
could be made by the government of already existing plans of private

agencies of long standing and experience for the further development of all natural resources.

As the administration opened, Hoover's attention was called to three matters which were to be of grave concern during his first year.

First, it was necessary to consider the plan for improvement of waterways, not only for economic reasons, but so the nation would not again suffer from floods such as occurred in 1927.

Second, there was a need to plan against lack of rainfall in certain regions. This was primarily an engineering problem, but it also interested Hoover because providing water for arid areas would increase their fertility; waste lands would become productive fields and orchards.

Third, in a new era of intense industrialization the problem of oil conservation led Hoover to take steps which culminated in the important Petroleum Conference in Colorado Springs in June 1929. This was a conference designed to improve interrelationships between the various oil-producing states and to create more satisfactory working agreements between the private interests involved in oil production and the state governments.

Hoover knew that his views on the most efficient use of natural resources ran counter to the opinions that had gathered support in the preceding twenty years, namely, that there should be greater public development of such natural resources as oil. The issue was three-cornered, however, for, if government were to take over the development of oil resources from private enterprise, it would mean that both state and federal governments would be involved. The issue would be sharply revealed in Colorado Springs.

Soon after taking office, Hoover stated that government oil lands would not be leased or disposed of except as required by law. "In other words, there will be complete conservation of Government oil in this Administration."[2] Shortly, he canceled permits on thousands of acres granted to companies that had not carried out their plans for drilling and that had been holding the lands for speculative purposes. This policy of the administration caused much opposition in those western states which had oil reserves. But, said the president, "the time will come when the Nation will need this oil much more than it is needed now."[3]

The "oil scandals" of the Harding administration had done much to inflame public emotion. The early months of the Hoover administration witnessed the relentless unfolding of the drama involving the former secretary of the interior under Harding, Albert B. Fall, oil operator Edward L. Doheny, and chairman of the Sinclair Consolidated Oil Corporation, Harry F. Sinclair.[4]

The record of Hoover in these matters is known. Together with Secretary of State Hughes, Hoover had urged Coolidge to remove Attorney General Dougherty. His immediate policies as president "undoubtedly swept Teapot Dome beyond all possible recall as a campaign issue."[5] Later, he would refuse to pardon Albert Fall, and he denounced the man who had betrayed both Harding and the country.[6]

Quite apart from the judgments upon unsavory and illegal private conduct of some public officials, there appeared unassailable evidence that public sentiment had never been satisfied on a deeper question: could the national government effectively protect the interests of the masses of the people without resorting to public ownership and operation of great enterprises engaged in developing public utilities? That is, could socialism be avoided? That was the basic question as millions envisaged it. This issue was ignored by those who advocated increasing governmental activity. Hoover's basic proposition was that the economic progress of the United States throughout its history had depended upon the acceptance and functioning of private enterprise. Thus had transportation and industry been revolutionized. Every phase of human existence had been miraculously uplifted by the use of oil and water power, and by the improvement in living standards that had accompanied private enterprise. A new industrial age had emerged. Nor had conservation practices been totally lacking within the new century.

It was perhaps normal that a president who approached the national problem of the use of natural resources with a knowledge of the great sources of wealth which lay in Europe, Asia, and Africa should see the American situation in a world setting. This was important, because he would think of American interests in relation to the interests of other parts of the world. Thus the president would be led to formulate a position toward other nations. Especially involved in this was his firm belief in the efficacy of private enterprise in the United States.

In the basic division of American public opinion between supporters of private enterprise in development of natural resources, and supporters of government in this task, the president naturally favored private enterprise.

An important distinction must be made between the need for basic conservation of natural resources and the method chosen for their use. Hoover's position on both of these matters was very definite. In his view, every step taken in the conservation of oil, coal, and mineral ore resources, and in the preservation and proper use of these resources, should be in the interest of future generations. He urged government improvement of waterways. Moreover, he believed that the development of the land resources of the nation for agricultural purposes should be met by the efforts of individuals and groups devoted to individual or private group enterprise. Indeed, the deepest division between those who followed Hoover's leadership in the years to come and those who did not was on this very issue. One who regarded the national estate as the property of its citizens, yet distrusted the efficacy of government ownership and operation, clearly favored economic rather than political processes. This was fundamental with Hoover.

It is difficult to see how any party organized as the Republican party was, on a national scale, could expect to find a solution that would be satisfactory to all groups within the party. If the party stood by its earlier record, government would leave to private groups the development of the national wealth. Government was supposed to protect those engaged in private enterprise and in particular regulate unfair practices. Conversely, government was supposed to protect the people as a whole against exorbitant costs. But this did not mean government intervention in the operation of private enterprise.

A deep division thus developed between those within the Republican party who as traditionalists adhered to the philosophy of earlier years, and the more daring, who now felt that the party should take a different position in the new industrial age. This cleavage has been grossly misunderstood not only by the American people but by interpreters of the political developments of the Hoover administration.

In the early months of the administration, Hoover furnished his press conference with considerable "background material" on the matter of oil conservation, a subject which interested the American Petroleum Institute. As Hoover said, the questions raised by the institute were not concerned with administrative action related to the public domain (which at the time supplied less than two percent of all the oil of the United States). Hoover had been a member of the Federal Oil Conservation Board appointed by President Coolidge to study the problem as a national issue, and the American Petroleum Institute cooperated with this board. According to Hoover's description of these joint activities, the board had studied the problem from two points of view: the scientific methods that would assure the longest life of American oil supplies, and the economic measures that were desirable to attain this end.[7] Hoover explained that one of the causes of great waste in oil production was overdrilling, which resulted in a rapid exhaustion of the fields. Intense drilling caused the relaxation and exhaustion of the gas pressures of the oil pool, with the result that less total product came from a given pool of oil. The waste of gas itself into the air also was a problem. The board had recommended regulation of drilling to secure the maximum production of oil from a given pool and to correct the feverish drilling of offset and competition wells and the overdevelopment of fields at the initial stages.

The board was concerned with the economic aspects of waste, and predicted that periods of intense overproduction of oil would be followed by periods of famine and consequent extravagant prices for oil. But the main concern of the board was with the possibilities of government regulation of drilling. A committee comprised of three representatives each from the American Bar Association, the American Petroleum Institute, and the federal government had been assembled by the board to study the problem of governmental action.

The committee concluded, as had the advisers of the Federal Oil Conservation Board, that drilling for oil was an intrastate matter over which the federal government had no authority. Constitutional provisions for national defense or interstate commerce were explored but did not provide any authority for federal control. The board suggested that the solution to the problem lay in the control of drilling, not in the stifling of production through interstate agreements that would be in violation of the Sherman Antitrust Act.

The Petroleum Conference that met in Colorado Springs on June 12 ended in an uproar of criticism and misunderstanding. The tempest revealed most of the liabilities of democratic governance in a scientifically minded administration, many of the facets of divided responsibility, and not a few actors in characteristic roles.

There were two classes of invitations to this conference. California, Texas, Oklahoma, and Wyoming were asked to send "representatives." New Mexico, Kansas, Colorado, Utah, and Montana were given an opportunity to send delegates *if interested*. Secretary Wilbur realized that no final compact could be signed at this meeting, and hoped that the public would not expect any agreement to be reached.[8]

The conference met under the chairmanship of Mark Requa of California to consider Hoover's plan of "regional interstate compacts" for control of physical and economic waste in the oil industry. He reported to the president that the official delegates from Texas, Oklahoma, and California were not prepared to make recommendations for immediate action. They believed further study of the problems necessary. Requa felt that the governors of Kansas, Colorado, Montana, and Wyoming had presented a much more cooperative attitude, but, because Texas, Oklahoma, and California produced 85 percent of the oil, they agreed to accept the "Big Three" position. Thus Hoover's plan for stabilizing the industry failed. The alternative was federal control.

Hoover assured the governor of Texas that it was the aim of the conference "to discuss general policies" in order to discover what might be done in the public interest of conservation. There was no intention to interfere with state authorities or negate antitrust acts; federal action would be avoided, and the states would be supported.[9]

Requa felt that much had been accomplished despite the bitterness of the Rocky Mountain states over withdrawal of the petroleum land permits, and the "frankly hostile attitude of the Texas delegation and . . . of a portion of the Oklahoma delegation." In his report to the president, Requa remarked that "the word 'compact,' seems to be the quintessence of everything mysterious, tyrannical and undesirable," and concluded that "there is a great deal of educational work that will have to be done."[10]

The "educational work" should have begun in the Senate. The day before the conference, Hoover issued an order that barred further prospecting on the public lands. Senator W. H. King of Utah went so far as to say that the conference was "largely in the interest of some plan or scheme that will tend to the creation of a monopoly by the large oil producers in the United States."[11]

Requa claimed that the governors and delegates praised the handling of the conference. Scott Heywood, the representative of Governor Huey Long of Louisiana, who came to the conference as an unreconstructed rebel, said before leaving that he would cooperate in every way possible with any program that Requa would endorse.[12]

It was clear that the parties to the discussion represented divergent views: those of the oil company representatives; those of Secretary Wilbur, who represented the administration; and those of the state representatives.

It later appeared that the opposition to Hoover's proposal concerned "conservation," rather than production control and price-fixing.

Requa later wrote regretfully that "struggling with a hostile Congress, unable to secure cooperation with the governors of the oil-producing states (in a compact resembling, perhaps, the Colorado River compact), President Hoover was forced to stand by and watch the disintegration of a great industry, the dissipation of natural resources. . . ."[13] Hoover wrote Requa: "Considering the situation, I think you got through with this conference extremely well. We should have realized that calling a conference at that point only invited difficulties, but it did not occur to us that people would try to misuse the conference."[14]

The president found it necessary to make clear that the resolutions passed by this conference were not to be thought of as embodying a final solution. The conference had been held to bring together various views as a preliminary step in a broader investigation. It is noteworthy that the plan presented by the governors of the most interested states did emphasize the basic objectives of the conference and then recommended that several commissions be empowered to investigate and recommend action to the states, the private companies, and the federal government.

This procedure was not new to Hoover, but it confirmed early in the administration his belief that government should aid private business in every way possible, yet not actively participate; that in matters of local concern or sectional interest, it was important that the states be consulted and that their views be presented and widely understood. The national government was, in effect, merely aiding the smaller units in their own proper activity.

Hoover's interest in the conservation and protection of the national estate continued to find expression in his press conferences. He found that conservation of the cattle ranges never had been considered. Neglected during the whole history of the government, the ranges had been over-grazed. At the time they were probably not worth as pasturage 50 percent of what they had been twenty years earlier. Hoover had been advised that in another twenty years they would be ruined beyond remedy.

He suggested to a Western Conference of Governors meeting that a commission be appointed to examine public land problems. This idea, he felt, was fundamentally a proposal not only to simplify federal relations with the states but to promote a particular conservation program under state rather than federal management.[15]

When Hoover announced subsequently the appointment of the Commission on the Conservation and Administration of the Public Domain (suggested by Secretary Wilbur), he emphasized that destruction of the natural cover of the land would imperil the water supply. But the commission was to consider as well the conservation of oil and coal, and other problems that arose in connection with the public domain. Later, concern in Congress with the economy prevented action at that time on the commission's recommendations, particularly for saving the grazing lands, but their report contributed focus and facts for later discussion and laid a basis for action.[16]

How difficult such a program could be was seen in Hoover's description of the problems facing the Reclamation Service. Most of the lands in the West available for reclamation had passed into private hands. The Reclamation Service had secured agreements with private landholders whereby the landholders agreed to contribute under the Reclamation Act. Voluntary agreement had proved very unsatisfactory. The states were the only political entities possessing the power to enforce contributions in the matter of reclamation of private land.

More than a month before the October stock market crash, Hoover announced a public works program which he described as greater than the construction of the Panama Canal. At his press conference on September 17, 1929, he said that, with the appointment of General Lyttle Brown as chief of engineers (on the recommendation of the secretary of war), he proposed some important alterations in the organization of the office of the chief of engineers.

As Hoover saw it, the large increases in public works programs since 1927 and the probable increases to come meant that there should be more definite responsibility and continuity in the direction of public works than had existed to date. He therefore proposed to appoint an engineer who would have direct responsibility for all of the new flood control and related projects on the tributaries of the Mississippi (the Ohio, upper Mississippi, Missouri, Illinois, and others, comprising a great inland transportation unit). Thus the administration of this vast project, including work on the Great Lakes and probably on the Saint Lawrence Seaway, would be on the spot rather than through centralization in Washington.[17]

Reporters were told that it would have been possible to save one hundred thousand head of cattle in the 1927 flood, if there had been adequate maps of the flood area of the Mississippi. Inasmuch as Hoover estimated it would take about eighty years to complete the basic survey of the country at the current rate of work, he was pleased to receive a report from the secretaries of interior and commerce which indicated that this enormous program of surveys could be completed within approximately eighteen years.[18]

Hoover said this would not require a very large budget increase. He estimated that the time compression from eighty to eighteen years might cost an additional $1 million, but the early results would be of great economic importance both to the states and to federal activities within the states.

The significance of the new surveys would be their accuracy—elevations as low as one foot over the entire country would be displayed. About 43 percent of the accurate mapping of the country had been accomplished over a period of seventy years, but the new chief executive was not inclined to wait another eighty years for completion!

Hoover felt at this time that he had made some headway with the plan for the appointment of the Commission on the Conservation and Administration of the Public Domain. The real problem was a problem in water conservation. The overgrazing of the unreserved lands had removed the cover and denudation had resulted, with serious inroads into the water supply.[19]

It was the president's view that additional reserves should be set up, and that the grazing lands should be turned over to the states, but that other lands should be administered by the national government. Some progress was made in the course of the administration.

Three of the states objected to taking over responsibility for the conservation measures the administration wanted to effectuate. Apparently seven or eight of the eleven principal public land states were prepared to do so, however. James R. Garfield, secretary of the interior under Theodore Roosevelt, was appointed chairman of the commission, which included Secretaries Wilbur and Hyde as ex-officio members.

The report of what now came to be called the Garfield Commission was twofold: (1) additional Federal reserves should be set up to include "all possible oil and coal reclamation areas, forests, parks, bird refuges and national defense areas"; and (2) the remaining grazing lands should be granted to the states; or, if not acceptable to the states, they should be placed under federal administration. But legislation to implement these recommendations was still pending when the president sent a special message to Congress on February 17, 1932. The grazing law that was eventually passed under the New Deal (without giving control to the states) was nevertheless an outgrowth of the work of this commission.

It was in dealing with the water power of the nation that Hoover's conservation program was to be most clearly visible. This was a subject to which, as a professional engineer, he had given much attention before he entered the presidency.

President Hoover was intimately concerned with the Boulder Canyon Project Act that had been approved on the eve of his administration (December 21, 1928), for he had been chairman of the Colorado River Commission appointed by President Harding years before (1921). On June 25, 1929, Hoover announced the Colorado River Proclamation which made effective a compact among the seven states in the Colorado River basin (Arizona excepted) that in turn facilitated the construction of a projected dam on the Colorado River. Hoover said that the proclamation was "the final settlement of disputes that have extended over 25 years and which have stopped the development of the river. . . . And it has an interest also in that it is the most extensive action ever taken by a group of states under the provisions of the Constitution permitting compacts between States."[20]

Soon after entering upon the presidency, Hoover started the Reclamation Service to work on the Grand Coulee Dam project on the Columbia River. Some months later, Hoover suggested to Governor Young of California the appointment of a joint federal and state commission to study the engineering and economic problems connected with the Central Valley project of California.

Hoover told his press conference on August 13, 1929 that Governor Young in the last session of the legislature had arranged for an appropriation from the state government to carry out an investigation of water supply problems. Hoover had agreed to the appointment of a commission, upon which the federal government would be represented by delegates from the War Department, the Federal Power Commission, and Department of the Interior. The governor would appoint representatives of state government departments and some leading citizens. The commission would determine facts and develop some coordinated policies on developing California water resources in connection with irrigation, navigation, flood control, and power.

It was in the development of the water resources of the Tennessee Valley, however, that political controversy became acute. The president took the basic position on the expansion of the Muscle Shoals Dam project in Tennessee (an electric power project begun in the Wilson administration) that he had displayed in similar cases; that is, that private power companies should distribute the power generated by dams built with government aid. The governors of Alabama and Tennessee had gone along with Hoover in his plans.

The proposal associated with Senator George W. Norris of Nebraska that the government produce water power, distribute the resultant electric power, and manufacture fertilizers at Muscle Shoals met with the president's energetic opposition later expressed in his veto of the Muscle Shoals Joint Resolution on March 3, 1931.[21] Hoover stated at that time that "the first essential of all business is competent management.... Although the bill provides for the management by three directors, the Congress must from the nature of our institutions be the real board of directors and with all the disadvantages to a technical business that arise from a multitude of other duties, changing personnel, changing policies, and regional interests."

The president pointed out with gentle irony the political absurdities of appointing a board of administrators for this project "on the basis of their beliefs rather than their experience and competency," for the plan for the board provided that not more than two should be of one political party. Apparently "the entire working force is likewise to have such a basis of selection, as the usual provision for the merit service required by law in most other Federal activities is omitted." Hoover concluded that "three men able to conduct a one hundred and fifty million dollar business cannot be found to meet these specifications." The veto message provided Hoover with the opportunity to declare:

> I am firmly opposed to the Government entering into any business the major purpose of which is competition with our citizens. There are national emergencies which require that the Government should temporarily enter the field of business, but they must be emergency actions and in matters where the cost of the project is secondary to much higher considerations. There are many localities where the Federal Government is justified in the

construction of great dams and reservoirs, where navigation, flood control, reclamation or stream regulation are of dominant importance, and where they are beyond the capacity or purpose of private or local government capital to construct.

Hoover was convinced, moreover, that the Norris bill raised an important issue confronting the American people, namely, whether government should remain government, with regulatory functions, or become involved in "barter in the markets." That, said Hoover, "is not liberalism, it is degeneration." At the same time Hoover made the distinction that in cases where power was a by-product of dam construction by the federal government, such power should be disposed of by contract (which had been the case with the Hoover Dam).

The reaction of Senator Norris was vitriolic. The President had taken Muscle Shoals from the people and given it to the trusts by "his wicked, his cruel, his unjust, his unfair, and his unmerciful veto."[22] While Norris would finally triumph on the Tennessee Valley Authority (TVA), the basic structure of electrical power distribution would remain in the nation, a third of a century later, in the hands of privately owned public utilities companies. Nevertheless, the Hoover position enjoys nearly universal disapproval if not scorn in the history books, while Norris often has the stature of "a folk hero in the finest traditions of American political life."[23]

Hoover had been interested, long before becoming president, in movements to bring about a more effective public building program. Less than a week after his inauguration, the president was invited by Treasury Secretary Mellon to address the members of Congress and their wives and the American Institute of Architects at their annual meeting in Washington on April 25.[24]

While speaking about the great building program that Congress had authorized and that would have to extend over many years, Hoover recalled:

> Our forefathers had a great vision of the Capital for America, unique from its birth in its inspired conception, flexibility, and wonderful beauty. . . . It is on this national stage that the great drama of our political life has been played. Here were fought the political battles that tested the foundations of our Government. We face similar problems of our time, and here centuries hence some other Americans will face the great problems of their time. For our tasks and their tasks there is need of a daily inspiration of surroundings that suggest not only the traditions of the past but the greatness of the future.[25]

Several months later, the president told the press that he and Mellon

had been making a study of the building program. The $50 million appropriation, to be spread over ten years, would not, he thought, meet the
necessities of the government for space. He said he would like to rotate
construction by continuous excavation of foundations and the placement
of steel in turn in one building after another, followed by stone and
refinishing, so that a very large amount could be saved on construction
costs. By bringing all the buildings into rotation, federal accommodations
would be practically completed at the end of the ten year program.
Although this was, of course, subject to congressional authorization,
Hoover thought it was a "good-sense" program that would appeal to most
people.[26]

The director of the National Park Service in the Hoover administration was Horace Marden Albright, a civil servant who moved up to this
position after serving in Yellowstone National Park and elsewhere during
the Coolidge years.[27] Regarding his desire to save historic sites, Albright
recalled:

> We kept on trying to get control of the historic sites in the Park Service,
> and President Hoover was with us. When he worked up his program of
> reorganization in the latter part of '32 he gave us everything we wanted in
> that proclamation. He assigned all the parks to us, and also all the parks of
> the District of Columbia which were also under the Army.

Congress would not approve, however. Said Albright, "It was disgusting.
I was there all the time and it was disgusting."[28]

Albright was still in office during the Roosevelt administration and
seized the opportunity to tell Roosevelt of Hoover's efforts to transfer the
military areas and the parks of Washington, D.C. to the Park Service.
Roosevelt was at once interested and implemented his wishes.[29]

Herbert Hoover was directly responsible for the idea of the Skyline
Drive in Virginia, for he personally worked out the details with Albright.[30]
Said Hoover on the scene: "There's nothing like it in the country, really,
where you can see such vistas first one side and then the other, and sometimes both ways. I think we should have a survey made here." He then
had the work performed by hand in such a way as to give maximum local
employment, in order "to get as much money (as possible) back in there
where it is needed," Albright recalled. This, too, was agreed to by Roosevelt, after he visited the site at Albright's request.

The famous Rapidan Camp of the Hoover years was sited by Hoover
and paid for through the cooperation of various jurisdictions. He later
arranged for its use by the Boy Scouts and as a park.[31] (A famous log on
which Ramsay MacDonald and Hoover sat to discuss British-American

relations eventually rotted away, and several buildings were torn down over the years.)

Hoover spent a good deal of effort during his administration on the George Washington bicentennial celebration, finally proclaiming the period February 22, 1932 to Thanksgiving Day as a time to do honor to Washington. As Hoover judged, "To contemplate his unselfish devotion to duty, his courage, his patience, his genius, his statesmanship, and his accomplishments for his country and the world refreshes the spirit, the wisdom, and the patriotism of our people."[32]

As fisherman in primitive wild rivers and wilderness areas, on "retreat" among the redwoods of Bohemian Grove, and as an on-the-spot concerned observer of floods and drought, Hoover was keenly aware of the American environment. As secretary of commerce he had worked to save the fisheries of Alaska, despite the furor such policies then occasioned. But he won, remarking at the time: "I can stand any amount of personal abuse with all the amiability of the winner. . . ."[33]

In 1921 Hoover had noted that "pollution of the coastal waters by industrial wastes is yearly becoming a graver menace to the fisheries, shipping, and use of our pleasure beaches." Hoover strongly encouraged the development of fish hatcheries and called for the release of more mature fingerlings. Always there was the personal fervor:

> I . . . insist that no other organized joy has values comparable to the outdoor experience. We gain less from the other forms in moral stature, in renewed purpose in life, in kindness, and in all the fishing *beatitudes*. We gain more of the constructive, rejuvenating joy that comes from return to the solemnity, the calm and inspiration of primitive nature. The joyous rush of the brook, the contemplation of the eternal flows of the stream, [and] the stretch of forest and mountain all reduce our egotism, soothe our troubles, and shame our wickedness.[34]

Hoover had often visited and had long been interested in the national forests and their streams, the national parks, and private undeveloped lands—in Virginia, Pennsylvania, California, and Oregon in particular. Early in the administration he determined to get a National Timber Conservation Board appointed. Of all of his administrative efforts, however, this proved one of the slowest. It took all of the year 1930 to get a full board appointed, despite the president's numerous proddings of subordinates. Finally, the privately financed board began to meet. Aided considerably by a Forestry Service report made for them, "The Forest Situation in the United States," the board presented its report on June 18, 1932 with the following recommendations: substantial additions to the national forests should be made ("Public forests should be administered primarily as a timber supply to be sold and cut only to meet public needs; and, so far as consistent therewith, to promote permanent forest industry operations."); federal and state forest fire prevention allotments should be increased; timber taxation should be modified to prevent unnecessary cutting; yield management should be sustained to prevent timber exhaustion; government permission should be given for "reasonable agreements to adjust production to consumption," thus stabilizing employment; research of forest products by the federal government should be used to aid industry; wisely planned mergers of timber holdings should be in the public interest; studies should be made on interstate compacts and shipments, and on selective logging; marketing standards should be improved and made uniform; industry ethics should be adhered to. It was also recommended that the board's surveys should be continued indefinitely. Finally, tribute was paid to the Forest Service report, which had provided the board with "the most comprehensive investigations ever undertaken."[35]

The Bureau of Fisheries was far from idle during the Hoover Administration. A treaty for the preservation of the sockeye salmon fisheries in the Fraser River system was signed with Canada in 1929, and a revised convention on halibut in the Pacific became effective in 1931. A study of possible adverse effects of a Passamaquoddy dam was undertaken. A new law-enforcement division of the Bureau was created to oversee conservation of black bass, and provisions of a 1928 act to conserve fish in canals and when bypassing high dams were implemented. A convention to conserve whales was ratified on June 17, 1932. The bureau stocked streams with 7 billion fish and eggs in one year; work on selective breeding went forward. The bureau also worked to improve oyster cultivation and to propagate mussels artificially. A new and important industry in domestic fish oils was established, and a study of mackerel led to suggestions on their use to the industry. The population of the fur seal herd of Pribilof Islands, 130,000 in 1911, rose to 1,220,000 by 1932, although the take of skins was up. A report on such progress on many fronts must have given the fisherman-president great satisfaction.[36]

Hoover was to find, as he had anticipated, that his views on the use of the national estate and the methods by which conservation should be accomplished were not acceptable to two groups of citizen, each well organized and convinced of the soundness of their respective views.

The first group included individuals who had played important roles in the development of natural resources. These constituted the leadership in companies engaged in oil and coal production and the utilization of water power. The private enterprises that had been built up by utilizing these resources had prospered while providing necessary services to the public.

The second group had been growing in number in the years since Theodore Roosevelt's early struggles for conservation. They felt that conservation was a fundamental political problem: private interests had despoiled the national resources, had used them selfishly, had not held the future of the nation clearly in mind, and would not reform or change.

These conservationists were opposed to the participation of private enterprise in the development of natural resources. They shared their opposition with those who for other reasons objected to the private ownership and operation of public utilities. Nearly always had they sought remedy in the federal government.

Those who opposed private ownership and operation of public utilities were growing in strength, and some of the most powerful of these persons were in the Republican party. Thus Hoover found himself, as manager of the national estate, circumscribed by powerful groups among his fellow citizens. Instead of a problem in economic planning and technical administration that could be solved in the light of his conviction that government should only arbitrate between the various private economic interests, the president found before him a political (and emotional) problem that would be a basic cause for controversy throughout his administration. Here was a football of politics not only within the Republican party but also within the Democratic party. Nor was the argumentative Socialist Party silent.

It was here that Hoover found a growing conviction on the part of such leaders as Senator Norris of Nebraska, that land and what lay beneath the land as well as the soil and forests above it—indeed, all the wealth which the nation could claim—should in some fashion be returned to the federal government. The government, having taken possession of its own wealth, should then arrange for the utilization of it in the best interests of the people of the United States.

Thus the president was confronted with three issues: the present versus the future use of resources; private versus public development of resources; and state versus federal action. He was concerned chiefly with the division in sentiment between those who adhered to the familiar American practice of permitting citizens, individually and as groups, to continue to organize and develop the enterprises that had built a great industrial civilization, and those who would turn over to the government for ownership and operation the enormous legacy of natural resources within the national boundaries. This was the fundamental issue which Herbert Hoover often referred to in later years as a division in social philosophy.[37]

— 6 —

Hoover and the Farmer

*Wonderful. We will now solve that vexing farm
problem.*

Charles L. McNary to Herbert Hoover,
November 7, 1928 (telegram),
McNary Papers, Library of Congress

The background of the agricultural crisis, as it existed in 1929, was an
important part of the history of the United States. The crisis had long
been gathering force.

When President Hoover on April 16, 1929 sent his special message to
the 71st Congress, convened in special session "to redeem two pledges
given in the last election—for farm relief and limited changes in the
tariff," he recalled, as was his custom, a long background of historic
causes:

> The difficulties of agricultural industry arise out of a multitude of
> causes. A heavy indebtedness . . . from the deflation processes of 1920.
> Disorderly and wasteful methods of marketing . . . growing specialization
> . . . congested marketing at the harvest . . . Railway rates . . . increased . . .
> growth of competition in the world markets . . . expansion of production
> from our marginal land during the war . . . Local taxes . . . doubled and in
> some cases trebled.

The United States had early developed as an agricultural society.
Every step in the journey, from the feeble beginnings on the Atlantic
seaboard at the opening of the seventeenth century, to the establishment
of a continental nation at the end of the nineteenth century, had been
possible because of the use of the land upon which the people could earn
their livelihood. Wide distribution of land ownership and general partici-

68

pation in government of an ever expanding population had created a democratic people characterized by initiative and independence, and a belief that the interests of the common man were paramount in the American way of life.[1]

In so vast an area discernible sections appeared at once, not because of population differences, but because of the growth of different economic interests in a variety of geographic environments. Not all of the North American continent lent itself easily to subsistence farming. Certain areas lent themselves better to wheat than to corn; to dairy farming rather than to cattle raising. Cotton, sugar and tobacco required special situations.

All these differences were expressed in political organizations at home in the county or state communities, and differences were also well marked in the national forum—the Congress of the United States. The economic history of the century from 1789 to 1900 had been written in terms of these conflicts.

Farming in any area, including the plantation South, had been a way of life. The family was always the unit of American society, and until the end of the nineteenth century the farm had made this distinctly possible.

In due time, the farmer as an economic unit in society found himself dependent upon the agencies that had developed in the life of a continental nation. He depended upon the banker for credit, upon the grain elevator for local storage, and finally upon the railroad for transportation of his crop to market. He could not rise above the stage of subsistence farming except in association with those who did not live as the farmer lived, and who did not see economics or politics as he saw them.

Ever since the Civil War the country had before it a so-called plight of the farmer. In essence, this problem had two economic aspects: one arose out of the rapidly enlarging farm area resulting from the opening of the West; the other had to do with the dramatic expansion in communication which in turn arose out of the problem of transporting products to market. Every decade witnessed angry protests from the farmers that they had a diminishing portion of the ever-increasing wealth of the nation. Naturally both political parties tried to deal with these protests. So ineffectual were the solutions tried, however, that third parties arose to make the farm problem the paramount issue; but in the decisions of the American people it never was the leading issue.

The gradual emergence of the United States as an industrial nation at the end of the nineteenth century did not at first alarm the farmer. Soon, however, it became evident that industrialism presaged a different way of life for millions of Americans who had been farmers, and that industrial interests were taking control of the farmer's means of livelihood as he moved over the continent. The last thirty years of the nineteenth century witnessed the efforts of the farmer—through his own organizations, through independent political procedures, and through campaigns within the two dominant parties—to win protection, aid, and understanding.

The aftermath of World War I emphasized the plight of the farming population in an increasingly powerful industrial society. The farmer was the victim of heavy indebtedness, deflation, increased production costs created by the necessity for more and more specialization, and insuperable problems of marketing, complicated by shifts and uncertainties in American participation in a world market.

In the early twenties, following tremendous farm expansion due to the demands of the war, the problem became increasingly acute. Nothing that was done by the Republican party under Harding and Coolidge served to remove the problem from first place in the minds and emotions of the farming population in every section of the country.

Even before 1928, the basic divisions within the Republican party in Congress were those that marked the different stages of society that had actually existed in the United States at the beginning of the third decade of the twentieth century. In economic terms the United States was not one, but several, nations.

If, in imagination, we could think of the states of the upper Mississippi Valley, and the states of the lower South, as nations separate from the East in 1930, we could with greater understanding comprehend why a senator from North Dakota and a senator from Alabama seemed to be speaking of citizens and interests quite different from those discussed by senators from Pennsylvania and Massachusetts.

Republicanism did not mean in North Dakota, where the frontier was recent, what it meant in Pennsylvania. Hence the difference in views between such spokesmen as Gerald Nye of North Dakota and David Reed of Pennsylvania.[2] The rival interests of agriculture and industry divided the west from the east, and this division was reflected in the Republican party.

Hoover inherited the farm problem, as he did the Prohibition problem, compounded by his immediate predecessors. The pressure to do "something for the farmer" in the Coolidge administration had forced the issue in Congress, and in both instances—in 1924 and 1927—the proponents of farm legislation failed. The crux of the matter rested in the economic fact that farming was a losing business, and that attempts to industrialize it thus far had not been made palatable to the farmer.

At the Republican National Convention of 1928, the attempt to write the McNary-Haugen Bill into the platform was defeated. Surplus control legislation had been favored by Frank O. Lowden, candidate for the presidential nomination; when he withdrew from candidacy, "parity for the farmer" was not provided.

The economic problem of the American farmer was one on which Hoover long had ideas of his own.[3] As secretary of commerce, he was wont to remark that some western senators were looking backward, not forward. In their rush to protect the farmer, they envisaged remedies which, he believed, did not effectively meet the demands of the modern agricultural world.

Hoover supported President Coolidge's veto of the McNary-Haugen Bill, which embodied a plan for a Farm Board to buy up farm surpluses and sell them in foreign markets at world prices, resulting, it was hoped, in a rise in domestic prices. President Coolidge, following the recommendation of leading farm organizations, had proposed a Farm Board to consider such problems as, for example, cooperative marketing. The farmers' organizations advocated it at the Republican National Convention of 1928. The farm leaders' own plan was adopted as a primary part of the Republican platform. Hoover accepted it when he was nominated.

The presidential candidate had envisaged the problem as national in scope, and the basis of his analysis rested in the realization that the farm problem was not the same in every section of the continental nation. Thus, farm legislation as such was not his first interest. He wished, as he said, to provide through legislation a governmental structure that would be able to do for agriculture what the Tariff Commission, in his view, could do for the problem of the tariff.

His position in the campaign of 1928 had been presented at West Branch, Iowa, on August 21:

> . . . A Federal Farm Board is to be set up with the necessary powers and resources to assist the industry to meet not alone the varied problems of today, but those which may arise in the future. My fundamental concept of agriculture is one controlled by its own members, organized to fight its own economic battles and to determine its own destinies. Nor do I speak of organization in the narrow sense of traditional farm co-operatives or pools, but in the much wider sense of a sound marketing organization.[4]

This was a call to the farmers to solve voluntarily their own problems with the aid, but not the subsidy, of the government. "It is not by these proposals intended to put the Government into the control of the business of agriculture," Hoover cautioned, "nor to subsidize the prices of farm products and pay the losses thereon either by the Federal Treasury or by a tax or fee on the farmer." His August 21 proposal for government assistance included, however, "an initial advance of capital to enable the agricultural industry to reach a stature of modern business operations by which the farmer will attain his independence and maintain his individuality."

Hoover said later that his overall reform for the farmers was "for the Farm Board to withdraw the excessive acreage of marginal lands which had been brought into cultivation during the war." He felt "the farmer deserved the same treatment that had been extended to manufacturers in compensation for overexpansion."[5]

For twenty-five years there had been in the Senate an important "insurgent" group, characteristically in the Republican party, although not limited to it. Some divisions in party membership might be expected, but this was a group revolt, and it was sectional.

It was a revolt centered in the agricultural states of the Middle West and Far West, and it reflected the differences between two stages of American society: agricultural and industrial. Western Republicans had been dissatisfied with the "eastern" views of Harding (his Ohio origins notwithstanding) and of Coolidge, as they had been dissatisfied with Taft's views.

The party split found additional strength in a tradition of respectable, often highly regarded irregularity in the Senate that had appeared sporadically as early as 1869. Throughout the ensuing thirty years, several types of "irregularity" appeared in the Senate on matters of machine control, on issues of patronage, and sometimes, through personal hostility, on general disagreement with presidents in office. In the annals of the Republican party, Hoar of Massachusetts, Platt of New York, Edmunds of Vermont, and Pettigrew of South Dakota had been nationally known for their independence of party organization. It was not, however, until Robert M. LaFollette entered the Senate from the state of Wisconsin in 1905 that disagreement on the nature of party government in a democracy came to national attention.

By 1909 a group of insurgent Republicans became well defined within their party: William E. Borah of Idaho; Albert Cummins of Iowa; Moses Clapp of Minnesota; Joseph Dixon of Montana; Jonathan Bourne of Oregon; Albert Beveridge of Indiana; Jonathan P. Dolliver of Iowa; and, of course, LaFollette himself.

Eleven of these insurgents, who came to call themselves "progressives," conducted an independent fight upon the Tariff Bill of 1909. They opposed the *method* of the party in writing the tariff into law by secret caucus. The states represented in this "revolt" were the agricultural states of Iowa, Kansas, Idaho, North and South Dakota, Minnesota, Nebraska, and Wisconsin.

Underlying the activities of the "insurgent" senators from these states was their growing conviction that (1) government functions should be extended; (2) private monopoly was intolerable; and (3) the legislative methods of the federal government should be improved. It was this group which, under the leadership of LaFollette, had spearheaded the preliminary movement that led to the Progressive third party in 1912. In more powerful terms but with less popular backing, some members of the group had supported the independent candidacy of LaFollette for the presidency in 1924.

So it was that, despite Republican incumbency in the executive branch of the government, supported by the House of Representatives, and despite the Republican majority in the Senate, no one congressional leader in 1929 was the generally accepted leader of that Republican party identifiable as the powerful political organization that had governed the nation with few interruptions since the Civil War.

As a result of the election of 1928, fifty-five members of the Senate were returned as Republicans, and, in the House, two hundred and sixty-eight representatives. Inasmuch as these duly elected Republicans constituted a majority in the legislative branch, they, like the President, had a mandate from Republican voters; their mandate, however, was from whole states or single districts, not from the nation as a whole. After election day, nevertheless, the senator or representative—especially the senator—thought of himself as representative of *all* the people (even though at the very same moment he kept "in touch with constituents").

If the essential purpose of the Senate was to legislate on great problems (and that alone) then speed of action could be demanded quite properly in the name of efficiency. If, however, the function of the Senate was "to examine, to question and to interpret," then action was subordinate to debate. As the insurgents who were progressives returned to the Senate for repeated terms of office, and as the years passed by, "debate" and "independence" became their weapons in welding legislation to support a program that they publicized as of especial benefit to the farmers who were their constituents.

As this program developed, it was revealed as sectional, in that it represented the interests of two successive "western" recent frontier areas as opposed to the eastern industrial and financial areas. It was apart from the South with its differing agricultural interest. To say, however, that the wheat and dairy states were claiming a cause separate from that of the cotton and tobacco states would be to simplify the situation.

Herbert Hoover, as candidate for the presidency, had been supported by Senator Borah, a moderate Progressive, because he said he thought of Hoover likewise as a moderate Progressive who would take care of the farm problem—and of Prohibition. But neither Norris of Nebraska nor

Blaine of Wisconsin thought of Hoover as a Progressive, because they knew he was not in sympathy with their belief in giving more power to the people, who would in turn protect themselves from private business by turning power over to the government. Hiram Johnson had personal reasons for suspecting everything that his rival in California politics might do.

Between March 25 and April 6, 1929, 370 witnesses appeared before a House committee to offer their views on proposed legislation. At his press conference on March 22, President Hoover explained that he felt the general principles of farm relief had been determined in the last political campaign. There now remained nothing to do except to draft those principles. The proposals of the president, presented in detail, did not, however, lend themselves easily to compromise.

First, he called for continued analysis of problems and recommendations from time to time on the basis of new facts. Second, he proposed to deal with agriculture as an industry in an industrial civilization. Finally, he indicated that there was to be no concession to those who would place the government in competition with private enterprise.

President Hoover based his program on a theory of government as a regulatory power and as an aid in investigation and guidance, as clearly as had his predecessors Theodore Roosevelt and Woodrow Wilson.

On April 12, 1929, the subcommittee of the House Agricultural Committee called upon the president and presented the draft of their farm relief bill, H.R. 1. This was to establish a federal farm board to promote the effective merchandising of agricultural commodities in interstate and foreign commerce, and to place agriculture on a basis of economic equality with other industries. It was introduced by Representative Gilbert N. Haugen of Iowa on April 15.

This bill had been in the making over a period of two months in conferences with various agricultural associations and interested individuals, and the subcommittee believed it was a sound measure conforming to the pledges of the Republican party. The bill, which emphasized farm cooperatives, was acceptable to the president, and he was gratified to learn that the House Agricultural Committee was by a large majority opposed to the Export Bonus plan or the debenture plan, which was to be a dominant feature of a Senate Farm Bill (S. 1.) introduced by Senator McNary on April 18.

Senator Smith W. Brookhart of Iowa expressed the extreme view of the dissident Republicans on the proposed farm legislation when he told the Senate that the House bill, which the President favored, did not keep the pledges of Hoover's campaign speeches. "I have not surrendered my responsibility on the floor of the Senate to the seat in the White House,"

Brookhart said.[6] Well known for his opposition to the railroad interests, Brookhart maintained that the farmers were losing financially through federal favor to "these financial combinations." By May 1, Brookhart could say:

> I believed in Herbert Hoover because I found that he had actually done these things that I want done in the Food Administration and in the Wheat Corporation. I found that he had asked the Congress for a billion dollars to handle wheat alone, to buy and sell wheat; and I told the farmers what his record was, and I told them that that was the best record that had ever been made for the farmers, and I believed that they could rely upon that in time of peace as well as in time of war. This bill repudiates that record.[7]

The proposed Federal Farm Board was to provide adequate warehousing and storage, aid marketing organizations, provide clearing houses for perishable products, correct wasteful methods of distribution, eliminate unfair practices, investigate fields for economic betterment, eliminate the use of unprofitable marginal lands, develop industrial by-products, and, most important, set up limited cooperatives and aid them. For the first time in American history, there was to be for the nation's principal activity a national organization comparable to the Interstate Commerce Commission and the Federal Reserve Board.

Hoover asserted in his message to Congress on April 16, 1929, that "there should be no fee or tax imposed upon the farmer." And warning of the need for safeguards against "bureaucratic and governmental domination and interference," he argued that "Government funds should not be loaned or facilities duplicated where other services of credit and facilities are available at reasonable rates."[8] He declared his belief in the farmers' own market organizations "which now embrace nearly two million farmers in membership and annually distribute nearly $2,500,000,000 worth of farm products. . . . In order to strengthen and not to undermine them, all proposals for governmental assistance should originate with such organizations and be the result of their application."[9]

It was the long view of the president that the difficulties would not disappear in a day, nor be easily removed by any one method. But he said, "We must make a start. With the creation of a great instrumentality of this character, of a strength and importance equal to that of those which we have created for transportation and banking, we give immediate assurance of the determined purpose of the Government to meet the difficulties of which we are now aware, and to create an agency through which constructive action for the future will be assured."[10]

On the same day that he received the House Agricultural Subcommittee, Senators McNary, Capper, Heflin, Norbeck and Ransdell, acting as a subcommittee of the Senate Committee on Agriculture, called to request the president's opinion of the Senate's export debenture plan for agricultural relief. As a bounty on agricultural exports, a debenture would be exchangeable for United States import duties, the amount being that percentage of the latter thought most likely to discourage over-production of staple crops.[11]

The president replied, in a letter of April 20 addressed to Senator McNary, that he was convinced the export debenture plan would bring disaster to the American farmer:

> The issue of debentures . . . amounts to . . . a gigantic gift from the govern-ment and the public to the dealers and manufacturers and speculators . . . [It] would stimulate overproduction . . . which would in turn depreciate world prices . . . and thereby defeat the plan. . . . It offers opportunity for manipulation in the export market none of which would be of advantage to the farmer.[12]

This decisive opinion of the president was supported by attached letters from the secretary of the treasury and the secretary of agriculture and by a lengthy memorandum from the Department of Commerce drawn up by John D. Black, professor of agricultural economics at Harvard University.[13]

The picture of the president sitting back and waiting for action, after he had made his recommendations to the Congress, is wholly false. Yet it was a picture frequently presented in later months by those intent upon discounting presidential leadership. Hoover, in private conversations, in a succession of meetings with members of Congress, in correspondence, and in statements to the press, continued to present his views. He met opposing views with arguments that stressed the party platform declara-tions of 1928, as well as economic facts. Of these facts, which he collected and used in great quantity, it can be said they were the product of careful and efficient analysis by experts.

The president also conferred with members of various farm organiza-tions, and with many personal advisers. In particular he corresponded widely in gathering information about the personnel proposed for the Farm Board.[14]

In pushing the farm program to which he was pledged, Hoover did not neglect his interrelationship with the proposed revision of the tariff as far as it was of interest to the farmers. On this he repeatedly stated his belief in enlarging the powers of the tariff commission.

At his press conference on April 19, the president developed his view of the importance of public opinion, a view that was to become so familiar in years to come:

> I regret to see that some of our farm organizations are again divided on measures of agricultural relief. One primary difficulty in the whole of this last eight years has been the conflict in point of view in the ranks of the agricultural organizations and the farmers themselves. A definite plan of principles for farm relief was adopted by the Republican Convention at Kansas City. It was the plan of the party; it was not then or now the plan of any individual or group; it was necessarily the result of a compromise. . . .[15]

This comment, as quoted, was in answer to a direct question. A statement amplifying this position was issued the same day.

Early in May 1929 the issue of retention of the debenture provision in the Senate farm bill came to a crisis in the Senate. On Senator Watson's motion of May 8 to strike out the section in the Senate farm bill calling for export debentures, the alignment against the president was clearly revealed. The motion to omit the debenture plan was lost, with thirteen Republicans joining with thirty-four Democrats to defeat it (47 to 44). The insurgent Republicans were Blaine and LaFollette of Wisconsin, Borah of Idaho, Brookhart of Iowa, Frazier and Nye of North Dakota, Howell and Norris of Nebraska; Johnson of California; McMaster and Norbeck of South Dakota; Pine of Oklahoma; and Schall of Minnesota.

The same alignment, with the addition of Senator Couzens of Michigan, was revealed in the strategic vote of June 11 on the conference report on the disagreeing votes of the two Houses on the amendment of the Senate (including the debenture plan) to the Bill (H.R. 1.) to establish a Federal Farm Board.[16]

But the refusal of the House to accept the debenture plan forced it out of the bill; and the Agricultural Marketing Act, creating a Federal Farm Board with a supporting fund of $500 million was passed by the Senate on June 14 and signed by the president the following day.[17]

It was thought that the votes on the measure revealed two things: that Hoover's presidential victory in certain southern states carried no weight with Democrats representing those states, and that the nine-year-old coalition of Progressives and Democrats might still hold the whip hand over a nominal Republican majority. Both political realities had deep meaning for the president's hopes.

Through the insistence of his supporters in the House, the president had won the first battle in his conflict with his own party members in the Senate. This, however, was but the beginning of a struggle whose nature was less clear at the time than it was later in the session, as will presently be seen.

The triumph of the president left many political scars on his own party. What would happen in the application of the remedy to "sick" agriculture was yet to be seen. For a brief time it was expected that the "cure" would be based on economic needs rather than on political expediency.

Senator Brookhart of Iowa defended debentures, but proposed that they be issued to the Federal Farm Board for optional use. To this proposal the president replied that "the tendency of all boards is to use the whole of their authority and more certainly in this case in view of the pressure from those who would not understand the possibility of harm. . . ."[18]

Two days prior to passage of the Farm Bill, Brookhart defended his position and stated:

> If the debenture . . . can not be put into the farm bill. I think the bill should be permitted to pass without it. . . . I believe we shall be able to put the debenture into the tariff bill in the form I have here suggested. In order to make sure that this be possible, we should at once organize to put up a progressive candidate in every congressional district and for Senator in every State who will fight for this program; and if the bill should be vetoed, we should follow this with a progressive candidate for President.[19]

In the two months which terminated in victory for the president, there was ample opportunity for the press, for members of the Congress, and for representatives of interested groups to learn how Hoover proceeded as president. His actions aroused great interest. They promoted a preliminary conclusion that here was a strong executive in charge of the government who could also direct the warring interests in the Congress and reach and guide public opinion.

After the passage of the Farm Bill, the president asked the secretary of agriculture to canvass farm organizations throughout the country for proposals of members for appointment to the Federal Farm Board. Secretary Hyde telegraphed these organizations, and a summary of proposed persons and their sponsors was prepared.[20]

The long search made by the president for those who would administer the fund at the disposal of the Farm Board resulted in the appointment of: Alexander Legge, president of the International Harvester Company, chairman; James C. Stone, founder and former president of the Burley Tobacco Growers' Co-operative Association; Carl Williams, Farmers' Co-operative Marketing Association; C. B. Denman, National Livestock Producers' Association; Charles S. Wilson, professor of agriculture, Cornell University; William F. Schilling, Minnesota, National Dairy Association; ex-Governor Samuel McKelvie, publisher of *The Nebraska Farmer*; and C. C. Teague, Fruit Growers' Exchange.[21] In announcing to the press on July 2 two acceptances on the Farm Board—Teague of California and Legge of Chicago—Hoover remarked that, in the selection of an outstanding businessman for the board, some 150 farm organizations were consulted and their leaders were very desirous that Legge should be secured if possible. He added that all of the men invited to serve on the board considered that here was an opportunity to do probably as great a service as would come to their generation. With the exception of Legge, all of the members thus far chosen were proposed by farm organizations.[22]

The president admitted later in the month, in response to questions from the press, that no conclusion had been reached about the western member of the Farm Board. He noted that there were two or three divisions in the wheat groups over the marketing of grain, so it had been difficult to find anyone who commended himself to all groups. In ten of the states, organized wheat pools represented one form of cooperative activity of great importance. Two or three different categories of farmer-owned and farmer-controlled elevators provided another phase in the cooperative marketing of grain, and there had hitherto been some conflict between these groups.

The board met with Hoover one month after the bill became law on July 15, 1929. The long view of the president was again the heart of his admonition to them:

> I know there is not a thinking farmer who does not realize that all this cannot be accomplished by a magic wand or an overnight action. Real institutions are not built that way. If we are to succeed it will be by strengthening the foundations and the initiative which we already have in farm organizations, and building steadily upon them with the constant thought that we are building not for the present only but for next year and the next decade.[23]

Hoover had known what he wanted, and he used a method that had been successful. His views were known. The members of his party in the Congress were divided—and had been divided for many years. They had fought this battle again despite the earlier battles. They divided on their support of Hoover's proposals. The president won only by insistence.

Moreover, the farmers themselves were doubtful; evidence on this was voluminous. Hoover proceeded to deal with these discordant elements. His correspondence covered the country as he sought advice from many leaders. His files bulged with this correspondence, and with the record of his efforts to obtain proper representation of various organizations and experts.

Lowden supported the president's farm bill when he returned from

Europe in late 1929. The secretary of agriculture had requested Lowden,
following passage of the bill, to suggest "at least twenty men whose
experience and place of residence qualified them for membership on the
Board." Lowden had hastened to respond. Hoover selected two of his
nominees.[24]

The Farm Board was barely under way when the stock market
crashed and the board was turned into an emergency relief unit. The
board successfully "eased" the farmers over the winter of 1929–30 marketing hump by stabilizing prices. Hoover later recalled that "the bulk of
the 1929 crop harvest was marketed at fair prices."[25]

The problem of marketing farm products recurred with the harvest
of 1930; thus that autumn the board renewed its support of prices until
the following April, when again it allowed prices to readjust themselves
to natural levels. The Chicago Board of Trade, hitherto not very friendly
toward the Farm Board, reacted favorably toward this policy, intimating
that "these actions had alone prevented widespread panic in the agricultural markets."[26]

On June 10, 1930, the president signed another important measure in
the new marketing act for licensing dealers in perishable commodities, a
step which he had advocated for some years. This found support among
most of the responsible commission men, as well as among agricultural
organizations. Hoover felt that it was a very important step in the protection of the farmer, the honest dealer, and the consumer. The matter
attracted little public attention, however.[27]

The "problem" of the farmer became a different problem with the
onset of the financial crisis of November 1929, the successive crises in
business and industry, and finally the complete alteration of the farmer's
status in the world market in 1931 and 1932.[28]

It was perhaps an irony of national growth that, as the president put
it to his press conference on September 4, 1931, the result of improvements in wheat cultivation had been a constantly accumulating surplus of
wheat year by year since 1923. This revolution in the production of wheat
was, Hoover thought, as important as the revolution in transportation
when steam was applied to draw cars.[29] Yet the plight of the farmer was
undiminished in a world of economic contradictions.

At the conclusion of the Hoover administration, the Farm Board conceded that the agricultural surplus was in itself not the cause of farm
troubles. Low farm incomes due to lowered consumer income, shrinkages
of foreign markets, disorganization of world trade, unemployment, and
reduced European purchasing power were the causes of trouble. Recovery, in the view of the board, depended upon recovery in domestic
business, recapture of foreign markets, reduced interest rates, taxes, and

freight costs, expansion of cooperation, and a better balance of production and consumption.[30]

That the Farm Board was not tailored to deal with financial crisis and depression would seem self-evident, and that the farm problem was not to be easily solved was amply demonstrated during the following administration.

As the president himself remarked two years after the passage of the Farm Bill: "We are giving aid and support to the farmers in marketing their crops, by which they have realized hundreds of millions more in prices than the farmers of any other country."[31]

The president had to enter upon a campaign of defense of his farm policies at a time when there was no solid basis in the national economy for determining what was or what was not successful in bringing adequate return for the labor of producing food for the nation. By the autumn of 1932 (and its election day), the farmer had a class interest—as always in the American story—but he also had a sectional interest in the fate of his favorite political party (the Republican). He did not see, and President Hoover was unable to make him see, that more important than his stake in the national economy was his place in the world economy of an increasingly industrial civilization.

The Palsied Hand of Prohibition

The worst evil of disregard for some law is that it destroys respect for all law. For our citizens to patronize the violation of a particular law on the ground that they are opposed to it is destructive of the very basis of all that protection of life, of homes and property which they rightly claim under other laws. If citizens do not like a law, their duty as honest men and women is to discourage its violation; their right is openly to work for its repeal.

Herbert Hoover, Inaugural Address, March 4, 1929

Nothing excited so much violent language from first to last in the campaign of 1928 as discussion of enforcement of the Eighteenth Amendment prohibiting the "manufacture, sale, or transportation of intoxicating liquors . . . for beverage purposes" within the United States and territory subject to its jurisdiction.

 Ever since the Eighteenth Amendment went into effect on January 16, 1920, implemented by enforcement legislation known as the Volstead Act, the American people had become increasingly obsessed by the fear that the federal government could not handle the problem thus created. At the time of President Hoover's accession to office, a decade of experience had revealed a population seriously divided not only on the wisdom of liquor laws, but on the enforcement of law against all nonconformists. No one who read newspapers, journals, or books could be unaware of the shifting standards in personal conduct. Implicit in such an attitude was growing distrust of, disregard for, and disbelief in government.

The president was not slow in indicating his line of action. Indeed, he stated in his acceptance speech:

I do not favor the repeal of the eighteenth amendment. I stand, of course, for the efficient, vigorous, and sincere enforcement of the laws enacted thereunder. Whoever is chosen President has under his oath the solemn duty to pursue this course. Our country has deliberately undertaken a great social and economic experiment, noble in motive and far-reaching in purpose. It must be worked out constructively.[1]

Not so well known as this familiar (but often misquoted) statement is Hoover's later explanation of his personal conception of this problem:

My innumerable contacts in life had confirmed that alcohol was one of the curses of the human race. The immediate problem was whether the widespread devotion to it as an escape or a road to happiness could be controlled by a Federal law. At the time the Eighteenth Amendment was adopted, I was at the Peace Conference in Paris. I had expressed to my friends the reverse of enthusiasm for that method of advancing temperance, saying that I did not believe that the Constitution was the place for sumptuary legislation.[2]

The control and restriction of the alcoholic liquor traffic in the United States had been the subject of controversy for many years. A continental nation presented confusion in practice resulting from divided authority, which in turn was a reflection of diversity in public opinion. Prior to passage of the Eighteenth Amendment to the Constitution, the manufacture, sale and transportation of alcoholic beverages had been strictly regulated in two-thirds of the United States. Local licensing systems, it is true, had developed in the colonial period. State prohibition, however, was an outgrowth of the temperance movements of the nineteenth century. It was in rural America that this "greatest social experiment of modern times" had gained the strength to become national policy.

While the nation was still engaged in World War I twenty-five states had statutory or constitutional prohibition, and this was background for the adoption, on January 16, 1919, of the Eighteenth Amendment to the Constitution of the United States. The amendment was subsequently ratified by forty-six states and became effective on January 16, 1920. The implementation of enforcement was provided by congressional action in the Volstead Act passed on October 28, 1919. This gave to states concurrent jurisdiction.

The force of a dominant public opinion supporting such extensive control of individual action had been met, particularly in urban areas, by vigorous denial of "prohibition" as justifiable policy under the Constitution of the United States. This conflict had deep roots and vividly revealed a basic issue in American life that must be met as the nation emerged, with shattered nerves and confused philosophies, from the agonies of war. In the new America, plagued by inadequacies in peacemaking, many attitudes of mind familiar through long acceptance were destined to be reexamined.

Evasion of a law that had come out of a traditional American rural society would become a marked characteristic of every metropolitan area in the nation, particularly in states which had been "wet" prior to the national legislation for Prohibition. Disregard of law in the twenties came to be associated with the aftermath of war. As bootleggers, highjackers, kidnappers, and racketeers monopolized the daily news, those elements in society desiring liquor by license, as well as those desiring it under any circumstances, were sufficiently strong to call for repeal of the fateful amendment.

When he assumed presidential office, Hoover was confronted with a fantastic situation in the nation: two citizens of Michigan, within one week of each other, had been sentenced to life imprisonment for four convictions of selling liquor; the Maryland House of Delegates killed a prohibition enforcement bill; the Massachusetts State Senate passed (twenty-six to six) a resolution asking Congress to repeal the Eighteenth Amendment; the Wisconsin legislature approved a national referendum on the question of modifying the Volstead Act; and the House of Representatives passed (283 to 90) the Jones Bill, previously passed (65 to 18) by the Senate, to punish first offenses against Prohibition by a $10,000 fine or five years' imprisonment, or both, at the discretion of the court.

If confusion was compounded in legislative halls, it was no less dominant in the city of New York where thirty conspiracy charges against "booze-selling" night clubs had to be dropped because the average jury would not convict, and Police Commissioner Whalen insisted that Prohibition aggravated by 32,000 "speak-easies" was responsible for the increase in crime and vice.

A month after President Hoover was inaugurated, it was officially disclosed that, since the Eighteenth Amendment had come into effect in 1920, the number of persons killed in the enforcement of Prohibition laws had risen to 190, of whom 135 were citizens, and 55 were Prohibition agents who met death in the line of duty. Following several killings of automobile drivers who failed to stop at the command of border patrolmen assigned to liquor smuggling duty, the United States Prohibition Bureau in Washington announced it would limit its agents to service pistols and would bar guns and rifles.

The controversy over Prohibition was many sided. It was first of all a moral problem for millions of Americans who believed that the consumption of hard liquor was injurious—physically, mentally and socially.

Others believed the liquor trade was injurious economically as well. All who favored Prohibition recognized that its enforcement was both necessary and difficult. The controversy was not altogether within the federal structure, however, for a number of states had prided themselves on various degrees of "dryness" over a considerable period of years. The problem of states' rights or duties versus federal responsibility in enforcement was a constant source of conflict. Hoover later stated that during the nine years prior to his administration, "the officials of the states most clamorous for national prohibition, including Iowa, Kansas, Ohio, Indiana, Alabama, and Georgia, steadily abandoned their responsibilities and loaded them upon the Federal government."[3]

As was to be expected, advocates of repeal proposed various methods for accomplishing their desired result, including state control of the liquor traffic and, again, state referendum on enforcement within the states.

By the time the Eighteenth Amendment was ratified, thirty-three states had adopted state-wide Prohibition. Fifteen states were "wet," one in the South (Louisiana), and one in the West (California). Attempts in the ensuing ten years to change this general picture had failed, but efforts within both political parties were redoubled in such states as New York, Pennsylvania, and Illinois.

In the Congress, whenever any proposed method reached a vote, in committee or in full session, the political parties were shown to be divided. On some votes the division was fairly even, but never overwhelmingly for a "wet" proposal. By March 1932, in a proposal calling for a constitutional amendment providing for state rather than federal enforcement, the Republican members divided evenly. This foreshadowed the Republican platform position in the campaign of 1932.

In a press conference on March 19, 1929, President Hoover denied the rumor that he proposed to initiate some kind of drastic, dramatic Prohibition drive, startling in character. He said that his purpose was to build up the enforcement of the laws of the United States as rapidly as possible, whether these laws were related to prohibition of narcotics or any other subject. In that effort the president hoped to reorganize both administrative and judicial activity to the ultimate purpose of reducing crime in the United States. In this effort he expected the support of the press and of every decent citizen.

In his inaugural address Hoover said that it was essential that a large part of the enforcement activities pertaining to the Eighteenth Amendment be transferred from the Treasury Department to the Department of Justice as a beginning to more effective organization.

The following month, members of the press presented him with a number of questions bearing on the transfer of the Bureau of Prohibition to the Department of Justice. On April 12 he commented that, while the two departments were engaged upon a joint study of the method of transfer, there had been some suggestion of delaying action. The president said he did not see how this could be undertaken in the Congress then in session in view of the organization of the House.

The press inquired whether the transfer could be made by executive action, and the president said it could not.

In addressing the annual meeting of the Associated Press in New York City on April 22, the president said:

> I have accepted this occasion for a frank statement of what I consider the dominant issue before the American people. . . . That is the enforcement and obedience to the laws of the United States, both Federal and State.
>
> I ask only that you weigh this for yourselves, and if my position is right, that you support it—not to support me but to support something infinitely more precious—the one force that holds our civilization together—law. And I wish to discuss it as law, not as to the merits or demerits of a particular law but all law, Federal and State, for ours is a government of laws made by the people themselves.
>
> A surprising number of our people, otherwise of responsibility in the community, have drifted into the extraordinary notion that laws are made for those who choose to obey them. And, in addition, our law-enforcement machinery is suffering from many infirmities arising out of its technicalities, its circumlocutions, its involved procedures, and too often, I regret, from inefficient and delinquent officials. . . .
>
> In order to dispel certain illusions in the public mind on this subject, let me say at once that while violations of law have been increased by inclusion of crimes under the eighteenth amendment and by the vast sums that are poured into the hands of the criminal classes by the patronage of illicit liquor by otherwise responsible citizens, yet this is but one segment of our problem. I have purposely cited the extent of murder, burglary, robbery, forgery, and embezzlement, for but a small percentage of these can be attributed to the eighteenth amendment.[4]

The president took early action toward appointment of the National Law Enforcement Commission he had mentioned in his inaugural address. He had said:

> I propose to appoint a national commission for a searching investigation of the whole structure of our Federal system of jurisprudence, to include the method of enforcement of the eighteenth amendment and the causes of abuse under it. Its purpose will be to make such recommendations for

reorganization of the administration of Federal laws and court procedure as may be found desirable.[5]

The purpose and scope of the commission, as he told his press conference, was:

> . . . to critically consider the entire Federal machinery of justice, the redistribution of its functions, the simplification of its procedure, the provision of additional special tribunals, the better selection of juries, the more effective organization of our agencies of investigation and prosecution.[6]

The president's correspondence with Charles E. Hughes at this time reveals how serious was the need, in Hoover's view, of the reorganization of the judicial function of the national government.[7] So completely was the public preoccupied with the problem of the Eighteenth Amendment that there was little comprehension of the scope of the president's plan in appointing the National Law Enforcement Commission. The people were under the impression that this commission was to deal primarily with enforcement of the provisions of the Eighteenth Amendment, despite the president's intention, expressly stated, to have the commission investigate law infringement in general.

Hoover endeavored to secure for membership on the commission those who represented not only the public interest, but also a variety of political party affiliation and various views on the question of Prohibition. He sought the advice of two men of high judicial position, Charles Evans Hughes and Harlan Fiske Stone.[8]

The commission appointed in May 1929 included former Attorney General George W. Wickersham, chairman; former Secretary of War Newton D. Baker; U.S. Circuit Court Judge William S. Kenyon; U.S. District Court Judges Paul McCormick and William Grubb; former Chief Justice Kenneth MacKintosh of the Washington Supreme Court; Dean Roscoe Pound of Harvard University; Dr. Ada Comstock; and Messrs. Henry Anderson, Monte Lemann, and Frank J. Loesch.

As was natural, public discussion of the problem in the early months of the administration centered upon the *views* of the members of the commission rather than upon their qualifications for the task.

In speaking to the initial meeting of the commission at the White House on May 28, the president said:

> A nation does not fail from its growth of wealth or power. But no nation can for long survive the failure of its citizens to respect and obey the laws which they themselves make. . . . Nor is this a problem confined to the enforcement and obedience of one law or the laws of the Federal or State

Governments separately. The problem is partly the attitude toward all
law.[9]

The president had had before him the comments of several advisers
on the suggestion that the Bureau of Prohibition be transferred from the
Treasury Department to the Department of Justice. William J. Donovan
(who had been asked for his opinion) stated that he believed "transfer"
of administration of the Volstead Act to the Department of Justice would
be a major error. American tradition, he said, had followed the Anglo-
Saxon practice of separating the office of sheriff from the office of prosecuting attorney. If the district attorney were to be liquor administrator,
no self-respecting lawyer would take the office.[10] Although not acceptable
to the administration at the time, this reasoning foreshadowed the recognition later that the Eighteenth Amendment created an insoluble administrative problem.

It was fortunate at this juncture that the president had the advice of
Secretary Mellon, who wrote the following to him:

> . . . with reference to the organization of a special corps of attorneys in the
> Department of Justice with its own investigating staff, I enclose herewith a
> memorandum outlining the duties of the Special Agents of the Bureau of
> Prohibition. This force, with or without such additions as might be deter-
> mined upon, could be detailed to the Department of Justice without the
> necessity of any legislation. . . . The advisability of carrying out such a
> program is, of course, closely connected with your plans for the ultimate
> disposition of the prohibition enforcement agencies, but the above suggested
> program might well, pending the enactment of legislation, constitute a
> preliminary and logical step looking to the ultimate transfer of the Bureau
> of Prohibition to the Department of Justice.[11]

Later, Secretary Mellon advised the president that the problem was
fundamentally an administrative one. All of the facts were within the
knowledge of the executive departments.[12]

In a special message to Congress delivered on June 6, 1929, the president stated:

> In order to secure the utmost expedition in the reorganization and con-
> centration of responsibility in administration of the Federal bureaus con-
> nected with prohibition enforcement . . . I recommend that the Congress
> appoint a joint select committee to make an immediate study of these
> matters and to formulate recommendations for consideration at the next
> regular session. . . . As the question embraces numerous laws and regula-
> tions in several bureaus, it will require extensive consideration which if

given jointly by such committees of the Congress and the Departments prior to the regular session will save many months of delay.[13]

Nowhere in all of the early discussion of Hoover's leadership has there been greater misunderstanding than on his attitude toward the Prohibition issue. Much attention has been given to the fact that he, personally, had an open mind as to what could be done in the national emergency over this question. This was looked upon by zealots on both sides of the question as an element of weakness.

It should be clear that it was not an element of weakness except as that weakness was revealed in political terms. It was an element of strength that was inherent in Hoover's approach to public questions. He saw, as not everyone did, that this was by no means a question that could be dealt with simply in terms of investigations and facts and recommendations. It was a question that would be violently discussed, no matter what recommendations were made by whatever commission, and no matter what congressional action was taken upon it.

But the president had an abiding faith that the first principle that should guide the executive in office was enforcement of the law. The president was therefore bound to seek information about the possibility of the enforcement of the law, and information as to better enforcement of the law. If commentators upon this matter who dealt with the president's position had been wise enough to confine their attention to this approach, they would have produced something more than the confused state of the public mind and the violent denunciations that were so characteristic throughout this period of discussion.

The president continued to point out that the increase in crime throughout the nation was general. The largest group among the federal prisoners was the violators of the Narcotics Act, he said to his press conference several months later: "They comprise now about thirty-three per cent of the inmates at Leavenworth and Atlanta . . . while prohibition contributes about fourteen per cent."

In his message to the Seventy-first Congress on December 3, 1929, President Hoover again said that his first duty "under his oath of office" was to secure enforcement of the law. Since the enforcement of the laws enacted to give effect to the Eighteenth Amendment was "far from satisfactory," partly because of inadequate organization of the administrative agencies concerned, he again called for the transfer to the Department of Justice of the "Federal functions of detection and to a considerable degree of prosecution, which are now lodged in the Prohibition Bureau in the Treasury. . . ."[14]

Subsequently on December 27 the president took his press conference

behind the scenes and discussed the situation at length. Investigation of
the problem had revealed a no man's land between the executive and the
judicial branches of the government which obviously challenged Hoover's
keen interest. He had found that for some twenty-five years or more the
government had been steadily falling behind in its criminal work. The
District of Columbia, for example, was eighteen months behind in the
criminal docket. It was obviously impossible to enforce the law, he
thought, when it was necessary to wait eighteen months before a criminal
could be brought to trial.[15]

Whereas an increasingly cumbersome court procedure might account
for some of this delay, the growth of population would naturally add to
the burdens upon the courts, but Hoover felt that probably more important than any other factor was the very large expansion of the federal
government's activities into criminal control. This involved not only the
Prohibition laws but the laws controlling narcotics, and (curiously
enough) to an extraordinary degree the interstate theft of automobiles.
The Mann Act and the Immigration Act also gave the federal government responsibility for a very considerable area of criminal activity.
Although the enforcement machinery of the country had grown tremen-
dously, the machinery was far behind its load.

The Law Enforcement Commission, the President reported, had been
investigating the different phases of this problem with a view to arriving
at some sort of broad and effective solution. He was clearly troubled by
the revelations of abuse and uncertainty that had been uncovered.

One effect of this enormous piling up of the criminal activities of the
courts had been the tendency of district attorneys to try to get relief by
wholesale confessions, and the net result of that was the establishing of
a sort of licensing system by which the various offenders could confess
and be assured of a small fine, which put them in a position of considerable safety. There seemed to be some misunderstanding of the position
of district attorney. He was not a police officer; he could not go out himself and find a criminal and bring him into court. He had to wait until
various instruments of the government brought cases to him. Sometimes
the cases were not well presented, and the district attorney was not able
to get effective action. He blamed the police or the prosecuting agencies,
whatever they might be, for his failure, and they in turn blamed him and
blamed the Department of Justice.

Further confusion, Hoover found, was inevitable in the shifting of
responsibility among district attorneys, police, and state and federal
authorities.

Of the two or three alternatives possible in solving the problem of
overcrowding of the courts, the president felt that not one of them

escaped difficult constitutional as well as practical questions. To add to the number of district courts, to create subsidiary courts, or to increase the authority of the court commissioners would be alike impossible in this emergency. Furthermore, the president remarked that prohibition was not enforced by the Volstead Act, but by twenty-four different statutes, extending over forty years.

The president's prodigious efforts to coordinate the activities of the Law Enforcement Commission, the Congress, the Department of Justice, and the Bureau of Prohibition (originally in the Department of the Treasury) were partially rewarded when on May 27, 1930 he received authority to consolidate all the agencies dealing with Prohibition in the Department of Justice.[16]

When President Hoover finally, on January 20, 1931, received the report of the National Law Enforcement Commission, he found that two of the members were for repeal of the Eighteenth Amendment, six for its modification, and four for further trial of enforcement. The lack of unanimity and the lack of clarity in the recommendations, reasons, and conclusions of the report were distinctly embarrassing to the president, who stated:

> The Commission, by a large majority, does not favor the repeal of the eighteenth amendment as a method of cure for the inherent abuses of the liquor traffic. I am in accord with this view. . . . I . . . must not be understood as recommending the Commission's proposed revision of the eighteenth amendment which is suggested by them for possible consideration at some future time if the continued effort at enforcement should not prove successful. My own duty . . . is clear—to enforce the law with all the means at our disposal.[17]

Here, to the "drys," appeared a positive declaration in favor of the amendment as it stood. The "wet" Republicans took it that way, too, and quickly pressured the White House. The *New York Herald Tribune* was able to say the next day, however, that the president was still open-minded on the matter.

Hoover later revealed that his "personal difficulty was something that did not appear upon the surface," and that he had considered whether he "should . . . recommend repeal," but was advised by former Secretary of State Elihu Root that the president could not in effect veto a constitutional amendment as he could veto other forms of legislative action.[18]

Of course, Hoover's open-mindedness on the merits of Prohibition and on possible methods of enforcement was not pleasing to realistic politicians or to cynical commentators, and it certainly seemed inexplic-

able to a great number of the American people who were passionately
aligned on one side or the other of the controversy. This matter could not
be dealt with in terms of the president's declaration that he would
enforce the existing law, for it was impossible to do so.

The mood of the people, at least in urban areas, was described by
two commentators. Harvey O'Higgins noted "the new status that has
been conferred on drunkenness. Instead of being despised as a sign of
weakness, it is now esteemed as an evidence of strength. It marks the
proud rebel who will not be cowed by authority and is the fine free
gesture of the hero who proposes to be master of his fate."[19] Katharine
Fullerton Gerould took a more despairing view: "We sit at the feet of
the hobo, the bruiser, the criminal. . . . The fact is that luxury like Rome's
and ours always brings people back to the eternal crudities. . . . Only
aristocrats can make a spiritual use of leisure. . . . We are, by and large,
the mob enriched."[20]

Meanwhile, the people showed neither a change in practice nor in
attitude toward lawbreaking in general. Indeed, a disregard of law
seemed to suit the mood of the time.

When the Wickersham Commission made its report early in 1931, the
president was faced again with the dissatisfaction of the Republican
party on this issue. And in view of the rapid development of anti-
Prohibition sentiment over the nation as a whole, which seems to have
increased with rising unemployment and economic depression, the president had to deal with this change in the public mind as well.

The chief executive's approach to this matter was that of a public
official dedicated to the enforcement of the laws that were on the statute
books. It was inconceivable, however, that, as president and as leader
of the Republican party, he could recommend drastic change in the law
with any hope of a united party response or, for that matter, any hope of a
united nonpartisan support.

Yet Prohibition did not cease to be a political issue and it was one of
the crucial issues in the second campaign that Hoover waged for the
presidency. The "wets" and the "drys" were powerful in both of the great
political parties. The outcome of the election in 1928 seemed to many to
indicate that the "wets" had definitely been defeated. Nevertheless, it
was not at all evident that the "drys" had been successful, for the Republican party membership was seriously divided upon this question, and it
continued to be. A considerable number of Republicans did wish to
change the law.

Senator Borah was not one of these. As early as December 1929
Borah's criticism of the president for not making prohibition legislation
effective drew from the attorney general a sharp reminder that when

Congress was ready to consider and adopt legislation to carry out the administration's recommendations those whose duty it would be to enforce the law would be able to accomplish more.

The relations between Hoover and Senator Borah on law enforcement at this time were prophetic of Borah's uncompromising attitude in the campaign of 1932. The president was well aware of Borah's opinions and of their influence upon the public mind. Their contacts were frequent and they discussed in conference and by letter such matters as farm relief, flexible tariff, conservation, foreign relations and—especially, at this time—prohibition and law enforcement.[21]

On December 26, 1929, Borah had lunch with the president, and their conversation centered exclusively on Prohibition enforcement. There was a difference of opinion on the quality of enforcement personnel.[22] Shortly thereafter, Hoover wrote to Borah in painstaking detail to defend the personnel of the judicial system Borah had criticized:

> The question of appointments is a most important one, but it is nevertheless but one segment of a much wider problem which confronts us. . . . Our conclusions . . . are that the first and urgent steps are the expansion of court facilities; divorce of the permit system from the detection and prosecution system by transfer of the latter to the Department of Justice with concentrated responsibility; the consolidation of border patrols; enlargement of our prison and reformatory parole system; an increased salary basis for prosecuting attorneys and their assistants in order that we may command a better body of men without such a large degree of self-sacrifice; and a rigid day to day improvement in our law enforcement personnel by selection upon a basis of fitness; a tightening in enforcement processes without the dramatic drives with only evanescent effect, and with scrupulous adherence to lawful methods of law enforcement; and above all we need larger cooperation from the states, upon whom the major responsibility must rest in criminal matters.[23]

Hoover then hinted that "it would seem to me helpful if senators who believe in enforcement would inaugurate campaigns for more vigorous action by state authorities in their own states; . . . the greatest difficulty is in securing men of the necessary caliber for district attorneys. . . ." The president was firmly convinced that Borah was "greatly misinformed as to the character of the personnel of the Department of Justice and the results which they are obtaining." Subtly he suggested:

> You have often said that enforcement of law will never be perfect, but these men deserve encouragement instead of blame for failures in a system

which no one but Congress can remedy. . . . I do not understand your proposal to be different from that which I hold, unless you mean that I should publicly announce that the Attorney General shall disregard all recommendations from individual senators. . . . We cannot overlook the fact that confirmation obviously implies Senate reliance upon the views of senators from the states concerned. . . .

The candor and persuasiveness of this important letter was emphasized in the president's concluding statement:

In any event, I think you will agree with me that the problem of law enforcement is one which requires wide-spread reorganization of the federal agencies; that its machinery is of extreme delicacy which cannot be summarily dealt with; that we must develop its improvements step by step, and that we would not be able to overcome in any short term of years the difficulties which have accumulated over a period of a quarter of a century.[24]

Senator Borah's reply to the president was immediate:

What I fear is that one by one the states will vote themselves free of the obligation to enforce the law, or as nearly free as they can do so. . . . I am thoroughly convinced myself that the major portion of the fault lies with the officials who are charged with the duty of enforcement. . . . I cannot believe, Mr. President, that I am misinformed as to the personnel. . . . And I do not think I am in error. If I had had any doubt about the matter, I would not have spoken. And if I am convinced I am in error, I shall be only too happy to retract anything I have said.[25]

Then, as was his habit in political statement, Borah assumed an attitude of aloofness:

But, Mr. President, I look at this matter from a governmental standpoint. I am interested in this matter primarily from the standpoint of constitutional government. I cannot conceive of anything more destructive of the faith of a people in their government than to see the fundamental law daily and monthly and yearly trampled under foot. It demoralizes the whole people. And while I trust I shall be careful not to do any faithful servant an injustice, I promise you I shall not hesitate to expose from this time on men who compromise with duty when the Constitution of the United States is involved.[26]

A Borah correspondent at the time referred to the Idaho senator as follows: "Great and dear friend of the long years, I covet for you the supreme leadership in the maintenance of the Constitution and the

reestablishment of American liberty in this generation."[27] This seems to
have been Borah's self-image.

Although Borah had revealed that he had no intention of meeting the
basic issue in their discussions, the president continued to probe his
antagonist gently:

> I have the grave responsibility of keeping the Government clean and honest.
> Whoever the men are whom you mention, they have never placed their
> information at my disposal. It would help me greatly if you would give to
> me the names of the men you mention. . . . Any good citizen should be glad
> to inform his President. . . .[28]

Now it was Borah's turn. He declined to give the president any names,
but said he had suggested to the "parties" that they present the facts to
the president and thought that would be done in time. The remainder of
Borah's reply was devoted to a first, second, third, fourth, fifth, sixth, and
seventh series of attacks on the "industrial permit system" and "illicit
liquor," and concluded with a pronouncement that certainly would meet
with the president's hearty approval:

> I want to say again that it is my view no really successful, efficient enforce-
> ment of the prohibition law will be brought about until there is an entire
> divorcement between law enforcement and the political machines. . . .
> Machine politics and law enforcement do not go together. . . .[29]

There is reason to believe that the invisible curtain that fell between
Hoover and Borah soon after the election of 1928 was reinforced, on
Borah's side, by his uncompromising view of the Prohibition issue. This
issue was one of the last legacies of rural America to the national tradition. The movement that resulted in the Eighteenth Amendment drew
its strength from the agricultural districts. Opposition came from the
cities. Senator Borah prided himself upon symbolizing the rural morality,
as well as the rural economy, of the nation. President Hoover, though
himself derived from Borah's ideal community, had long been a citizen
of the world, a position which demanded deeper insight into economic,
social, and political problems, domestic and foreign alike. The two met
on a high plane of conflict, to be sure, but Borah did not comprehend
his antagonist. Possibly he did not wish to do so. The clash between the
two on Prohibition was a symbol of more to come.

A contemporary biographer has summarized the extent of disagreement:

> The Senator found it necessary to differ strenuously with the President on

the tariff, farm relief, unemployment relief, judicial appointments, the World Court, Prohibition, Andrew Mellon, high government expenditures, the creation of bureaus and commissions, silver and the currency, and the independence of the Philippines.[30]

Borah saw himself as consistent before and after 1928. Gone, however, were the days of the campaign of that year, and the Borah who would extravagantly praise "the miracle man." Gone too, for the president, was one more aspect of hope that insurgent senators would support his program.[31]

— 8 —

Legacy in Foreign Relations

I am not of those who have an impatience of honest debate. I believe that the debate over the League of Nations going on in the United States is building the very foundations of the League. It is bringing home to every household in the country the necessity and possibility of providing for our own safety and of providing for the safety of the world as a whole without great armies or navies. Nor do I believe in the criticism of the Senate for not accepting out of hand this document so laboriously evolved by five hundred conflicting minds in Paris. It is a fundamental part of our institutions that the Senate shall scrutinize these matters.

Herbert Hoover, Address on The League of Nations,
October 2, 1919

Hoover had early thrown his support to American entrance into the League of Nations. But in the campaign of 1920, his support of Harding caused many League supporters to begin to doubt him. He was, after all, a man who envisaged the United States as a powerful national force in international affairs. In any case, his fundamental views on foreign policy were known then and during the election of 1928.

Upon assuming office, President Hoover hoped, as he later expressed it, "to pull the people of the United States out of the extreme mental and spiritual isolationism which for years had made impossible a proper American participation in the constructive building of peace in the world."[1] His concern that the United States should assume greater responsibility in world affairs had been demonstrated by his frequent addresses and messages on the subject. He had said in 1919:

Those who think we can isolate ourselves seem to ignore the fact that modern communication has shortened our distance from our neighbors from a month

97

to an hour. A vast amount of our civilization and the daily improvements of life that come to our people are the products of the ideas and intelligence and labor of our neighbors. . . . We are an overseas people and we are dependent upon Europe for the surplus products of our farmers and laborers. Without order in Europe we will at best have business depression, unemployment, and all their burden of troubles. With renewed disorganization in Europe, social diseases and anarchy thrive, and we are infected with every social wind of Europe. We are forced to interest ourselves in the welfare of the world if we are to thrive.[2]

The League of Nations had been proposed "by leading spirits in all civilized nations. It belongs to no one man, it comes from the heart and mind of the world." He regretted that "this council of nations" should be termed a "league," for, he said, "the term smacks of military alliance." And he warned that in "the desperation to which Europe has been reduced," if the League should break down, "we must at once prepare to fight."

Nevertheless, he was as wary of being "dragged into European entanglements" as he had been when advising Wilson in April 1919.[3] And he was as alert to the development of communism in Europe as he had been while secretary of commerce. Although Hoover had saved millions of Russians from starvation in his relief work abroad, he had supported the administrations of Harding and of Coolidge in withholding recognition from the Soviet government. "I often likened the problem to having a wicked and disgraceful neighbor," Hoover explained later. "We did not attack him, but we did not give him a certificate of character by inviting him into our homes."[4]

President Harding appointed Secretary Hoover a member of the Advisory Committee of the Naval Arms Conference that met in Washington in 1922, and of the World War Foreign Debt Commission. Hoover was intimately concerned with the deliberations of the commission on German Reparations. At one stage in the work of the War Debt commission, Hoover proposed "that we cancel all the debts incurred before the Armistice and require the payment in full of loans made after the Armistice, with a rate of interest equal to that which we paid on our own bonds." He felt that "this would have strengthened our moral position, as we should have been asking repayment of advances only for reconstruction and not for war."[5]

Two beliefs animated every utterance and action of President Hoover throughout his White House years. One was his native devotion to peace which had been compounded by the horrors of war that he had witnessed. The other was his belief in American democracy and in the possibility of the expansion of its accepted practices beyond the borders of the United

States. His language a decade earlier had been forceful:

> I believe that if the intelligence of the world can be aggregated around a table, the pressures from the responsibility of these men for the possible enormous loss of life and the fabulous amount of human misery created by their failure to prevent war are such that no body of decent men in these times can fail to secure some sort of solution short of war. We have now seen the most terrible five years of history because the reactionaries of Europe refused to come into a room to discuss the welfare of humanity.[6]

It followed that Hoover believed in fair dealing among nations as the insurance of friendship and cooperation. He believed the guidance of established law was essential to international justice. In case of international disagreements, reasoned judgment on the part of a court of arbitration should be the solution. That force should not be used except to resist criminal aggression was his deep-seated conviction.

Hoover was nevertheless bluntly realistic. He knew that beliefs and principles, and adherence thereto by nations and their representatives, were not enough to preserve peace. Threats to absolute freedom in presidential decision lay in events beyond our borders that could not be foreseen nor controlled, and especially in the words and actions of innumerable Americans abroad and at home. Such persons—some of them in official positions, like Secretary Stimson—represented a view of the role of the United States in the world that conflicted to a degree with Hoover's view.

Moreover, the president was bound by the Constitution in his exercise of the powers of the presidency, and bound by commitments of previous administrations. His action was always limited by public opinion in the United States. Popular conception and knowledge (or lack of it) were of immeasurable importance to this president who always conditioned his final judgment upon his faith in the American people.

Power politics were repugnant to President Hoover. He early served notice to the world of his attitude by establishing a new relationship with the countries of Latin America. His good will trip to Latin America prior to his inauguration was an indication of this. He took early occasion, after entering office, to dispel "one sinister notion . . . as to policies of the United States, . . . that is, fear of an era of the mistakenly called dollar diplomacy." He rejected intervention by force to "maintain contracts."[7]

Hoover later explained:

> As Secretary of Commerce I had developed an increasing dissatisfaction with our policies toward Latin America. I was convinced that unless we displayed an entirely different attitude we should never dispel the suspicions

and fears of the "Colossus of the North" nor win the respect of those nations. An interpretation of the Monroe Doctrine to the effect that we had the right to maintain order in those states by Military force, in order not to give excuse for European intervention, created antagonisms and suspicions which dominated the politics of much of the Latin area. . . . The policy of military intervention practiced by the Wilson Administration had been continued by Harding and Coolidge.[8]

He proceeded to act along new lines. In 1930 he directed the release of the so-called Clark Memorandum which had been written at the request of Secretary of State Kellogg by international lawyer and former Under-secretary of State J. Reuben Clark near the end of the Coolidge adminis-tration. This memorandum denied to the United States the role of inter-national policeman in Latin America once assumed under the Monroe Doctrine. President Coolidge did not see fit to make the memorandum public, but Hoover, who was in accord with its pronouncement, had it published as a public document early in 1930.[9]

In his first annual message to the Congress on December 3, 1929, the president reviewed the situation in some detail:

> We still have marines on foreign soil—in Nicaragua, Haiti, and China. In the large sense we do not wish to be represented abroad in such manner. About 1,600 marines remain in Nicaragua at the urgent request of that government and leaders of all parties pending the training of a domestic constabulary capable of insuring tranquility. We have already reduced these forces materially and we are anxious to withdraw them further as the situation warrants. In Haiti we have about 700 marines, but it is a much more difficult problem, the solution of which is still obscure.[10]

Four days later, Hoover requested that Congress authorize a commission to investigate conditions in Haiti. (A treaty of 1915 under which forces of the United States were to be present in that country to assist in restora-tion of order was to terminate in 1936.) By December 1930, Hoover reported that the commission had completed its investigation, recom-mended future policies, "and proved of high value in securing acceptance of these policies."[11] The president then ordered withdrawal of the marines remaining in Nicaragua; this began on June 3, 1931.

Another result of Hoover's preinaugural visit to Latin America was the settlement of the long pending Tacna-Arica dispute between Peru and Bolivia, which the United States had been asked to arbitrate. Learn-ing "by cautious inquiry . . . the approximate limits of concession that both sides would make,'"[12] he was able, upon his return to Washington, to effect a compromise which disposed of the matter.[13]

President Hoover regarded his new policy toward Latin America as strictly nonpartisan, and he referred to it as the attitude of the "good neighbor." The later adoption of this term by President Franklin D. Roosevelt, first with reference to Latin America and afterwards to American relations throughout the world, accompanied by much publicity, led to considerable popular ignorance of the pioneering role essayed by President Hoover.[14]

Early in his administration the chief executive let it be known that he favored the removal of political appointees from the list of ministers and ambassadors in Latin American countries and the appointment of career men, preferably those who knew the language and the people of the countries in which they were sent.

Secretary of State Stimson later stated, in summarizing the policies of the administration:

> We have sought to make our policy towards them so clear in its implications of justice and good will, in its avoidance of anything which could be even misconstrued into a policy of forceful intervention or a desire for exploitation of those republics and their citizens, as to reassure the most timid or suspicious among them.[15]

In carrying out his policies in Latin America, the president had the warm support of both Secretary of State Stimson and of Undersecretary William R. Castle, Jr., who remarked that "in the protection of American interests in Latin-American countries, the Monroe Doctrine has no more place than in the protection of those interests in the Orient."[16] Castle also neutralized criticism of the Hoover policy in Latin America as a Republican party policy by declaring: "Our relations with Latin America are, above all, not in any way partisan. It is the United States which has duties and responsibilities, not the party. To be sure, the party in power has to carry out those duties and responsibilities. . . ."[17]

Most of the Latin American countries, but Argentina and Uruguay in particular, reacted unfavorably to the Smoot-Hawley Tariff Act.[18] It is judged that in reality "the new duties did not greatly affect trade relations with most of Latin America; nevertheless, they undeniably had a bad effect on inter-American relations."[19] This was inevitable.

Still, one of Hoover's critics concluded at the time: "On the whole, Mr. Hoover's record in regard to Latin America is excellent."[20] Overall, Hoover pursued his belief that the principles of American democracy may be applied in dealing with other nations, and this meant uprooting the mythology of American imperialism in the various forms in which it had been emphasized ever since the beginning of the century.

President Hoover had indicated already his interest in naval limitations.[21] Prior to his inauguration he conferred on the matter with Ambassador to Belgium Hugh Gibson who was called to be his new "Ambassador
at Large." Gibson was to attend a meeting of the League of Nations
Committee on Disarmament and deliver a speech (on the framing of
which the president worked). "The League had never seriously dealt with
this question, and I thought to inject life into its discussions by having
Mr. Gibson deliver a bold and unexpected proposal," Hoover wrote later.
"In this speech Gibson dealt with 'yardsticks' which might be used." In
this manner the president countered British opposition based on grounds
of impracticality.[22]

With the active support of Ambassador Dawes, President Hoover laid
plans for a British agreement with the United States on naval limitations.[23]

Now Prime Minister Ramsay MacDonald chose to come to the United
States as President Hoover's guest. The MacDonald visit marked in some
ways a coming of age in American power and was a first. The president
greeted MacDonald via radio: "As you near the shores of the United
States I send to you a most cordial welcome not only in my own name
but on behalf of my fellow countrymen as well."[24] MacDonald replied
from the *Berengaria*: "Greetings and hearty thanks for your message. I
greatly value your kind words of welcome on behalf of yourself and your
fellow countrymen and they will be highly appreciated by mine."[25]

The talks were general but, in longhand memoranda presented to the
prime minister at the outset (October 5, 1929), the president made clear
that his interest was primarily in "measures for prevention of war." He
hoped that treaties of conciliation and arbitration would become more
common. The League of Nations Covenant, he thought, was inadequate
in that "it does not provide for such action originating in the parties in
the controversy or for their being represented upon such commissions or
for friendly suggestion that they should set up such inquiry themselves."[26]
In another memorandum Hoover urged full and frank examination, by a
body of jurists chosen from maritime nations, of the question of neutral
trade with belligerents during war. "As to myself, I should be glad to see
food ships declared as irrevocably free from interference. Nothing can be
more hideous than starvation of women and children. None of the great
naval powers including ourselves have been free from the use of this
weapon."[27]

The talks lasted for ten days. Some were at Rapidan Camp. Press
releases tended to emphasize "moral" understandings and influences. But
there was progress toward good Anglo-American relations. MacDonald
later told Ambassador Dawes, in the latter's words, "We threw aside all
the old rectitudes of mid-Victorian and still more ancient clothes; we

never beat about the bush; we never employed the methods and the language of circumlocution. We went straight at it. We were informal."[28] In a note to the president the prime minister said, "I think and feel that with the help of the local brigade—between us but not entre nous—we have done something to insure our citizens against conflagration."[29] Hoover's own recollection was that "on the 6th at the Rapidan Camp we went down the creek and on a log threshed out the points as yet unsettled in the naval agreement."[30]

Hoover's view of the practical consequences of the forthcoming conference on naval limitations was reflected in a press conference where he said the American people should understand that current expenditures of the army and navy totalled the largest military budget of any nation in the world, even though there appeared to be less real danger of extensive disturbance of peace than at any time in more than half a century. The hope of tax reduction lay very largely in the ability to economize on military expenditures while maintaining an adequate defense. The national situation was considerably modified by the Kellogg-Briand pact, he believed. Moreover, an international agreement on reduction of naval arms would bring savings.[31]

Hoover told the reporters he agreed with the secretary of war that the general staff needed a commission of leading army officers to reconsider the army program over the next four years to see what services and other outlays had become obsolete, and what developmental programs could well be considered over long periods—in view of the general world outlook—while completely maintaining adequate preparedness. The investigation would be entirely constructive and not in any sense negligent of defense.

To President Hoover's suggestion that the British consider selling the United States British Honduras and the islands of Bermuda and Trinidad, Prime Minister MacDonald did not respond, Hoover recalled. Nor would MacDonald agree to support Hoover in a proposal to "devise stronger diplomatic teeth" for the Kellogg-Briand Pact.[32]

The American delegation to the London Conference on Naval Limitation was to consist of Secretary Stimson as chairman, Secretary of the Navy Adams, and Senators David Reed and Joseph T. Robinson. Three ambassadors were to participate: Dawes, who had prepared the way under the careful direction of the president; Gibson, a close friend of the president; and Dwight Morrow, ambassador to Mexico. Admiral William V. Pratt was to be Chief Naval Adviser.

Dawes later recalled with satisfaction the time in preparation:

My three days in Washington were, of course, devoted chiefly to naval matters. My conferences were with Secretary Stimson and Assistant Secretary Joseph B. Cotton, but chiefly with the President. As his guest at the White House during my stay, opportunity was given for hours of consideration without distraction. My admiration for his grasp of the problem, both in general and in detail, already great, was heightened by this continued contact. He has had a constant struggle to get fair play from the Naval Board, and he would never have got it, in my judgment, had he not mastered the technical elements of the question as thoroughly as the Board. To mislead him was impossible. Every report made was checked over with at least the same if not greater competency than that with which it was prepared.[33]

Senator Borah, chairman of the Senate Foreign Relations Committee, declined President Hoover's invitation to serve on the American delegation to the London Conference on Naval Limitation, pleading his preoccupation with tariff legislation and farm relief at home. He was certain that "in the long run" he could be of "more service off the delegation than by being a member of it."[34] It is doubtful that the president was disheartened by Borah's decision, for the chairman of the Senate Foreign Relations Committee was cast in the role of isolationist and a leading adversary. Borah had long interested himself in the results of the Limitation of Armaments Conference that had met in Washington in 1922, and he naturally had had a part in the early preparation for the London conference. But it was difficult to reach his sympathy, even on routine matters of foreign relations.[35] That Borah early in the Hoover administration had submitted a resolution in the Senate to the effect "that the Senate of the United States favors the recognition of the present Soviet Government of Russia," emphasized his differences with the president.[36] Borah's was "the diplomacy of abstinence."[37]

The Conference on Naval Limitation began in London on January 21, 1930 and continued until April 22. There followed a period in which it was necessary to obtain from the United States Senate a ratification of the resulting Treaty for the Limitation and Reduction of Naval Armament. The president transmitted the treaty to the Senate on May 1, 1930. Opposition there delayed ratification, and the president called a special session of that body on June 13 and issued a biting statement in defense of the treaty. His analysis of opposition in other countries, as well as in the United States, was clear and prophetic. He said:

The real issue in the treaty is whether we shall stop competitive naval building with all the destruction and dangers to international good-will which continuation on these courses implies; whether we shall spend an enormous sum in such a race to catch up with competitors, with no assurance that we will reach parity and proportionate strength even with such an expenditure; and whether the present agreement gives us a substantial parity and proportionate strength and therefore with our army absolute defensive power, and accomplishes this by an agreement which makes for good-will, for decrease in the naval armament of the world, and puts our program of naval renewals and cruiser construction at a cost far less than would otherwise be required.[38]

Hoover's friends rallied to his defense on the treaty during this session. Dawes, who was in Washington at this time, felt that the situation was favorable.[39] Henry M. Robinson of Los Angeles, one of the president's most loyal supporters, was not so sure and was in a mood to call for an amendment to the Constitution to provide for the approval of treaties by a majority of the Senate and the House, if the Senate should continue to delay ratification.[40]

The special session of the Senate called by the president on July 7, was told:

> It is folly to think that because we are the richest nation in the world we can outbuild all other countries. Other nations will make any sacrifice to main-tain their instruments of defense against us, and we shall eventually reap in their hostility and ill will the full measure of the additional burden which we may thus impose upon them. The very entry of the United States into such courses as this would invite the consolidation of the rest of the world against us and bring our peace and independence into jeopardy.[41]

Meanwhile, it had become clear that opponents of the president on other matters were at the front of the battle against ratification. Senators Borah and Johnson led in this. To a Senate resolution asking the president to submit to the Senate all letters, cablegrams, minutes, memoranda, instructions . . . and other information touching the negotiations of the London Naval Treaty, the president replied that the preparation of the treaty had involved a great deal of confidential interchange. "To make public in debate or in the press such confidences would violate the invari-able practice of nations," said Hoover. The treaty contained "no secret or concealed understandings, promises, or interpretations. . . . No senator has been refused an opportunity to see the confidential material referred to, provided only he will agree to receive and hold the same in the con-fidence in which it has been received and held by the Executive."[42] In all this, it would appear, "Hoover did not take lightly his duties and his constitutional obligations. There is no evidence that he was willing to allow the Senate to usurp any of his powers."[43]

The treaty was ratified by the Senate on July 21, 1930, by a vote of fifty-eight to nine. Senators Borah, Norris, LaFollette, and Walsh (Montana) were among those who voted for ratification; Senators Hiram W. Johnson, Bingham, Hale, McKellar, Moses, Oddie, Pine, Robinson (Indiana) and Walsh (Massachusetts) voted against it.[44]

Long in the making, this treaty was regarded by the American delegation as a great triumph for President Hoover. Although France, Italy, and Japan were not satisfied, the British and the Americans emerged with satisfaction. Ambassador Dawes reflected that "Anglo-American relations reached a level of cordiality in the year after the London Conference that was not equalled again until 1940."[45] In retrospect, "the victory went to Hoover, and it showed the world that the United States was not adverse to all forms of international cooperation."[46] Moreover, it marked a victory by the civil authorities over the military experts.

The good envisaged by Hoover in the early months of 1929 as emerging from an agreement with Great Britain, in particular, had been attained. And it was accompanied by a very good feeling between the governments of the two nations. But it must be added that subsequent events in Japan, and the development of distrust in Italy and France, were traceable in part to the deliberations and decisions of this conference. Dawes noted on October 18, 1930, that "President Hoover is confronted with what seems to be a well-nigh irrepressible conflict between France and Italy, but, as in the past, he is preserving initiative."[47] The Navy League, pressure group for Navy prestige, at first attacked the treaty but finally gave cautious support.[48] Vessels were to be scrapped, and plainly, some could—and would—be built, but a reading of the *New York Times* shows that people in general felt there had been accomplishment toward peace.[49] The treaty was well received at home.[50] Anglo-American relations were improved. If indeed a moral victory for the president, it would still prove ephemeral in a world replete with competing nationalism. Still, for the first time, all of the naval weapons of three great nations were limited, and national freedom of action was relinquished in favor of an international agreement.[51] The importance of this is better seen in the perspective of years.

In furtherance of his moves for the maintenance of peace, Hoover had long advocated adherence of the United States to the World Court of International Justice. American membership in the court had been opposed by a large number of members of both political parties, and their representatives in the Senate had prevented action. Mr. Hoover reflected later: "When I took office America was so isolationist that our proper responsibilities were neglected. Congress was adamant against the World Court, and even to suggest that we would collaborate with the League of Nations in its many nonpolitical activities brought storms of protest."⁵² President Hoover had enlisted the interest of Elihu Root, who drew up a formula for American participation that was incorporated by the president in his recommendation to the Senate on December 10, 1930.

It was not brought to a vote, and the president renewed his appeal in his message to Congress on foreign affairs of December 10, 1931: "I need not repeat that for over twelve years every President and every Secretary of State has urged this action as a material contribution to the pacific settlement of controversies among nations and a further assurance against war."⁵³ The opposition was again successful in preventing the issue from reaching a vote in the Senate.

It should be remembered that a large segment of American public opinion construed membership in the World Court as a stepping stone to membership in the League of Nations. As a correspondent of the *New York Herald Tribune* wrote on May 9, 1929, "... the attempt to bring us into a World Court under the Root formula is as truly a fight to enter the League of Nations ... as was the first effort which the advocates of the League made in 1919 and 1920. . . . Every leading individual in this country now urging the Root formula is pledged to our joining the League."

Nevertheless, during the four years of the Hoover administration, there were concluded twenty-five arbitration treaties· and seventeen treaties of conciliation with individual nations.⁵⁴

In international problems not included in Hoover's thinking at the beginning of his term, but forced upon him by the world-wide economic depression, the president achieved positive results. He had a plan to aid the western European nations in the crisis of the spring and summer of 1931. His proposals for relief of Europe were similar to his proposals for relief of the United States in the Great Depression: reliance upon national initiative and self-help. In any case, the determination to act could be termed a real advance toward genuine international action, always Hoover's chief objective. He welcomed any indication of realization that fundamental economic questions were, as he would put it, "world questions."

The maintenance of stable currencies, world-wide reduction of armament to release more means of livelihood to the peoples of the world; and making "productive enterprise" the object of international lending and borrowing—these were Hoover's favorite themes of economic statesmanship. Furthermore, he believed that American aid to a disordered world was not enough; there must be American interest and participation in settlement of questions outside American borders.

Hoover was later to give his support to the work of the World Disarmament Conference that met in 1932, proposing through the American representative the abolition of all offensive weapons and the reduction of existing armament by nearly one-third. These revolutionary proposals were antedated, however, by the development of the military crisis in the Far East.[55]

The president did not favor the use of economic sanctions against an offending power. He argued that this policy led inevitably to war. He attempted to develop the idea of moral sanctions. It was, indeed, an extension of the American idea of withholding recognition of the seizure of territory in violation of principles previously agreed upon. This was a basic principle in the Hoover thought pattern.

President Hoover's efforts to bring about a reorganization of the foreign service were predicated on the belief that "an able and experienced American diplomatic representation abroad had been neglected as a factor in preserving peace."[56] He succeeded in obtaining "career men" for thirty-three countries and established an Ambassador-at-Large in Europe in the person of Hugh Gibson, Ambassador to Belguim.

Characteristic of Hoover's belief in calling upon energy and resourcefulness in the conduct of the foreign service was his appointment of Nicholas Roosevelt, an experienced foreign correspondent of the *New York Times*, as minister to Hungary. Roosevelt's experience in central European affairs during the armistice following World War I equipped him to render the State Department unique service in warning of the collapse of central European finances in the crisis involving the Viennese Credit-Anstalt, at a time when career diplomats in adjacent capitals did not share his interest in financial and economic problems.[57]

Quite apart from his pronouncements on foreign policy and his reference to particular items in foreign programs, President Hoover from time to time talked at his press conferences about the position of the United States in the world. He talked in terms that those who knew the world understood perfectly. He was less well understood by those who had had no experience outside the United States and who had no clear-cut conception of the part played by Great Britain in the continent of Europe, for example, or of the undermining influence of the rise of dictatorships in western Europe. The careful planning of the administration program in Haiti was beyond the comprehension of those who had given little thought to the subtleties of race relations.

Repeatedly Hoover made it evident that one who early had urged American entrance, with proper restrictions, into the League of Nations was one who naturally took for granted that the United States would participate in the World Court.[58] By insisting upon an aggressive policy of international participation, President Hoover endeavored to make it possible to protect the interests of growing democracies throughout the world.

From his vantage point of great influence the president hoped that in the Asiatic world emerging from dependence upon a declining Europe the United States could provide an example in its social and political system and in its economy that would serve as an antidote not only to violent revolution but to the lure of both Communist and Fascist philosophy.

Perhaps a broader understanding of what the president believed and a clearer comprehension of what he intended would have been available to the representatives of the press who reported what he said to them from time to time, had more of them, in that day, had a wider knowledge of world economics and politics. The problem was inevitable, but one effect was a gap, in understanding, between newspaper readers and their president in the realm of world affairs.

— 9 —

A Hostile Senate: The Tariff

*. . . the essence of accomplishment in government lies
in that threadbare expression—cooperation. I wish
sometimes our language afforded us a few more syno-
nyms for the word, because we sometimes become so
weary of repetition of phrases that we would defeat
great purposes and abandon great ideas because of our
annoyance with words. Our form of government can
succeed only by cooperation—not only by cooperation
within the administrative arm of the Government and
with Congress, but also by cooperation with the press,
cooperation with business, and the cooperation in
social leadership.*
Herbert Hoover, Address before the Gridiron Club,
Washington, D. C., April 13, 1929

The president had made it clear in his inaugural address that he looked
upon the declaration of the party in favor of a limited revision of the
tariff as an important part of his program. In calling for a special session
of the Seventy-first Congress to proceed at once with this matter, Hoover
merely repeated the views that he had stated in the course of the campaign.

On May 9, 1929, the House Committee on Ways and Means reported
a tariff bill (H.R. 2667). Hearings had been held in the short session of
the Congress. Now appeared a great number of new proposals under
limited revision. These perhaps could go properly to a tariff commission
with added powers. On May 12, the president met with several members
of the House Committee on Ways and Means and protested many items.
On May 22, in conference at the White House, he urged House leaders
to get changes on farm products and reject industrial changes. On May
23, the House agreed. The tariff bill passed the House.

110

It became evident, after many weeks of debate, that there was no possibility of securing from the Senate either approval of the tariff bill prepared and passed by the House or approval of added powers to the tariff commission advocated by the president and urged by him in repeated conferences. A detailed account of this struggle between the president and the Senate is essential to an understanding of all that was to follow in the depressing winter of 1929–30.[1]

As is well known, the United States Senate is continuous, not only from administration to administration, but from generation to generation —"an undying body with an existence continuous since its first creation." Thus, the Senate cannot express the mandate of the voters declared at a particular election, because as a rule two-thirds of its members are "holdovers." A state often has senators of divergent views or even of opposing parties. Most striking is it that the majority of the Senate membership does not represent the majority of the nation's population. Nine states in 1930, for example, each had a smaller population than the city of San Francisco; yet these states sent eighteen senators to Washington. The power granted the Senate by the Constitution in the ratification of treaties, the approval of appointments, the passage of legislation—in addition to the investigation of public business—is so great that the Senate has again and again dominated the life of the government.

In the closing years of the Wilson administration, the Senate had achieved prominence, not only in the United States but in the world at large, by its aggressive attitude and final negative action on the League of Nations Covenant. This was a striking illustration of a general condition. A powerful Senate opposition effectively stood across the path of presidential leadership.

The Senate continued to set its will against Wilson's successors, Harding and Coolidge, particularly on foreign relations. The danger to effective government at this time came not from the Republican party organization—supposedly in control of the Senate—but from individual senators and particularly from the so-called insurgent group, some of whom had been fighting the dominant party leaders for more than twenty years.

Yet despite this familiar situation, the political complexion of the Senate of the United States was not understood by the public at the time of President Hoover's inauguration. It was a condition fully understood by the president, however, who had been in Washington during the previous eight years and had been a very careful observer of the processes by which legislation had been secured and denied.

He knew that a group of experienced legislators in the Senate were in a position to support him effectively, as it was hoped might be the case, in the major matters which he urged upon them. But he also knew that they were in a position to do what was more their habit: to limit the programs of the president, and, indeed, more often than not, to destroy them.

It had long been the view of many experienced senators that it was the duty of this never-ceasing body to lead the president, whoever he might be. James E. Watson, the titular leader of the Senate Republicans for a considerable period, tried to tell President Hoover what to do on the frequent occasions when the senator was at the White House. To the Senate, Watson made clear his conception of the severely limited duty of the president:

> I think it is the business of Congress to legislate, and it is the business of the President to fill his place and either to approve or disapprove the legislation when it reaches him. I do not believe that it is the business of the President of the United States constantly to be mixing up in legislative matters. Where would a President be if he would undertake to send for Senators on every schedule [of the tariff] that comes up [;] to give his advice, or his direction, if you please, for the purpose of controlling the action of the Senate of the United States on any propositions before this body. Time and again I have suggested to him . . . that he keep out of this contest until the bill reaches him, unless something absolutely necessary forces him into some kind of a statement. . . .[2]

On two points the utterances of well-recognized leaders of the Republican party made the president's task no easier: they repeatedly asserted that the western insurgents were really not Republicans except in name; and, in bitterness and derision, the party conservatives reminded one and all that the western leaders were not only "irregular," but were representative of undeveloped and backward areas. "Sons of the Wild Jackass," said Senator George H. Moses. Wherever the conservatives happened to be—in Omaha, Chicago, or San Francisco, as well as in the older cities of the eastern seaboard—they were united on their side of the party conflict. To the vast number of habitual Republicans in the Middle West and Far West the situation was regrettable, but they did not actively resent it. And it was this that strengthened the insurgents in opposition to the party organization in Washington.[3]

Moreover, the titular leaders in the Senate were conservatives; in fact, they were so far to the right of the president as to warrant the term *reactionary*. But of course the most conspicuous Republican members of the Senate at this time were the rebels against party rule. Therefore, except in those matters wherein his own initiative, planning, and activity could determine the issue (at least in obtaining the attention of the country), the president was at a great disadvantage.

Senators believed they advanced the views of their constituents. Thus the final word in every discussion was *politics* rather than *policy*. A senator could not easily subscribe to the statement of President Hoover in his inaugural address that "the animosities of elections should have no place in our Government, for government must concern itself alone with the common weal."

Furthermore, throughout the preceding decade of peacetime presidents, members of the Senate, conscious that they were in positions of power for periods of time longer (and perhaps much longer) than the president, realized they had determining power in legislative matters in that they could quite easily deny, delay, and often determine action by inaction. An outburst of Senator Hiram Johnson, however, on October 2, 1929 was illustrative of the realization that the situation had changed: "... God knows, none upon this side [Republican] would dare say that we have a weak Executive today."[1]

The Senate of the Seventy-first Congress that had convened in special session on April 15, 1929, was a self-sufficient and aggressive group, powerful in all governmental affairs. It was known to the nation as a body of "independents." Yet not more than one-half of its members were known beyond their own communities, even though some of them had served for more than a quarter of a century.

Continuing in the administration of President Hoover were five senators who had begun their service prior to the inauguration of President Taft in 1909. Four, Francis E. Warren of Wyoming, Furnifold M. Simmons of North Carolina, Reed Smoot of Utah, and Lee S. Overman of North Carolina, had served in the Senate for more than twenty-five years. Thirteen others had entered the Senate prior to 1913 and twenty-four during the administration of Woodrow Wilson. Just one-half of the Senate of the Seventy-first Congress had entered between 1921 and 1929. Only ten had entered upon office with President Hoover.

Here was a body of experienced legislators. One-half of them had already been through two tariff sessions. Smoot and Warren had served on the Finance Committee under Nelson W. Aldrich. Such senators as George W. Norris of Nebraska, Thomas J. Walsh of Montana, and William E. Borah of Idaho had long been familiar with every aspect of the work of the Senate.

Although twenty-five members had come to Washington without previous experience in politics, the remaining seventy-one had considerable political experience. Thirty-seven had served in state legislatures and twenty-eight had served in the House of Representatives. Eight had served as judges; twenty had been governors; one had been in the diplomatic service. Sixty were lawyers.

A Senate has been defined literally as "an assembly of old men." At the beginning of the special session of 1929, one-fourth of the United States Senate were sixty-five years of age or more, and two-thirds were past fifty years. All except sixteen had been voters for thirty years or more, and their political direction had been set before the opening of the century. More than one-half had entered the senate when past fifty years of age, nine when past sixty years. Theodore E. Burton of Ohio and Frederick H. Gillett of Massachusetts were seventy-seven; Simmons and Overman, seventy-five; Carter Glass of Virginia, seventy-one; Walsh of Montana, sixty-nine; Norris and Smoot, sixty-seven; Watson, sixty-four; Borah, sixty-one; George H. Moses of New Hampshire and Smith W. Brookhart of Iowa, sixty. The average age was 57.8 and the spread of years was just a half-century from Francis E. Warren (eighty-four) to Robert M. LaFollette, Jr. of Wisconsin (thirty-four).

Such an assembly was not to be easily moved in matters of politics or public policy. There had developed within this body an unusual esprit de corps, particularly evident among those who had served long, even though they were on opposite sides of the Senate chamber and opposed on most public questions. It was the recently arrived recruits who were likely to meet sharpest rebuke on policy as well as procedure.

Senators of known independence were in positions of committee control because of the rule of seniority. It was this that had given members from western states important committee assignments: Charles L. McNary of Oregon, Francis Warren of Wyoming, Peter Norbeck of South Dakota, Wesley L. Jones of Washington, Smoot of Utah, Borah of Idaho, Johnson of California, Lynn V. Frazier of North Dakota, and Norris of Nebraska.

Except for Warren and Smoot, and possibly McNary and Jones, these were not men who had in the past followed the party organization in the Senate. In vain did new arrivals of unimpeachable regularity protest, for there was no authority, that is, party authority, which the outstanding figures in either party were bound or disposed to acknowledge.

Although the Republican party had fifty-five members at the opening of the session (fifty-six when Joseph R. Grundy was seated), twenty-two of these came from less populous states and represented only seven million inhabitants. Of thirty-nine Democratic senators, only six came from states with small populations.

What manner of men were these ninety-six senators? All except a dozen were born in the country or in small towns. More than one-half were born in the Mississippi Valley; the majority of them were born in the Middle West (nineteen coming from four states: Michigan, Wisconsin, Illinois, Ohio). Thirty-four represented the states in which they were born. This was particularly true in the South.

Five of the ninety-six were farmers. Twenty-one were Methodists; one-half were members of evangelical churches. Seventy were college men. A few were very wealthy. Many came from the ranks of the poor.

Some had traveled far: Hiram Bingham from Hawaii; Robert Wagner from Germany; P. J. Sullivan from Ireland. Two had come from Canada. Within the United States there had been at that time little movement in the East and South, but of course much movement from the older Middle West into the newer mountain and Pacific West. For example, Borah came from Illinois to Idaho; Walsh, from Wisconsin to Montana; Samuel M. Shortridge, from Iowa to California; and Norris, from Ohio to Nebraska.

To suppose that this Senate in the summer and autumn of 1929 was waiting upon the action of the president would be a mistake. The Senate was, in truth, asserting that it had the power to determine the political action of the people of the United States.

Hoover, on the other hand, must proceed as if the Senate were powerful but disposed, on the whole, to work with him. He must ignore glaring divisions; he must assume a party loyalty; and, above all, he must maintain aloofness, yet show that he would cooperate at every step in legislation and patronage if the Senate were disposed to do so.

A party pledged to protection of industry, labor, and the farm was understandable in American practice. And a party pledged to revision of the tariff in the interest of the consumer was understandable. Each had won victories in American politics. But Hoover's proposal that tariff rates be based upon government statistics and adjustable to changing conditions was politically unrealistic. The president might build his program upon the facts provided by experts in government who searched for facts, but this would not appeal to the spokesmen of constituencies interested in special provisions in the tariff.

The president's relations with the leaders of the Senate therefore became a matter of the gravest importance. He conferred with the titular leader, Watson of Indiana, later with Jones of Washington, and still later with Fess of Ohio. But President Hoover conferred repeatedly with such independents as Borah of Idaho and with veteran legislator Smoot of Utah. In the ensuing conflict that emerged there was an ever-present personal byplay which was of greater interest to the public than actual differences on policy or principle.

The president himself was the only element in the Republican party who was actually at the time in a position of strength. He was an executive of initiative and determination. Ideally, one would have thought he would be able to bring members of his party in the Senate as well as in the House to his standard by providing them with factual information for their discussions, with the expectation that they would follow him in the national interest.

What actually happened in the Senate during this struggle with President Hoover in the summer and autumn of 1929?

Between April 15, when the special session opened, and December 2, when the regular session opened, there were ninety-eight votes in the Senate, fifty-two of them on the tariff. In that period the Republican membership was not united on a single vote; the Democratic membership united on only seven. The Republican minority varied in size from three to twenty-two. Considering a majority of the party members as constituting the majority will, we find that seventeen Republican senators voted against the Republican organization a sufficient number of times to be termed definitely *irregular*.[5]

In contrast, six months of experience had shown that Hoover was fairly successful in dealing with the leaders of the House. One reason for this was that the members of the House, representing limited constituencies, supported the president because of the support he in turn had from their constituents. The majority Republican membership of the House had been elected on the Republican platform in the Hoover campaign of 1928. The House Republican organization would therefore keep in line with the president's policy.

Considering the relations of the president with the members of the Republican majority in the House, it is of importance to note that at the close of the first portion of the special session at the end of June, Walter H. Newton, who had been a member of the House for ten years, ceased to hold that position and became, by appointment, secretary to the president. In discussing the fact that Newton was leaving the House, Speaker of the House Tilson said: "I believe that Walter Newton will make for himself a great place in the position to which he is going. It is a new position, without a precedent to hamper or guide."[6] Mr. Newton replied thus: "I look forward to seeing you frequently, of retaining that friendship and comradeship, for I hope to be able to promote without reference at all to the middle aisle of this House the heartiest kind of cooperation between the executive and the legislative branches of the Government to the end that those principles of government to which we all subscribe can be carried on."[7]

It was clear, however, that as Hoover developed a policy or group of policies which might be termed his platform in the presidency, he would require—for success—support from both Houses of Congress.

The House of Representatives proceeded with dispatch in voting on the tariff bill. Committees had worked upon the provisions of the bill for many weeks. The leadership in the House felt confident of their ability to enact a bill that would meet the wishes of the president. There was much talk of responsible government and a responsible party majority carrying out the party platform.

Whereas there had been considerable outcry against this bill—which contained ten thousand items when it was first reported—much of this protest (even on the part of Democrats) had subsided.

When the bill had been debated in the House over a period of some three weeks and a vote was taken, Tilson remarked that "neither branch of Congress in any session of any Congress in our history ever more promptly, thoroughly, or more in the public interest, completed the work for which Congress came together than has the House of Representatives in the present session."[8] Later he said: "If we may judge from the limited amount as well as the source and character of the criticism both in the House and in the press of the country . . . it must be by far the best bill ever written in the history of modern tariff making."[9]

This was not the view that President Hoover adopted in his discussions of the House bill, or later of the Senate amendments. In elaborating his view to his press conference on September 24, 1929, he explained his position. In the message which he had sent up to the special session on the tariff he stated what he thought were the general principles upon which to proceed. He had not thought that the president was ever in a position to discuss individual schedules—which necessarily must be the result of long hearings and debates and the determination of hundreds of thousands of facts concerning thousands of commodities entirely beyond the capacity of the chief executive to consider.

President Hoover wanted to make clear to the press that his advocacy of a flexible tariff, to be administered quite apart from the executive power by a tariff agency or commission, was simply the amplification of a principle which he considered to possess "great vitality." It was, he thought, the business of the executive to limit himself to consideration of principles which he thought were of public concern.

Thomas Marvin, chairman of the Tariff Commission, congratulated the president on his message to Congress. Marvin hoped that the Tariff Commission could be made "a more effective instrument of public service and that a more flexible tariff" might be adopted.[10]

Marvin's views were of course known to the members of the Senate in their debates upon the bill, so that Senator Borah—who, like other progressives, had favored the "principle"—became alarmed and on September 26, 1929 said in the Senate:

The chairman of [the tariff] commission, a man of very exceptional ability,

I should say, was for years the representative here of those interests which doubt the feasibility or the wisdom of duties upon farm products at all. He comes from that region of the country where has originated every time the movement to put farm products upon the free list. . . . It is too much to expect him to put aside those convictions which he had long entertained and long promulgated before the people.[11]

Marvin, in a letter to the president, denied that he had advocated placing farm products on the free list. Borah's view was "not correct."[12]

As late summer moved into autumn, the temperature in Washington was better, but the temper of Congress was not. Effective party government in the most substantive of matters had ceased to exist less than six months after the inauguration of the president. Thereupon, as far as events could be determined by executive action, everything depended upon the wisdom of the president and his immediate advisers.

The Congress was of course in a position to challenge any plan of the president that required legislation, and it was in a mood to do so. The party impasse in the Senate on the tariff question threatened to be more consequential than the basic Republican-Democratic division. This was not a repetition of such party divisions as had appeared in Cleveland's day nor in the more recently attempted revision of the tariff in Taft's administration. It was clear that no such party support would be accorded Hoover as had been accorded Wilson in his successful tariff fight in 1913. Party discipline in the Senate had been difficult to enforce in the Harding-Coolidge administration. It had failed utterly in 1925 following the presidential campaign.

Democratic leaders viewed the Republican party debacle with satisfaction. It was to be expected that the Democratic party that had polled such a national vote in 1928 would present in the Congress a party opposition to the presidential leadership of Herbert Hoover. It was not at first clear what form this would take or what means would be used to present it to the country.

Neither the inchoate character of the national Democratic support in 1928 nor the record of the Democratic minority (1921–29) indicated a logical or coherent program. Nor was it necessary that it should be so to attract attention.

It had long been the belief of students of politics that in the functioning of the American government there was need for the clear-cut organization of party opposition to the "party in power."[13] This view gave great weight to the need, now, of formulating Democratic opposition in the Congress. It was found, further, that a national agency should be set up to correlate and present to the nation, through all avenues of public information, the alternative program which the Democrats would offer in opposition to the president's. It was on June 15, 1929 that Charles Michelson was chosen to do this.

The decision to set up permanent national headquarters in Washington, the plans of the chairman of the executive committee, Jouett Shouse, and the choice of Michelson as director of publicity all marked the beginning of a serious effort to take an aggressive role in opposition to the ruling Republican power.

How far this well-prepared plan for using the Democratic national organization in opposition to the Republican administration would have laid the groundwork for a return of the Democrats to majority power in "normal times" cannot be determined. It is significant that the early moves excited little attention. But by the end of the first three months of the Hoover administration, it was evident that the conservative elements in the Republican majority grudgingly admitted the need of reply to the charges of the Democrats. It was also evident that insurgent elements in the Republican membership in the Senate would be used by the Democrats, and they in turn would use the charges of the Democrats. It was clear that the Democratic high command would attempt to destroy the president's power by destroying his party support. The stock market crash and the ensuing confusion were to give the Democrats their great opportunity.

Basic in the Democratic organization attack was criticism of the administration as personified by the president. Thus early in the period 1929–33 began the campaign that presented to the country the picture of an executive "unfit" for the presidency and unable to carry on the business of party government. An organization devoted to "politics" used every means to distort the public view of public questions, public policy, and the record itself. A proposal endorsed by political scientists as a means of informing the electorate and of developing more efficient government procedures became, in the hands of the Democratic National Committee, an engine of destructive criticism (although strong partisans rejoiced).

By the end of President Hoover's first six months in office, therefore, a major political crisis had developed. It was clear that the support he might obtain from his own party would be won only after continuous contest against the two clearly marked divisions in the membership of the Republican party in the Senate and, to a less extent, in the House.

The insurgents, who thought of themselves as progressives and who came from western agricultural states, were, they said, disillusioned by the president's failure to prefer the agricultural interests to the industrial interests of the nation. They found him interested in establishing for the farmer "equal opportunity in our economic system with other industry."[14]

Furthermore, the president, in whose political ideas the western Republicans had placed their faith, was revealed as dealing in friendly fashion with the conservative eastern elements of the party who seemed to the westerners often decidedly reactionary. The eastern conservatives had found that Hoover was a man with whom they could cooperate and in whom they had confidence. Repeatedly, around the council table, it seemed to them—and to the president—that they spoke a common language. But how far President Hoover, wishing to proceed as if he had a united party, could hold the support of the progressives in Senate and House at the same time that he carried on much of the business of government in close cooperation with eastern conservatives was a question of great moment. He could not unite the party because it had split upon sectional lines. He was dealing not with one party but with at least two Republican alignments which, paradoxically, found not only sectional but national supporters. Confusion was compounded.

As for the president's personal supporters in the party, as distinguished from the conservatives or progressives, few of them were in public office and none of them in the Senate was clearly representative. The president had no prime minister to speak for him.

It was in November of 1929—when this picture of party disunity appeared already so disheartening—that William Allen White urged upon the president a course of action based upon White's knowledge of previous disunity and his analysis of the present situation. After pointing out that the Republicans were facing a situation similar to that which existed in 1909, but that in 1929, twenty years later, "all the cards were in the hands of the President," he urged Hoover to make overtures to the independents and "bring order out of chaos." The progressives should then rally to his leadership "to save their cause," for "the Republican party is their refuge and strength."[15]

But the sectional divisions envisioned by White at this time were not all-important, although they had been in the previous half-century. This can be seen in light of the change that was coming over a large portion of agricultural and small town America. The division between large business and small business was deepening. It had been there and had been important in bitter battles for more than fifty years. But now the national aspect of all issues had called into being national organizations of rural as well as of urban interest. Farm and labor organizations came to compete with industrial and financial organizations as national groups.

Consequently, a western insurgent, speaking for his constituency that remained loyal to him in his independence, could also attract a sympathetic national audience. Everywhere it seemed increasingly important to have every economic interest represented in Washington.

Hoover was well aware of this change and of the need for a political party organization which would effectively represent these interests and provide an opportunity to work out *a party policy* in convention and before the people that might be enacted in Congress. As in all other matters, so in party government the call, as far as Hoover was concerned, was for men of divergent views to iron out their differences in the light of ascertained facts and then to unite in a program of action. There was little place for the dissident within the party after such steps had been taken.[16]

But neither conservative nor liberal, any more than reactionary or radical, in the existent Republican party could accept such a point of view. All were familiar with the old lines of conflict, and these would appear upon any issue that arose.

As this became apparent as a fixed fact of politics in the conflict over the tariff, the president more and more insisted upon his point of view. But even now this would not indicate encroachment upon the domain of representative action in committee or in debate on the floor. Those who wished him to do so were ill informed as to the intensity of party feeling, or blind to the inadequacies of party discipline. The president was without a powerful party organization upon which he could depend for action. In its absence, he could only wait until the final stages of legislation to exert his influence on the full Republican membership of the Senate.

In the midst of the tariff debate of the autumn of 1929, the Senate was distracted by a personal controversy that became by design a political issue. Senator Hiram Bingham of Connecticut had brought into the deliberations of the Senate Finance Committee an industrial expert who clearly belonged to the high tariff lobby. Both Democrats and Republicans who opposed high tariff personalized the issue and called for censure of Senator Bingham's conduct. This of course attracted much attention. The investigating committee condemned Binghams' action, and he in reply attempted to make it a party issue. His conduct was condemned by a vote of fifty-four to twenty-two on November 4, 1929.[17]

So the tariff debate dragged on and the nation became increasingly dissatisfied. In good time the rift in public opinion upon this unmistakable conflict revealed several shades of opinion: some blamed the president; others criticized the Senate organization that did not function; yet others were impatient with the insurgents or the coalition of Republicans and Democrats who made progress in debate only to lose the final vote. A few saw the weaknesses in American governmental practice that afforded opportunity for such division of responsibility. Few realized that party government had failed, because no one except the president was speaking for the American people as a whole.

The year 1929 demanded effective and prompt government action not only on farm relief and tariff, but on innumerable questions that pressed for consideration. Only as the people would in time see issues in party terms—not in factional or sectional terms—was it probable that a strong executive could provide successful leadership. A strong executive could win temporary success, but he would only postpone the day when Americans would have to forge party organizations on a truly national pattern.

In a period of normal, typical, or average economic activity, it might have been possible to carry on an experimental program in tariff administration despite the doubt of politicians. The tariff conflict coincided, however, with the economic crisis that struck the nation in the autumn of 1929. Henceforth, tariff policy was numbed by economic uncertainty and would inevitably come to be blamed for contributing to that uncertainty.

— 10 —

Financial Catastrophe: 1929–

In after years I often had reason to recall the scriptural text: "There ariseth a little cloud out of the sea, like a man's hand. Say unto Ahab, Prepare thy chariot, and get thee down, that the rain stop thee not."
Herbert Hoover, *Memoirs: The Great Depression, 1929–1941*

A financial crisis of the kind that came in autumn of 1929 was not unexpected by the president. He had long been aware of danger. As secretary of commerce, Hoover had reported to the Congress on the work of a Committee on Business Cycles and Unemployment:

The "business cycle" of course is not based alone upon purely economic forces. It is to some considerable degree the product of waves of confidence or caution—optimism or pessimism. Movements gain much of their acceleration from these causes, and they in turn are often the product of political or other events, both domestic and foreign. . . .[1]

His alarm over the credit inflation "deliberately created" by the Federal Reserve Board, which in his opinion had misused its powers in an effort to aid European finance, led Hoover, while still secretary of commerce, to seek—though unsuccessfully—the intervention of President Coolidge and Secretary of the Treasury Mellon. Hoover later wrote: "I do not attribute the whole of the stock boom to mismanagement of the Federal Reserve System. But the policies adopted by that System must assume the greater responsibility."[2]

In 1927 as secretary of commerce, Hoover organized a Committee on Recent Economic Changes. One of the conclusions of this committee, reported the following year, was that "from our very increase in efficiency we might get some readjustments." The committee described the economic situation which had come into existence prior to the crisis of 1929:

> ... from an increase in production efficiency of some 30 per cent per person during the 1920's, very little had gone to decrease prices of industrial products. The average price level had remained about the same from 1922 to 1929. . . . About three-fourths of the gains from increased efficiency and decreasing costs had gone to increased industrial wages and one-fourth to increased profits. The buying power of the industrial workers had been increased, and increased profits had become a stimulant to speculation. But as labor and business absorbed the benefits of increased efficiency, such other groups as the farmers and the "white-collar" classes benefited only by a small increase in buying power. Therefore, these groups could not absorb the increased production of industry. To put it another way, had there been a decrease in price levels, the nonindustrial groups could have bought more goods, thus sustaining production.[3]

Never before, however, not even in the greatest boom days of expansion that characterized the nineteenth century, had the economics of plenty so excited the citizens' eager attention as in the decade following World War I. For ten years there had been an unhealthy and nerve-racking development of "speculation."

It came to be said in explanation of new levels in the stock market that we had experienced a "mighty revolution" in industry, in trade, and in finance. To many *this* was the New Era. The greatest change had taken place, however, in the minds and emotions of Americans. Stocks, not bonds, had become the investment media, for there was no limit to what a citizen might have—not earn—in this new day. He was an investor in New America. One million held stocks on margin in 1929. The broker and the speculator became the outstanding figures in this new life.

It need not be a preoccupation here to determine certain controverted matters concerning what has been said above. In his *Memoirs*, Hoover stressed his contempt for New Era economics (or the new economic era),[4] and he related efforts he made while secretary of commerce, despite Coolidge's disinterest, to minimize the speculative fever.[5] Hoover's efforts to prevent the boom and possible crash have not impressed some observers;[6] indeed, some have been unforgiving toward Hoover.[7] "Who should have stopped it [the boom]?" one asks; the answer: "Hoover was in the boat and, as he himself tells, he knew where it was headed. But, having warned the man at the tiller, he rode along into the reef."[8] Hoover was clearly, in that critic's eyes, one who applauded Coolidge.[9] The matter cries to be settled by any who will take seriously (rather than frivolously) what Hoover wrote, said, and did, all within the limits of a cabinet post.

Fortunately, one can now judge, "we are at last moving beyond the 'conventional wisdom' of the liberal stereotype."[10]

"The stock boom was blowing great guns when I came into the White House," Hoover stated later. "It was obvious that there had to be vast liquidation of paper values, and especially a liquidation of the mental attitude of people mesmerized by the idea of speculation as a basis of living and of national progress."[11]

After his inauguration, nevertheless, Hoover maintained that the government must remain aloof from participation in banking as well as business, although he realized, as he later commented, that "our banking system was the weakest link in our whole economic system."[12]

Believing that self-interest would bring financial leaders to take the course needed, he tried by various means to persuade them of the seriousness of the situation. He conferred individually with editors and publishers of influential newspapers and magazines. He attempted to reach bankers and stock market promoters, including Richard Whitney, president of the New York Stock Exchange. He supported Federal Reserve Board Governor Roy A. Young's efforts at this time to curb loans for speculation.[13]

President Hoover felt that he had no authority to take direct executive action and he did not recommend additional legislation from Congress during the early months of the administration.[14] The government's financial condition was sound. The government had closed the fiscal year on June 30, 1929, "with its finances in a highly satisfactory state. Receipts again exceeded expenditures by a substantial amount," according to the announcement prepared by the Treasury Department for release to the morning papers on July 1.[15]

"The initial difficulty was a lack of government authority," Hoover later commented, "except such as could be exerted by the Federal Reserve System. To ask Congress for powers to interfere in the stock market was futile and, in any event, for the President to dictate the price of stocks was an expansion of Presidential power without any established constitutional basis."[16]

Had the Republican party been known to be readily responsive to the president, the fact in itself would have been a deterrent to ill-considered action in the business world. As it was, thirty years of unsuccessful agitation for reform in finance, ten years of party turmoil, and the rapacity of human nature typified by the misdeeds of Charles E. Mitchell, president of the National City Bank of New York, and Richard Whitney produced a natural result. Selfishness in politics and dishonesty in private enterprise had blindly worked toward self-destruction in both government and business. The results were for a time obscured by the general confusion.

——The stock market crash of late October 1929 was a blow first of all to the financial process that in the view of the people had hitherto provided a prosperity identified with the Republican party. It was felt that the government was to blame for the overwhelming disaster to big business and should be punished. In the realm of public opinion, the situation was that simple.

Yet more than a few members of the financial world seem to have realized a crash was inevitable as the stock market boom reached unprecedented heights in 1928 and 1929. The demand for stocks had increased so prodigiously that the value of the 1,100 New York Stock Exchange seats increased from $319 million in January 1928, to $653 million in December.[17]

On the whole, there was expectation of disaster on the part of those who held conservative economic views. "This panic, in my judgment, is the beginning of a major depression," recorded Charles G. Dawes on November 5, 1929. Six days later, on his way to Europe, he wrote:

> It occurs to me to say something about the great stock panic and credit contraction through which our country is passing. It is long overdue. For several years I have been expecting it, getting my house in order to meet it. It should have occurred two years ago, and for at least that length of time I have been warning my friends to get out of the stock market.[18]

Bernard Baruch was another who saw the end in sight. After helping Arthur Krock in 1928 with plans to found a strikingly innovative New York newspaper, he pulled back, saying, "I don't like the looks of this crazy bull market. There is a strong probability of a break. . . ."[19]

When the break came it was in the world of finance. The bull market reached its peak on September 3, 1929. The decisive slump in the market occurred on October 29, although the famous crash came five days earlier.[20] The traders on margin had reached their limit. The question then was how to save the situation. Faced with cries of "sell at the market," a group of bankers on October 24 bought $30 million worth of stocks so that October 25 and 26 were better days. The president's publicly professed confidence, expressed to his press conference on October 25, that the fundamental business of the country in the production and distribution of commodities was on a sound and prosperous basis, was reinforced by the emergency action of the Farm Board in "cushioning" wheat and cotton prices.[21] Tuesday, October 29 was the worst day. On November 13, after two weeks of uncertainty, the bottom prices for the year appeared.

Meanwhile, on October 17, on the eve of leaving for a trip to the

Middle West, the president had conferred with leaders of the Senate. It was not a pleasant conference. It is not clear whether this was because — of the strain of the long struggle over the tariff and the vehement charges of eastern industrial favoritism made against the president by members of the Senate, or because of the break in routine occasioned by this first extended trip from Washington since the president took office.

The president returned from his trip on October 24, and the following day faced the press.[22] He met inquiries about the "business situation" with whatever encouragement he saw. He believed that the business of the country was fundamentally on a sound basis because, although production and consumption were at a very high level, the average prices of commodities, taken as a whole, had shown no increase in the preceding twelve months; moreover, there had been no appreciable increase in the stocks of manufactured goods and no speculation in commodities. A tendency toward wage increases and a rise in output per worker indicated, the president thought, a healthy situation.

Hoover's use of the words "business situation" was a true reflection of the direction of his thought for many months. He carefully avoided "any appearance of attempting to predict the future trend of stock prices."[23] He emphasized that there had been no speculation in commodities. He admitted that the construction and building materials industries had been somewhat affected by the high interest rates induced by speculation in New York City, but felt that this was of secondary importance, as was the temporary drop in grain prices.

The direction of his thinking was further revealed in his frank and informative talk to the press on November 5 when he again elaborated on the "business situation." His statement was a revelation of the president's view of the situation at the time, when he was concerned primarily with economic conditions within the nation. He recognized in the period of widespread overspeculation one of those waves of uncontrollable speculation that ultimately results in a crash due to its own weight. He admitted that the crash was possibly somewhat expedited by the foreign situation, since the congestion of capital in the loan market in New York City had driven up money rates all over the world.

As the president saw it at the time, there had been a very great movement of capital out of New York City into the interior of the United States, as well as some movement out of the city into foreign countries. The incidental result of that was to create a difficult situation in the interior.

In explaining this situation, Hoover sought a parallel with the last great crisis of 1907–1908, when the same drain of money immediately took place into the interior. At that time there was no way to warn of capital movement over the country, and interest rates ran up to 300 percent.[24] The result was a monetary panic in the entire country.

But it was Hoover's view that the resources of the Federal Reserve System had made it possible to prevent the stock market crisis from affecting the rest of business in the country.

——President Hoover's initial view of the stock market crash was that for the first time in history the crisis had been confined to the stock market itself.[25] He believed that the effect on production was purely psychological. He found no evidence of cancellation of orders such as might be expected as the natural result of alarm from the shock of the crash. The lessening of buying in some of the luxury contracts he did not find to be significant in itself. In effect, Hoover did not believe that the crisis had extended into either the production activities or the financial fabric of the country. For this, he gave "major credit" to the Federal Reserve System, which he had previously criticized severely.[26]

The action that he took immediately bore no relationship to any action that might be taken within the Congress. Charged with the interests of the people as a whole, he was careful not to exceed the constitutional authority granted him. The weapon available to him was economic and not political.

President Hoover brought to Washington representatives of the various economic interests of the nation for consultation, and sought from them recommendations about what should be done not only by the national government but—more important from the president's point of view—by the various private economic groups in finance, in business, and in labor, each in its own way having a profound effect upon the national life.

In meeting a crisis that was economic, the president was on grounds with which he was entirely familiar. His course of action now reflected his earlier procedures in public life.

—— It cannot be stressed too vigorously that the president's action was taken in the area of economics rather than in the area of politics. To meet the situation by means of "politics" would not only be unnatural to Hoover, but the economic remedy appeared far more likely to succeed in view of the political situation that had developed in the first six months of the administration. Of course political action must be taken in due time. In statements to the press the president constantly indicated that he was preparing to deal with the Congress when it convened in December 1929.

—— The impact of modern industrialism upon the world had produced belief in coercion by many a dictator abroad and some of similar persuasion (bosses and their machines) at home. Hoover knew of this intimately. He was determined that coercion should not be the method used by the government of the United States. He was loath to believe that in the United States, with its tradition of self-government, either employer or laborer would refuse to use the offices of the government to promote *cooperation* as a solution in time of crisis. The welfare of society, that is, of the whole people—as he saw it—was paramount.

In his press conferences during the first six months of his administration, President Hoover had many times presented his view of the relationship of the government to the citizen. Yet he was not always understood. He turned aside in his press conference of November 15, 1929 to say that in market booms we develop over-optimism; but market crashes, of course, lead to acute pessimism. Both may be equally unjustified, but the sad thing is that many unfortunate people are drawn into the vortex of these movements with loss of savings and reserves. He added a sentence that, in view of what he was doing and what he continued to do, was obvious enough in its meaning not to be distorted (as it was by partisan critics then and later): "My own experience has been, however, that words are of no great importance in times of economic disturbance. It is action that counts."[27]

On November 19, the president again discussed the emergency with the press. He suggested that the situation was, to a very considerable degree, psychological, and "a question of fear," he added in this off-the-record statement.[28]

It is clear that President Hoover, in less than a month after the crash, saw its implications for employment. He said he was concerned with the vital question of maintaining employment in the United States and consequently the comfort and standard of living of the people and their ability to buy goods and proceed in the normal course of their lives. He hoped to disabuse the public mind of the notion that there had been any serious or vital interruption in the economic system, and to restore confidence not by talk, but by definite and positive action on the part of industry, business, and government.

That action was provided by the president in a series of ten conferences with industrial and business groups between November 19 and 28.[29] Those who planned the conferences, and those who participated were dead serious. For example, President Hoover wrote in detail to Julius Barnes, the president of the United States Chamber of Commerce: "Now that the various steps which have been in negotiation during the past few days for strengthening the security market have made good progress I feel that we should consider the next and most important step in business stabilization. . . . With view to bringing about such coordination I would be glad if you could suggest to me the names of a few leaders in the business world who would confer with Secretary Lamont and myself,

together with representatives from other sections of the community whom
I will invite, the purpose of this consultation being to formulate preliminary plans for such an organization."[30]

Hoover's announcement of his plan for business stabilization conferences was praised by financial experts including R. G. Dunn and Brad-
streets, Roger Babson, Irving Fisher, John J. Raskob, W. C. Mitchell,
Charles M. Schwab, and Julius Klein, who regarded the conferences as
"prosperity insurance."

Five thousand telegrams pledging support of the program were
received at the White House. Chicago labor and industrial leaders
endorsed Hoover's views. William Green, president of American Federation of Labor, remarked that labor's economic philosophy was vindicated
in the Hoover conferences.[31]

Criticism, however, was sharp. Democratic Senator Kenneth D.
McKellar said the conferences were "too late."[32] Socialist leader Norman
Thomas ridiculed a "wage truce."[33] The Hoover program was attacked
by the Young People's Socialist League.[34] The Conference for Progressive
Labor Action, meeting in January 1930, called the Hoover conferences "a
gigantic publicity stunt."[35] Philosopher John Dewey advised prevention
of economic evils rather than conferences after the crisis.[36]

A letter written by Thomas J. Walsh to William E. Dodd on November 15, 1929 reflected the bitterness of some: "If it were not that the
Secretary of the Treasury is sacrosanct, even more so than the President
and particularly his predecessor, the country would hold all three responsible in a large measure for the debacle in Wall Street."[37]

Lincoln Steffens, deep in his personal crisis of confidence in capitalism, later wrote of the conferences:

> That meeting of the heads of industry and finance with the heads of the
> U.S. government under President Hoover struck me as an historical event of
> some significance. It was a recognition, however informal and unaware, of
> the truth Stinnes had seen in Germany, Mussolini in Italy, and the Bol-
> sheviki in Russia, that the governments of business and the political govern-
> ment should be one. It confirmed the impression I got when I came home
> from Europe that big business had won in the long struggle which we muck-
> rakers had reported only the superficial evils of; we and the liberals, progres-
> sives, and reformers had been beaten. The process of corruption had culmin-
> ated in the comfortable establishment of the big bribers in power. The
> summoning of big business men to the White House to a public conference
> in broad daylight was a logical acknowledgment of the meaning of the
> election that chose Hoover for president.[38]

Thus the line was drawn between those who favored voluntary effort on the part of business, industry, and labor together with government *assistance,* and those who wished government itself to do the whole job. It is clear that at the time the conference plan had wide support. A weakness lay not in what the leaders said in the conference, but in their inability to utilize a political means to present solutions to the people. Self-government broke down at this point.[39]

A year before the crash, Governor Brewster of Maine, at a conference of governors, referring to a plan said to have the approval of President Hoover, remarked: "Picture the approach of an economic crisis with unemployment on every hand. The release of three billion dollars in construction contracts by public and quasi-public authority would remedy or ameliorate the situation in the twinkling of an eye."[40] Right or wrong, the president did not have such a sum available.

Hoover sensed a further difficulty, which he expressed to his press conference on November 29, 1929: Overdoing the job might create a sense that the situation was more serious than it really was. He was anxious to have "news" that might be a definite statement of accomplishment without exaggeration. He told the press he did not believe such caution was "censorship."

This was the clue to much that was to follow in the president's program. He did not want to alarm the public by overstating the case. To maintain national morale, therefore, he was inclined to minimize in public the seriousness of successive crises. This dedication to the public welfare was often mistaken by his critics, then and later, for inaction.

Ultimate solutions were not available in a complicated society. Of this the president had long been convinced. He commented later that "it is not given even to Presidents to see the future. Economic storms do not develop all at once, and they change without notice.... [In] three years of the slump and depression they changed repeatedly.... We could have done better ... in retrospect."[41]

To the Congress, meeting in regular session in December 1929, the president outlined his program. It contained a blueprint of the future of the United States as he envisaged it. He asked for long-range activity on conservation, construction, and better facilities for a full life (including education and housing, particularly for the underprivileged). He called again for efficient, less expensive government, a balanced budget, and ultimate relief from heavy taxation.

It was a reasonable, efficient, sensible plan to bring together the leaders of labor and pledge them not to strike; to bring together the leaders of industry and pledge them not to cut wages; and to organize the voluntary spirit of the United States—in states, counties, cities—to help the unfortunate in the national emergency by the expansion of public works from local community enterprises to nationwide projects under the control of the federal government. One would expect, in the perspective of time, with decline in partisan emotions, some concessions on the matter.

——In their extremity the American people had looked about for a savior. Instead of having to find and elect one, they already had a potential one in high office. Herbert Hoover was a student of business, a superior organizer, and an experienced director of public affairs. As a private citizen, rather than as president, he would have volunteered to aid his fellow citizens.

—— In the crisis, his program as president was nevertheless a radical departure from the policy—or lack of policy—of his presidential predecessors faced with similar crises. It was not the old Republican conservatism that he brought to bear upon the situation, relying on big business to carry the nation through the emergency. Big business—perhaps, more accurately, big finance—had failed the nation. Yet under Hoover it was not big government that came directly to the rescue, but government at every level as an indirect agent of economic arbitration and economic stimulation. This program was not understood at the time, nor has it been generally understood since.[42]

Still, as early as 1939 there could be thoughtful appraisal from those who knew their national economic history. Wrote historians Charles A. and Mary R. Beard:

> Though [Hoover's] program, as a matter of course, came within the framework of his experience and social philosophy, it was none the less radical in its implications, for it marked a departure from the renunciation of his predecessors. It accepted a responsibility on the part of the Federal Government for breaking the clutches of the crisis and for seeking ways and means of overcoming the violent fluctuations of such cyclical disturbances. Instead of greeting the visitation with the old cry, 'God wills it,' or 'Nature decrees it,' Hoover invoked intelligence and took action in conquering the periodical 'black death' which had so often disrupted industrial processes. In so doing he drew upon himself the easy criticism of those who said that he did not do enough or did the wrong thing, but such strictures in no way obscured the fact that he broke from precedents and made precedents in the discharge of his duties as Chief Executive of the United States.[43]

The whole period of early winter 1929–30 was witness to the fact that in the Congress representatives particularly of the Democratic party were disposed to debate the responsibility for the crash rather than the remedies which might now be taken to alleviate the injuries sustained. Here, in contrast to the president's willingness to provide an economic cure for economic ills regardless of political considerations, politics became active.

Yet the president could not reach the state of mind or perhaps the state of feeling of those who did not or perhaps could not face the collapse of their dreams. This deeply troubled him at the very outset of the crash. He wrote to William Allen White on October 28, 1929: "What I really need are some suggestions as to practical device and method by which the American conscience can be awakened and led. You might devote your odd moments to this and advise me about it."[44]

A close reading of his public addresses at the time shows how he struggled to bridge the communications gap between the president— advised and informed by legions of individuals and groups—and the citizen who increasingly gazed at the nation's status with uncomprehending concern. Hoover concluded a letter at the year's end with the following credo of conviction: ". . . my resolutions for the new year include a continued effort to keep pure the wells of wisdom, and to reassure you that I have faith that the people want the truth determined even if it takes time and patience."[45]

The winter was one of increasing uncertainty. This was partly the result of increasing unemployment as well as a growing apprehension that perhaps the results of the crash were to be far more serious than had been anticipated.

As the spring of 1930 approached, somewhat relieving the distresses of the winter, there was little diminution of uncertainty about what would take place. On the basis of a survey made by government agencies, the president issued an optimistic statement on March 7, 1930, concluding with these words:

> All the evidences indicate that the worst effects of the crash upon employment will have been passed during the next sixty days, with the amelioration of seasonal unemployment, the gaining strength of other forces, and the continued cooperation of the many agencies actively cooperating with the government to restore business and to relieve distress.[46]

This hopeful view was contingent upon the outcome of the tariff controversy in the Congress and the willingness of leaders of finance not only to follow the president's advice but to support him in his long-range planning for economic distress. In the realm of politics, where the president was finding it increasingly difficult to obtain cooperative action, the outcome was dependent in large part upon the senators in his own party.

— 11 —

The President's Party Abdicates

*I am the keeper of neither the dignity nor the honor
of the United States Senate. I represent a bloc of one,
just one. . . . There is no law that requires us to be
here. . . . We are here because we like it, and because
we fight to get here, and because the job is attractive
and ministers to the egotism and the vanity that God
put in every one of us. We are here in the endeavor to
do some little service, it is true, and to do that service
as best we can in our own small way, but we are
here . . . primarily because we fought with both fists
to get here, and every one of us is fighting with both
fists to remain here.*
                    Senator Hiram Johnson, November 21, 1929,
                                           speaking in the Senate

It was in the midst of the winter of 1929–30 that such serious rifts in the
Republican party were revealed that the president's entire program was
jeopardized. The presidential victory of 1928 was not a reliable indicator
of Republican party strength. The Republicans had enjoyed a similar
experience eight years earlier, when they learned that the unprecedented
vote cast for Warren Harding was no real indication of the health of the
party organization. For more than thirty years the party in the Congress
had been held together by makeshift arrangements, especially by the
ineffectual opposition of the Democrats who suffered from the same
malady that made the prospective life of either party a concern of every
politician.

Between September 10, 1929 and March 24, 1930, 257 votes were cast
in the Senate. Of these, 228 were on the tariff. The fact that Senator
Hiram Johnson voted against the party only one-fourth of the time during
this session is an indication, perhaps, of independence rather than insur-

gency. During the tariff session, eleven Republican senators voted against the majority of the party members more than one-third of the time. Some had a greater record of irregularity than that: McMaster voted against the party two-thirds of the time; Schall, Frazier, and Howell, one-half of the time; and Brookhart, Nye, Norbeck, and Borah, more than one-third of the time.[1]

Senator Walsh of Montana reminded a correspondent that "in order to accomplish anything in connection with the pending tariff bill we [the Democrats] must work in harmony with the insurgent Republicans, but they are all protectionists wanting high duties on agricultural products, though willing to go along with us in preventing increases, and in some instances to secure decreases in the duties on industrial products.... It is rare that any party can count on 100 percent support from its members on a tariff bill. The party is to be judged by the general results, not by occasional operations." Walsh felt that the Democrats had done "very well."[2]

Even more detrimental to the president's tariff program than the rift in the Republican party was the spectacle of a self-appointed tariff "commission" of ninety-six members completely preoccupied throughout the winter of economic uncertainty with highly technical discussion and argument. In the final sessions the proponents of extended debate took the position that the Senate, rather than a commission, was the proper body to fix rates and determine schedules. Another view was expressed by Democratic Senator Simmons of North Carolina:

> Think of a bill containing 4,000 items, involving taxes upon the people, imposing burdens upon the masses, granting favors to special interests, many of them dictated by special interests, received in that body [the House], traditionally regarded as the forum of the people, considered and passed after one week's discussion.... Upon what theory does the other branch of Congress justify its abdication of its obligation to the people? There is but one ... and that is the theory that when the bill gets to the Senate it will be given that consideration which it is entitled to and failed to receive in the other body. It is this burden which has been thrown upon us—the burden of rewriting a bill that deals with thousands of items and thousands of commodities. We have largely rewritten it, discussing the items as they should be discussed for the enlightenment not only of Members of the Senate ... but for the enlightenment of the people of the country as well.[3]

Hoover's position at the time—in the mind of the orthodox party member—is not easy to recreate for the modern reader, taught through the years to equate *Hoover* and *high tariff*. It is illuminating to read such

judgments as these: Senator Simmons, for example, could not see "invest-
ing the executive department with a power [flexible rate-setting] so vital
to the whole body of the country, and changing the practices and precedents of nearly 150 years, if, indeed, what was proposed to be done was
not in violation of the Constitution itself."[4] Another voice was that of
traditional Republican tariff advocate Leslie M. Shaw, with whom Hoover
often exchanged letters. Shaw confided to National Committee Chairman Fess:

> Heretofore, whenever the country has been in industrial extremes the people
> have turned to the Republican party, and protection, exactly as they have
> turned to God when on their death beds. Now that a Republican Congress
> has abandoned protection, and espoused competition—the Democrats go
> us one better, they declare for 'effective competition'—where will the people
> turn?"[5]

Shaw wrote to Hoover when the battle was over:

> ... but for your abandonment of the Republican doctrine of protection, and
> the espousal of the Democratic fallacy of competition, I would feel the
> country safe in your hands. But as certain as history repeats, your tariff
> theories are sure to bring ruin. America has several times survived a Demo-
> cratic victory, and it can again, but my heart sinks within me when I con-
> template both parties struggling for front place on a single tariff plank
> designed by Woodrow Wilson, and fashioned in a Democratic convention.
> Still I congratulate you much, and love you notwithstanding.[6]

Such a view is simply not comprehensible unless one sees the Hoover
tariff views and hopes for what they really were.

The president emphasized his concern in his press conference of
February 18, 1930, hinting that the tariff matter was one of pressing
character because the business situation of the country was more sensitive
than it normally would be to legislative reactions, and delays in legislation would have a tendency to slow down recovery.

In the course of the first session of the Seventy-first Congress (April 15–
November 22, 1929), President Hoover had shown that he adhered to his
initial position on revision of the tariff. He believed the tariff was a cor-
rupting influence in American life and hoped that *a semijudicial tariff
commission* might relieve the people of this dead weight. He was interested in the readjustment of rates wherever there seemed to be need. His
guide on agricultural and industrial rates was equalization of the differences in cost of production at home and abroad. A flexible tariff adjusted
by a strengthened commission appeared to be the solution to the problem.

This view brought him into opposition not only with traditional Republican tariff advocates, but also with high tariff industrial exponents such as Senator Joseph R. Grundy of Pennsylvania, and with the progressive Republicans—as well as with the Democrats. Could so sophisticated (and so modern) a position hope to prevail against such odds?

Senator Borah expressed the general western Republican point of view:

> The real fight here is between the agricultural interests and the industrial interests. . . . I am not speaking as a tariff-for-revenue advocate. I am not speaking against the protective system; but I do say . . . that the protective system with reference to industrial schedules has grown and expanded until it has reached the point where it is practically an embargo, and by reason of that fact there is an inequality between the agricultural and the industrial interests . . . . Where is that matter to be fought out? Are we western Senators to be asked to transfer our power in that contest to a Tariff Commission, where the West will have one vote at most? . . . We in the West are now a developing country, a growing country. . . . Protection is more applicable to us than to any other part of the country, and more necessary in order that we may develop; and it is because of that fact that we must necessarily guard the power that we have, and the rights we have, upon this floor. . . .[7]

Borah voiced another fear:

> I do not know what the future has in store, but the Tariff Commission, as it has been made up from 1921 has been composed to a dominant degree of lobbyists for the industrial interests of the United States. . . . Truly, as has been said, the President enjoys more power than any living sovereign. . . . But shall we turn over to the Executive, with all his tremendous powers, the additional power which enables him to levy duties as a practical proposition which the people of the United States are to pay. . . . Something is happening here . . . which the fathers of the Constitution never dreamed of. . . .[8]

Later, Senator Johnson reminded the Senate more specifically of such apprehensions when he repeated the Progressive party plank of 1912 referring to the tariff:

> We pledge ourselves to the establishment of a nonpartisan scientific tariff commission, reporting both to the President and to either branch of Congress, which shall report, first, as to the cost of production, efficiency, and the general competitive position in this country and abroad of industry seeking protection from Congress. . . . We believe that this commission should have plenary power to elicit information, and for this purpose to prescribe a uniform system of accounting for the great protected industries.[9]

Johnson believed that this tariff commission was visualized to be "advisory," for he continued: "No man had the temerity at that time . . . to argue . . . that the tariff-making power . . . of the Congress of the United States should be transferred to any other branch . . . of the Government."[10]

Johnson said he had been disillusioned by the Tariff Commission that had come into existence and believed that the Executive—Hoover, no weak executive—would keep his hand "upon every bureau and every commission he appoints." Although he admitted that the methods of Congress were cumbersome with "great and obvious defects," Johnson cried out: "Here is an immutable principle of whether we retain this Government in its present form or whether we surrender unto the executive branch the most powerful prerogative that belongs to the people."[11]

Old-line Republicans, like Smoot and Grundy, had no desire for a working tariff commission at all. Yet the president, in putting his faith in a commission and a flexible tariff, was doing precisely what would be expected of an executive who believed in the constant application of governmental principles to a changing economic situation.

Although the proposal of the president to enlarge the powers of the Tariff Commission had a precedent in the Progressive party platform of 1912, the insurgents in the Senate now feared that widening the powers of the commission would give too much power to the executive and his "experts." And the Progressives feared that Hoover would appoint a high tariff commission. Senator Simmons, from the Democratic side, asked if the people of the country, through their senators and representatives in the Congress, were "to continue to control the purse strings of the Nation, to determine and fix the taxes the people should be required to pay, by open discussion and vote after due deliberation of the rights and interests of the people," or were those taxes to be imposed by a single individual "with the help of a body appointed by him and subject to removal by him"?[12] The question was not personally directed "to the man who now happens to hold the great office of President of the United States."[13]

The progressive Republicans, wishing more and more aid to the farmer, would add the debenture feature—which had been rejected from the Farm Bill—to the Tariff Bill. The president vigorously attacked the high protectionists, and he stubbornly refused to placate the western bloc.

As the session advanced into February and March, the majority leader, Senator Watson, finally admitted that the other leaders were making no attempt to keep the party members in line. Thus delay was inevitable, and controversy resulting from loose party ties kept the Senate in constant turmoil and made the business of legislation a long, uncertain, tortuous road. Presidential leadership being rejected, the tariff session finally resulted in a complete abdication of party government. Tariff sessions in the United States have usually been productive of the expression of divergent political philosophies, but this session witnessed a struggle to the death.

Senator Watson had reminded the Senate in the fall that he had not asked the president whether he approved of the tariff bill "for the very reason that the bill as reported is not the one which finally will be presented to the President of the United States. . . . The Senate committee changed the bill and the Senate will change the bill still further, and how could any President of the United States, or anybody else, say as a finality that he intended to favor the bill that ultimately will reach the President of the United States?"[14]

Senators on both sides of the chamber, however, proceeded on the assumption that the Tariff Bill was to be formulated much as a group of businessmen might arrange their enterprises and lay plans for development. These senators supported vigorously the position that the recommendations of the Finance Committee should be accepted without debate. Others, especially prominent among the Republicans, maintained that the tariff was public business to be handled in the Senate in accordance with the rules of evidence. They asked that the Senate act as a body of experts, if not upon separate schedules, at least in matters of general legislation.

Moreover, they turned to the composition of the Finance Committee and asked why a bill emanating from eleven members of *that* committee should be accepted without debate.[15] Senator Walsh of Montana pointed out that three members of the committee came from states with a population of less than 500,000, two of these in New England. The chairman of this important committee, Senator Smoot, and one other member of the committee came from the country west of Illinois. The population represented by majority members of the committee was but thirty million.

Senator Capper summarized the situation as he saw it. In 1928, he recalled, there had been a great Republican victory. It included promise of tariff revision. Fifteen congressmen had proposed a tariff bill. Eleven senators had rewritten it. The Senate had refused to accept either action. It was equivalent to a vote of lack of confidence in the party organization in Congress. This party organization was believed not to represent properly either the Republican voters who had won the victory of 1928, or the president they elected.

The basic rift among Republicans outdistanced other sectional and economic divisions as the session moved to its conclusion. It was at work even in the "trades" that marked the session's closing weeks. It revealed that, whether as cause or effect, there had reappeared in the Senate at this time a basic division in American political thinking. The time was ripe for it. Division in basic sentiment transcended the issues of water power, the tariff lobby, even the issues arising out of foreign relations at the time.

The political alignment that had existed prior to the outbreak of World War I had reappeared, and divergent philosophies that had been the outgrowth of American development were actuating the opposing members in their acts and utterances. Should the federal government extend its activities into areas hitherto considered the responsibility of private business? That was the basic question. On this question the position of the president was well known.

When Hoover's flexible tariff policies were defeated in the Senate by the high tariff, old guard Republicans, the insurgents, and the Democrats, and the bill was in conference after passage by both Houses, the president insisted that the flexible provisions again be incorporated. This was done, for Hoover was willing to sign the bill only on the condition that it contained provision for continued amendment by a bi-partisan tariff commission.[16]

The final vote on the Smoot-Hawley Tariff Act in the Senate reflected the fact that neither of the political parties had enjoyed agreement on the tariff issue in general. Eleven Republicans voted against it, and five Democrats voted for it. The final vote was forty-four to forty-two. Before the vote was taken, Senators Reed and Grundy of Pennsylvania denounced the bill but later voted for it, as did the Republican independents Couzens, Cutting, and Johnson.

The president had not only participated in the process of legislation (in conference with members of the Congress), but also had corresponded widely with those interested in it. His files now bulged with comment for and against, and advice to sign or to veto. The bill itself was by now no work of art. J. F. Burke wrote to the president in mid-May: "The bill itself is an abortion. With the flexible power eliminated, it would have been an atrocity. Time and aim your shots carefully."[17]

It has been customary in narrative accounts of this tariff act to give considerable attention to a statement by "over a thousand economists" allegedly *asking Hoover to veto the Smoot-Hawley Tariff Act.* Generous space has been given to this enterprise, and the reasons advanced by the economists have been quoted or paraphrased fully.[18]

Actually, the economists appealed to the Congress not to pass the bill and to Hoover not to sign it. Their appeal was given publicity on May 5, 1930, at a time when a draft bill was still in the Congress. Thus the statement began by urging that an upward revision bill "be denied passage by Congress." If it should be passed, however, it should then "be vetoed by the President." The final bill did not achieve passage by the Senate until June 13. Here was a period of thirty-nine days in which the people's representatives could have heeded the counsel of the American Economic

Association signatories. They quite obviously did not, but the entire opprobrium for the Smoot-Hawley Tariff Act is almost invariably placed on Hoover alone.[19]

Contemporaries knew better than this. An editorial, "Economists and the Tariff," in the *New York Times* of May 7, 1930 stated that political economists had called on the president to veto the tariff bill, "should it come to him for signature. . . . It may well be that most members of Congress will listen with scorn to this unprecedented protest. . . . The President may yet feel constrained to sign the bill, *if it reaches his desk* [italics added]. But he will frankly be influenced by political motives, not by economic. And we may be sure that if he does sign, it will be with a heavy heart and haunting apprehensions."

The May 5 statement was signed by economists from 46 states and 179 colleges; clearly, it was written long before that date and certainly was prepared in ignorance of the success Hoover would score with his insistence on a flexible tariff provision.[20] In any case, no opponents, said Hoover in retrospect, "gave credit for taking tariff making out of Congressional log-rolling, by the 'Flexible Tariff.' "[21]

Clearly the economists' statement was one opposed to protective tariffs in any form; their arguments showed this. Supporting the bill was the American Federation of Labor. As Republican Senator Hatfield of West Virginia remarked, the economists "seem to be more concerned with the prosperity of the foreigners than the welfare of our own people."[22]

When Matthew Woll, AFL vice-president, head of the Wage Earners Protective Conference, and a supporter of Hoover in 1928,[23] was asked about the economists, he replied:

> With few exceptions they are free traders. They are neither producers nor creators of any commodity or article of trade. They are generally cloistered in the atmosphere of the schoolroom and their mental wares do not enter into the competition with producers where lower wage levels and longer working hours prevail, and where standards of living are not only lower, but in other respects much inferior to the standards of our own country under the American tariff policy.[24]

Needless to say, protests came to the State Department from interests in more than thirty nations and were forwarded to the Senate Finance Committee. American-owned exporting corporations overseas also protested.[25] Among those favoring it were the American Farm Bureau Federation, the Farmers' Union, and the National Grange.

The president signed the bill on June 17, 1930, as he had announced he would do a year earlier (June 15, 1929) once it had been passed by

the Senate and House. Before signing he issued a long public statement
giving his reasons for doing so. It included this characteristic sentence:
"On the administrative side I have insisted, however, that there should
be created a new basis for a flexible tariff and it has been incorporated in
this law."[26] Repeating what he had said many times of the necessity of
fulfilling campaign pledges and about the gains inherent in the flexible
feature, Hoover found it urgent that the year long debate be ended and
that there be assurance that politics would no longer interfere with the
resumption of normal economic conditions. These were gains seen at the
time but little noted or valued by later critical observers, nor has interest
been shown in his principled remark, "Platform promises must not be
empty gestures."[27]

The mood of the president as the final bill lay before him for signature
or veto appears in a letter written the day before his final action:

> I am afraid you are disappointed over the Tariff Bill. . . . I am sending you
> the statement in full which I issued. Perhaps it is idealistic to believe that
> we could get this eternally corrupting influence out of American life by put-
> ting it into the hands of a semi-judicial body, but it seems to me it is worth
> trying. . . . If it succeeds it will be one of the most constructive things done
> for the American people in many a long day.[28]

An intimate of those years later described and explained the Hoover
concerns and decisions:

> During this time of legislative wrecking of his tariff policies, Hoover steadily
> fought to maintain his principles. At one time, by the combined action of
> the Republican high tariff Old Guard, the so-called Progressives, and the
> Democrats in the Senate, the flexible tariff provisions were defeated in the
> Senate. While the bill was in conference after it had been passed by both
> Houses, Hoover demanded that the flexible provisions be incorporated again
> in accordance with his views. This was accomplished. Hoover was only
> willing to accept the bill provided it contained the necessary provisions for
> its continued amendment by means of the flexible provisions at the hand of
> a bi-partisan Tariff Commission. Under these conditions he signed the bill
> and, under his direction, the Tariff Commission promptly began its work
> of revision.[29]

At his press conference on August 22, 1930, the president indicated
his view of the potential world-wide influence of the new Tariff Commission, whose chairman was to be Henry P. Fletcher, a man who had been
in the Foreign Service of the United States government for several decades.

The president's signature on this tariff bill was to be more severely
criticized than any other single act of his administration. It has been

asserted that it at once cut the United States off from economic sanity in a world of economic strife; that it united foreign opposition to us in reprisals by thirty nations; that it was altogether bad, economically, for us and for the world. Naturally, free traders took this view, but so too did the majority of economic opinion aroused by what was thought to be impending disaster.

Such opinion is worthy of careful examination, but it is impossible, in view of the changed financial situation after December 1930, to prove what might have been. Veto of the bill might have produced chaotic results in other directions. Reputable voices, including some from trade union leadership, so predicted.

To many, Hoover's signature of the Tariff Act proved that he was a conservative, high tariff Republican. Yet his repeated expression of views, his long struggle to obtain a flexible tariff provision, his dependence upon tariff concessions—marked him akin to many in the progressive bloc. But he could not, in view of his relations with them from day to day, embrace their view of party (which they termed independence, and he considered irresponsibility). It would have been party suicide to have vetoed the bill.[30]

It has been asserted, further, that President Hoover should have openly disowned extremists such as Grundy and Smoot, and should have supported vigorously Borah's resolution to limit tariff revision to agriculture. With the president backing this, agricultural revision would have been carried out. Here, again, the president believed that he must work with the national party organization, dominated though it was by opponents of western insurgency.

In any event, historians would do well henceforth, if inclined to blame, to include Congress as target of the economists, and to note that the economists petitioned before the bill had a flexible provision incorporated in it. Hoover has carried this unilateral burden long enough.

In the aftermath of the long struggle, the Republican party was to lose control of the government in the November 1930 elections, when a Democratic majority was returned to the House. The rising storm of economic crises on several continents—predating the rise of American tariff rates—showed that the results of higher tariff legislation could not be measured years later with any exactitude. On the one hand, it was asserted that the legislation tended to increase economic disturbance abroad; on the other hand it was maintained at the time, in the White House and by the majority in Congress that voted "aye," that we had set our house in order. The latter was the president's view. But he did not consider that winning this much of the battle would remove the tariff issue permanently from American politics.

In the course of the long struggle over farm relief and tariff revision, no criticism of the president was more often repeated than that he was an engineer and an economist, seeking facts and not primarily interested in getting political results.

President Hoover repeatedly stated that his predecessors had called for investigations and recommendations based upon the reports of commissions. He himself had placed his seal of approval on such procedures in the appointment of the Law Enforcement Commission, but the best example was his plan for engaging in a scientific investigation of social trends. This was announced on December 19, 1929, and the report was finally prepared and issued in January of 1933.[31] After summarizing at length the findings of the report, a historian of social work has concluded:

> No more compelling summary of the complex, sweeping new agreement [on social intelligence and social engineering] in American life is available. In the four years of its labors, the committee drew upon the resources of hundreds of leaders in business, government, philanthropy, education, labor, public service, research. Its massive two-volume report, together with separate monographs, constituted a thorough and profoundly critical self-analysis of the quality of contemporary civilization in the United States. The committee's findings furnished masses of information and guide lines of social policy for the events of the next decade.[32]

Here was presented a guide for national self-appraisal and planning.

*   *   *

Disagreements involving persons are of more interest to the average voter than divisions in party ranks concerning issues and problems such as the tariff. Consequently the president's difficulties with the Senate reached the peak of popular discussion in the Senate and in public debate over the appointment of two justices to the Supreme Court, Charles Evans Hughes and John J. Parker. A vigorous minority in the Senate opposed the former and a coalition majority of the Senate rejected the latter.

In each case, the basic attack was much the same, and it revealed, as perhaps nothing else could, how violent was the feeling of the western Republicans on matters of popular control versus what they called entrenched wealth and special privilege.

If representatives of agriculture and labor could unite to reject a nominee to the Court, it would be clear that economic interest, not constitutional belief or achievement before the bar, was the test.

Early in his term, President Hoover had sought to bring Hughes into the administration. When, in February of 1930, a vacancy on the Supreme

Court was caused by the resignation of William Howard Taft as Chief Justice, Hoover proceeded at once to consider the appointment of Hughes. On January 31, Hughes came to the White House at the President's invitation and was offered the appointment.[33] The debate upon confirmation revealed again the character of the opposition maintained by the insurgents. Their language was extreme; their reason for rejecting Hughes was a summation of an ingrained belief that the real struggle in America was between *reactionaries* and *progressives*.

The evidence indicates that Chief Justice Taft and Justice Butler, both of whom were conservatives, had expected the president to elevate Justice Stone, and did not look upon the appointment of Hughes with much approval. To many at the time, Stone appeared to be a liberal, whereas Hughes appeared definitely to be a conservative.

Senator Borah spoke to this on February 11, 1930 in the Senate: "When during the last 16 years has corporate wealth had a contest with the public, when these vast interests claimed advantages which the public rejected, that Mr. Hughes has not appeared for organized wealth and against the public?"[34] It was recalled, furthermore, that Justice Hughes had resigned his place on the Supreme Court bench in 1916 to become a candidate for president of the United States in opposition to Wilson. That he had had wide political experience including the governorship of New York, and that he had served as secretary of state—together with his acknowledged leadership of the American bar—contributed fuel to the Senate discussion of his qualifications. Might he not wield influence on behalf of organized wealth as chief justice in the Supreme Court of the United States?

In the final vote, fifty-two senators voted for the confirmation of Hughes, and twenty-six against, with eighteen not voting. Among those who opposed confirmation of his nomination were Blaine, Borah, Brookhart, Frazier, Johnson, LaFollette, McMaster, Norbeck, Norris, and Nye, the nominally Republican senators who were the backbone of resistance to the party on the Tariff Act.

Some weeks later, the president, despite his usual precaution in insuring endorsements, found that his proposed elevation of Parker to the Supreme Court was opposed by elements that could not be defeated. Attorney General William D. Mitchell explained the background of the appointment in a letter of May 3, 1930 addressed to Senator Hubert D. Stephens:

> Upon the death of Justice Sanford, in response to the President's request . . .
> I undertook an inquiry into the qualifications of a number of judges and
> lawyers, particularly from . . . circuits, which are not represented on the

Supreme Court. An impressive showing was made as to the qualifications
of Judge Parker. He has been indorsed by 2 ... circuit judges, district
judges, a large number of State judges, the president and 5 former presidents of the American Bar Association, 22 presidents of State and county
bar associations, a number of United States Senators, including ... [those]
from his home State, and the governor and former governors of that State,
and by hundreds of members of the bar and prominent citizens, not only
from the fourth circuit, but from the country at large. These indorsements
come alike from members of both political parties and are evidence that no
narrow politics entered into the matter.

I made a painstaking inquiry into Judge Parker's judicial work and examined
all of the opinions he has written as a circuit judge, numbering over 125. No
fair-minded lawyer could read these opinions without being satisfied that
Judge Parker has legal ability of the highest order, qualifying him to sit on
the highest court. . . . His personal character was shown to be above re-
proach and his integrity unquestioned.

This information was laid before the President with the recommendation
that Judge Parker be nominated. Justice Sanford was from the South and a
Republican. While locality is not controlling, it is never ignored, and the
fourth circuit had not been represented upon the court for 60 years. It
seemed that the appointment of Judge Parker to succeed Justice Sanford
would be in accordance with tradition and should be well received throughout the country.[35]

The appointment may have seemed routine enough at the time, but it
became both personal and partisan.[36] In the ensuing struggle in the
Senate, the intensity of language used indicated the growing resentment
toward the president of both insurgents and Democrats. When the president on March 21, 1930 told his press conference of the appointment of
Parker, he remarked that while fitness was of course the primary requisite
for service on the Supreme Court all the other circuits had been represented during the last twenty years except that circuit.[37]

Organized labor opposed the appointment, as did the National Association for the Advancement of Colored People. The American Federation
of Labor opposed the appointment of Judge Parker because of his decision in the case of the United Mine Workers of America v. Red Jacket
Coal & Coke Company to the effect that it was unlawful by any means,
however peaceful, to attempt to persuade an employee to join a labor
union if he was working under an alternative agreement or yellow dog
contract within the employer's establishment. Negro opposition arose out
of Parker's statement when accepting the nomination for governor of
North Carolina in 1920 to the effect that the Negro was neither ready for
the burdens and responsibilities of government, nor did he desire to

participate. Parker suggested that the Republican party in North Carolina did not want the Negro in politics; still, the flame of racial prejudice or hatred must not be kindled, he said. Other problems arose during the Senate debate, even though the Judiciary Committee favored Parker by a two to one vote. Southern Democrats became increasingly restive as they sensed Southern Republican advantage in confirmation.

The outcome was a rejection of the Parker nomination. In a letter to Senator Glass, Oswald Garrison Villard, editor of the *Nation*, stated:

> Personally, I am not sure that the colored people are united enough to make quite certain the punishment at the polls which the Senators from the border States and those having large masses of colored voters fear. But, more important by far than the willingness of some Senators to bolt in fear of punishment, is the fact, now established, that the Senate hereafter will take a different attitude toward nominations for the Supreme Court than the purely negative one it has held to heretofore, and the truth that the negroes for the first time since emancipation have demonstrated to the entire country that they propose to use their political power hereafter in safeguarding their rights. If they succeed in defeating Judge Parker, it will be an epoch in the history of the race.[38]

The campaign against Hughes had, in a way, anticipated the battle that had followed, and Parker's rejection was a kind of aftermath.[39] He was an unfortunate victim of circumstances and of words spoken a decade before.

Contemporaries, of course, could not know what kind of high court justice Parker might have made. An historian long resident in North Carolina has judged: "When one evaluates Parker's record as Circuit Court judge especially in the twenty-five years after his failure to reach the Supreme bench, one might wish that he had been confirmed."[40] The *New York Times* would finally judge in 1958 that refusal to confirm Parker had been one of the "most regrettable combinations of error and injustice that has ever developed as to a nomination to the great court."[41] In any case, the discussion of the Parker appointment emphasized not only the growing intensity of the issues between capital and labor in the United States, but also the position of the Supreme Court in the United States government as a rival of the legislative branch in determining social and economic policies.[42]

The adjournment of the Congress on July 3, 1930 was occasion for review of what had been accomplished since it had come into being in April of 1929.

Despite preoccupation with the tariff, Congress had made some progress upon important bills called for by the president.[43] Yet throughout his efforts to secure support of his proposals from members of the Congress, his listeners did not seem to believe that their constituents wanted what the president proposed; nor were they interested in trying to change the public mind. Repeatedly it was clear in the executive-congressional interaction that both congressmen and senators looked to their constituents, rather than to the president, for leadership.

In theory, there were opportunities in all this. A close friend wrote:

> The country likes the idea that a patriot President may also be a fighting President. Just as a matter of strategy, enlisting public support behind you and your administration, apparently nothing could be more effective than a continuing contest with the Senate on questions on which manifestly common sense and fair play are on your side.[44]

But such advice was perhaps better suited to less emotional times and to a much different kind of president.

Contemporary commentators made much of the activities and utterances of those who disagreed with the president, especially those within the group of insurgents. The most perceptive knew, however, that it was a group of independents rather than insurgents. There was therefore little possibility of a new party emerging from this group.

Norris, sitting in the Senate as a Republican from the state of Nebraska, had not supported the Republican national ticket in 1928, nor had Blaine of Wisconsin. But other independents, notably Borah of Idaho, had supported Herbert Hoover in the campaign. The president and Borah had had frequent conferences in 1929 and 1930, but it was not known by the casual observer how long and persistently the president had sought in correspondence and conference to come to a working agreement with the Idaho Senator.

In truth, no comprehensive agreement between Hoover and Borah was possible. The continuing danger to ordinary party procedure did not lie in the possibility that Borah would displace President Hoover in determining government action—for Borah could not seize executive power. Nor could he seriously thwart the president by pushing legislation contrary to presidential programs. To the people of the United States as a whole, Borah appeared as a national figure of long service, distinguished accomplishment, and positive views. He was, as some caustic critics asserted, a political party in himself and, unlike other independents (except Norris to a lesser degree), he stood for a national program known to every section of the nation.

The progressives in the Republican party had failed in their possible opportunity to capture control of the party in the economic crisis that overtook the nation in the autumn of 1929. Diverse in leadership, they had not developed a unified program. The Republican party was far-flung and continental in membership, and had experienced increasing conflict since the opening of the century. The electorate had accustomed itself to the quarrelsome spectacle (1912 and 1924 brought high visibility). Events quite outside the determination of party leaders had finally struck a decisive blow at such a diverse, chaotic, and inefficient organization and had removed it at last from its longtime influence in the national government.[45]

The tariff session had revealed additionally the results of presidential pressure on legislation. The president had conferred with congressional leaders day by day and week by week. Textbook commentaries on "Hoover vs. the Democratic Congress" tend to obliterate memory of all this. A knowledgable newsman recalls Hoover saying in those years, "There are some fine people up there on the Hill, and some very, very shrewd politicians."[46] The first to be mentioned was Jack Garner—termed shrewd and effective as a politician. Above all, it is contended, Hoover liked the "old pro's."[47]

Although Hoover had won on Hughes and had won his hard-fought campaign for a flexible tariff commission, his own party had failed to respond to his presidential leadership. The Republican progressives and conservatives had not united even in the face of emergencies. As an agency of unified, constructive action in the national government, the long established senior leaders of the Republican party had abdicated; thereby they lost the great opportunity that had been theirs. An extraordinary individual elected overwhelmingly to the presidency only a few months before could only reflect on what might have been.

— 12 —

The Voters Turn Away

*All our institutions are under scrutiny. He would be
blind who did not see that insurgency is stronger and
more successful in the present Congress than it has
been since 1921. This is more than a method of ob-
structing legislation. It is a move, almost a movement,
of protest.*

Anne O'Hare McCormick, March 2, 1930

The 1930 congressional election campaign began early in the year. Political surveys in the spring—devoted especially to a review of Hoover's one
year in the presidency—indicated that the political situation had so drastically changed since November of 1928 that any estimate of the proba-
bilities in the midterm elections was impossible.

As was natural, one year following the opening of the administration
many summaries were made. "Hoover's First Year" was the title of an
article by Anne O'Hare McCormick in the *New York Times*, March 2,
1930. None reached as deeply as did this one into the causes for the
growing chasm between those who had placed their faith in the Hoover
type of procedure and those who, following older party methods, felt
that the solution of the pressing problems that had arisen in the first year
of the Hoover administration was to be found in the Congress.

Another article which attempted summary was by John Pell, associate
editor of the *North American Review*, who wrote an article in mid-1930
entitled "Mr. Hoover's Hair Shirt," which was published in *The Readers'
Digest* for August 1930 and reached millions. "Seldom," it was said, "has
an off-year election become so personalized as the one in which Hoover
is made the issue." Hoover and the Depression—the Democrats strove to
make the words synonymous. The case against Hoover was summarized

by Pell: (1) the bankers and brokers had voted for Hoover in 1928 in order to avoid a weak market; (2) the "drys" voted for Hoover to get prohibition upheld; (3) the internationalists voted for Hoover because he advocated entering the World Court; (4) many farmers voted for Hoover because of his promises of farm relief; and (5) millions voted for prosperity. With Hoover as President, everything had "gone wrong."

There was no doubt that the President's personal supporters believed in the wisdom of his course and in the ultimate justification of his policy. Yet a considerable minority of the Republicans in the House and Senate did not share this view.

It was absolutely necessary in view of the party split in Congress that the Republican national organization make known a determination to support the President's policies. Hoover was, to a decisive degree, like it or not, all that the party had in common.

To his press conference on January 21, 1930, President Hoover reported that the Department of Labor had that day informed him that for the first time since the stock market crash the tide of employment had changed in the right direction—with a very distinct increase in employment all over the country during the previous ten days.

By early March 1930 Hoover felt that he could draw certain conclusions about the results of his measures taken November 1929 to counteract the stock market crisis. Unemployment amounting to distress was centered in twelve states, the president told his press conference on March 7, 1930. In the remaining thirty-six states either normal seasonal unemployment existed or abnormal unemployment was rapidly vanishing. Hoover felt at this time that the low point in business and employment had been reached in the latter part of December and early January 1930. The nationwide response to his request for increased construction programs by the railways, utilities, and other industries showed material results. All the facts indicated that the worst effects of the crash on unemployment would be passed during the next thirty to sixty days.

At this time, when the president frequently stood aside—at least as detached as any commentator—and discussed the background situation with the press, it was evident that the potential, that is, the conceivable seriousness of the economic situation was not clearly understood either by members of the press or by the public.

Whereas numerous Chicago bankers and businessmen, including some members of the grain trade, had declared that without the intervention of the Farm Board a serious panic in agricultural commodities would have taken place, the necessarily experimental efforts of the Farm Board under adverse circumstances following the stock market crash were not understood by business leaders.[1]

Nevertheless, the spring of 1930 witnessed an unprecedented drive for new legislation and for the expansion of old services, which would entail very large additional burdens on the government; but only a very small percentage of this arose from members of Congress themselves, reported the president as he discussed with the press on February 25, 1930 the appeals for financial support that swarmed in from different sections of the country. He hoped the people would realize that the government could not undertake every worthy social and economic proposal. The public should support the members of Congress as they cooperated with the administration in an endeavor to keep expenditures within the resources of the government.

Hoover's first principle of government was that it should pay its way. This principle was being applied to a federal government that in 1930 was but a miniature of the huge and vast governmental organization of today. (This is easy to forget.) For example, on April 29, 1930, the president reported to the press that the public works program had been augmented by some $12 million over and above the annual expenditure. Altogether, the government was meeting the situation one way or another by increasing its program for construction by somewhere in the neighborhood of $100 to $125 million. The Electrical Utilities Committee that was set up in December 1929 reported that their construction program had increased by May 1930 from $865 to $900 million.[2]

The president tried to correct misunderstandings of his actions or apparent inaction. Thus he told the press on May 2, 1930 that the body of representative men appointed to study economic developments during the previous eighteen months was not to be a high-powered group that would direct economic life in the United States. It was merely to make an examination of experience in line with a study that had been made of the financial boom and slump of 1919–1920. The earlier study had amounted to a crystallization of the ideas of economic conduct in the country since that time.

In line with his promotion of efficiency in government, the president was much pleased with the passage by Congress of a bill authorizing the consolidation of all veterans' agencies (the Pensions Bureau, Veterans Bureau, and Soldiers' Homes) into one agency, the Veterans Administration.[3] This consolidation, as Hoover saw it, would effect considerable economy, although a budget of $800 million would be required for the new agency. Hoover told his press conference on July 8, 1930 that the Veterans Administration would perform "one of the most important functions in the government," and he regarded this reorganization as the most significant step taken since the beginning of his administration.

Hoover frankly condemned the veterans bill (the Rankin Bill) which promised what he called "discriminatory" aid to a particular group of 75,000–100,000 men while neglecting to help over 200,000 more veterans who suffered from similar disabilities. Congress passed the Rankin Bill, but the Hoover veto was sustained by four votes. Congress then passed the president's bill—"the most sweeping, equitable, and generous proposal that had been made."[4]

The midsummer of 1930 was occupied by attempts to alleviate the effects of a prolonged drought, chiefly in the area in a belt east of the Mississippi and south of the Ohio and the Potomac. The president was characteristically determined to provide relief after Secretary of Agriculture Hyde and Chairman of the Farm Board Legge studied a survey by the Department of Agriculture. The president promised that no stone would be left unturned by the federal government in its assistance to local authorities in dealing with the situation.

On August 8, 1930, Hoover received the preliminary report from the Department of Agriculture and determined to call in the governors of the states most seriously affected. The shortage of animal feed crops was most acute in southeastern Missouri, northern Arkansas, southern Illinois, southern Indiana, southern Ohio, together with Kentucky, northern West Virginia, and northern Virginia, as well as in Montana, Iowa, Kansas, and Nebraska. The acutely affected area contained approximately one million farm families, about two and a quarter million horses and mules, six million cattle, and twelve million hogs and sheep—about 12 percent of the entire animal population of the United States.

The drought mainly affected animal feed, as the bulk of the food for human consumption had already been safely brought to harvest. Nevertheless, the president thought there would be much privation among families in the drought area caused by loss of income and inability to carry their stock over the winter.

The president's concern with the situation was increased by the difficulty of making the truth known to the nation. The publication of the national figures given in the crop report, Mr. Hoover told the press on August 12, 1930, tended to obscure the real situation to some extent because the shortage in corn, in the amount of 700 million bushels, was felt most acutely in certain areas. The effect of such a shortage was to deprive great numbers of people of their entire livelihood. A great many families would have to have assistance to live over the winter. Furthermore, the entire wheat carry-over and surplus of the year would be required for immediate use, whether human or animal, to get the country through the emergency.

Asked by the press whether he would carry out his projected trip to the West, the president replied that in view of the drought situation and his feeling that he could be of greater service in Washington, he would not go west, at least during the next month or two.

By August 15, Mr. Hoover was able to report that "organization" to meet the crisis was well on its way to the individuals in distress. He said that the governors had gone home to appoint their state committees and to set up the organization of county committees. The three great farm organizations would cooperate. As soon as the governors appointed the banking representatives to their state committees, they would be asked to come to Washington to take up questions of finance organization. The Red Cross had already given directions to their chapters in every one of the distressed counties to take care of the situation. The secretary of agriculture was advancing allotments for federal aid to those states. The secretary of war had directed that the flow of the Illinois River through the Sanitary Canal should be increased for a time. He had also proposed to the governor of Virginia to use the artillery ranges in that state for cattle pasturage.

Although rains late in August stemmed the spread of the drought, the ground crops of more than three hundred counties in the worst affected areas were "pretty far gone," reported the president to the press on August 19, adding that the real burden of the drought would of course be more evident during the winter to come.

——Energetic measures were thus taken to meet the need. By December 19, 1930, the president was able to report to his press conference on seven different methods of relief: (1) loans to farmers provided by the Drought Bill; (2) increased highway construction provided by the Emergency Construction Bill; (3) participation in the accelerated rivers and harbors work in the drought states; (4) accelerated public building; (5) extension of intermediate credit activities through creation of a considerable number of Agricultural Credit Corporations that had been started four months earlier; (6) reduction of railway rates by which some 60,000 carloads of feedstuffs were poured in at half rates; and (7) effective methods set up by the Red Cross to look after personal distress.

Meanwhile, the Cabinet had discussed the financial situation in which the government found itself as a result of appropriations made by Congress during its last session. Budget estimates for the fiscal year beginning July 1, 1930 showed an increase of about 5 percent. The largest part of this was for the increased building programs, rivers and harbors, public works, "Boulder Dam," and veterans' relief.

All the Cabinet members and the heads of independent establishments had undertaken a searching survey to see what economies could be imposed during the current fiscal year, without interference with the employment program. Hoover felt confident that economies would provide a large cut in the $209 million increase in the budget as a protection against the fall in revenues which would result from the economic crisis.

At this time Hoover found, as he told the press on August 1, 1930, that commercial bills, industrial loans, installment buying, and to some extent farm credits, all had very substantial reservoirs that had maintained the flow of credit through the depression. Home building, however, had been almost stifled by inability to secure financing.

The president therefore decided to call a White House Conference on Home Building and Home Ownership to consider on a nationwide scale all the problems involved. His hope was to ameliorate some of the conditions that seriously limited home building and home ownership. Not only were finance, design, and equipment involved in the problem, but city planning and transportation were as well.

Hoover added that the purpose of the conference was not to bring forward recommendations for legislation, as the problem was rather one of coordination, stimulation of private agencies, and better development of ideas. The conference would need to cover the question of state mortgage laws, which limited the credit facilities of home builders very seriously. (The president assured the press that ample funds had been provided from private sources for the entire cost of the research and expenses of the conference.)

Despite the increase in the federal budget, which the president had estimated at 5 percent, he felt confident that it would be possible to continue tax reductions during the following year. After reviewing the fiscal situation with Secretary Mellon and Undersecretary Mills, he found that despite decreasing revenues and increasing expenses, it would be possible to bring about an economy cut of about $75 million. In reducing expenditure, Hoover recalled that about $2 billion out of the $4 billion of estimated expenditure for the year consisted of fixed charges for such things as interest and debt redemption and pensions, so that the amount open to economies was less than one-half of the total.[5] And on August 22 he told the press that the amount allocated by departments for construction was being increased to alleviate unemployment.

Knowing how small a ratio existed between the national economy and the "business" of the federal government at the time, the president nevertheless insisted upon working within the accustomed limits. He felt that the establishment of cooperation between government and business would materially relieve the unemployment situation since "systematic information" from the government would not only provide a "barometer of business," but would contribute to methods for placing people in employment or on unemployment relief. He therefore appointed a committee to consider the matter. Members of the committee represented the

American Federation of Labor, the United States Chamber of Commerce, the Railway Employees and other labor organizations, the National Bureau of Economic Research, the Committee on Economic Changes, and other economic bodies which had been interested in the problem for many years. The Statistical Division of the Department of Labor, the Department of Agriculture, and the Bureau of the Census were also represented. The chief executive warned the press on July 29 that the problem was not as simple as it appeared to be on the surface, although an accurate determination of the amount of unemployment had been obtained in the formal census taken April, 1930. This fortunately provided a far better basis on which to formulate plans than was usually the case. The president warned that such an accurate determination of employment once every three months would require a house-to-house canvass of the entire nation, however, and would cost $10 or $15 million a year.

The president reminded his·audience that the appointment of temporary committees and commissions for advisory, fact-finding, coordinating, or negotiating purposes was not a new necessity in government. President Theodore Roosevelt created 107 of them, President Taft, 63, President Wilson 160, President Harding 44, and President Coolidge 118. President Hoover had not as yet gone that far. In view of the need for the best brains of the country to assist in government and in the coordination of public efforts, he said he intended to appoint other committees. He said he appreciated enormously the willingness of the American people to give their time and specialized knowledge in voluntary service to assist in the solutions to the multitude of problems the nation faced. This, Hoover thought, was a fine attribute of American citizenship.

By September 16, Hoover reported that the Department of Commerce had made a study of how far imports and exports had been affected by the fall in prices. The results indicated that United States exports decreased about 20 percent in quantity during the first seven months of the year, whereas imports decreased about 5 percent, indicating that the nation's buying power had held up much better than buying power abroad. Therefore, concluded the president, the foreign trade of the United States was somewhere between 80 and 85 percent of its normal condition.

Looking toward the second winter of unemployment, Hoover reported to the press on October 17, 1930 that in his Cabinet meeting that morning a thorough discussion was held on the unemployment situation in the country.[6] He had requested Secretaries Lamont, Davis, Wilbur, Hurley, Hyde, and Mellon, and Governor Meyer of the Federal Reserve Board to formulate and submit plans for continuing and strengthening federal activities for the unemployed during the winter. He had communicated with the governors of several states on methods of further cooperation;

the Cabinet Committee would take up and expend those methods. They were also to review interaction on problems with the national industrial groups—railways, utilities, and manufacturing industries. The situation in federal public works would again be reviewed. Governors and mayors had indicated a very strong feeling of local responsibility and a determination to meet the situation during the winter. The president said he believed it was the national responsibility to prevent hunger and cold among those of the nation's people who were in honest difficulties.

On October 21, 1930 Hoover described an unemployment organization that was being formed. Although not ready to make a formal public statement as yet, he described to the press the proposed organization for cooperation with industry, and especially for cooperation with local welfare bodies. On federal public works there had been some limitation in the amount of money expendable in any given period, the president admitted, and he intended to ask Congress to remove those restraints so that public works could be developed to the fullest extent, wherever engineering and architectural design and other plans were complete. (Hoover recalled that accompanying and related to the unemployment problem was the drought problem of the current year.)

Characteristically, the president warned the press ("just privately") that all these difficulties could be very much exaggerated, and exaggeration would not help the general situation of the country. The actual amount of unemployment (taking the base of the census of April 1 and applying to it the factor of employment as shown by the Department of Labor employment index) probably at that moment was somewhere about 3.5 million, he conjectured. "I am not minimizing the problem at all," he said; he estimated that the degree of unemployment amounted to a good deal less than half of that being borne by countries abroad. At the conclusion of the conference, when he said ". . . we shall get through with it and we shall get through without any actual suffering," a probing member of the press inquired, "You mean without actual individual suffering?" The president replied that the object of organization was indeed "to prevent individual suffering, and we ought to be able to accomplish it."[7]

Three days later the president was again confronted by the pressing question, Should a special session of Congress be called to deal with the unemployment problem? Hoover stated that there would be no special session. He believed the sense of voluntary organization in the community had not vanished altogether. The spirit of such service had been strong enough to cope with the problem for the past eleven months and he was confident that it was strong enough to serve the occasion in full measure. Hoover said he found most gratifying evidence of support from the

governors, mayors, industrial leaders, and welfare organizations throughout the country.

By October 31, the public works in progress, including ships for the
Shipping Board and navy war-vessel construction, amounted to roughly
$1 billion. (The number of government employees had increased, the
president observed, from 990,000 to 1,033,000 since January 1, 1920.)

If the public had known the full facts about the president's thoughts
and activities throughout this trying year, it is doubtful that they would
have comprehended—at the time—their significance. The days of big
government were in the future. All the "bigness" in the public mind was
confined to business, unemployment, and losses from the drought.

Yet, by midsummer of 1930, the president had rounded out a record of
accomplishment which led many to feel that he now had greater strength
for his own program. He had achieved a degree of control over the
Republican party organization. At the same time he had gained legislation
on the Federal Farm Board, and had procured a Tariff Bill after great
difficulties. He had won from the Senate ratification of the Naval Treaty.

That the president was clearly not representative of either of the
extreme wings of his party was to become clearer as the congressional
campaign advanced. Of course, he was "candidate" in the elections only
by proxy. But his leadership to date as president, more than any other
single issue, dominated the canvass. So divergent were the issues in the
various congressional districts, especially in senatorial contests in fourteen
of the states, however, that the outcome was certain to be inconclusive.

A considerable number of the candidates for Congress—notably national
figures who were candidates for reelection to the Senate—were running
for office in opposition to the president's program. This paradoxical political situation was nowhere so clearly revealed as when the issue was
drawn between the Republican National Committee and the Republican
voters of the state of Nebraska wishing to support for reelection insurgent
Senator George W. Norris.[8] Although he was supported by a considerable
number of his Republican colleagues in the Senate, he was known to be
opposed for reelection by the president and by those who were close
to him.

The president believed that Norris was not entitled to be considered
a Republican because he was not supporting the Republican administration. Norris, however, believed that his Republicanism was to be determined only by the voters of the state of Nebraska. Here was the familiar
division between those who maintained that the test of party was adherence to the president and those who held that the real test was support
by the voters.

Despite rumors to the contrary, neither the president himself nor members of his administration publicly supported or opposed individual candidates for nomination in the Republican primaries held throughout the nation.

The struggle surrounding the election brought into sharper focus what had seemed clear enough to the president's supporters during the sessions on the farm and tariff bills. They asked whether it was possible to deal with new problems in the old familiar way: when voting for candidates, could the voters deal directly on the basis of self-interest with the farm problem, tariff revision, prohibition enforcement, or steps toward world peace?

The Hoover method was a research method and much slower than the political method. On the tariff, for example, the president would not only present the facts, but as more facts might be forthcoming, he would let debate upon the matter reveal the actual situation. He would not only ascertain the causes of the panic, but would propose objectively those methods of dealing with the results of panic that seemed to him most practicable.

In this the president seemed too subtle and elusive to be understood by his press correspondents. Much less was he understood by people at a distance. Despite the fact that President Hoover saw and conversed with more people than the presidents who preceded him, he did not reach out to the public in image or reality. To many people he seemed to lack the "human touch" that he had demonstrated by his activities in food administration during and after World War I. Many who still thought of Hoover as a great engineer questioned whether he was also a "fighter" who could lead them out of their economic distress.

A qualified public relations specialist judged that "Hoover had the right idea of public relations—that was to do things and let one's acts speak for themselves, but that isn't the modern way it is done. You must let people know. He never quite learned that knack."[9] As John W. Hill remarked, "There are two sides to the coin of public relations—words and deeds. President Hoover gave greater weight to deeds...."[10]

Hoover's friends knew that he was sensitive to hostile criticism. Writing in his diary for December 4, 1930, Henry L. Stimson stated: "I do wish he could shield himself against listening to so much rumor and criticism. If he would only walk out his own way and not worry over what his enemies say, it would make matters so much easier. He generally comes out all right, but he wastes an enormous amount of nerve tissue and anxiety on these interruptions."[11]

To comment that Hoover's administration was intended to be an "educational administration" sheds considerable light upon his method and, incidentally, upon the difference between the approach to a political problem as something to be used to obtain popular support and as something to be solved by examination and discussion by those in government concerned directly with it.

Nevertheless, the contemporary press agreed that the president still had huge popular backing despite the violent attacks upon him by outstanding Progressives and the fact that big business was divided in its support and critically watchful of his procedure in dealing with the depression. These were indeed liabilities. It was generally supposed, however, that President Hoover had not lost sight of the objectives he had had when he entered office. Such undertakings as the White House Conference on Child Health and Protection, and the work of the president's Research Committee on Social Trends were witness to Hoover's broad objectives.

The day-by-day, even hourly, White House effort to meet successive crises was completely unknown to the public;[12] so also was the president's activity in the daily assessment of all available information on the state of the nation.

The basic factors in the overall economic situation are now known to us as they were not known even to the commentators at the time. We have before us the reports made at the end of the decade (that is, in 1930 and 1931) and distributed then and later. We have not only statistics indicating the extent of the financial debacle and the continuance of increasing unemployment, but also reports showing government expenditures for 1930 and the expenditures planned for the ensuing years. All of these facts enable us to see now, as was not generally possible at the time, the dimensions of the economic situation.

Practically all of this information was available to the president *at the time*. It was his great advantage that he had the basic facts upon which to build his policies. He regretted that it did not seem possible to present the picture effectively to a great number of people, although attempts were made to present the facts to the many different groups who called on the president.

Judging from statements made in the press at the time, there was no real appreciation of the facts which the president had before him day by day in reports which came to his desk. This is a factor of great importance in estimating the voters' understanding of what the president was doing. Public understanding or its absence was most significant in forecasting the extent of votes that might be given Republicans in the elections now to be held.

In the absence of any general knowledge of the president's program and accomplishments, it was claimed by many that the enemy of public welfare was the government itself. Had it not failed in this emergency? A few claimed that Congress had not properly assumed responsibility because of unstable party conditions. But the most compelling view was that the government—under the leadership of President Hoover—had failed. Conspicuous was the impression that the president had dealt with Congress with little success, however much he might have achieved by way of executive action in coordinating means of resisting the depression. And of those constant efforts far too little was known to the voters.

The congressional elections of 1930 took place under these unusual conditions. Both those who knew of the president's leadership behind the scenes, and those who did not, agreed that the president was the issue. So unusual had been the distribution of political forces in the presidential election of 1928 that any congressional election a mere two years later would have occurred under unprecedented circumstances. Two conditions further altered the situation: one was the profound economic upset which had affected all of the people of the United States; the other was the hopeless division of the Republican party upon questions that seemed of pressing importance to a majority of the people.

When it was fully appreciated inside the administration that in the November elections the issue was to be the Hoover leadership, plans were made for a handbook which would review the accomplishments of the preceding sixteen months. Each of the executive departments in Washington would present a review of what had been accomplished.[13] The direct purpose of the handbook was to furnish information to speakers who were to appear in the congressional campaign. The constructive work of the administration was emphasized to minimize the congressional conflict that had been widely publicized. As the campaign progressed, aided in part by radio, some inroads were seen. One local assessment was: "Many people telephoned expressing their surprise at the many things Mr. Hoover has accomplished and that they now have a better understanding of Mr. Hoover and his ability as a real executive and leader."[14]

Late in the campaign attempts were made to revive what might be termed the idealism that had accompanied the campaign of 1928. But the national atmosphere was one troubled by sentiment against the Agricultural Marketing Act that had created the Farm Board and against prohibition.[15] "My faith in Hoover was great. Almost unlimited. I still have great faith in the man, but somehow he doesn't seem to be the great man we elected President," wrote one correspondent to the White House.[16] In response, the president's special secretary wrote:

I think if I were at a great distance from Washington I probably would share your feelings until I had fully considered the alterations in the proportions of the man that were inevitable when he came into the White House. . . . He took over a whole series of new and vast responsibilities to which he must devote the major part of his time. . . . To me certainly, and probably to you, the tariff is a bore, but the President of the United States must devote many laborious weeks and months to its consideration and to practical dealings with Congress and public opinion upon it. It is not a subject from which idealistic natures can derive any inspiration. Nevertheless it is one of the humdrum and exhausting tasks of the leader of our political economy. In the same way a President's time must be liberally given to the consideration of such other uninspiring subjects as postal deficits, development of the merchant marine, plans to expand aviation. . . . Besides all this the President is the political leader of his party and must exhaust many hours and much nervous and intellectual energy in dealing with its problems. . . . Nowhere nearly so high a proportion of the man is left for devotion to the things that really are nearest to his heart. . . . No President before Mr. Hoover ever thought of creating the position which I have the honor to occupy in the White House, which he invented solely to permit him to continue upon an enlarged scale his activities in behalf of projects of social well-being by having one secretary whose whole time should be given to this side of his interests. Such undertakings as the White House Conference on Child Health and Protection, the President's Conference on Home Building and Home Ownership, the President's Research Committee on Social Trends, national work sponsored by him to combat illiteracy on an intensive and nation-wide scale—these and a dozen other enterprises are on a scale of magnitude beyond anything in the past. . . . These things have had little relative notice as yet because as usual the President has been doing the careful foundation work upon which real accomplishment must rest. I am convinced, however, that long before his Administration is over, when these things have had the time to flower and bear fruit, they will be universally known and will give his Administration an outstanding place of decisive fresh leadership in the very field of our enthusiasm. . . . I do wish it were possible for you to sit at my desk and see the stream of enthusiastic people who by personal contact and by letter, more than five thousand of the leading people in the fields of child health and protection, social work and home betterment, who are actively engaged under the President's inspiration in intensive work to formulate new programs of advancement in these fields.[17]

As the campaign reached a climax, one of the closest adherents to the president's point of view summarized his impressions of the factors operating against the administration:

The mass. . . . acting in a burst of fury against the failure of the financial and business leadership—considered to be mostly Republican.

A surprisingly accelerated swing away from Prohibition and its enforcement.

The action of the Senate and Congress and the long delayed tariff battle with a Bill which was not satisfactory to any group; the type of leadership the party has had in the Senate.

Nine months or longer, when because of the failure of the National Committee to properly function, the opposition was able to paint a picture in lurid colors that, in the short time the Committee has been functioning, has not been particularly modified.[18]

What could the president himself do in this situation? His inescapable daily, weekly, and monthly problems were those of economics and of government. Winning the congressional elections, however, was a problem of politics. What alternatives did he have?

The president might in theory insist upon a national committee equipped to do intensive fighting upon behalf of the Republican administration. And the president might wish the defeat of the senators who had not supported his program. To bring about such a defeat, he would have to reach grass roots Republicans who had been priding themselves for years on their "independence" in electing and reelecting these senators.

Yet the odds were against him because of the political power of the insurgent senators, which rested upon their popularity *in the states*. The real question was not whether a man was a "good" Republican or not, for there were many degrees of Republicanism. The real question was whether a Republican was for Herbert Hoover, the president. In the light of American party practice, the chances for Hoover were poor indeed.

Sensational charges against the administration were published in the *New York World* late in October 1930. The president dignified the charges by replying personally to them, even though the attack was made not upon him but upon the secretary of the interior.

The president reported to his press conference on October 28 the findings of the Department of Justice on its examination into the sensational charges made by Ralph S. Kelley, an employee of the Land Office, to the effect that Secretary Wilbur and other officials of the Department of the Interior had been guilty of dishonesty and misfeasance in the adjudication of titles to oil shale lands, running into hundreds of thousands of acres, with alleged losses to the government of billions of dollars. Attorney General Mitchell and Assistant Attorney General Seth Richardson, after a painstaking examination of the records on every item in Kelley's charges, were able to pronounce every one of them baseless and without merit or substance. Kelley had negotiated for the sale of his fabrications to a journal identified with the opposition political party in order that they might be used in the campaign.[19]

The Democratic opposition naturally made much of Republican disunity, and it was assisted by all those who were outside the Republican fold. Because the Democratic party was itself seriously divided not only upon public policy but upon the nature of social structure, the Democratic attack concentrated upon the leadership of the president. More than any other individual now in office, he had been the symbol of Republican victory in 1928. Every rule of the politician's craft led to one conclusion: to defeat the Republicans in 1930 by attacking the president who continued to lead that party would prepare the way to defeat the president himself when and if he stood for reelection in 1932.

By midsummer of 1930 the president's friends were planning to work for his reelection in 1932. The president was told by Dwight Morrow "he was fortunate in having this depression—for which he is in no way responsible—come in his first year, rather than a little later."[20]

Hoover had said many times—and he was reminded of it later—that he believed the two-party system was a great bulwark of American political freedom. Although he believed in complete independence of expression in discussion and in the formulation of a program, he felt that, when a decision was made by a designated group, all members of the group should support that decision.

Speaking to the American Bankers' Association on October 2, 1930 the president, reviewing the financial history of the preceding twelve months, asserted that the credit system had withstood the shocks of the panic and that bankers had dealt effectively with the emergency. He emphasized that such crises in no way disturbed the nation's "fundamental assets in the education, intelligence, virility, and the spiritual strength of our 120,000,000 people," nor our fundamental resources in lands and mines. While pointing out that the depression was worldwide, Hoover dealt at length with domestic overexpansion and the need for retrenchment, for he felt that the United States certainly should not wait upon the recovery of the rest of the world. "It is not a problem in academic economics," said the president. "It is a great human problem. The margin of shrinkage [in production and consumption] brings loss of savings, unemployment, privation, hardship, and fear, which are no part of our ideals for the American economic system." The standard of living should continue to increase.[21]

A reminder may be in order at this point regarding the national psychology. The word *depression* was not yet capitalized as in the later expression *Great Depression,* and, indeed, the memory of earlier temporary setbacks in the capitalist system of America meant that there was simply no one in 1930 who would care to predict a forthcoming decade of economic woe. "I don't think that anybody at that time realized the extent and depth of the Depression—I mean until it became an avalanche," recalls a political scientist. "They felt sure it was temporary."[22]

Lost in the drive for electoral success in the midterm conflict was the outline of a program that Hoover had presented and continued to present. But it was not a program that conservatives were willing to accept, nor was it a program that enlisted the basic convictions of the progressives. His campaign addresses to the American Legion Convention and the American Federation of Labor Convention on October 6, 1930 were as fruitless as was his spirited campaign utterance at King's Mountain Battlefield, Tennessee, the following day. There, Hoover spoke eloquently of the principles and ideals of American life, rooting his conclusions on his lifetime of world experience. He referred particularly to "that ultimate goal of every right-thinking citizen—the abolition of poverty of mind and home."

Had the nation been in a more prosperous condition, the assertion of leadership by the president might have caught and held public attention. But his farm program had not produced expected results because the depression had changed the basic premises on which it was constructed. The serious depression that had weakened the conservative as an effective force in American society had raised the radical doctrines of easy money and strong central government to first place in public interest.

Progressive Democrats had looked forward to this development for many years. It was an inheritance from the Bryan influence and it had enjoyed a brief opportunity in the early years of the Wilson administration. The subsequent years had witnessed the frustration of the Democrats because of divisions in their national party organization. Now, however, aided by economic depression and equipped with a masterful publicity agent, the Democrats thought that 1930 might be a real training ground for 1932.[23] Democratic attacks had been well publicized throughout 1930. Jouett Shouse, the director of the Democratic National Committee, gave full time to the work of the committee; press releases of the publicity director, Charles Michelson, were designed to make Hoover "the issue." Michelson worked closely with Democratic members of the Congress.[24]

Progressive Republicans knew that inability to wrest control of the party organization from the eastern conservatives meant a loss for them. If the progressives had supported Hoover on his terms; had Hoover, in turn, worked with the other progressives (as he had tried repeatedly to work with one of their leaders, Senator Borah); and had it been possible to work toward progressive control of the party organization, looking forward to the campaign of 1932, the result might have been different, at least in degree.

Individual progressives scored personal successes. Appraisal of these victories was also personal. "How proud I am that you have won," William Allen White wrote George Norris. "It is an indication of the wisdom of your people and vindication of the political intelligence of Nebraska. I hope I may be here six years from now to lend some small aid again to your victory.... Always depend on me to help when you need it."[25] So it was that Norris could boast a few years later that "the people of the country are tired of good party men."[26]

The drastic results of the election of 1930—a Democratic House—gave that party increased opportunity to present its views to the nation. Although the majority was small (220 Democrats, 214 Republicans, and 1 Farmer-Laborite), it was sufficient. In the Senate, the Republicans had 48 members, the Democrats 47, and the Farmer-Labor party 1. As yet there was no real indication of an overwhelming shift from two-party allegiance. Democrats captured the governorships in Ohio and Massachusetts, and Franklin D. Roosevelt was reelected governor of New York by a large majority. The Republicans retained 22 governorships; the Democrats had 25; and the Farmer-Labor party had 1.

The outcome of the election was judged to be a failure of the president to hold previous support from the nation. It was also an indication that the Republican national organization had failed to win a supporting majority in Congress for the president.

Yet the elections of 1930 revealed—as nothing else had done—the continuing shift of popular sentiment throughout the nation. Almost all commentators sensed the outline of the future—in particular the approaching alignment for the presidential election of 1932 and its probable outcome. Consequently, attention centered upon three points of greatest interest. There was the program of the president and his use of it, not only in alleviating widespread distress but also in explaining his procedures to the nation. Then there was the conduct of the progressives, not only in Congress but also in selling their program of dissent. Most of all, perhaps, there was the successful organization work of the Democratic National Committee in healing the party breach on Prohibition and farm relief, and its skill in uniting all elements in the party to find a candidate for the presidency who would capitalize upon the Republican debacle. Evidence was multiplying, furthermore, that "wet" sentiment was increasing in every section of the nation.

At a dinner at the Gridiron Club on December 13, 1930, the president portrayed the realities in the new situation. He called attention to a new need for excitement to arouse the interest of the electorate. With sardonic humor he imagined a Gridiron Club platform declaration ending with, "We, the people, demand entertainment and sensation from our government. The good do not stimulate our curiosity or our emotions, our happiness or our jokes. . . ."[27]

The election results were, of course, a source of distress to the president. A cabinet member recorded that he saw them as a lack of confidence in him personally. He was "rather sad and depressed" initially.[28] Publicly, Hoover minimized the importance of the election results. He called upon the Democrats who were to come into office to cooperate, and promised to work with them. Yet there was a new sting in his adverse comments on the suggestion that an extra session of Congress should be called into being. President Hoover believed that the executive was the proper source of leadership. This would be tested.

— 13 —

A Political Impasse

*I have the feeling that if you could sit in the middle
of the Government and see the tools with which we
have to work and the disasters which confront us at
all times in the use of these tools, you would not want
us to extend the area of government but rather to keep
the government as nearly as we can in its greatest
function—the safeguarding of human rights. Also, if
you could sit in the middle of the government you
would be even more disheartened than you are
now by the wrongs and cruelties that take place
through greed and selfishness. To steer a straight
course through these rocks is no ordinary task, and is a
task that will not be wholly accomplished in one
generation.*

Herbert Hoover to Richard Lloyd Jones,
March 11, 1931

Seldom has the inflexibility of the American electoral system been so
completely revealed as in the political situation that emerged from the
congressional elections of November 1930. The Republican party had
suffered some form of defeat, yet the Republican congressional majority
elected two years earlier were obligated to govern and to hold the initiative in the government for another five months, until March 4, 1931. The
Congress elected in 1930 (in which Democrats would have a majority in
the House) would not meet, unless called into extra session by a Republican president, until December of 1931. A political impasse was therefore accepted in fact, and the events of the year 1931 are best understood
in light of that singular situation.

The winter months from November to March were bleak in every
part of the country. With local defeats in state and city elections, the
Republican party had become a symbol of failure and futility, whatever

its performance in executive or legislative branches of the national government.

By Christmas Day, 1930, it was apparent to some—and certainly to the president—how isolated a figure he had become in the Republican party. As his friend Secretary Stimson wrote,

> The very stars seem to have turned in their courses to make your path difficult; the world has been embittered by losses and in their suffering men have been tempted to strike out at any mark; but not even the shadow of a suspicion has attached to your single-mindedness and lofty purpose. When I see how rare such qualities are in political life, I feel that this alone would be a triumphant success, and that the country is fortunate indeed to have a man of your personal character at the head of its government during this crisis.[1]

Never having been the first choice of the party organization, Hoover had not been fully successful in his efforts to take over or to provide a new organization. Outstanding Republicans of long experience in all parts of the country were not "Hoover men" by appointment, election, long friendship, or perhaps even inclination.

Had Hoover attained the presidency as a man of military reputation, it would have been much clearer why he stood apart from the old-line political personnel. Yet in a sense he had come to the presidency as a war hero and he was reaping, as others had before him (and would again), the benefits of such an entrance upon the position of first political importance: the presidency. His personal following in and out of the party was as loyal as ever, and the members of his group were scattered throughout the nation, to be sure. But in no state, not even in his own state of California, was he in control of the political forces (the national, state, and county committees) that made party government possible. It could be said that in general these persons were in charge before his election and would still be after his departure from office.

Loss of control of a house of Congress by the president in office has not been common in American political history.[2] When it has occurred, apparently basic causes have afforded temptingly easy explanations. Neither causes nor explanations have much importance, however, for presidential government does not suffer the vicissitudes of parliamentary government. In a word, endorsement from or repudiation by the public has no positive and clear-cut result in our system, except as it reshapes the lines of preparations for the next genuine test—a presidential election.

Intense political discussion at this time took various forms. One of them was the suggestion by a considerable number of Republican leaders that the president should plan to call an extra session of the new Congress. Hoover indicated that he would not call the new Congress into special session, however, emphasizing his conviction that quick political action in dealing with the continued economic crisis was not the step that could most profitably be taken.

By the end of 1930, fourteen months after the crash, business was 28 percent below normal. Six million were unemployed. Stock prices had gone up a little in July, but went down again in September. Brokerage houses, joined by investment companies, began to go under in the fall. There were 1,345 bank failures in 1930. On December 12, the Bank of the United States, a state bank in New York City (with a highly unfortunate title), closed its doors.

Of the unemployment situation, the president spoke at length to his press conference on December 5, 1930, when he explained the background of the Emergency Employment Bill. Remarking that there seemed to be some misunderstanding of the fact that large sums of public money could not be, applied to construction work in times of depression, he emphasized that all construction required a large amount of technical preparation. Most government work required acquisition of titles involving condemnation proceedings occupying eight or nine months at best before an authorized project could be brought to actual employment of labor. If the government were to take up new projects at the time of emergency, there would be all the delays of preparation and legislation; undoubtedly another period of very active log-rolling of projects of interest to different states would terminate in a hopeless morass.[3]

Although this was said to the press "not for quotation," it was certainly most unusual for the president of the United States to appear in the role of economic analyst and critic. This role was not a difficult one for Hoover. Despite his long-time reputation for initiative and direct action, and his record of constructive accomplishment, he found it easy to state obstacles, to detect pitfalls and, in particular, to see through glittering generalities that did not bear promise of making a good program, a good policy, or an enduring contribution. But was such a display "good politics"?

There was to be ample opportunity for a display of such talents in the ensuing two years. The *Congressional Record* reveals much evidence of the multitude of plans, the multiplicity of devices, and the ceaseless ingenuity of men to find easy solutions and short-cut methods of dealing with pressing economic problems. Americans were accustomed to this, but not for many years had there been on Capitol Hill so many men devoid of basic conviction on economic theory, financial stability, and budgetary honesty. The Congress was not composed of economic experts but of men with political experience and a great deal of acute insight into public opinion. Even those in high committee positions, some of whom posed as economic experts, had been accustomed for many years to dealing with a country passing through a period of inflation and growth. Adversity was a new milieu for most of them.

From his independent, critical point of view, Hoover was satisfied with the budgeted federal construction program, to aggregate for the calendar year (1931) around $650 million, which, said he, was nearly three times any ordinary program of building construction. To the suggestion that the federal government might borrow money for new projects, his answer was that—in addition to the difficulties inherent in new projects—for the federal government to take money from the investors of the country to put into governmental works would only shorten the amount of private construction that would be undertaken with the same sum of money. He insisted that this would have no economic advantage. He maintained that for the government to overspend itself and increase taxation for public works of this nature would produce an even more disastrous effect on employment in the country as a whole.

The president saw that the same difficulties accompanied rapid increases in public building in the states and cities of the nation. The selection of a site, for example, became a matter of moment in practically every town of the country. There almost certainly would be disputation on the matter, and the government would have to make peace only then beginning the long delayed processes of building. Hoover felt that every agency of the government was exerting itself to the utmost on a very extensive program ever since authority had been received the preceding June for expanding work on rivers and harbors.

Hoover had been pushing for the consolidation of the railroads into four independent systems, under the Transportation Act of 1920, to maintain broader competition, more equitable rates, and lower operating costs. The hope was to contribute to recovery by enlarging opportunities for employment while increasing the financial stability of the railroads.

Good news came from California, where a Golden Gate Bridge bond issue of $35 million would stimulate other expenditures, while $20 million in veterans home and farm state bonds would be helpful. Hoover was notified, "This is the best way we know in San Francisco and California of relieving unemployment."[4]

He was able to announce at the end of the year (December 30) that the basic understanding that leading employers would maintain wage scales was providing some of the most constructive action during the depression thus far. The president felt that federal policy had to emulate this wage policy. It had been followed everywhere by the government.

In the economic situation that existed in the months following the election of 1930, great political advantage rested with those who, in the atmosphere of uncertainty, called for formation of a new political party.

It now became absolutely clear what the more pronounced insurgents in the Republican party would prefer to do. Facing the obvious fact that they could not do what they had repeatedly hoped to do in the previous twenty years, that is, capture the party organization, they now turned their attention to the "need," as they saw it, for a third party. A few, among them both Borah and Norris, considered it essential to furnish an alternative program to that of the president. Such a program would emphasize something more than the protest activities of the previous quarter century. Those years had witnessed repeated efforts.

The progressive movement within the Republican party, dating from 1900 to 1915, which appeared in 1905 with LaFollette as leader, was for a time lost sight of when Theodore Roosevelt headed the third party, the Progressive party, in 1912. Many progressive Republicans did not support him, although most did. After the failure of the new party in 1912 and the upheavals of the war years, this party simply disappeared as an organization. With the opening of the Harding administration the line-up of progressives appeared again under the label *insurgency* as well as *progressivism*. The insurgent movement of the Hoover presidential years had been the heart of the Progressive party efforts of 1912 and 1924. Representatives of this movement in the Congress called themselves progressive Republicans, insurgent Republicans, and liberal Republicans.

The driving idealism that animated that movement was less in evidence in 1930, but only gradually were American liberals to realize this. In the twenties there had been no real rebirth of the earlier spirit. The effort of 1924 died abruptly. Little political writing of the 1920s embodied the hope that had sustained progressive writers of the prewar years. Attempting to meet the charge of failure, the People's Legislative Service compiled a list of accomplishments of the "insurgency" of the previous twenty years.[5] Not even in the presidential campaign of 1924, when the candidate of the Progressives polled five million votes (helped by Socialists and organized labor), could it be said that the mood had been restored.

To an extent only partially realized at the time, World War I had changed the home-grown American dream of 1900–1915. Prior to 1915 it had been an American product, stated in American terms, dictated chiefly by the leaders of middle western democracy.

Many citizens who belonged to a younger generation, not bound in politics to either of the great parties, thought they saw in this situation the beginnings of a new development not only in politics but in economics. "It may be that the whole money-making-and-spending psychology has definitely played itself out, and that the Americans would be willing, for the first time now, to put their traditional idealism and their genius for organization behind a radical social experiment," wrote an observer.[6]

The country resounded in the winter of 1930–31 with proposals for monetary reform, for taxation reduction, and altogether (it might be said) for economic change of some sort not too clearly visualized. It was a day of revolutionary thought for those who were anxious for opportunity not only to meet the mounting dangers of depression, but also to break the hold of those who had controlled in time of prosperity.

Never before had discussion of party failure reached so promising a stage at so critical a time. So it was argued that all parties were much too conservative, could not be moved, could not be captured. There must be a young party. It was argued further that the insurgency that had been a practice for many years did not do effective work. Insurgents were rebels and inciters, but they did not constitute a party.

Why not then turn to the Socialists? This was not sufficiently appealing at the time, because the Socialists hoped to change the whole economic basis of American life.[7] Those who favored a major third party were not yet ready for this. Nor were many people ready for parties with an economic connotation such as "Labor Party" or "Farmers' Party." What, then, was this new party to be?

In this winter of 1930–31 attention was given the fact that in the state of New York the governor, Franklin D. Roosevelt, who had been reelected by a great majority, was being considered very generally over the country as the possible Democratic nominee of 1932.[8] Consequently, not only his program of action in New York but the reaction of different parts of the country to his program and to his personality were given close attention. Yet outwardly he seemed to promise little to the progressives; he was so definitely a "Democrat."

Insurgent members of both parties in the Senate called a conference to meet in Washington soon after the adjournment of Congress. In this call appeared the statement: "In the midst of depression this country is without effective political or economic leadership." Although the subjects for discussion were all economic, the basis for this movement to bring insurgents together in one political party lay in the assertion that "economic privilege has taken possession of the government." This, then, was an attempt to revive for current use the slogan used by progressives throughout the preceding thirty years.

The conference was begun on March 11, 1931. On this occasion Senator Borah, in an extemporaneous address opening a round table on agriculture carried over the Columbia Broadcasting System, identified himself with the agricultural interest and referred to worldwide depression and financial trouble as "accentuated and deepened by a coterie of capitalists who inaugurated the most vicious era of speculation and inflation of which the world gives any record." Saying that he would not take from the 4 percent who "have the wealth," Borah called for a political party or at least a "political voice, which shall worry more about the 96 per cent than they are worrying about the four per cent." Borah said he believed the Farm Board had failed for lack of a permanent policy, inasmuch as between 1929 and 1930 farm bankruptcies had increased 470.5 percent. Still advocating the debenture system, Borah ventured to say "there is no difference in principle between the protective tariff for manufactured goods and the debenture for the American farmer."

Senator Borah was not, however, the standardbearer of any party. He had written on December 23, ·1930: "I believe in political parties, but their jurisdiction is limited and it can never be made to include the right to control the votes or the conscience of public men in matters of legislation."[9]

About the same time, Borah made a notation with reference to the farm problem, the Parker case, and the power problem:

> But if we were agreed upon all questions, if there were complete harmony, if the solidarity of the old days were here, still the task confronting the party is a staggering one. It would tax to the utmost the leadership and the constructive genius of the party in its best days. We seem to be at the crossroads in the economic life of the American people. The mechanician [sic] of American industries imposes upon this generation the problem of finding a place for millions of men and women and readjusting their lives to entirely new conditions—mass production piles up goods in the sight of those whose purchasing power is daily diminishing. People talk of surpluses. And the thing that is haunting us is really the under-consumption upon the part of millions who are no longer [able] to buy. . . . The Power problem, the transportation problem, the farm problem, press for consideration. . . . It is task enough for any party. The Republican party is in power. The Republican party can not shirk. It must either present a program or go out of power. If it does not present a program. it ought to go out of power.

Senator Borah was very active at this time, creating an atmosphere of doubt and fear of administration policy. In the proceedings of the Senate for February 20, 1931 he asked permission to have printed an article from the *New Republic* of February 18, 1931, in which the following appeared:

> Fear is the dominant motive of the bipartisan coalition which is stifling action in a national emergency, which is preventing the American nation

from taking even the most elementary measures to make its business order behave in a barely endurable way. The President, the great Republican and Democratic newspapers, and the sinister forces behind them are really trading in human misery. They are telling the country that it cannot have relief from depression unless reaction is allowed to have its way, but those among them who are capable of disinterested thought should reflect on the longtime risks they are taking. How long can our civilization continue to creak along with a governmental machine which is so nearly prevented from functioning.[10]

It was in eulogizing George Washington in the Senate on February 23, 1931, that Borah remarked on Washington's alleged attitude toward the French Revolution, saying:

No one in the Cabinet approved of the principles or of the practices of the French Revolution but Washington saw, as he afterwards said in effect, that while it was a bloody road over which they were traveling, it was the only road to a sane and stable democracy. It was a marvelous exhibition of courage and vision that under those circumstances he should recognize the French Revolution.[11]

Borah's own interest in the Russian Revolution and in Bolshevik rule was no secret. Ideas of revolution were in the air. An eastern view that was widespread was expressed by a correspondent of Borah's following the election of 1930:

I hate to see you associated with those other Senators who are generally spoken of as the "blatherskites." With you associated with them, they have a power which, without you, would fade away. Mr. Hoover may not have personal magnetism, but he has the tremendous respect of the average thinking man here in New York, and that is something which the so-called "blatherskite" Senators decidedly have not got. . . . Those other Senators are looked upon as playing politics at the expense of the Nation, and are causing a bitterness toward, and distrust of, the Senate, which is fraught with danger. You, the only one of the so-called insurgents to whom credit is given for strength and sincerity, are being associated with them, to the grief of us, who hold you and your ability in respect. You did such clean and magnificent work in electing Mr. Hoover, it distresses us to see you now in such constant opposition to his general program as the papers report you to be.[12]

Senator Norris was identified with insurgent protest in his own way. Following his reelection, Norris was in receipt of telegrams and letters of congratulation from a great number of his colleagues in the Senate—

Democrats as well as Republicans—and from others in public life known
for their independence of party, like William Allen White. In particular
did William Green, President of the American Federation of Labor, take
opportunity of sending a telegram that stated:

> Your campaign for reelection to the United States Senate in Nebraska was
> of national and international interest. Because of the terrific opposition of
> special interests laboring men and women were attracted to your campaign.
> There was great rejoicing among the officers and members of the American
> Federation of Labor and all their friends throughout the nation when we
> learned of your triumphant election. Your great victory has strengthened
> the faith of the masses of the people in the virtues and efficacy of popular
> government.[13]

It was clear to many an observer in the spring and summer of 1931
that the break in the Republican ranks was so serious that nothing could
bring about the unity necessary to party success either in Congress when
it should meet in December, or in the presidential election of 1932. Only
a few of the insurgents were willing at the time to admit it but, in pursuing their cause of independence and in pushing programs of protest,
they were, in their continued repudiation of the President, giving up
hope of retaining standing in Republican circles. They could not capture
the organization; they therefore faced having to give up the name.

This name meant much to a large number of voters in the Middle and
Far West, for however they had modified its meaning by prefixes, they
still preferred—locally and nationally—the name *Republican* to any other.
Republicanism for almost 100 years had stood for stability, respectability,
and intense nationalism. It was the party that led in saving the Union.
Yet no amount of eastern conservatism or reactionary philosophy could
make the insurgents believe that Wall Street rather than Main Street
ought to be the real Republican stronghold. Accordingly, when leaders
in the movement in Congress embarked upon their agricultural conferences in 1931, they knew that the outcome might defeat their own programs for the time being. The conservatives would repudiate them.

When disturbed citizens in 1931 contemplated a third party as a
means of achieving results, their memories of earlier failures plagued
them.[14] Theodore Roosevelt in his revolt of 1912 had at length justified all
the warnings of traditional politicians. When in the adventure of 1912
Roosevelt had led a movement outside of the party in his effort to reach
the presidency, it was notable that millions believed in him personally as
a symbol of revolt, but he was never again accepted by party-minded
politicians.

Woodrow Wilson was another who was never satisfactory to his party organization, and it would be a mistake to assign his great popular acclaim, even in the election of 1916, to convinced party support. His later overwhelming repudiation came from the electorate chiefly because the public was attuned to the acceptance of party methods. Taft had been acceptable because he was constitutional and dependable. Harding and Coolidge filled the picture for the party bosses, and, it should be added, for the party-minded voters. In the persons of these men, the Republican party became synonymous with the interested citizen who considered economic prosperity, political tranquility, and social fluidity sufficient in the face of calls for reform.

The president was well aware of such developments. On February 3, 1931, he was asked at his press conference a long and involved question concerning party as an agency of government:

> What is your conception of the effect of the present business situation on the future politics of the country? Will it operate to bring about clearer views of basic economic problems such as agricultural rehabilitation, better distribution, conservation of resources, etc. and less sectionalism and political bias in the consideration of such problems?

> Are we, in this period of economic distress, giving any indications of political growth or are we drifting further toward dismemberment of the two major parties with a consequent strengthening of the bloc system based upon sectional advantages?

The president did not discuss this issue, although he stated clearly the relief policy of the administration in referring to "certain Senators" forcing an extra session of Congress.[15]

Meanwhile, the Democrats were not offering a radical alternative to the administration program, however critical of Hoover they might be. It was said of them at the time that "they want . . . to step into the Republican shoes for the next thirty years, become another Republican party . . . [and] win the safe negative victory which they expect as a result of the revulsion against the present administration."[16]

Indicative of the political irresponsibility of the time was Democrat Walsh's appeal to Republican Borah to help him in the congressional election:

> I have in mind your keen interest in my reelection, which you generously expressed to me in the spring and of which I should have had no doubt even though you had not mentioned the matter to me at all. The hope has been expressed by your many admirers in this State that you might come to talk in my behalf. I hesitated to ask you to do so, knowing of the embar-

rassments that usually attend or follow from the open advocacy by a member of one political party of the candidate of another. You occupy, however, a unique position and would, as I know, be little concerned regarding what might be thought of such a departure by you. If you feel, under the circumstances in which you are placed, you could justifiably come to Montana to make one or two addresses I should feel under very great obligations to you, and your doing so would be of inestimable value, indeed I am confident my reelection could no longer remain in doubt.[17]

To the end of the administration, Frank Lowden of Illinois believed that Hoover was identified with the eastern conservatives of the Republican party. This must be, in part, the explanation of his coldness toward the Hoover candidacy, and the explanation of Lowden's failure in 1928 to respond to the request of his friend Dawes that he come to the support of Hoover. Nor did Hoover have the support of those who worked closely with Lowden, and this helps explain the suspicion with which a number of men who worked with Lowden looked upon Hoover.

A thoughtful and somewhat perplexed American voter, with some knowledge of the factors in political protest that have filled the pages of American history since the foundation of the American government, might well have remembered Lincoln's phrase, "We cannot escape history." Plenty of reasons could be presented—and were presented—in the spring of 1931 for a national movement to provide a national vote apart from either the Republican or Democratic parties.

In his call for new party formation, John Dewey departed from cool philosophy with these judgments: "President Hoover's constant appeal to self-reliance, enterprise, private initiative, is simply puerile; it is a voice from the grave in which human hopes and happiness are buried."[18] The words to which Hoover resorted might represent "excellent qualities," but Dewey thought their exercise under existing conditions had brought social catastrophe. Governmental action would give them a new chance.

Typical of those who had experimented with a new party in 1912 (or 1924) but would not in 1932 was Paul U. Kellogg, editor of *Survey Graphic*. We are told that "for awhile he was tempted to support a move on the part of old insurgent Republicans to seize control of the party from Hoover and nominate some such candidate as Gifford Pinchot."[19] He wrote Harold Ickes that a movement of calibre would be attractive. But he ended up voting for the Socialists.

Searching for a new political party led almost all who engaged in this interesting pastime to one conclusion. A new party simply could not be organized in the United States in time to be of the slightest value in the presidential contest of 1932.

— 14 —

Hoover's Leadership in the World of 1931

*These acts do not imperil the freedom of the American
people, the economic or moral future of our people.
I do not propose ever to sacrifice American life for anything short of this. If there were not enough reason,
to go to war means a long struggle at a time when
civilization is already weak enough. To win such a war
is not solely a naval operation. We must arm and train
Chinese. We would find ourselves involved in China
in a fashion that would excite the suspicions of the
whole world.*

Herbert Hoover, memorandum in mid-October 1931

The longest period during the Hoover administration when the Congress
was not in session was from March 4 to December 7, 1931. It was a
period of crises calling for presidential action—in Europe, in Asia, and
particularly at home in the United States. The year cannot be treated as
one of either purely domestic or purely foreign concerns, for both were
important.

During this nine months of presidential leadership, Hoover made it
evident that (*a*) he had a domestic program of relief and reconstruction
and was prepared to push it as far as he could within the powers of the
President; and (*b*) he had a program in foreign relations, especially with
nations in economic distress, and was disposed to proceed in this as far
as the executive might, strengthened to a degree with the advance
approval of the leaders of Congress. This, then, was the plan.

The first (special) session of Congress (April–November 1929) had
revealed deep division among Senate Republicans. In the second session
(December 1929–July 1930) this division had deepened with the panic
and depression. The entire House and one-third of the Senate had been

involved in the elections of November 1930 that resulted in repudiation of the former Republican majority in the House. The third session of the old (Seventy-first) Congress, from December 1, 1930 to March 4, 1931, included 140 members who would not sit in the new (Seventy-second) Congress which would not meet in regular session until December 1931.

"Certain senators," the president told his press conference on February 3, 1931, had issued a public statement to the effect that unless the president and the House came to an agreement upon appropriations to relieve unemployment before the end of the session in March, they would force an extra session of Congress. Hoover, indicating that he would not call an extra session, gave newsmen his reasons for believing that the situation could be handled without additional legislation.

He reiterated his views at length, comparing the situation of the United States with conditions elsewhere:

> It is a question as to whether the American people on one hand will maintain the spirit of charity and mutual self help through voluntary giving and the responsibility of local government as distinguished on the other hand from appropriations out of the Federal Treasury for such purposes. My own conviction is strongly that if we break down this sense of responsibility of individual generosity to individual and mutual self help in the country in times of national difficulty and if we start appropriations of this character we have not only impaired something infinitely valuable in the life of the American people but have struck at the roots of self-government. Once this has happened ... we are faced with ... reliance in future [sic] upon Government charity in some form or other. The money involved is indeed the least of the costs to American ideals and American institutions.[1]

Referring to President Cleveland's warning in 1887 against "expectation of paternal care on the part of the Government," President Hoover reminded the American people that "the help being daily extended by neighbors, by local and national agencies, by municipalities, by industry and a great multitude of organizations throughout the country today is many times any appropriation yet proposed," and that federal help would be likely to stifle this giving and thus cut off more private resources than would be equaled by government appropriation.

As President Hoover saw it, there were two entirely separate and distinct situations in the country, one in the drought area, and one in the large industrial centers where unemployment was severe. He felt that efficient methods of combating unemployment outside the drought areas had already been established through agreements between industrial and labor organizations, and within local and state governments. He recalled to the people that he had indeed spent much of his life in fighting hardship and starvation. "I do not feel that I should be charged with lack of human sympathy for those who suffer, but I recall that in all the organizations with which I have been connected over these many years, the foundation has been to summon the maximum of self help." He said further:

> I am proud to have sought the help of Congress in the past for nations who were so disorganized by war and anarchy that self help was impossible. But even these appropriations were but a tithe of that which was coincidently mobilized from the public charity of the United States and foreign countries. There is no such paralysis in the United States and I am confident that our people have the resources, the initiative, the courage, the stamina and kindliness of spirit to meet this situation in the way they have met their problems over generations.[2]

Hoover did promise, in this same statement, that if voluntary agencies and local and state governments were unable to meet the situation, he would "ask the aid of every resource of the Federal Government because I would no more see starvation amongst our countrymen than would any senator or congressman." He had faith that such a day would not come.

He was to return to these themes in late May when pressures were renewed for an extra session of Congress. Senator Alben W. Barkley of Kentucky had spoken for the Democrats when he said in the Senate on February 28, 1931: "How can we inject any more courage into Congress than we have displayed all during this short session? . . . Now Congress is about to adjourn and go home and leave the United States Government helpless in the midst of this great tragedy, and powerless to render any real relief. . . ."[3]

The insurgents let it be known that during this period (March–December 1931) they had no intention of letting the president "run the country." Although Congress would not be in session, they thought they had other means of accomplishing their purpose. A round-table conference that met in Washington on March 11 was an example of what they could attempt.

As the session of Congress ended, Hoover envisioned national emergence from the depression (as he wrote Ambassador Dawes) without financial, industrial, and social disorganization and upheaval, and the human suffering, which accompany economic recession. With wages and farm prices in the United States held at levels 30 percent to 40 percent higher than in the rest of the world, the president was hopeful about the immediate future.

Wrote the president: "Our people have organized and taken care of destitution through the winter; we have no doles and no action which permanently undermines our social system."[4] But greater trials and suffering lay in the year ahead, the immediate cause of which was financial collapse in Europe.

Early in March it was announced that the president would take a brief vacation, the first in many months. He proposed to go on the trial run of the U.S.S. *Arizona* for ten days, with visits to Puerto Rico and the Virgin Islands. He was to be accompanied by a small group of newsmen.

On March 24 the president made a formal address at San Juan, Puerto Rico, and at a subsequent press conference on board ship he answered questions on Puerto Rican problems and on the policies of the United States toward that island. In Puerto Rico things went well.

> Hundreds of thousands of citizens welcomed the Chief Executive with shouts, cheers, and music. A correspondent wrote, "In lonely mountain passes, secluded villages, lowland plains, and the capital and its suburbs, men and women from the humblest workers to the heads of Government gave the President such an ovation as the island had never seen or heard."[5]

Soon, however, Hoover discussed the status of the Virgin Islands:

> The Virgin Islands may have some military value sometime. Opinion upon this question is much divided. In any event when we paid $25,000,000 for them, we acquired an effective poor house comprising 90 per cent of the population [and] it was unfortunate that we ever acquired these islands. Nevertheless, having assumed the responsibility we must do our best to assist the inhabitants." [6]

This statement brought much criticism, and both in and out of context the words "poor house" sounded harsh. But as Secretary of the Interior Ray Lyman Wilbur stated later, "Nowhere in the world had any government made so philanthropic an experiment in the aid of a people whose sovereignty it had acquired, without gain to itself."[2]

The president's true concern for the people of the Virgin Islands was soon to be demonstrated when he transferred their administration from the Navy Department to the Department of the Interior in February 1931, and made Paul M. Pearson the governor.

Those close to the president, and who had followed his thoughts from the day of his inauguration, realized that no pressure of domestic politics ever removed from his mind the implications of United States relations with the rest of the world—and particularly with the nations of western Europe. His associates knew that the problems of agriculture, industry, and finance were seen to be part of the world economic situation. That situation was watched with care, and was aided by information furnished by the secretary of state and a body of experts of long experience and positive conviction.[8]

The president's actions of the spring and summer of 1931 can only be comprehended after a brief recital of the international economic stresses of the time and the headlined events which brought such concern to financial circles on the continent and at home.[9]

World War I produced devastating political, economic, social, and psychological dislocations: the breakup of the Austro-Hungarian empire, the division into victor and vanquished, the determination of the British and French to collect reparations from the defeated, and an equal determination on the part of the United States to collect war debts from the allies. At the same time a new program of profitable short-term loans overseas preoccupied American financial circles and facilitated in Europe an illusion of prosperity.

Thus there was dislocation in national economies, in international trade, and in currency stability in the 1920s. Conversion from peacetime to wartime production—and back again—left its toll. One could say that payment of national installments by debtors to creditors was a form of "one-way dumping" of wealth.[10] (Even in the aftermath of the Franco-Prussian War, the payment of reparations gave rise to problems within the borders of both giver and receiver.)[11] There was an "utterly hollow structure of finance" in Europe.[12] Gold would flow from the continent to New York City and the very integrity of paper currencies would come into question. Said President Hoover in appraisal of the events of early 1931,

> When . . . the financial systems of Europe were no longer able to stand the strain of their war inheritances and of their after-war economic and political policies, an earthquake ran through forty nations. Financial panics; governments unable to meet their obligations; banks unable to pay their depositors; citizens, fearing inflation of currency, seeking to export their savings to foreign countries for safety; citizens of other nations demanding payment of their loans; financial and monetary systems either in collapse or remaining only in appearance.[13]

Announcement of a customs union between Germany and Austria on March 21, 1931 would prove the spark that would ignite a new world crisis equal to the American stock market crash of 1929. France, joined by Great Britain, was determined to block this step, and thus insisted on immediate payment of short-term bills by the banks in the defeated states. A wild financial scramble ensued, with ramifications as apparently remote as cancellation of European orders for American wheat and cotton. Soon the Kredit-Anstalt, the Austrian national bank, closed its doors. German Chancellor Bruning, followed quickly by President Von Hindenburg, called on Hoover for help. Said Hindenburg, "You, Mr. President, as the representative of the great American people, are in a position to take steps by which an immediate change in the situation threatening Germany and the rest of the world could be brought about."[14] Recorded Secretary of State Stimson at the time, "We have been saying to each other that the situation was quite like war."[15]

The German banks closed on July 14 and 15, as did many banks elsewhere, for "financial panic is no respecter of national frontiers."[16]

In late summer there would be what Hoover recalled as "a new and worse blow from Britain."[17] French withdrawals of gold deposits started a run on British resources; the repercussions in politics included the fall of the Labour government in late August. International banking proved inadequate to the heavy obligations imposed by events of 1931, as Britain, followed by twenty-five countries, would go off the gold standard on September 21, 1931.[18] World trade dropped abruptly, and economic conditions in the United States deteriorated sharply.[19]

Faced with such terrible world-wide economic disasters, President Hoover kept himself well informed. The public knew some aspects of the debacle at home and abroad, but a full comprehension might have led to greater disquietude or even panic. The president made it a point, as usual, that the most vital conferences on the matter were never known to the public. Joslin reminds us that on many occasions highly qualified advisors were able to visit him at Rapidan Camp or very late in the evening at the White House without occasioning press comment. In this way needless public concern was avoided, but the extent of presidential effort and alertness was not given credit then or later.

Even the press representatives, often in the president's confidence, did not manage to realize how important was the scale of values set up in the vast enterprise which President Hoover conceived of as inherent in his office. He was now moving toward a position in which additional action in the European crisis would be taken by the United States.

Early in May 1931, the meetings of the International Chamber of Commerce in Washington, D.C. had brought together many who were interested in the business situation both at home and abroad. Prior to the meeting, at his press conference on May 1, the president was asked whether he could give the press some advance information. He replied that a great many distinguished men were coming to the conference and they would likely have a very illuminating session on the business depression and the international relations that had grown out of it. When asked if he could give any guidance about the American attitude on proposals to restore international prosperity by currency control, the president was firm in stating, "Our policy in that matter is not changed at all." He was noncommittal in declaring, "We are glad to cooperate, but we have no governmental connection with it."

It may be recalled that early in his administration the president had refused to accede to a request of a group of American bankers (including Owen D. Young, J. P. Morgan, Thomas N. Perkins, and Thomas W. Lamont) for a declaration of American participation in a World Bank. What were the circumstances which would presently lead Hoover to reverse his position on assumption of American governmental responsibility in European financial affairs?

The news of the situation in Germany led President Hoover to take steps hitherto thought impossible. He consulted the secretary of state and the secretary of the treasury, as well as a number of bankers. The method has interest. The president wrote, for the record,

> I had a definite proposal to lay before them. That was that we should postpone all collections on allied debts for one year in consideration of all the allies making similar postponements of reparations and all claims during the same period. I further explained that the world needed some strong action which would change the mental point of view and that I felt perhaps such an action might serve the purpose of general reestablishment of courage and confidence. I read them a rough memo I had prepared.[20]

Stimson was for it. Mellon was unqualifiedly opposed. Mills posed some problems. Said Hoover, "I stated that I feared we were in the presence of a great crisis." Later in the day there came a call from Thomas W. Lamont of the Morgan Company, querying about the German situation. "I did not communicate to him any feature of my plan for a year's deferment," recorded the independent chief executive.[21] He then prepared a statement which became the basis for postponement of payment on war debts owed the United States.

Long and complicated had been the road since October 21, 1930. Then, in response to a suggestion of Charles D. Hilles that, "inasmuch as one of the fundamental faults is the economic and financial distress in Europe and throughout the world, this country should propose to postpone for a period of two or three years the payments due us on the war debt," the president replied:

> The question you mention is one of extreme complexity. Under the Balfour note the British have no direct interest in our attitude on the subject. It mostly concerns the French. In any event I doubt whether it would be possible to carry through any kind of arrangement which acknowledges

the principle of German Reparations as lying at our door. However, we must keep our minds open to any eventuality in these times.[22]

Preliminary steps leading to a proposed moratorium on war debts had to be taken with great secrecy. Otherwise, a critical banking situation realized at the time by only a few would become generally known, and then the president's proposals would be jeopardized.

It was rumored that the president had talked directly by telephone with the British prime minister or the French premier or the German chancellor. This, however, was not the case. His conversations were with accredited diplomatic officials or members of the president's official family who were abroad.[23]

A careful distinction should be made between two kinds of inter-governmental debt: debts arising out of reparations owed by Germany to the victorious allies, and debts owed by the allied nations (mainly to the United States). By the spring of 1931 it was generally agreed that there must be a decided change in both kinds of debt payments. It was in this situation that Hoover presented to Secretaries Stimson, Mellon, and Mills his plan for the postponement of debts. They simply would not be collected for a year, or perhaps two years!

Stimson wrote of Hoover's plan in his diary on June 5, 1931: "It involved a bold emphatic proposition to assume leadership himself, and I myself felt more glad than I could say that he was at last turning that way. He told me that he always believed in going out to meet a situation rather than to let it come. Altogether it was one of the most satisfactory talks I have had with him in a long time."[24]

Prior to the events which in time were to lead to Hoover's formal proposal of a moratorium, two developments of striking interest had taken place. The first concerned members of the Congress, while the second concerned the general public.

Leading members of the Congress, seconded by a considerable body of public sentiment, had renewed their demand that the president call an extra session of Congress. At his press conference on May 22, 1931, the president said:

> I do not propose to call an extra session of Congress. I know of nothing that would so disturb the healing processes now undoubtedly going on in the economic situation. We cannot legislate ourselves out of a world economic depression; we can and will work ourselves out. A poll of the members of Congress would show that a large majority agree with me in opposing an extra session.[25]

Turning to the public, the president embarked on a trip into the

Middle West, which had been planned many months before. His statements in three formal speeches on this trip were a reflection of his determination to deal with the increasing public turmoil. At Indianapolis,
Indiana, at Marion, Ohio, and at Springfield, Illinois, he addressed himself particularly to Republican gatherings.

Dawes had learned that the president was to deliver a series of important economic speeches in different parts of the country as early as May
and June, and he believed this would be a mistake. "The country will
inevitably regard these speeches as the *beginning of your campaign for
re-election,*" Dawes warned. "These speeches . . . should be made at the
time they will best 'sink in.' *That time is later.*" Saying that he felt
Hoover's renomination was certain and his re-election "chiefly dependent
on the time element in the business recovery," Dawes wrote as a friend,
he said, to urge that "nothing now needs a more careful consideration
than this time element." He continued at length:

> Plans, proper and effective under normal conditions, may, in times of
> depression, have a very adverse reaction if in their consummation the time
> element is ignored. . . . You are dealing with a situation in mass attitudes
> which has been determined, not by reason, but by instincts. The mass
> reaction, the full extent of which was evidenced by the stock collapse in
> 1929, was not a "return to reason," but a reaction from one set of extreme
> feelings to another. . . . You long ago set out on the right track to influence
> business revival, not by reasoning with the masses, but by initiating relief
> measures. When, you "reasoned" for instance, with the heads of the leading
> business enterprises of the U.S. and organized under your leadership the
> great programme of building construction, you were reasoning with *individ-
> uals.* The actual employment of men, and the expenditure of money to carry
> out construction programmes is something the mass feels, and that is why it
> is contributing to an earlier revival of business, which without it, still is inevi-
> table later under natural law. *For an interval,* reason is now at a discount
> with the masses, just as it was before 1929. . . . Your speeches when de-
> livered will be effective just in proportion as "better feeling" exists.[26]

Dawes reminded Hoover that in his "strenuous work and unparalleled
achievement in relief organization building during the last year," his
mind "naturally and properly was not concerned with politics." Thus,
while his speeches to relieve public apprehension were "commendable"
from the point of view of the public, they were "unwise from the personal
political standpoint." Dawes felt that "the minimizing of the severity of
conditions was calculated to lessen an eventual proper appreciation of
the real results" of Hoover's effort to better them. Having ignored the
"time element," Hoover should not, Dawes believed, repeat this political

indiscretion. "The mass little comprehends, nor ever properly gauges in advance, the relation of time to the securing of results from constructive effort in depressed periods. Premature arousing of expectations is always resented. . . . Your campaign 'opening' (in effect) would seem best not earlier than October. I am glad to come to America any time you deem best prepared to say something along the lines you suggested [in a letter of March 11]."

Hoover's most revealing reply to his ambassador's forthright advice was a bit rueful:

> What you say is exactly true. . . . There are certain appearances that the President has to make—which just cannot be avoided. . . . In that case I shall accept your wise suggestion and keep away from dangerous ground. One of the large points which the opposition makes, of course, is the optimistic attitude which we deliberately assumed in the early stages of the depression. It was vitally necessary in order to prevent a monetary panic. But we necessarily pay a certain amount of political price for it.[27]

The president felt that the situation had "materially changed in the last sixty days, as the country is very much better in spirit although there is very little of a statistical character to back it up." He enclosed with his letter to Dawes in London a copy of the Department of Commerce graphic index of business "plotted on the same basis for four major depressions since that of 1894," and told Dawes:

> There is from a business point of view a very considerable difference between this depression and all others in that the various activities of the Administration produced a more gradual descent on this occasion, which has enabled the business and agricultural world to constantly readjust itself without the acute stress of general bankruptcy. The economic machine is in good running order, although it is out of gas. You will notice that in the three previous depressions the collapse has taken place over periods of from four to six months, whereas this time it has been gradual over a period of nineteen months. You may be interested to note that this depression has only one parallel in its acuteness, and that is 1873. If your reading or recollection goes back that far you will find it was a period of general bankruptcy and of wild social disorder, both of which we have so far avoided on this occasion.[28]

The president had contemplated a trip across the continent to his home on the Stanford University campus but was counseled by his friend Henry M. Robinson to forego it. Robinson wrote to Walter H. Newton, the president's secretary:

> While it is true that conditions in California are troublesome, and while it is true that some of those could be straightened out if the President were here, it is my opinion that the trip across the continent would be a very difficult one. The pressure to go through important centers would be great. This would mean a trip full of difficult encounters, as the temper of the people generally is quite unreasonable and unreasoning. It would mean the necessary preparation of speeches. It would mean pressure to go here, there, and elsewhere, either coming or going, all of which constitutes a very serious strain and in my opinion, no advantage could arise. . . .[29]

The president's trip into the Middle West was brief. Only his Indianapolis address, at a dinner of the Indiana Republican Editorial Association, was "political." It was, however, a blunt and comprehensive summary of his view of the business depression as "the dominant subject before the country and the world today." None hitherto had been so widespread; its main causes were outside the United States—malign inheritances in Europe of the Great War. Hoover reminded his hearers that the United States was "economically more self-contained than any other great nation," but that "repeated shocks from political disturbance and revolution in foreign countries stimulate fear and hesitation among our business men." So, speaking on June 15, 1931, he judged, "We are suffering today more from frozen confidence than we are from frozen securities."[30]

He could not have described more aptly the background for the coming moratorium, although he did not mention it—for it was still a secret. It was continually on his mind. "With no desire to minimize the realities of suffering or the stern tasks of recovery, . . ." the president said, "[we] must not look only at the empty hole in the middle of the doughnut." He described the material advantages possessed by the American people and the "extensive and positive part" taken by the federal government in "mitigating the effects of depression and expediting recovery." He emphasized the coordinated action between the Treasury, the Federal Reserve System, the banks, and the Farm Loan and Farm Board systems. He described the relief work of the federal government: "over two billions of dollars is being expended, and today a million men are being given direct and indirect employment. . . ." Concluding that "we shall keep this ship steady in the storm," he paid tribute to all the voluntary forces in business, industry, labor, and agriculture that had entered into efforts to bring recovery.[31]

The concluding note of this revealing address was forthright: "If, as many believe, we have passed the worst of this storm, future months will not be difficult. If we shall be called upon to endure more of this period, we must gird ourselves to steadfast effort, to fail at no point where humanity calls or American ideals are in jeopardy."

Dawes was in America in June and went to Marion, Ohio, to attend the dedication of the Harding Memorial.[32] He joined the presidential train on Tuesday, June 16, 1931, writing in his journal:

> On the train going to Columbus Hoover went over the financial situation in Europe which is critical. At that time he expected the National Bank of Austria to fail as the relief measures under negotiation seemed likely to fall through. . . . The New York bankers had been telephoning Hoover before he left Washington requesting governmental assistance in the European difficulty. In this situation Hoover was considering what he could do to relieve it. His present thought was to suggest a reparations moratorium all around for one or two years, funding the payment to the United States for that time. France, in this case, would have to forego receiving reparations, at present amounting to more than she is paying the United States. Hoover could not propose such a plan without being assured by the leaders of the opposition in the Senate that his proposal would be ratified by the Senate next December. He asked my opinion on this course and if he took it, said that he wished to call me to Washington to help in securing Senatorial agreement. I approved the plan but urged the period be made two years instead of one.[33]

At Springfield, Hoover's spoken contribution to Lincoln's memory dealt with the burden of leadership. And he singled out characteristics in Lincoln worth special mention:

> Nothing that we may say here can add to the knowledge or devotion of our people to the memory of Abraham Lincoln. . . .
>
> No man gazes upon the tomb of Lincoln without reflection upon his transcendent qualities of patience, fortitude, and steadfastness. . . .
>
> Time sifts out the essentials of men's character and deeds, and in Lincoln's character there stands out his patience, his indomitable will, his sense of humanity of a breadth which comes to but few men. . . .[34]

On the same day, June 17, Mr. Hoover reminded the joint session of the Illinois Legislature that, as a student of American politics and government, he could speak from long experience. He said he retained his confidence in the value of the governmental process in the states:

> A study of national legislation and national action will show that an overwhelming proportion of the ideas which have been developed nationally have first been born in the state legislatures as the result of the problems which have developed within the states. They have been given trial; they

have been hammered out on the anvil of local experience. . . . Ours must be a country of constant change and progress because of one fact alone amongst many others, and that is that the constant discoveries in science and their product in new invention shift our basis of human relationships and our mode of life in such a fashion as to require a constant remodeling and the remoulding of the machinery of the Government. . . . And in these great processes our state legislatures occupy a position of dominant importance to the Nation as a whole.[35]

Upon his return to Washington on June 18, President Hoover made his final decision on the moratorium. He now secured by telephone the support of thirty leading members of the House and Senate, and on the following morning at a cabinet meeting the matter was presented in its final stage. The president determined to propose the moratorium openly in advance of any discussion by the foreign governments concerned. It was to be "open diplomacy openly arrived at."[36] Secretary Stimson was instructed to call in the ambassadors and ministers of the nations concerned in order to give them opportunity to inform their governments in advance that the proposal had been made. But the press, learning of the pending announcement, forced the president's hand into a premature announcement on June 21.

To his press conference the preceding day, Mr. Hoover had said that he did not approve "in any remote sense" of the outright *cancellation* of the debts. The moratorium was, in his view, a way to insure *postponement* of payment. This was not, however, the French view.

There have been many discussions of the delay in telling the French, who were most deeply concerned, of the earlier steps in the plan. Stimson later felt that it was necessary to act before a possibly hostile verdict could be reached by the American public. He reports that on June 19 he explained President Hoover's plan to the French ambassador, who was pleased that the president would go so far. He promised to urge his government to support the plan.

Although this moratorium on all intergovernmental debts resulting from World War I was thought by many to be "the boldest and most constructive step" taken by the United States in its dealings with European nations since 1918, evidence at once appeared that the action taken by the American government would not be satisfactory to France.

On June 24, 1931, Ambassador Dawes telephoned from Chicago that he had received word from Jean Parmentier, the leading French delegate to both the Dawes and Young Committees, that while "President Hoover's most generous proposal is likely to check the present crisis," the suspension of payments for a year would so profoundly modify the agreement that it was doubtful whether payments could or would ever be resumed. It might never be brought to life again.[37]

The immediate domestic reaction was favorable. Americans at this time were, in the view of Anne O'Hare McCormick, "so abnormally subdued in spirit, manifesting so little boldness of initiative in the highest ranks, and so little tendency to rebellion in the lowest, that if Mr. Hoover had announced the cancellation of the war debts instead of a year's moratorium, if he had annulled the latest tariff, recognized Russia, given one good feed to China with all our surplus wheat, set up a supreme economic council, done half a dozen things he cannot be imagined doing, public acquiescence in these revolutionary changes (supposing Congress still out of session) would probably still be as unanimous, and as passive."[38]

Not only had the moratorium announcement been well staged; its economic significance was immediately perceptible, and it appeared to be "good politics" as well—in fact, "a bull's eye," as Secretary Wilbur wrote the president. By July 6, the president could tell his press conference that the moratorium had been accepted by the creditor governments and that he had personal assurance it would be approved by the United States Congress.[39] With such almost unanimous support in the United States, Hoover could say, "We simply pass it over to the State Department."

But it proved to be not at all simple, as one crisis after another unfolded during the ensuing weeks and months. On July 14 the president told his press conference that the reparations postponement had taken the most dangerous strain off the whole situation, but that there were elements of popular panic in the failure of a German bank the preceding day.[40]

In the critical German situation, the president stood firm for voluntary cooperation of the bankers of the world rather than government loans. The conference of representatives who met in London on July 20 finally accepted his plan. Ambassador Dawes warmly congratulated the president for preserving the full benefits of the reparations moratorium arrangement: "By your recent statement from Washington you again assumed leadership . . . and preserved confidence. . . . Your intervention was necessary to preserve the full benefits of your reparations moratorium arrangement. In financial crisis nothing is more important than central leadership, with definite opinions, and which acts without delay."[41]

The German attitude, in claiming continued bankruptcy and imminence of collapse even after the debt moratorium had been announced, not only destroyed the usefulness of the moratorium in rehabilitating confidence in Germany, but brought about a mirror reflection of discouragement in the American press. This deterioration in German morale was a source of continuous concern to the president. Following the London conference of governmental representatives, the same claims of insolvency by Germany tended to destroy their own credit and nullify the president's efforts to help. Yet the Reichsbank was now holding its own, and, if it would but give to the public a hint of progress, rehabilitation could be in sight. President Hoover felt that nothing more could be hoped to come from Washington unless this were done. The American government would make no further effort if the only result should be humiliation of the United States.

Dawes wrote in his diary on July 21, 1931, "I believe no one concerned with the whole situation in Europe had at his command more authoritative information than did the President.... His clearness and quickness of comprehension, his equipoise and calmness and his command of knowledge of every element in this diversified and world-important problem, were remarkable." One notes the behind-the-scenes effort by President Hoover; by no means was all of it visible even to Dawes. For example, Hoover dictated a telegram to Henry M. Robinson on July 27 as follows:

> In amplification of our discussions, it seems to me these points should be made strongly to Warburg, and if you desire you can say that you reflect my views. Now, first, German attitude by claiming continued bankruptcy and imminence of collapse after debt moratorium announced by President destroyed its value and usefulness in rehabilitating confidence in Germany. The same tactics by Germany following the London Conference are destroying the confidence which could have been relieved through maintenance of $1,200,000,000 short term credits. Aside from destroying their own credit they are rapidly destroying the ability of the President to give them help. The reflection in the American press that the President's efforts have been futile is the direct result of the German attitude. Yet the Reichsbank is now holding its own. If they would give to the press the atmosphere of progress, ventilate the relief from drain, we could in two weeks rehabilitate what has been now lost. Unless this is done nothing more can be hoped from Washington as our government will make no further effort and then be humiliated as is now the case. The attitude of Wall Street and Grain exchanges that no good has come of our efforts will infect the entire country in a week and her attitude is due to Germany's attitude solely. If attitude of Germans is not changed we cannot hope to hold banks to cooperation in maintaining present credit lines open. Second, commodity purchases should be pursued by Germans vigorously but move must come from Germans. Third, Warburg should vigorously back up purchases of governments....[42]

The president's action in the European crisis had been spectacular and decisive. It won the approval of his closest advisers as one of the

most effective he had ever taken. To those who, like Secretary of the
Treasury Ogden Mills, had rendered extraordinary service during the
trying weeks of preparation for the debt postponement, the president
was deeply grateful and said so:

> I feel that any form of verbal or written appreciation for the extraordinary
> service you have given in the last three weeks in the matter of the debt post-
> ponement is wholly inadequate. I just want you to know I appreciate it.[43]

The response of Congressional leaders to whom he had appealed for
support in advance of his announcements indicated that they had realized
the gravity of the crisis and were willing to follow presidential leadership. Democrats, as well as Republicans (including some insurgents), had
given approval. Here was another example, however, of American policy
determined by events beyond our borders and consequently distasteful to
some isolationists.

Senator Borah, who had endorsed the president's plan for the moratorium, sent a message from Boise, Idaho in late July that the program
outlined by the committee of finance ministers at London was feeble and
wholly inadequate. He felt that France proposed to wreck the plan and
hoped to draw the United States as far as possible into the political affairs
of Europe—a result which he said he had not foreseen in his earlier
endorsement. The president explained that the report of the finance
ministers was solely and absolutely devoted to economic relief of Germany and that there was not a phrase or sentence of a political order in it,
much less any involvement of the United States in the political affairs
of Europe.

Later, on September 2, Borah wrote the president that he wished to
withdraw from the United States delegation to the forthcoming meeting
of the Disarmament Conference. (Hoover had suggested that Borah serve
as chairman of the delegation.) On the pretext that he did not see how
he could be absent during the next session of Congress, Borah pushed his
withdrawal. The president replied shortly,

> I hope you will come to no conclusion in this matter until I have had an
> opportunity to discuss it with you in all its aspects. It seems to me the situa-
> tion is one which even more urgently requires your leadership than ever
> before. I do not believe it will require a long absence from the Senate.[44]

Such were the president's trials with some whose help and cooperation
he needed.

As summer advanced into autumn—and the situation in Europe did
not improve—it became clear to many that the dramatic action of the

president had really come too late. The European situation, both economically and politically, was so serious that it called for action on the part of the United States that would carry the nation much further than a moratorium on the debts for one year.[45]

All of the president's planning of the moratorium—as presented to the Congress and to the press—indicated his continuing belief that the nation must deal not only with a national economic crisis, but with a world crisis in economic relations.

"Words fail to give an understanding of the pressures centering upon the White House," stated Secretary Joslin a few years later. "Crowded hours became more crowded. Long days became longer. No sooner did the President attend to one crisis than another swept down upon him. There was no relief whatsoever. . . . The nature of the impending disasters did not permit confidences. Any revelations would have accentuated panic. This he prevented."[46]

When Great Britain went off the gold standard on September 21, and the Bank of England defaulted on gold payments, another international crisis was thrust upon the president. Over most of Europe commodity and security markets closed; prices dropped in the United States.

On September 4, the president had reminded his press conference of the flow of gold to the United States which amounted to over $5 billion. He said this gold situation was abnormal in light of the whole history of the world and was fundamentally caused by the people's lack of confidence in their own governments, and by their own circumstances in their home countries.[47]

❖   ❖   ❖

Hoover was no stranger to affairs in the Far East. In 1899 he went to China to engage in exploration for minerals on behalf of the Department of Mines of the imperial Chinese government.[48] For three years he and Mrs. Hoover soaked up impressions of Chinese customs and culture, and they lived with the disorder and danger of the Boxer Rebellion. Hoover had indeed seen China as few American political leaders have ever seen it, and his travels took him even to Manchuria. He wrote later, "The impression I have held of the Chinese people is one of abiding admiration."[49] The personal Hoover position toward Japan and the Japanese was essentially neutral. When a decade after the presidency someone tried to portray Hoover as "pro-Japanese," William Castle wrote,

Nothing could be further from the truth. During his residence in China and thereafter, he had many long friendships with Chinese officials and others. He disliked the Japanese character [that is, at *that* time] because he hated

militarism and could not lose sight of this trait in many Japanese. I think
that ten years before Pearl Harbor he was fearful that Japan might bring
war on the world.[50]

Over the years there would be circulated both extravagant praise and
despicable charges about the Hoover years overseas. As to China there
exists this Chinese judgment, "Mr. Hoover's record in China is clean and
honorable, highly creditable, and in many ways remarkable."[51]

As a member of the cabinet from 1921 to 1928, Hoover had been in a
position to keep an eye on the struggle in the Orient for resources, trade,
territory, and power. He had witnessed the conduct of the Japanese
representatives at the Limitation of Armaments Conference in Washington in 1921–22; thus he had realized the possibility of war in the Far East.
Against his background of early experiences in China, he could foresee
that the expanding interests of Japan in the outlying areas of Asia would
attract the attention of the world—including the United States. Secretary
of State Henry Stimson, during his service as governor general of the
Philippines, had come to know firsthand the pressing problems of Japan's
population growth, its economic penetration of China, and the mounting
threat of militaristic elements in Japan.

The Russo-Chinese clash over Russian rights in the Chinese Eastern
railway in northern Manchuria in 1929 led Stimson and the president to
call to the public's attention the renunciation of war pledge provided in
the Kellogg-Briand Pact of the previous year. But this only served to
emphasize American distrust of the League of Nations, the natural world
forum for discussion of any outbreak of nationalistic military action. As
near as the United States would come to lending its influence there would
be the presence at League of Nations Council meetings of an American
representative when matters arose under the obligations of the Kellogg-
Briand Pact.

September of 1931 was a fateful month. Two days before Great
Britain defaulted on gold, Japanese army forces occupied Mukden and
other cities in Manchuria. This well-organized coup could not be ignored.
Although the situation was "very confused," as Secretary Stimson noted
in his diary on Saturday morning, September 19, it nevertheless threatened
damage to "the new structure of international society provided by the
post-war treaties." The results might prove to be "incalculable."[52]

As Japanese military elements seized various cities along the South
Manchurian Railway, the president and his secretary of state reacted
indignantly. In retrospect, Hoover termed it "an act of rank aggression":

It was a direct violation of the Nine-Power Treaty of 1922, by which Japan had joined in guaranteeing the integrity of China. It was a gross violation of the John Hay agreement of the Open Door in China. It was a cynical violation of the Covenant of the League of Nations of which Japan was a member. It was an impudent violation of the Kellogg Pact to which Japan was a signatory.

Hoover recalled that he "fully realized the great seriousness of the situation and determined that we must do everything possible to uphold the moral foundations of international life."[53] Thus:

> At once I agreed with the Secretary of State that we must protest to the Japanese government, which he did on September 24. When, on September 21, China appealed to the League of Nations, I authorized the Secretary to cooperate fully with the League as it furnished a central point for coordination of action with the European nations. I insisted that we encourage the League to take the lead, and that we would cooperate with them.[54]

But in his message to Congress on its reassembly in December 1931, Hoover pointed out that the United States had maintained complete freedom of action. Reassuring though this was to the isolationist sentiment of a great number of Americans, it gave little satisfaction to those in America as well as in the western European countries, or in China, who wished that the United States would play an aggressive role in the ever-expanding crises in the Orient.[55]

Proceeding quite outside of the League, Secretary Stimson, in consultation with President Hoover, ultimately announced that the United States did not intend to recognize "any situation, treaty or agreement brought about by means contrary to the covenants and obligations of the Kellogg-Briand Pact." This emphasized *moral* sanctions against aggression rather than *economic* sanctions.

What ought to be termed the "Hoover Doctrine" can be described as follows: it rejected the idea of enforcement of peace by the use of force; it did not accept the idea of joint action of nations in an official boycott; and it declared that any nation guilty of breaking the terms of the Kellogg-Briand Pact would find that the fruits of its aggression would go unrecognized. Consequently in theory it rendered valueless either agression or the attempt to suppress it by force.[56]

Any discussion of the leadership of Herbert Hoover in foreign affairs must at this point include his relations with his secretary of state. It was first of all a close personal relationship, although Hoover afterward referred to his "able Secretary" as "at times more of a warrior than a diplomat." For his part, Stimson once recorded in his diary the comment that "the President being a Quaker and an engineer did not understand

the psychology of combat the way Mr. [Elihu] Root and I did."[57]
Nevertheless, Stimson could say of Hoover:

> His is a keen and ever-ready power of analysis. His is a well poised and
> balanced intelligence. Behind those qualities is the most unceasing mental
> energy with which I have ever come in contact. And again behind that,
> although they are shy and never paraded in official discussions, lies the
> guidance of the human sympathies of one of the most sensitive and tender
> natures which has ever wielded such official power.[58]

And Hoover could call Stimson "a man of integrity, sagacity, loyalty, and
patriotism," yet, he added, "I was obliged to take over more duties in
this field than otherwise would have been the case," because Secretary
Stimson "was not in good health" at the time he entered the administration. Stimson ultimately assumed strong control of his department, however, and wielded great influence through his grasp of public affairs, his
obsession with the position of the United States in the world, and his
resistance to the isolationist attitude of members of Congress, especially
in the Senate.

Yet, overwhelmed with the sheer bulk of the Stimson Diary and its
unavoidable magnification of the Stimson participatory role, it is a mistake to assume that the president assumed a peripheral role. Judges a
well-informed central figure of that time, "As a matter of fact, Mr.
Hoover's knowledge of the Far Eastern situation, from his visits and his
long residence there, from his experiences at Versailles and after made
him probably the best informed man in Washington on Oriental questions."[59] Moreover, "I am certain that no one ever drafted a memorandum
for Mr. Hoover on public policies. He was always ready to seek advice
but he did his own thinking and his own drafting."

This truth can be seen with clarity in an exchange of letters between
Hoover and Stimson in 1936 after Stimson sent the ex-president the
galleys of *The Far Eastern Crisis* for review. While noting below his
signature, "I omitted to say that the book is a grand lucid and needed
job," Hoover was outspoken on sanctions:

> On the whole question of the economic sanctions there is one reason
> for refusal that I think might be stated definitely (Galley 60A) and else-
> where. That was the President's flat refusal to be drawn into them, irrespec-
> tive of Congress, the public, Europe, or anything else, for what that might
> be worth as moral pressure. I find a note written at the time among my own
> papers which I enclose. I do not have the precise date of it.[60]

In view of the considerable dispute that has arisen on this subject among historians, this contemporary presidential memorandum is given in its entirety:

> The Secretary of State informs me that certain groups in the League are pressing for the application of economic sanctions against Japan. He seems to feel we would need to go along. Otherwise we would defeat the efforts of the League and place ourselves in a full responsibility for failure. He feels deeply and rightly that the whole fabric of cooperation to preserve peace and the whole fabric of international obligations are at stake. I agreed with that, but I could not agree to take any part in economic sanctions. My view was that they would likely lead to war; that I had told President Wilson that at the time the League was set up. I also felt that we were the exposed party and we would bear the brunt of it. I had no confidence in the League, in the present state of Europe, going further than to get us well involved along that path. I felt that we must first make up our minds whether we were prepared to go to war to support these treaties. If we were not we should take no steps that could possibly lead there. My own view was that war with Japan was unthinkable in our situation or for the stake we had in jeopardy. That after all China must defend herself; that if 300,000,000 people could not defend themselves from 35,000,000, it was hardly a moral obligation on our part to go to war in her defense. Moreover, I was sure that no matter what the Japanese did to China the passive resistance and superior number of Chinese would ultimately either absorb or overwhelm Japan. It might take fifty years, but for us to risk destroying our civilization, already in sufficient dangers, to speed this period up say seven years, was not particularly inviting. This was not, of course, the whole question. But the big question of enforcement of treaties it seemed to me would have to rest where they start—a moral obligation to be met by moral pressures. I felt we should refuse to recognize any territorial acquisitions.[61]

Stimson replied at once, and at length, saying he was "very mindful" of the Hoover position at the time on economic sanctions and had just reread his own diary entries on the matter; he wished that Hoover might read them; excerpts for December 6, 1931 and January 26, 1932 were attached. Hoover's position had long been clear to him, he wrote, and he had agreed about the danger noted by his former chief, but he thought it "after all a relative one," for dangers had to be weighed off against each other. As a tactic, he had begged at the time that Hoover not reveal publicly his position on sanctions in those months, and the president had not until the secretary of state was away—at which time Castle had been instructed to announce that a boycott would not be used. Thus the League for a time, at least, had not been discouraged from invoking sanctions. If the president insisted, said Stimson, he would insert in his book the strong private position the chief executive had taken at the time

against sanctions. But he did fear that Hoover's opponents would somehow twist this and use it against him.[62] Years later Hoover would place in
his *Memoirs* two pages of strong prose identifying Stimson with sanctions,[63] and it is worth noting that the Stimson letter of June 6, 1936, did
not deny that in 1931–1932 the secretary of state was vigorously opposed
to public renunciation of sanctions.

In summary, the differences between Hoover and Stimson were substantive. Under practically no circumstances would Hoover contemplate
sanctions, for he saw them as a step on the road to war.[64] Stimson, for his
part, did not wish to forswear sanctions publicly, for he thought the time
might well come when they should be used; moreover, he considered
them a legitimate and proper method of bringing Japan to heel. He
wanted the public posture of the United States to be such that sanctions
could be resorted to if need be.

It was the Hoover position that prevailed, and in his memoirs the
former president was at pains to point out that "Secretary Stimson and I
agreed to disagree on the sanctions point, and I must say at once that he
loyally carried out my policies in his negotiations with the powers.[65]
It is important to recognize, in any case, that the early thirties were a
time when efforts to exert American leadership in international affairs
had to consider the fact that Britain and France would have to be consulted and their support enlisted as a precondition to mobilizing world
opinion.[66]

Eventually, on March 3, 1932, when the assembly of the League of
Nations met, adherence to the doctrine of nonrecognition was expressed,
with both the British and French voting for it. This action came after
Japan, in its continuous march of aggression, had established additional
areas of interest on the Chinese mainland. It would be Hoover's conclusion, years later, that:

> Our long and earnest negotiations both with Europe and with Japan, and
> the European acceptance of the nonrecognition declaration, possibly were
> responsible for halting Japan's attack on Central China and inducing their
> subsequent withdrawal. But it did not restore Manchuria.[67]

European representatives at Geneva might scoff at such a program of
nonrecognition as unrealistic but at home the real problem for the president, as always, was the attitude of the American public toward any and
every move of political association with non-American powers. Comment
upon the Geneva conference at the time was acid (whatever might be the
attitude of internationalists years later) and growing apprehension of
developments that could bring about war in the Far East gave increased

publicity to both pacifist propagandists and defenders of military preparedness. Both groups found the possibility of agreement with foreign powers on armament dangerous to American interests. Hoover's moderate attitude did not inspire confidence in either group, and this is fully reflected in the magazine articles of the day.

The Hoover doctrine of nonrecognition of "any situation, treaty, or agreement" brought about contrary to the Kellogg-Briand Pact, a doctrine that did not include threat of economic boycott, was later applied by the United States to conquests by nations in Europe. Little support was given to it, however, by other nations, and it "failed to become a part of international law."[68]

There should also be mention here of the letter Stimson sent to Borah on February 23, 1932, which referred to the Nine-Power Pact of 1922 and made clear that treaty rights must be honored. The nation's attitude toward China was characterized as based on "the principles of fair play, patience, and mutual goodwill."[69]

President Hoover's attitude throughout, while one of outrage against Japanese aggression, was uniformly opposed to either military intervention or economic sanctions. It was the president's intention to withdraw troops from Nicaragua and Haiti; he certainly would not countenance sending troops or naval vessels to fight in the Far Pacific.[70] In a dictated memorandum of mid-October 1931 Hoover stated:

> The United States has never set out to preserve peace among other nations by force. . . . Our whole policy in connection with controversies is to exhaust the processes of peaceful negotiation. But in contemplating these we must make up our minds whether we consider war as the ultimate if these efforts fail. Neither our obligation to China, nor our own interest, nor our dignity requires us to go to war over these questions.[71]

Hoover concluded: "We will not go along on war or any of the sanctions either economic or military, for those are the roads to war."[72]

Castle wrote years later about the Hoover position: "He was certainly opposed to economic sanctions because he knew that they were the road to war."[73] Hoover and Charles A. Beard exchanged letters on the matter toward the close of the war against Japan (1945). Wrote the ex-president:

> . . . there were never personal conflicts between Mr. Stimson and myself. We agreed to disagree—and my views prevailed—over economic sanctions. We were in agreement over non-recognition. . . . You have no doubt noted that Secretary Stimson in his book (p. 161) says he wished in 1932 for Congressional authority for sanctions. Out of courtesy for my pig-headedness he did not mention that I stopped it.[74]

In his notes, said Hoover, he had a record of a 1929 discussion with Kellogg on the possibility of adding "moral teeth" to the Kellogg-Briand Pact. "The proposal I made to him was non-recognition of spoils or territory seized, withdrawal of embassies, united public denunciation by other powers, exclusion of membership to such aggressive powers in world conferences, etc. The depression and other reasons made it seem impossible to secure general agreement at that time." Replied Beard, on the basis of his own research on the post-Hoover period, "It was the Stimson version, with sanctions and war, that was pursued to the end by the Roosevelt administration in the ultimate showdown."[75]

While Secretary Stimson wanted to keep open the option of economic sanctions by not publicly renouncing the possibility of their use, he loyally went along with the president. To him, the Manchurian situation was "one of the thorniest and most difficult I have ever tried to envisage."[76] He did not reveal publicly that sanctions were being discussed within his inner circle, and even in a seventeen-page letter to his dear friend and confidant Elihu Root marked "strictly personal and confidential," a letter devoted entirely to policy toward Japan, he did not mention sanctions.[77]

The secretary was fully aware that the Manchurian matter comprised a real crisis. To Walter Lippmann, in a letter not mailed, he wrote, "If we were free from the danger of a sudden conflagration at any time in Manchuria, I should have little doubt that we would work out a solution. As it is, all our plans may be upset at any moment by the act of some hot-head."[78] His public posture was cool and restrained, and in his correspondence he tended to indicate that he held in reserve, in case of additional Japanese aggression, not sanctions but possible public release of various warnings delivered privately to the Japanese during the year.[79] It was behind the scenes, in debates with Castle and Hoover, that the idea of sanctions was aired, and to such effect that years later the former president could write of Stimson's apparent desires at the time, "He who brandishes a pistol must be prepared to shoot."[80]

Four years after leaving office, in 1937, Stimson proposed in a letter to the *New York Times* that economic sanctions be invoked against Japan. Still later, as secretary of war in the Roosevelt cabinet he supported anti-Japanese sanctions even to the point of confiscating Japanese assets in the United States. Wrote Hoover reflectively of the situation in 1941, "The economic paralysis of Japan was complete with huge unemployment and destitution. She struck back four months later at Pearl Harbor. Here was ample proof that 'economic sanctions' not only failed in their purpose to restrain Japan; they probably had some part in precipitating war." But it must be said that Henry Stimson sought peace both in 1931 and 1941, whatever his ardent desire to roll back aggression on both occasions.[81]

As commander in chief, Hoover saw the possible use of naval vessels in the Orient as limited. He would use them only "to protect the lives of Americans," so "strict orders were issued that our forces should confine themselves to the task of protecting Americans."[82] The protection would be from both Chinese and Japanese combatants. Stimson, judges one historian, "wanted to bluff and threaten Japan." Moreover, "Japan should fear this country."[83] Secretary of War Hurley said the nation should put up or shut up. The cabinet was warned by the president, however, of the "folly of getting into a war with Japan on this subject," and he said he "would fight for Continental United States as far as anybody but would not fight for Asia."[84] Feeling as he did, the president nearly made an official public statement that under no circumstances would the nation go to war over the China situation.[85] On this, the secretary of state confided behind the scenes to a senator that the nation "would not go to war unless Japan attacked us, but in that case we would fight like the devil."[86]

Nonrecognition did not roll back the Japanese, but the doctrine lived on. The League of Nations would also live on, but without Japan. There would be no war between Japan and the United States in the Hoover years, and this was clearly a major objective of the president—and the public as well. President Hoover, a man who had experienced war in China and its effects in Europe, had successfully avoided taking steps he thought likely to lead toward conflict, all the while using a method, nonrecognition, that would leave no doubt about America's repudiation of aggression and its rewards.[87]

❊   ❊   ❊

The world financial picture remained grim. On the same day that Britain went off the gold standard (September 21, 1931), the American Legion, at its annual meeting in Detroit, was threatening to demand the cash payment of the remaining half of the veterans' bonus from World War I. But the legion voted to forego the bonus, so that Hoover could observe, "The Legion has set an example to other voluntary bodies in the country in its determination to make no demands on the next Congress." The example proved a good one, for within the next two weeks the president obtained pledges of cooperation not only from the financial leaders of the nation, but from congressional leaders representing both parties. Following upon the stock market crash of 1929 and the central European collapse of the previous summer, this third crisis inaugurated by the default in Britain called for bold measures to bolster the

American people against similar financial collapse.

It was not the credit of the national government that was at stake, it should be noted, but the credit of private financial units. The danger at this time was very great. So it was that Hoover expressed his appreciation to the press in his conference of October 9 for their handling of "the pretty difficult situation" during the four or five days of early October. They had helped produce "unity of action," essential in times of national difficulties.

The president believed that one of the things that had undermined the stability of England had been the flight of its capital to the United States during the preceding eight years. He wrote to Ambassador Dawes that the British had invested in the United States upwards of $1.5 billion at a time when interest rates were lower on the average than they were in England. Thus England had been denuded of that much of her available working capital. The British were not, in general, supporting sterling, however. But the president felt that this was "not our business." He nevertheless recognized the obligation of a friendly interest toward Great Britain and the world as a whole. He was much troubled as he watched the British sell their securities in America. "It is difficult to see where it is all going to lead."[88]

Meanwhile, France was still on the gold standard and continued to withdraw gold from the United States. President Hoover invited the French Premier Pierre Laval to visit Washington for a discussion of the world economic situation.

It was in this period, when the president was carrying on, with as much secrecy as possible, intensive negotiations with private business and government leaders, that his meeting with Laval on October 23 attracted great interest.

"There was much speculation about whom he could have with him at the Conference as an interpreter," Secretary Joslin later stated. "He [Hoover] had decided long since that Ogden Mills would be at his side. The Undersecretary had a good command of French, but he was to be present primarily, if not so announced, because of his exceptional understanding of the international financial problems. It is an open question whether the president really needed an interpreter. His French was sufficiently good to permit him to understand most of, if not all, the conversation."[89]

When Senator Borah was interviewed by the seventeen French journalists who accompanied Laval, he spoke "frankly," with "determined and unequivocal" replies.[90] He told them that he favored wiping out all debts and reparations; that he was opposed to any consultative or security pact; that he believed there could be no real disarmament until the United

States recognized the U.S.S.R.; and that he wished to revise the Treaty of Versailles. Thus were the French apprised of the vast distance that separated "Idaho and Auvergne." But of course Borah spoke not for President Hoover but for the outposts of isolationism in the United States in this, "the most dramatic press conference held in Washington in recent times."[91] It "created a sensation" in the European capitals as well as in every American newspaper. Most American press comment was caustic in the extreme: Borah was characterized as "childish" and "immature," although the Hearst press thought he should be the next president. The *Boston Transcript* reporter noted:

> The Senate is always there to act as a brake upon the Executive in its international dealings; and that, after all, is the main function of Borah. He has enormous power to stay the Executive's hand in the conduct of foreign relations, even tho he has little opportunity to initiate anything. His power is that of an obstructionist.[92]

The Hoover-Laval communiqué stressed "the importance of monetary stability as an essential factor in the restoration of normal economic life in the world in which the maintenance of the gold standard in France and the United States will serve as a major influence." Hoover and Laval reported that they had "canvassed the economic situation in the world, the trends in international relations bearing upon it; the problems of the forthcoming conference for limitation and reduction of armaments; the effect of the depression on payments under intergovernmental debts; the stabilization of international exchanges and other financial and economic subjects." The announcement indicated that with reference to intergovernmental obligations, it was recognized that "prior to the expiration of the Hoover year of postponement, some agreement regarding them may be necessary covering the period of business depression, as to the reparations."[93] The statement had been rewritten a dozen times, newsmen were told. The French had achieved no security pact, however.[94]

Following Laval's visit, President Hoover worked with Hugh Wilson, the emissary extraordinary and minister plenipotentiary to Switzerland, on what could be done to "save the European situation." At that time, in the opinion of J. P. Moffat (first secretary of the legation at Berne), the president did not exclude the possibility of "divorcing American recovery from world economy and getting on as best as we can by ourselves."[95]

The president found it necessary to declare repeatedly that the reparations were a strictly European problem and that at no time had the United States committed itself in any way to surrender on the war debts, however inclined it might be to ease the situation temporarily. This was the general expectation of the Congress as well.

The isolationist sentiment both in Congress and in the country as a whole was strengthened by the intrusion of the European situation upon American consciousness. At the same time Americans were shocked by the advance of the Japanese into Manchuria. The League of Nations moved without success to put an end to this undeclared war in the Far East.

Meanwhile, the president had exerted every influence at his command in the formation of a National Credit Association which, by mobilizing the banking resources of the nation, would make loans to those banks ineligible for aid through Federal Reserve Banks. It was Hoover's intention to propose to Congress legislation that would broaden the scope of the Federal Reserve System, as well as strengthen the Federal Land Banks. He had in mind also a plan for a national system of mortgage discount banks, which he presented to a committee of leaders representing insurance, mortgage, building and loan, and construction interests.[96]

A meeting of thirty financial leaders, including Thomas W. Lamont, George Whitney, Winthrop Aldrich, Mortimer Buckner, Harvey Gibson, Walter Fleur, Percy Johnson, David Houston, and Jackson Reynolds, was held at Hoover's request at Secretary Mellon's apartment on October 4, 1931.[97] It was at this meeting that the President proposed the creation of a national credit association. Those present agreed to work out this voluntary plan and did so the following day, although several leading bankers were extremely reluctant to move in this direction.

President Hoover called into conference on October 6 thirty members of the Congress of both parties. Before the conference began, he received a message from the bankers with whom he had privately conferred, saying that they were agreeable to the proposal he had made, and were initiating action. The conference lasted until midnight. Objections were raised by Speaker of the House John Nance Garner and Senator Borah. But Hoover's proposal was accepted, and he issued a statement the following morning.

Response to the formation of the National Credit Corporation was immediate. "In twenty-four hours the impending panic was dissipated. The prices of wheat and cotton, and of all securities generally, rose at once. Hoarding diminished rapidly. By the end of the month currency was returning to the banks."[98] Said the *Literary Digest*, "Here at last is a way out." Here was Hoover the engineer, the leader, the great administrator in action.[99] Editorial comment was laudatory.[100]

Soon, Henry M. Robinson sent to Lawrence Richey for the president a telegram received by a friend in Los Angeles "from a man of standing and a fairly good judge of opinion" who described the situation at this time on Wall Street:

Normal reactions will of course take place but the bear market is over. . . .
While it will take a little time for actual improvement in general business
to follow the present united efforts of government and bankers, the higher
prices will be justified by the certain improvement in agricultural and commodity prices and sales volume. Wall Street is cheerful for the first time in
years. Everybody is working like a Trojan down here and are looking forward to better times in all lines. Evidently we are doing the sound thing of
fixing our own domestic situation now and then figuring out what we can
do further to help in Latin America, Europe and the Orient. We have been
excessively deflated. Recovery to date is only to the stock level prior to the
smash occasioned by the British abandonment of the Gold Standard. We
have stopped standing around talking European politics and are no longer
afraid of shadows. There is genuine public buying in this present market.[101]

By October 30, the president could tell his press confernce that a very
great change in the credit situation had gradually taken place following
the announcement of October 6. When England went off the gold standard, Hoover reported, a great wave of apprehension spread over the
United States as the hoarding of currency rose to $200 million a week
and country bank failures rose to more than twenty-five a day. Simul-
taneously, the drain of gold caused by the alarm of foreign holders of
American credits had risen to more than $200 million a week. With the
last week in October, hoarding had ceased and $24 million had been
returned to bank deposits, while small bank failures had almost completely ceased. Not only had foreign exchange returned to the point where
it was no longer advantageous to ship gold, but there had also been a
recovery of ten to twelve cents in the price of wheat and a fifteen to
twenty dollar increase per bale of cotton.[102]

As a result of presidential leadership in the twofold European crisis
of the spring and autumn, foreign observers and critics were clearer in
their perspective on Hoover's basic policies. Until October of 1929, he
had seemed to them to be making plans for a new United States. After
the stock market crash and the controversial outcome of the tariff fight,
he appeared to be holding to a status quo for the United States. This had
been confusing. Now, in late 1931, it seemed that possibly President
Hoover was again "champion of the cause of all mankind," in that he was
using emergencies at home and abroad to strengthen the economic structure for all nations. It was clear now to critical observers that politics had
been pushed aside for the advantages of economic statesmanship. Here
was much needed leadership for the world.

— 15 —

A Program for a New Congress

*From this national revival of interest in the history
of the American Revolution and of the independence of
the United States will come a renewal of those inspira-
tions which strengthened the patriots who brought
to the world a new concept of human liberty and a new
form of government. . . . What other great, purely
human institution, devised in the era of the stagecoach
and the candle, has so marvellously grown and survived
into this epoch of the steam engine, the airplane, the
incandescent lamp, the wireless telephone, and the
battleship?*

Herbert Hoover, Address to the Joint Session
of Congress, February 22, 1932, opening the
Bicentennial of the Birth of George Washington

Meanwhile, it was time for politics in the nation's capital. "It goes without
saying that Washington is the most political city on earth. It talks politics
as Detroit talks automobiles," wrote Anne O'Hare McCormick. In immediate retrospect of fall, 1931, commentator McCormick wrote:

Now it appears to many Americans that the bankers (with, of course, many
notable exceptions) were as lacking in foresight and wisdom as were the
politicians. This discovery has done something to America. It has shaken
the faith of the people whose cathedrals are banks, as conspicuous on all
downtown corners of America as churches were of Old Moscow and Old
Rome. The average citizen always suspected the morals of the financial
hierarchy, and now his distrust goes deeper. He doubts its intelligence.[1]

In a year that began in an atmosphere "far more hysterical and critical
than the days of 1917–18"[2] (and that was to end with hundreds of hunger

marchers milling about the Capitol while the Seventy-second Congress convened), everyone—inside the city and outside in the country—was discussing economics and politics.

On September 1, 1931, the president told the press that he did not yet know what the tendency of the national income might be. Any degree of economic recovery would entirely change the prospect of government receipts. He emphasized that the deficit in the previous fiscal year had been over $900 million, $400 million of which were caused by statutory retirement of the debt, whereas the actual increase in the debt was approximately $500 million. If the economic situation were to improve, obviously the government could live for a time on its "fat." But it could not go on indefinitely. And the economic outlook was dominated by the European situation. Hoover believed that the primary problem in governmental fiscal questions was maintenance of the social obligations of the government to a population in difficulties. He said that "no government of a substantial, humane character will see its people starve or go hungry or go cold, and every agency of a government, whether local, state, or federal, must be implemented to the end of maintaining complete stability and confidence in our federal government. . . ."[3]

Hoover's belief that economic considerations were necessarily primary was coupled with his belief in an economic structure based on capital, interest, profits, and wages. Hence his judgment of a governmental or international situation was invariably stated in economic terms.[4] That is, inflated prices had to be liquidated sooner or later; deflation meant losses in security holdings, in real estate, and in wages. No one class or group in a nation, or in the world, was unaffected by the economic sufferings of another class or group.

Hoover believed as firmly that the economic world could operate independently of government, except in times of crisis, and that this was, in fact, the only tolerable condition for free men. (On this principle men have differed, then and since.)

Certain results flowed from practicing such beliefs: the relation of government spending to government income, and unimpaired federal credit. President Hoover spoke from recent experience when he addressed the Pan-American Commercial Conference which met in Washington, D.C. on October 8, 1931:

> . . . no nation as a government should borrow . . . no government lend and nations should discourage their citizens from borrowing or lending unless this money is to be devoted to productive enterprise.
>
> Out of the wealth and the higher standards of living created from enterprise itself must come to the borrowing country the ability to repay the

capital. Any other course of action creates obligations impossible of repayment except by a direct subtraction from the standards of living of the
borrowing country and the impoverishment of its people.[5]

But the American people thought of the national situation not only
in terms of economics but also in terms of politics. Help had been given
to the farmer, the laborer, and the financier (each of whom presented a
separate economic problem). A debate was in progress throughout the
nation on economic *fundamentals* as well as on economic proposals. Such
matters as debts, credit, and tariffs must be dealt with in economic terms.

The success of the president's leadership in breaking the jam in international relationships by providing a moratorium on intergovernmental
debts, and by promoting the measures that grew out of this readjustment,
paved the way for a renewed effort to use the existent American system
of private enterprise to absorb unemployment and to bring back normal
economic life. The government would aid with certain emergency measures for recovery.

By the end of the summer of 1931, the country had been well informed
of the steps being taken and projected to care for the needy in the forthcoming autumn and winter. The president had collected a vast amount of
information about the situation in the country and on the success and
failure of efforts hitherto taken by various agencies throughout the nation.
This factual information was released in press statements in late August
and discussed at press conferences then and in September.

——To William Allen White's suggestion that a national emergency relief
corporation based on private subscription be established to buy the Farm
Board's wheat and other foods whose prices were sagging, the president
replied that "we are setting up as effective an organization as I can
command, placing the responsibility in a major sense up to the great
industries of the United States." Hoover expected that by mid-September
of 1931 the results of his efforts would become apparent, for "you will
see developments in the course of another month."[6]

The president constantly related the problem of need to the means by
which it was to be met—by federal construction, by federal subsidies, or
by local and state relief. On September 11 he spoke to his press conference about the seriousness of the problem.

He spoke with optimism about the rehabilitation of the three million
people who had been fed during the drought and who would no longer
be in need of help. He envisaged a serious problem in prospect, however,
in that the public was becoming seriously disturbed and fearful. One
result of such apprehension was the "tightening of belts" on the part of
those with resources, leading to a decrease in purchasing throughout the

nation and consequently to further unemployment. Hoover felt that nobody would starve or go hungry in the United States even though that might have happened in isolated cases during the previous winter.[7] The great humanitarian of the war years could not visualize in America, a land unmolested by war, the kind of distress and starvation he had witnessed among millions in Europe. Here was the basis for comparison. At this time he made it clear that he gave first consideration to maintaining governmental financial stability. This should be the test, as he saw it, for all legislation dealing with the relief of unemployment, the loosening of financial stringency, and the expansion of government construction.

There was a growing public conviction that the president had forged in the course of his nine-month period of unrestricted executive action a plan that might be effective. He appeared to have gradually developed a program that emphasized the importance of maintaining a government that, in emergency situations, would aid private interests in their efforts to deal with economic problems, whether in business or in the larger relationships involved in the use of public utilities by great masses of people.

Consequently, there were many who urged, in view of the divided political control of the government in 1931–32, a bipartisan approach to the solution of the most pressing problems of the depression. They did so with recognition of the hard political fact that the House of Representatives was under the control of the leaders of the Democratic party. But, as the session of Congress advanced, it was clear that this was a "paper" majority. Protests of individuals and presently of groups made Democratic party discipline impossible.[8]

In the autumn of 1931, throughout the country, increasing fear of the privations of the coming winter gave opportunities to would-be "saviors." In each section of the nation political salvation took on its own local manifestations. Divergent though the proposals were, all were based upon three well-worn devices in demagoguery: (a) the party in power was evil; (b) the way out was to place new men in office; and (c) officers of the government should be chosen to represent the interests of "the people in need," but certainly not the interests of the bosses, or the financiers, or those whose programs had been based upon the tried and accepted economic facts of recent years.

The officers of the United States Chamber of Commerce, following a vote of the members, advocated that the federal government suspend enforcement of anti-trust laws for two or more years. The purpose of this was to free business and to resume normal procedures without regulation. This brand of economics was anathema to the president, and he refused to support such a suggestion. He would not permit "fascism" to be smuggled through a back door.[9]

The Seventy-second Congress, assembling for the first time in early December 1031, had boon olootod more than a year before. Seventeen newly elected members appeared for the first time in the Senate, and ninety new representatives appeared in the House, seventy-four of whom were new to the Congress. Neither Republicans nor Democrats had a working majority in either house. These legislators were called upon to act in a crisis—the nature of which neither they nor their constituents had foreseen when they were elected. This meant that Congress was not committeed upon the great issues that lay before it. Its members were, in the words of Walter Lippmann, "free for once to consider themselves representatives of the nation and not merely delegates from their districts."[10]

In this Congress, it should be noted, the party distribution was wholly misleading. In the Senate there were 48 Republicans and 47 Democrats, and 1 Farmer-Laborite; in the House there were 220 Democrats and 214 Republicans. Although President Hoover advised Republican party leader Watson and the Senate Republicans to let the Democrats organize the Senate, this was not done. A dozen insurgents joined the regular Republicans in organizing the Senate but continued to hold the balance of power. In the House, Democrat John Nance Garner of Texas was selected Speaker and the Democrats organized the committees.

In the weeks prior to the convening of Congress in December 1931, the president had conferred with 150 members of the House and Senate, including a number of Democratic leaders. He made his position known to all. He was prepared to recommend a program, but he would listen to proposals from the Democrats, and he promised to cooperate with them. But to one observer, the Congress would "be a Congress of battles, battles in each House between factions and parties, battles between the Houses, battles of Congress with the President."[11]

Soon a group of Democratic leaders in and out of Congress announced that they would work with the president. Now he outlined in detail his plan of action in his message to Congress on December 8, 1931. He asked for cuts in government expenditures and increased taxes to make possible a balanced budget by the end of 1934. He asked for a revival, in effect, of the War Finance Corporation, greater freedom for home loan banks, and liberalization of the policies of the Federal Reserve Banks. The message was termed "businesslike," and "courageous" and "exceedingly welcome in a country beset by radicals and perfectionists," for hundreds of conferences and studies "by the most competent men in the country" lay behind it, said the *Washington Post*. Said the *Cincinnati Times-Star*:

Hoover has carried on his bleak battle against terrific business conditions with high courage and notable common sense. His plans and the natural resiliency of the country will bring a revival sooner or later. Whether it comes in time to persuade the people of the value of Hoover's services while he is still in office is the only question.[12]

But the *New York Times* sought a "stirring watchword or a symbol."[13]

The requests by the president, following hard upon his activities while Congress was not in session, produced sharp criticism from those who still felt that it was not a proper function of the president to attempt to determine the economic climate in which private business should be carried on. Many Americans had been shocked into a realization of the precariousness of the American financial and industrial system, but they still thought in political terms and of a simple economic order rooted in "capitalism." To them, an inactive president was desirable except as he exerted himself in "politics." Some felt that Hoover, in his unusual approach to economic problems, was exceeding his powers as president, for, as William Allen White judged, he was proposing "economic and financial legislation which in normal times would be regarded as revolutionary."[14] But some of the Democratic press saw the message as "stand-pat," while conservative Democratic circles felt the president was plunging the country into debt.[15]

President Hoover's point of view on parties was expressed most fully in an address to the Gridiron Club in Washington, D.C. on December 12, 1931. He began with a discussion of cooperation:

You have heard something tonight about cooperation between the political parties. The country needs cooperation. But do not forget that ours is a Government built upon political parties. There is no method by which the American people can express their public will except through party organization. The day that we begin coalition government you may know that our democracy has broken down. Constructive opposition is an essential to the very functioning of our democracy and no less certainly destructive opposition at this stage of the world's history is the road to the abyss. Political leaders can cooperate and maintain their identity. And political parties, having been elected to power whether in the Executive or in the Congress, have a definite and positive responsibility to the people and an expectation from them of patriotic action which overrides all partisanship. No party can stand among the American people which will not accept its full responsibilities.[16]

To his press conference at the time, the president explained his twelve-point, nonpartisan economic program for recovery which he con-

sidered to be a program to "turn the tide." He had consulted not only
with men in public office, but with leaders of labor, agriculture, industry,
and commerce. A considerable part of this program would depend on
voluntary action that had already been set in motion, and part would
require legislation that would be nonpartisan. The president showed
interest in the "principles involved more than in details." He appealed
for unity of action and its early consummation. He indicated that the
major steps to be taken were in the domestic field, although the reestablishment of stability abroad would be helpful. A summary of the twelve
points he had in mind is essential here:

1. Providing [relief of] distress among the unemployed by voluntary
   organization and united action of local authorities in cooperation with
   the Unemployment Relief Organization whose appeal for funds had
   met with a response unparalleled since the war
2. Encouraging employers to provide part-time work instead of discharg-
   ing a portion of their employees, with government continuing a very
   large federal construction program over the winter (over $60 million a
   month)
3. Strengthening the Federal Land Bank System in the interest of the
   farmer
4. Providing assistance to rural and urban home owners, "who are in difficulties in securing renewals of mortgages," by strengthening country
   banks, savings banks, and building and loan associations through creation of a system of Home Loan Discount Banks
5. Developing a plan to assure early distribution to depositors in closed
   banks, thus relieving distress among millions of small depositors and
   businesses
6. Enlarging "under full safeguards" the discount facilities of the Federal
   Reserve Banks in the interest of a more adequate credit system
7. Creating "for the period of the emergency" a Reconstruction Finance
   Corporation to furnish necessary credit otherwise unobtainable under
   existing circumstances, thus giving confidence to agriculture, industry,
   and labor against further paralyzing influences and shocks
8. Assisting all railroads by protection from unregulated competition and
   formation of a credit pool for weaker ones
9. Revising the banking laws to better safeguard depositors
10. Safeguarding and supporting banks through the National Credit
    Association
11. Maintaining public finance on a sound basis by drastic economy; by
    resolute opposition to the enlargement of federal expenditure until re-
    covery; and by a temporary increase in taxation, so distributed that the
    burden might be borne in proportion to the ability to pay
12. Maintaining "the American system of individual initiative and indi-
    vidual and community responsibility" [17]

"The broad purpose of all this program," said the president, "is to restore the old job instead of creating a new-made job; to help the worker at the desk as well as the worker at the bench, and to restore their buying power for the farmer's products. . . ." Hoover said that one of the purposes of such a program, in reversing the process of liquidation and deflation, was to start the flow of credit "now impeded by fear and uncertainty, to the detriment of every manufacturer, business man and farmer."[18]

Whatever the crisis in unemployment or the distress in any section of the country, Washington was to be the battlefield where the issue was determined while Congress was in session. Under the American system of self-government the verdict upon broad proposals of relief must come from Congress. Both House and Senate were engaged in continuous "warfare" upon most public questions. This was not unusual. Indeed, the warfare had become so acrimonious and unproductive in the preceding fifteen years that some felt the congressional method of bringing about legislation was no longer feasible. This viewpoint was growing.

An obvious cause of delayed and inadequate action was to be found in the rules of procedure in the House and in the Senate as well. Unquestionably most of the rules were satisfactory to whichever political power happened to be dominant in the House and Senate, yet unquestionably these rules made for delay, which was supposed to lead to wiser legislation. Obviously, the Rules Committees possessed great power. Yet delay did not appeal to voters in these crucial months. Consequently, attempts were made to hasten legislation by providing rules that were simpler; few positive results could be seen, however.

Lack of leadership in the Congress created further difficulty. In the seven months to come (December 1931–July 1932), no leader of either House was in control of majorities upon which he could depend. In the Senate, Republicans were still technically in control. In the House, Democrats had elected a Speaker and organized committees. But in neither Senate nor House were the majorities and the leaders they represented free from the risk of losing their power to a coalition of Republicans and Democrats. Most of the insurgents, earlier in the administration, had been in the Republican party. But in this Congress a large number of those who acted from time to time as an independent bloc were Democrats. It was thus obvious that party organization was weakened to such an extent that it could not accomplish the necessary results quickly and effectively.

Although this Congress was under unusual pressure from constituents "to do something," the constituents were by no means united in what they desired. The president told his press conference early in the autumn of 1931 that a review of the demands of "voluntary bodies" upon the Congress had uncovered 271 potential bills on which the executive agencies of the government were asked to pass judgment. These bills would have involved an expenditure of over $6 billion, an unthinkable sum for the era of balanced-budget government to consider.

In this situation, it was inevitable that the president of the United States, who properly makes recommendations to the Congress, was the one individual who could provide leadership. Such leadership, however, must extend far beyond the provision of definite recommendations, and far beyond bringing together members of both parties in the Congress to deal with proposed legislation. The president would somehow have to reach the voters with explanations of his program or individual proposals. The voters could then bring pressure to bear upon their representatives in the Congress. From this sequence would come action within the American system.

It was in this area, therefore, that President Hoover, during these very critical months, exerted an unusual amount of pressure. Hoover visualized the extremity of the crisis when, on February 12, 1932 in a radio address he said: "We are engaged in a fight . . . requiring just as greatly the moral courage, the organized action, the unity of strength and the sense of devotion in every community as in war."[19]

How the president went about his tasks is mirrored in his press conferences, in which, informally, he explained himself and his purposes. Hoover must have felt confident that his twelve-point program would meet with success, for he told his press conference on December 22, 1931 that the leaders of the House and Senate had assured him that Congress would devote itself to the expeditious passage of the emergency economic program he had proposed for the amelioration of the agricultural, employment, and credit situations.

Hoover asked that the creation of a Reconstruction Finance Corporation be the first item to receive congressional attention. As Theodore G. Joslin, secretary to President Hoover from 1931 to 1933, states, "He particularly sought enactment of the bill for the creation of the Reconstruction Finance Corporation, which he visualized as offering great possibilities in meeting the emergency." When Congress insisted on taking the Christmas holiday of two weeks after only a month in session, Hoover told legislators "with heat" that some essential legislation could be enacted during that time and that it would be negligence of duty to take the holiday. They did anyway; but the president was assured that there would be action after the holiday, "with the Reconstruction Finance Corporation bill being the first to be taken up."[20]

Joslin then says,

> Of all the projects he was sponsoring, he gave precedence to the Reconstruc-
> tion Finance Corporation bill, which would make two billion dollars avail-
> able for loans. He held party leaders, Democrats and Republicans alike, to
> their promise to expedite it through both houses. He waited impatiently for
> it the day it was supposed to reach him for his signature. He knew it by
> heart from the opening to the closing sentence. He wanted to receive it one
> minute and sign it the next.[21]

In fact, he literally did that, interrupting a meeting with Democratic
leaders to do so.[22] A little later he turned down the opportunity to attend
the National Press Club entertainment and ball. Says Joslin, Hoover
replied: "Gee, Ted, I can't do it. We must get the R.F.C. going. The
banking situation is much worse."[23]

A glance at the *New York Times* and its *Index* for this period shows
Hoover, on December 8, arranging for Senator Wolcott and Representative Strong to offer bills on the RFC; on the sixteenth he urged six representatives to push for the bill; on the twenty-second he obtained the
pledge of leaders to speed the program; on the twenty-sixth it was revealed
that he was planning personal conferences during the holiday to support
the RFC.[24] All of this shows intense interest and commitment on his part.[25]

The path the president took to reach his final position in support of
the RFC has great interest. Initially, in the crisis conditions of late
summer and early fall of 1931, Eugene Meyer and others sought to persuade the president to recreate the old War Finance Corporation, a
government agency utilized in World War I. Hoover, however, felt that
voluntarism should be given a chance to meet the nation's financial crisis.
Thus he rejected action such as the WFC solution, the idea of an immediate international conference, and the dramatic emergency action of
calling Congress into special session. Instead, Hoover saw possibilities in
a national credit association of bankers, using the credit and funds of
private banking as a prop for ailing financial institutions and a boost for
the public morale.

It was characteristic of Hoover to attempt a voluntary solution before
turning, in peacetime, to a wartime solution. He recalled that President
Wilson had offered a ringing veto message the last time the WFC
approach had been presented to him in peacetime. With Congress out
of session, in any case, the WFC approach was not feasible.

The banking fraternity seems to have been reluctant to try the voluntary approach urged by the president. In an automobile en route to the
formative meeting, the bankers apparently agreed to organizing and
funding a voluntary association only when promised by Meyer that he

would continue to press for a government organization.[26] They would give it two months of trial.[27] As time passed in fall, 1931, it became evident to Hoover that the financiers were unwilling to risk or sacrifice enough to make the voluntary National Credit Corporation solution a permanent vehicle for protecting the nation's financial institutions. This obviously troubled him very much. The time came when he told his secretary of state, privately, in deep irritation, that for the eighteen months remaining in his term he was really going to fight. "He was very bellicose," Stimson noted.[28]

The National Credit Corporation (NCC), incorporated in October, was very well received by a worried country. Innumerable articles publicized its deeds and its potential for financial services.[29] Meyer himself defended it forthrightly in public at the time, and a year's end summary of the banking events of 1931 called its creation a very important event of the year.[30]

Clearly, NCC performed a most useful interim role in 1931. It was Hoover's choice of a way for the chief executive to meet a crisis when Congress was not in session. But when it became evident between November 15 and December 4, 1931 that another approach would have to be asked of the incoming Congress, Hoover gave the idea of a Reconstruction Finance Corporation his full, whole-hearted, and unqualified support. This position was reached, of course, when the financial community could not or would not act to save itself with its own money.[31] Hoover appreciated the help given by Meyer in drafting a RFC bill, and was especially pleased with the quick aid of John Garner and Joe Robinson—asking each to nominate a board member (Garner chose Jesse Jones; Robinson named Harvey Couch, president of the Arkansas Power and Light Company.)[32] Passage of the RFC bill, pressed for so hard by the president, was rapid.[33]

Hoover should be credited with the success for a time in the fall of 1931 of the NCC—a voluntary mechanism of the private sector that as early as October 14, 1931 was termed "temporary" in the New York Times, long before it possibly could have failed in its mission. On December 5 it was announced that all loans requested to date had been granted. Says a close student of the matter, "The National Credit Corporation represented the ultimate embodiment of Hoover's personal philosophy." Thus private initiatives had been given their chance, and government had tried not to be a competitor with private organizations. "In calling upon the bankers to organize and operate the credit pool, Hoover expressed his optimistic belief in the efficacy of cooperative action." Moreover, the NCC was even a decentralized mechanism.[34] But the NCC did not have, *behind the scenes*, the full support of the bankers; Hoover and Mills by late October had to send telegrams to them criticizing their procrastination. There were due apologies, of course.[35]

Hoover should be credited with willingness, at length, to go along with the RFC solution; especially, he should be credited with fighting vigorously and successfully for it. There seems little or no appropriateness, however, for crediting him (as is too often done) with giving birth to the RFC of the long New Deal period—the opening wedge on gigantic federal financing efforts in a variety of areas previously in the private sector. Such certainly was not Hoover's intent, even though in the last weeks before leaving office he tried to broaden the RFC's power to meet emergency conditions.[36]

Hoover certainly did not intend for it to be said of the RFC in his administration—as it could be said, authoritatively, of the RFC in Roosevelt's administration—that "there was a disposition on the part of President Roosevelt to use RFC as a sort of grab bag or catchall in his spending programs...."[37] Possibly because of the NCC *potential*, bank failures and suspensions were less in evidence in late October and early November. Dollar figures on loans made are not the only index when one is dealing with the psychology of a nation. Success seemed in sight, but NCC directors chose to rest on their oars. Bank failures were up in late November. Thus one can say that the NCC "failed," although it certainly never got an adequate trial; "President Hoover ... was not responsible for the failure," it is entirely evident.[38]

One should, in quite another sense, speak of the NCC in terms not of failure but of success. The following spring, for example, Thomas W. Lamont wrote from Wall Street that he told assembled Harvard alumni that "in October 1931 when the extent of bank failures all over the country became so alarming President Hoover proposed the organization of what was almost immediately set up under the title of National Credit Corporation. This extended immediate and sorely needed relief to the banking situation. Hoarding let up, and banking failures diminished."[39] Hoover made clear the difference between the RFC of his years and of later years when in 1951 he testified in favor of abolishing the later RFC and transferring its functions to appropriate bureaus.[40] As early as August 1933, Hoover was distressed with the evolution of the RFC. "The whole change in the character of loans being made from those of positive security to loans which are practically gifts is of importance to the future history of this question," he wrote privately.[41]

Further testimony on the NCC's role can be found in a speech by Harry J. Haas, president of the American Bankers Association at the time, to New York bankers in June, 1932. If the NCC had not been formed the previous October, he judged, there might have been a national crisis.

It is not generally known, but I believe it is permissible to tell you now, that in no less than four states timely action by this corporation in relieving critical banking situations averted declarations of moratoria by their Governors.[42]

Bank casualties were therefore down to normal, he declared, and more than ten million depositors had been benefited. The NCA, as incorporated into the NCC, had indeed served its purpose of getting the weaker banks through the months from August to January without the shock to the nation of calling Congress into special session. More than that, to judge from public reaction, the NCC comforted a very worried country—and would have performed this function well even it if had not made a single loan.

By January 16, 1932 the enabling bill for the RFC was passed by both houses of Congress; a week later a board was appointed to meet with the president. (Members were Eugene Meyer, Charles G. Dawes, Ogden Mills, Harvey Couch, Jesse H. Jones, Gardner Cowles, and Wilson McCarthy.) The RFC was a reality, and it was also a symbol of the idea that, when the private sector cannot or will not meet critical public needs, government may well have to move to fill the void.

Throughout the winter calls for aid from the national government increased. Widespread defaults by taxpayers, the financial difficulties of states now overburdened by the necessity of local aid, bank emergencies —all of these threw an additional burden upon the federal government. Meanwhile, merchants could not get credit and more workers were losing their jobs.

Yet in this depression plight, many businessmen rejected the president's proposals for government retrenchment and a balanced budget. They still felt that business could be aided best by improving upon the basic structure of private enterprise, but they certainly wanted more government spending. At the end of June 1931, there had been a heavy national deficit. It was calculated that by June 1932 the deficit would be at least $3 billion. This meant that banks, as well as city and state governments all over the nation, were experiencing difficulties.

The country must realize that we cannot continue to live in a depression on a scale that was possible in times of prosperity, the president told the press early in January 1932; but he spoke reassuringly on January 8.

Hoover was encouraged at the moment by what he saw to be a "nonpartisan determination" by congressional leaders to cooperate with the administration in efforts to balance the federal budget for the coming fiscal year. He felt that the era of extravagant legislative proposals (which had totaled $40 billion) had ended. He saw that such spending spirit must be abandoned. Rigid economy was the real road to relief. The first duty of the nation was to put the national, state, and local governmental houses in order. With the return of prosperity the government could and would undertake constructive social projects and public improvements, but the president said that "we just cannot squander ourselves into prosperity."[43]

The widespread tendency to hoard currency had continued in the autumn of 1931. Hoover felt that here was "a real educational problem" that the press could do something about. Accordingly, he attempted to explain to his press conference on February 5, 1932 that, inasmuch as the United States currency was based on gold reserves, hoarded gold had to come out of the credit structure. Since gold multiplied itself into credit at the ratio of ten to one, anyone who was hoarding currency was actually depriving the community of employment, thus creating serious deflation. He believed that hoarding was an expression of fear and merely led to more fear. Here again it was revealed that the banks were potentially the weakest agencies in his elaborate plan for recovery, and he appreciated the fact.

On February 6, 1932, a conference of patriotic and civic organizations met with the president at the White House to consider the problem of "hoarding." On the ninth, he conferred with Meyer and Harrison of the Federal Reserve System, Dawes of the RFC, and Secretary Mills (aging Secretary Mellon had resigned on February 8, 1932) about the danger to the gold supply and the gold standard. In order to "enlarge temporarily the 'eligibility' of commercial paper" and otherwise "free" gold, the president requested the Senate leaders to meet with Meyer, Dawes, Mills, and himself at breakfast the following morning.[44]

Eleven days later Hoover told the press that the "turn of the tide" on hoarding had been reached. Again he emphasized that an effort was being made to open the channels of credit to dissipate fear and apprehension in the minds of bankers, businessmen and the public. This, he believed, was fundamental in ending unemployment and the stagnation of agriculture.

President Hoover was deeply concerned with basic defects in bankruptcy laws and practices, which he had directed the Departments of Justice and Commerce to investigate in July 1930. On February 26, 1932, Hoover reported to the press that an investigation of the situation showed that 23,000 bankruptcies in 1921 had lost $144 million to creditors; 53,000 bankruptcies in 1928 had lost $740 million to creditors; and 65,000 bankruptcies in 1931 had lost $911 million to creditors. These increases, according to the president's statement, were "not due to the economic situation, but to deeper causes."[45]

In an off-the-record interview with a newsman on February 29 the president shared his deep concern over hoarding. The bankers, he felt, could be helpful if they would. "We're going after the bankers next. They're the worst hoarders of all. They're all panic-stricken. We've got to combat that hysteria among the bankers themselves and get them to let their money go to work." Hoarding by bankers, he said, had the effect of not extending credit to merchants, farmers, and others "no matter what the collateral." Since the people were putting money back into the banks, the bankers were obligated to stop being "fear-stricken" and put that money to work. A nation-wide system of home loan discount banks would help, Hoover told the reporter, because it would "divorce banking more than ever from the stranglehold that New York has on it. I want to see that hold broken," he said, adding that it would be better if banks were independent in various states and localities.[46]

On the whole, at the moment, the president impressed the reporter as being jubilant over how things were going between himself and the Congress, for there were "public spirited men" in Congress in both parties even though individuals played politics. But the session would continue for many weeks.

The record of the Congress throughout this period was on the whole a sorry one. With party lines seldom drawn, great influence was exerted in the Senate by the independents who for years had opposed presidential leadership. Bipartisan action (so greatly needed) was always subject to dangers in a close legislative conflict, for each party hoped to claim success for any desirable outcome. Friction, not cooperation, was the dominant note in every conference. Yet again and again the participants themselves made it evident that they appreciated the deadly paradox: they must effect economies yet provide large sums for relief of nation-wide distress.

Moreover, events sometimes gave leaders grave worries. It is alleged that on May 16 Hoover himself had indicated the possibility of a crash in a few weeks.[47] So it was that in a personal appeal to the Senate on May 31, 1932, Hoover stressed the perils confronting the nation and urged that all emergency measures, at least, be considered on a non-partisan basis. By persistence, he did accomplish much in this six-month period. A review will show this.

Congress finally passed the Glass-Steagall Bill that provided for more extensive assistance to banks by the Federal Reserve System. The president, in signing this bill on February 26, called it a "national defense measure" without which he believed there would be widespread bankruptcy.[48] He took occasion to acknowledge the bipartisan support that had made this legislation possible.[49]

By March 11, credit had been extended to 2,395 communities; an increase in currency was thereby returned to circulation. The president felt that this massive effort was definitely dissipating fear and apprehension and was contributing to the general restoration of confidence. Here was, in effect, a "citizen's reconstruction organization."

In the belief that "to continue to live on borrowed money only postpones the difficulty," President Hoover was now trying to bring about retrenchment in government expenditures. Nevertheless, he believed that taxes would have to be increased. He was especially interested, however, in reducing appropriations within the authority of existing laws, or changing the laws if necessary. For example, he obtained from Congress special legislation making it possible for him to restore to the United States Treasury 20 percent of his own salary. The salaries of cabinet officers were reduced 15 percent at their request.[50]

The Department of the Interior and the Justice Department led the way in not requesting budget increases. "We had cut our Interior Department operations down to the bone to effect every legitimate saving," stated Secretary Wilbur later, "when Congress nearly wrecked things by a 10 per cent across-the-board slash in our budget. ... This slash was cutting below survival figures, since it was in addition to all the reductions we already had made." In the end, the budget of the Department of the Interior was cut 35 percent. "Some cuts were sound," commented Wilbur, but "many of them were cruel, foolish, actually wasteful, and pushed through in the hope of partisan advantage."[51]

Hoover had been working for many years on the problem of the reorganization and consolidation of government functions. He would remark to his press conference on February 16, 1932, that from fifteen to twenty administrative agencies in existence at that time could well be consolidated.

There was now very little room left for administrative reductions as matters stood. Further economies would have to be brought about either by reorganization of the federal machinery or by changes in legal requirements relating to departments.

The existence of "locust lobbyists" was a threat that Hoover found especially powerful at this time. He had warned his press conference on March 29 of another bonus bill that was on the way. Within two weeks, however, it became clear that Democratic leaders in the Congress were lining up with Republican leaders to defeat the bonus, and by May 10 he could refer to the "death and burial of the bonus" in the House Ways and Means Committee.

Not so easily disposed of was the Garner bill proposing to supply hundreds of new post offices throughout the nation. "This is not unemployment relief," remarked the president to the press in late May. "It is the most gigantic pork barrel ever proposed to the American Congress."

He added that the nation was "not founded on the pork barrel, and it has not become great by political log rolling."[52] (Needless to say, he vetoed the bill.)

The desperation the president now felt in the face of emergency, congressional delay, and congressional proposals is revealed in the address he made in an abrupt personal appearance before the Senate on May 31, 1932, haggard from a sleepless night and a five o'clock rising. "An emergency has developed in the last few days which it is my duty to lay before the Senate," he said.[53]

A continued downward economic movement in the past few days, he believed, was related to the financial program of the American government, uncertainty over which had alarmed foreign countries that "know from bitter experience that the course of unbalanced budgets is the road to ruin." He reminded his hearers, "They do not realize that slow as our processes may be we are determined and have the resources to place the finances of the United States on an unassailable basis." He added:

> The immediate result has been to create an entirely unjustified run upon the American dollar from foreign countries and within the past few days despite our national wealth and resources and our unparalleled gold reserves our dollar stands at a serious discount in the markets of the world for the first time in half a century.[54]

The president urged the members of the Senate to concentrate upon "three major duties in legislation," by (a) drastic reduction of expenditures; (b) passage of adequate revenue legislation which, combined with reductions, would undoubtedly balance the Federal budget; and (c) passage of adequate relief legislation to assure the country against distress. His analysis of the status of each of these three duties in the Congress indicated clearly how confused, vacillating, and uncertain the state of congressional business had become in his view.

In his plan to balance the budget the president certainly spoke for the financial community. A survey of bankers (with 3,726 returns) would shortly reveal a vote of 2,509 yes, 694 no on the question, Balance the budget immediately?[55] The peroration of the address to the Senate was vigorous, calling for speedy democratic action, national unity, solidarity before the world, and "the courage to look . . . difficulties in the face and the capacity and resolution to meet them."

Republican newspapers were pleased with this effort. He had gone as far as any president since Lincoln to safeguard the national integrity, said the *New York Herald Tribune*. But the *Baltimore Sun* wondered why the president had not made his move long ago.[56] Beyond doubt it was an election year!

Considering the session as a whole, the winter and spring relationship between president and Congress had not proven as unproductive as it seemed to many people at the time. The Hoover recommendations in the initial message of December 8 had been given consideration and many had been acted upon in accordance with the suggested plans. The president worked with Congress from December 8, 1931 through April 1932 in no less than twenty-one messages, statements, and addresses. He did not hesitate to threaten the veto and he used it seven times, including the case of a tariff bill (House Resolution 6662) and a relief bill (House Resolution 12,445). In doing so, the president asserted himself as a director of national policy.

"The President's attitude was not entirely consistent," commented one critic. "On some occasions he harshly called Congress to task for its dilatory actions and on others he refrained from comment in the face of chaotic conditions in the legislature. For the most part, however, he held to a conciliatory viewpoint."[57] Because the Democrats lacked a program in general, they did cooperate better with the president than he seemed willing to admit.

In his struggle with the Congress over unemployment relief, the president maintained that public works should be self-liquidating, income-producing, and self-sustaining, and that private as well as public enterprises should be encouraged to provide employment.[58] The object of all this was to get constructive work *started*.

When the Senate and the House disagreed on bills, the president called a conference at the White House to work out a compromise. Speaker Garner protested at this "unusual" interference in the legislative process, saying it had not been customary for the president to summon members of both parties to discuss legislation. Yet Garner, a "sophisticated politician," admitted that when the president of the United States invited members of the House to the executive office for the purpose of discussing the welfare of the Union, he did not see how they could refuse.[59]

The House and the Senate came to an agreement on the Garner-Wagner Relief Bill for expansion of public works, but the president vetoed it, saying: "This proposal violates every sound principle of public finance and of government. Never before has so dangerous a suggestion been seriously made to our country." Hoover reiterated his opposition to the broad authority to make loans to be granted the Reconstruction Finance Corporation. "Such action would make [it] the greatest banking and money-lending institution of all history, . . . a gigantic centralization of banking and finance to which the American people have been properly opposed for the past 100 years."[60]

Perhaps the most promising item wrung from the Congress was the first germ of authority to reorganize and consolidate the government bureaus. "The House recognized the importance of the matter, but felt that it should be again undertaken directly by the Congress instead of by the President," Hoover explained.[61] The core of economy lay in the reduction of the government payroll and in retrenchment to be effected through the coordination, consolidation, or regrouping of the administrative agencies of the government.

For example, as Secretary Wilbur described the possibilities in testifying before the House Committee on Appropriations, "the construction activities of the Reclamation Service and the Indian Service" might be transferred from the Department of the Interior to a proposed new Department of Public Works "under which would be consolidated all the public works functions of the government." Economy lay in establishing a common service agency specializing in various types of construction to carry out the plans of operating administrative bureaus. Obviously, "great savings in both money and in personnel could be brought about by such a pooling of engineers who would be constantly at work wherever and whenever needed."[62]

Intraparty divisions in both houses of the Congress were an all-important characteristic of this six months of continuous conflict. As one critic said, it was "perfectly evident that the two parties have long since ceased to have any sustained principles or vital points of difference. Every tariff and taxation bill proves that we are divided not into parties but into economic sections, so that the parties themselves have degenerated into little more than rival machines for electing a President and controlling federal patronage."[63] But here was a half-truth, to be sure.

It was obvious in the votes taken that both parties were seriously divided on the enforcement of Prohibition. Throughout the session, however, the center of attention was the relationship between the president and the Congress. On every matter which came before this Congress, whether of raising revenue, controlling lobbying, assuring economy, reorganizing the government, directing relief, providing methods of taxation, the president was able to push in the course of the session the conference method, that is, conference between the executive and the legislative branches.

It is certain that he pushed it further than had any president at any previous time in the history of Congress. On taxation, on relief, on reorganization—on the whole matter of the economy—it was the president's leadership in conference rather than any proposals he made that brought some success at the time and pointed the way to the future.

But in Democratic legislative circles all was not rejoicing. Observing, Hiram Johnson wrote, "The Democrats, I think, with some humiliations

and a great deal of irritation, realize what asses they have made of themselves."[64] Furthermore, a vocal rebellion against the Garner leadership
was under way. He had no policies and was dumbfounded by the depression.[65] "It is difficult, if not impossible to reconcile the different ideas
predominant among Democrats. . . . It cannot be done in the House,"
Johnson wrote to a confidant.[66] There clearly would have to be a change,
and soon, for 1932 was an election year.

As for Hoover at the time, the *Washington Post* said, "Even his opponents favor the sound measures which he has employed to combat the
depression. The election will probably turn upon the effectiveness of the
Republican campaign in making the achievements of Herbert Hoover
known to the electorate."[67] But summer and fall lay ahead, and there
would be developments.

With the adjournment of Congress in July 1932, signs of an upward
trend in the economic situation were perceptible to the president and
were announced by Dawes.[68] The battle against the depression appeared
in the White House to have been won.[69] Altogether, however, a session
which should have been concerned primarily with bipartisan economics
had revealed an aggravated case of pragmatic politics which, in the light
of second thoughts, forecast an uncertain future.

— 16 —

The Politics of Distress: Bonus Marchers

*Certain final observations can be made of a distressing
incident. A politically minded President never would
have permitted the District officials to involve the White
House in the first instance, let alone transfer the bonus
responsibility from the District Building to the White
House. The moment it was attempted it would have
been put right back where it belonged. Maintaining
peace and order in any city is a local responsibility,
not a state or a Federal responsibility, unless and until
the local authorities are unable to cope with the situation and find it necessary to call for outside aid. Again,
when the District officials had to ask the President for
Federal troops after the situation was beyond the control of the local police, a politician in the White House,
with an eye to the veterans' vote in the presidential
election only a few months away, might well have held
the Army to the letter of his written order and, if and
when it was exceeded, crashed down on the command-
ing officers, whose single responsibility it was to restore
order. Mr. Hoover was not the "buck-passing" type of
President.*

Theodore G. Joslin, *Hoover Off the Record*
(1934)

President Hoover's energetic leadership was undermined by unstable
financial, business, and industrial conditions at home and abroad. The
Democrats and the insurgents in the Republican party concentrated on
personal opposition to the president, and the close balance in distribution
of party power in the Congress reflected the unusual uncertainty of the
electorate. The president had not been able to convince many of his
fellow countrymen that a moderate and orderly program would provide

a solution for the economic crisis. The unbalanced budget, increasing bankruptcies, and staggering unemployment were reflected in emotional outbursts that in other nations would certainly have been portents of political revolution. In another nation, one lacking provision for elections at stated times—unlike the United States—there could have been in 1931–1932 an overthrow of the administration.

In the history of American politics, the eclipse of economic optimism has always been accompanied by pronouncements of political pessimism. While some such voices originated in unemployment or distress, one organized voice derived from a doctrinaire view of government and politics. The Communist party in the United States had operated underground prior to April 7, 1923, when it voted to dissolve itself in favor of its legal front organization, the Workers' Party of America. This, as the American section of the Third International, the world-wide Communist organization led from Moscow, became aggressive in the middle twenties.[1] As an organized party in the United States, the Communists were a group apart, and they anticipated the day when unemployment, strikes, and misery would somehow give them their chance to prove that their basic doctrines were sound. Although they reached very few people and polled only 43,917 votes in the election of 1928,[2] the Communists, by the extremity of their charges, helped to spread the myth, at least among themselves, that Herbert Hoover was the "agent of Wall Street."

The Communists became the object of attack in the Congress in 1930 as findings of a committee of the House of Representatives investigating communism (the Fish Committee) provided much factual data about the assertions and ambitions of Communists.[3] The Communists presented their case without restraint in the committee and elsewhere, but clashes between Communists and police in New York City and other places were normally minor incidents.

Radicals realized at the time that the only effective way to influence the national government was through the already existent organization of the Democratic party, for third party efforts had failed in 1912 and 1924, and minor parties were not catching the popular imagination. From their standpoint the Democratic party's position was good: it was already active on the national level; it had a majority in the House of Representatives; and it had the continuing opportunity of winning additional support in more than half of the states of the Union. Moreover, this party, with its traditional appeals to not only organized labor but the farmer, had always counted upon the electoral support of twelve states of the South.

It was a brutal fact that however distant the people of the United States were from any semblance of the extremes of revolution sweeping the world, they did not and could not—in view of their own history—

reject a hearing to those who sought to provide "a people's rule." In a word, in the mounting crisis of 1932, weakness of the first order attached itself to the program of any leader who insisted (as did Hoover) that the business of the executive or the Congress was government, not politics.

All of the radical programs—of whatever origin—were presented on behalf of special groups of people. It was President Hoover who continued to assert that he had the *whole* people in mind. Indeed, this might have been true of any leader in the presidency whose responsibility was the welfare of all the people of the nation, but it was emphatically true of Herbert Hoover. Repeatedly he emphasized the dangers of group favoritism. Of course his critics said that he seemed to be identified with the representatives of powerful economic units. And he did use such individuals in conference and in action. But he did not work *for* them.[4]

Hoover's interaction with the nation's ex-servicemen, the veterans, was a noticeable part of his term in office. Determined to bring efficiency to the government wherever possible, he was on July 8, 1930 granted authority to consolidate all veterans agencies under an administrator of veterans' affairs.[5] Yet on the whole the president's efforts to aid the veteran somehow failed to gain him the credit he deserved,[6] even though he sometimes enjoyed strong support from the press.[7] Although many failed to realize it, Hoover was the author of the World War Disability Act passed in the summer of 1930, a bill that was "exceedingly generous" even though not satisfactory to all.[8] Indeed, out of the byplay accompanying debate in the Congress and elsewhere there emerged late in the administration a feeling among many veterans that the incumbent president was a stingy roadblock to their hopes.[9]

In the nation's capital, in the summer of the presidential election year of 1932, occurred what some saw to be a manifestation of what radicalism might come to mean in the United States. Veterans in distress—always an object of public sympathy—motivated in part by pressure that had been accumulating for some years, used the year of the national party conventions to appeal for government help. Effort had been exerted already for the immediate payment of bonus certificates due and payable to veterans of World War I at a distant time (1945). In 1931, Congress had voted a partial fulfillment of this request, permitting borrowing upon the certificate to the extent of one-half of its value. The president vetoed that bill. He emphasized, in opposing the passage of such legislation, that "the country should not be called upon ... either directly or indirectly, to support or make loans to those who can by their own efforts support themselves."[10] This was strong language at any time; it was infuriating to many at that particular time. The bill was passed over the president's veto, in any case, on February 27, 1931.

A year later, a new bill proposed by Representative Wright Patman of Texas provided that the veterans should be paid immediately the full face value of their adjusted compensation certificates by issuance of $2 billion of treasury notes. As noted already, the American Legion in convention in September 1931 had refused to endorse this proposal. Their refusal was gratifying to the chief executive.[11] But on June 15, 1932, the bill passed the House by a vote of 209 to 176 (153 Democrats, 55 Republicans, 1 Farmer-Laborite, against 126 Republicans and 50 Democrats). The Senate committee on finance reported adversely, and on June 18 the Senate rejected the measure by a vote of 62 to 18 (35 Republicans, 27 Democrats, against 10 Democrats, 7 Republicans, and 1 Farmer-Laborite). There had been certainty of a presidential veto in any case, had the bill passed the Senate.

By the summer of 1932 the atmosphere in Washington had been grim for many months. The adjournment of Congress did not lighten the prevailing mood. "During this strange interlude when the national slogan is 'No Business As Usual' repeated everywhere with a certain grim gaiety, the nation's business is government," commented Anne O'Hare McCormick on June 26. "Ten to one the talk goes straight to the new question of America, 'What's the government going to do?' The tone is not tragic. . . . It never stops in despair. It is not revolutionary. The contemporary models of revolution are mentioned often enough, but as bogeys rather than as beacons."[12]

Presently it was national news that an "army" of petitioners would converge on Washington.[13] What was termed a "Bonus Expeditionary Force" (BEF) of perhaps 20,000,[14] accumulated from various parts of the country, assembled in Washington to push, by personal appeal, a request for government aid. About a thousand women and children were included. Meetings were held with every evidence of freedom of assembly and freedom of speech, together with freedom to petition Congress. Observers from the sidelines were numerous, as local citizens wondered when the occupation of their city would come to an end.

The president's secretary (Joslin) stated later that, when it was announced that veterans were coming to Washington, he necessarily ascertained Hoover's wishes in advance.

> The reply he made to me when I put the question to him is important because the common impression is that he flatly refused to let the veterans see him. He said, "If they ask you for permission to see me and they are veterans, tell them that I will receive a committee representing them. Make an appointment for the committee whenever it is ready to call. Bear in mind that advice I have received indicates there are many malcontents among

the marchers. I don't know whether this is so or not but I won't receive any communists. The committee must be composed of veterans.[15]

In view of the failure of the Patman bill and the adjournment of Congress, a stalemate was evident. Hoover quietly initiated a bill to provide loans to pay for the transportation of veterans to their homes; before adjourning, the Congress voted funds authorizing payment of railway fares. The people's representatives were keenly aware that here was the most massive (and the longest) protest Washington had endured.[16] Many veterans departed; but the remaining members of the "bonus army," housed in buildings being demolished near the Capitol and in shacks on Anacostia Flats near the Potomac, and of course not engaged in remunerative labor, were increasingly thought to be a menace to public health and the maintenance of law and order.

The administration was naturally anxious for the bonus group to leave Washington. A scholar summed it up well at the time: "The gathering of thousands of citizens in the very presence of the national legislature who say 'Here we stay until you pass legislation that is satisfying to our group,' is the most ominous phenomenon in many decades of our history." The right of petition definitely did not include "massed threat."[17]

The national government especially desired to clear the downtown Washington area of the bonus army because construction of major buildings was being held up. (The insurance of contractors was not valid under the conditions that obtained.) On July 21 the District of Columbia commissioners began a process designed to achieve federal goals by ordering buildings and parks vacated. Many maneuvers resulted. The police chief, Pelham D. Glassford, new to such duties but experienced as a former general in the army, sided on occasion more with the BEF and its declared leader, Walter W. Waters, than with his superiors.[18]

The nation had sympathized with the plight of the unemployed veterans, and some Congressmen had even encouraged their political pilgrimage. "We used to take food out to the Bonus people," recalled the White House butler later.[19] James Oliver La Gorce of the National Geographic Society said at the time,

> I visited all these camps . . . and talked to scores of the men just to make sure myself. True, they had a right to come here to see Congress as has every other American citizen, but when Congress adjourned and went back to their homes there was no excuse for this horde remaining here, for it presented a menace to health from epidemics as well as the danger of violence, and it was a serious situation.[20]

Hoover had at the outset ordered subordinates to provide ample tents, cots, blankets, rolling kitchens, and other army equipment to the veterans; barracks belonging to the marines were emptied for them; and medical care was provided to many.[21]

All hoped that force would not be necessary. After all, federal troops had not been called out very often in the century.[22] Because of changing circumstances "no two presidents have handled disorders in the same manner."[23] One must agree with an expert, however, that the inhabitants of a troubled area will welcome the arrival of federal forces, but are unlikely to forgive excesses. Thus the chief executive moves very deliberately in such instances.[24]

The bonus army did include some Communists (organized into a Workers' Ex-Servicemen's League) who hoped to capitalize on the situation by trying repeatedly to create what they traditionally called "a revolutionary situation." On several occasions they tried to take charge and failed, although there were arrests and publicity. Communist propaganda and a BEF newspaper vied for the attention of marchers, observers, officials, and the public.[25] But the bonus group was not championing the cause of poor people generally; rather, it was essentially middle class in origins.[26]

Hoover had viewed the matter of Communist activity in the United States calmly during the years subsequent to World War I. This has been demonstrated by one scholar who stresses the distinction between the tone of the Hoover *Memoirs* (written during the Cold War) and Hoover's conduct in office, 1914–1918 and 1921–1932. Even though in the twenties Hoover was a special target for Communist denunciation, "he did not think that rhetoric, even if it was an expression of revolutionary intent, constituted a serious threat to the nation." Thus behind the scenes he "discouraged overzealous police" anxious to arrest Communist pickets, and he avoided "red hunts" of the kind A. Mitchell Palmer had engaged in after the war. An assassination threat against him left him untroubled.[27]

Needless to say, President Hoover, Secretary of War Pat Hurley, Chief of Staff Douglas MacArthur, Treasury officials, three district commissioners, the chief of police, and newspapermen watched the events of July 21–28 attentively; most of them hoped that the veterans would melt away (as had those who had accepted free transportation home). But on the twenty-eighth there would be an incident and the police would lose control; contingency planning would have to be put into effect after all.

The descent into violence now seems clear enough. Some veterans refused to leave buildings being demolished to make room for new construction. Before long some 3,000 veterans were milling about in the general area. Now it was that the highly unfortunate availability of broken bricks and other building materials furnished ready ammunition.

At one point some police were seriously injured; there was a melee inside the old Ford Building, and then a policeman fired, clearly in self-defense. Two veterans died and three police went to the hospital.[28] The District government turned to federal authorities for aid.

Now, very reluctantly, the army would be called out by the president, but not until he insisted that the district commissioners put their request in writing.[29] General MacArthur, who was Hoover's own choice for chief of staff,[30] would not be in immediate command but would be very much on hand as things progressed and would issue orders on the scene.[31] Meanwhile, President Hoover was hard at work on both foreign policy and major domestic matters. At noon he was having lunch in the White House with a visiting sociologist. For weeks the president had been calm in the face of rumors of Communist plots, so that he can be credited with "defense of the marchers' civil liberties" and with "a firm faith in the democratic process."[32] Now a secretary came in to tell him that the civil authorities had phoned to ask that he take over administration of the city for the purpose of removing the bonus army from downtown Washington. Said Hoover tersely, "Please tell them to put that in writing." The secretary left, to return in half an hour with the written document.[33] (Stated Hoover a day later, "There is no group, no matter what its origins, that can be allowed to violate the laws of this city or to intimidate the government.")[34] The army's orders were to "cooperate fully with the District of Columbia police force which is now in charge." The area was to be surrounded, and any prisoners were to be turned over to the civil authorities.[35] Clearly, the army was not taking over the nation's capital, there was no state of martial law, and the president continued to be unwilling to issue a proclamation declaring a state of insurrection.[36]

The Army officers and men who forced the BEF from Washington were as good as the nation had at the time: "both men and horses were superbly trained," with almost all segments fifteen-year men or better, the officers above captain were all World War I veterans, and the lieutenants were West Point graduates.[37] There had been special training on dispersing crowds. It is not surprising, therefore, that the army pushed the bonus veterans before them in general compliance with the Hoover order relayed by Hurley that "any women and children who may be in the affected area be accorded every consideration and kindness. Use all humanity consistent with the due execution of this order."[38] Still, episodes occurred that made disturbing reading then and later.

Anacostia Flats, the major BEF residence area, was some two miles southeast of the Capitol and across the river. Because Hoover had seen no present need to disturb the camp, he ordered Hurley to see to it that the army did not cross the river. This key order from the president was not taken seriously enough by Hurley; in the forms he twice chose to transmit it, the order was not obeyed by General MacArthur, who apparently saw an opportunity to end the entire bonus army intimidation of Washington, once and for all.[39] Says a careful authority on the matter, "MacArthur intentionally disobeyed the President's orders and, on his own volition, decided to drive the B.E.F. out of the capital."[40] MacArthur said he thought there was "incipient revolution in the air."[41]

That night the camp at Anacostia Flats was burned by some of the marchers and certain members of the army, with later recriminations.[42] The veterans and some dependents fled, so that there was to be some national concern expressed subsequently about the mistreatment of citizens who had once served in uniform.

President Hoover privately upbraided General MacArthur over his violation of presidential orders.[43] Initial press reaction to the entire rout of the BEF was considered fairly favorable, however;[44] therefore, although the president asked Hurley and MacArthur to reveal their full responsibility, they felt no need to do so.[45] Oddly, because of the initial favorable national reaction, they were able to disclaim a desire to be made "heroes." Hoover let the matter drop and accepted responsibility.[46] Hurley and MacArthur held a press conference, where MacArthur in no way revealed that he had acted independently. To Secretary of State Stimson, busy with his own concerns, it seemed on the night of July 28 that the problem had been "the inefficiency of the District Government and the publicity itch of General Glassford [who] by handling it too loosely and easily in the beginning [had] allowed it to get a start which they now can't handle."[47]

As August closed, an incensed American Legion met in convention and this time declared in favor of payment of the bonus. The whole matter became a factor in the fall election, especially as Chief of Police Glassford (as upset as the Legion over release of data by the attorney general charging the bonus veterans with quantities of prior "criminal" convictions) wrote a series of vigorous anti-administration syndicated newspaper articles.

In general, Americans seemed to have ambivalent feelings about the bonus episode. They had not wanted the bonus paid; they had not liked the intimidation of government; but they did not like, either, the pictures of citizens versus United States Cavalry. The day after the riot a Californian wrote to the President:

> I wish to congratulate you upon your masterly handling of the so called "Bonus Army," at Washington. Every consideration was shown these misguided men up to the time violence and the breaking down of civil law was attempted. In the days that followed our Revolutionary War, our first Presi-

dent, George Washington, had a similar situation to meet. He met this
situation in a similar manner.[48]

Herbert Hoover was not to rid himself of public blame for the burn-
ing of the camp at Anacostia Flats, either in general memory or history
books. It was falsely recalled that the army had shot veterans. It was
falsely said that infants had died then or later at the army's hands.[49]
A president, who initially had tried to order that only sticks and no fire-
arms be carried by troops, was charged with the "fascist" suppression of
citizens who as memories faded seemed to have been merely petitioning.

In private retirement, Hoover was attacked by a civil liberties-violating
Governor Rolph of California, with various distortions of what had actually happened on July 28, 1932. Hoover replied with spirit that not a shot
was fired by the troops who ended the bloodshed between rioters and
police.[50] But there can be little doubt that between the riot and the election the busy and troubled president made serious missteps in handling
public relations aspects of the Bonus Army episode.[51]

At the time, this affair revealed the American public in a familiar
performance. Everyone was interested in this dramatic picture of Americans—veterans, congressmen, police, the army, and even the president—
engaged in a struggle for assertion of power. At no time was it clear what
the long-range outcome might be. Reports by the press, by radio, and by
moving pictures stressed every salient point of conflict and as time passed
minimized the necessities of law and order, and confidence in government during an economic crisis. The president's secretary recalled later
that the *Washington Times* had declared that "no group of a few thousand citizens, no matter how worthy, can be allowed to defy flagrantly
the rules and regulations which a hundred and twenty million have set
up for the preservation of peace, order and comfort."[52] Yet criticism of
the president increased among those already convinced that his actions
were unfeeling and despotic. Reaction to the release of Attorney General
Mitchell's not entirely accurate report on September 12, 1932, with its
allegations of criminal backgrounds among many of the veterans of the
BEF, added to Hoover's unpopularity.[53]

This was so, even though Hoover took special pains to say that there
was no intent "to reflect upon the many thousands of honest, law abiding
men" who had petitioned for aid.[54] And it appeared to make little difference to critics when Waters, leader of the bonus group as it gathered
briefly in Johnstown, Pennsylvania, attempted to mobilize the "army" as a
khaki-shirted activist group. If most Americans were naïve about such
matters, the president was not.[55]

The figure of Herbert Hoover that now appeared to the public was no longer one that appealed to a people in distress. This was the more strange because the Hoover of ten years—even two years—before had been envisaged as a savior of millions from starvation. Now he seemed to be remote from the realities of hunger and chiefly concerned with the honest dollar and a balanced budget. That many Americans of education, prestige, and leadership, who were removed from the insecurities of the depression, appeared to look upon him with approval only seemed to increase the distrust.

The full measure of uncritical response to the basic problems of distress and despair was the quarrel over the extent of Communist influence in the nation in the 1930s. Party leaders had organized certain hunger marches early in the year, to be sure. Their banners were used, of course, in various demonstrations. Yet they were thought normally to be more of a nuisance than a menace.

Violence was a different matter. It had earlier manifestations in American history, and not always without provocation. Attempts to "storm the government" had not previously attracted so much serious national attention at a critical time, however. Communist or not, the bonus veterans, rioters, or mobs (as the case may have been) greatly disturbed the nation. The *B.E.F. News* editorialized that "the first veteran killed might be the beginning of a national upheaval." And "behind the veterans encamped at the Capital were millions of other distressed Americans anxiously watching every move . . . ; a spark in the powder-keg might become a conflagration sweeping this land from ocean to ocean."[56]

The tone of the presidential campaign was altered by the entire bonus episode. The Democrats rejoiced at the tarnishing of the Hoover image. Charges of "conspiracy" were made by various interested parties then and for many years afterwards.[57] Meanwhile, as unemployment continued, the fact of mass protest and of recriminations worried all who hoped that orderly processes might suffice to handle the economic crisis. While the Communists naturally hoped to profit from all this, they did not, probably; their vote base of 1928 (10,876 votes in New York, 2,039 in Pennsylvania) was indeed small.[58] But they had more of a hearing than previously, and their words were heard far more often. A tiny Socialist Workers' Party (Trotskyites) was born in 1929 but grew only slowly.

By mid-summer of 1932 the cleavage in knowledge between those who governed on the "inside," and the people who waited and watched hopefully or campaigned on the "outside" was more clearly marked than in any campaign year since 1896. It was the administration's responsibility to provide government for the people pending a new election. On the "inside," Hoover's sources of information on national economic improvement were encouraging clear through to November.

On the "outside," the situation was different. There would be rever-
berations of Washington's violence among farmers in Iowa and among
urban dwellers in Detroit. Extremes on the left and the right were
strengthened somewhat, and attacks on Communists increased. Congressman Fish, as he investigated Communist activity, thought he saw a crisis
of major dimensions and called for strenuous methods of opposition. A
modest number of admirers of fascism could be noted.

Yet for decades an ever-increasing number of leaders and thinkers had
been applying their minds to the problems of democracy in the modern
world. Penetrating questions were raised by scholars, critics, journalists
and some occupants of public office. Reform as an idea, once so popular,
no longer held its appeal for various independents who now looked
toward socialism and in some cases beyond. Revolt was their mood but
not always what they advocated—revolt against the practice of orderly
(or at least slow) government, and revolt against the institutions of
government.

To a considerable extent, a merely conceptualized "democracy" was
exalted; constitutional "republicanism"—that is, confidence by the ruled
in the elected representatives—was the victim. Reform had always had
an easy American remedy: "throw the rascals out" at scheduled elections,
and "man the government with devoted public servants." Revolt, on the
other hand, had no clear-cut and definite goal unless it was the overthrow
of government and a remaking of society into a dramatically new pattern.

President Hoover, who in the early 1920s had displayed full awareness of the gradations between reform and revolt in his book, *American
Individualism,* was all too conscious of what might happen in America,
and the lines on his face deepened with the passage of the months.

Hoover in the Campaign of 1932

*In the financial storm Mr. Hoover had stood out like a
lighthouse. The years of strain and pressure had but
strengthened those qualities of his which I had found
in him during our Stanford student days together, and
which I called 'The Four I's' — Industry, Integrity,
Initiative and Independence. Now that we were finally
on the road to more prosperous days for our country,
there seemed to be a chance, if he could be re-elected
for the next four years, for him to carry forward, at last,
the many constructive social and economic projects
which he had long had in mind, but which had been
prevented or retarded by the depression.*

Ray Lyman Wilbur,
The Memoirs of Ray Lyman Wilbur

Pressures upon the president to provide leadership in formulating the
Republican program for the forthcoming campaign increased as the
spring of 1932 advanced. At the time, he maintained that he was too busy
carrying out the duties of his office to take any active part in this type of
"politics." He seems to have held the view, first expressed in the preceding year, that he would open his campaign late. But his correspondence
reveals receipt of wise counsel on the need to take steps to construct a
platform to suit his own wishes.

The party atmosphere in which this work must be done was not calculated to produce good results. For in the light of the November 1930
election results, the national committee of the Republican party was in
a mood of despair—producing a conviction widely shared by the president's friends that the committee could not "save the country."[1] This
obvious attitude aroused Republicans not in office or on the national

committee, who believed the real tests would be the attitude that the president would take toward this "political" task.

"Certainly," wrote the anonymous editor, T.R.B., "Hoover's voice does not ring through the nation." He judged that while the White House statements were sometimes "sound enough," they lacked conviction; while invariably failing to produce results, they always evoked partisan retorts. "It is unfortunate," T.R.B. reflected, "at a time like this that Hoover's personality should handicap his best efforts. . . ."[2]

An answer to this criticism was that Hoover was overwhelmingly occupied with the complexities of the economic situation. He was reticent, furthermore, because of his belief that blunt revelation of the serious economic situation would create widespread fear throughout the nation.

Rumors that prominent eastern Republicans had approached Coolidge in the hope that he might accept a presidential nomination if it were offered him circulated to the point of being denied by Charles D. Hilles (one of the supposed conspirators). Yet such a rumor in itself reflected a state of uncertainty among party leaders. Hilles wrote Hoover on March 26, 1932:

> Recently . . . a story has been publicly circulated in Washington which I think should not go unchallenged, because it is more specific than such stories usually are and may, in consequence, be more plausible.
>
> It is to the effect that Mr. Thomas Cochran, Mr. Julian Mason and I sought an interview with Mr. Coolidge for the purpose of persuading him to submit to a candidacy for renomination, and that the attempt was abortive. . . .
>
> The story is so utterly untrue that it must have been the result not of accident but of design. . . . I do not know that the report has reached you but I *do* know that men in the service of the party have been engaged in its circulation. On the chance that it may come to your notice, as that is clearly its destination, I write to brand it a falsehood.[3]

A prophetic evaluation of the chances for the Republican party in the coming presidential election was brought to Hoover's attention at this time by the warning of a leading economist, Thomas Nelson Carver of Harvard, that if the large financial interests were to desert the Republican party, a "soak the rich" campaign would lay them open to the attacks of a radical Democratic bloc. The strategy was clear. It would bring back the excess profits tax and super-taxes on income and inheritances as means of balancing the budget, besides endangering the tariff policy on which manufacturing interests of the East depended.

Furthermore, a "wet" plank in the Republican platform would mean that the Republicans would not carry a single southern state. They would lose a number of western farming states where the Democrats were trying, with some success, to profit from the discontent fostered by the belief that farmers were taxed by the tariff to increase the profits of big business. With the "dry" tie severed, there would be a Democratic landslide in the farming West including Minnesota, the Dakotas, and Montana; probably Nebraska, Colorado, Missouri, Kansas, Washington, and Oregon; and possibly Iowa. With the help of discontented radicals in the cities and in the agrarian West and South, the Democratic party would then come into power. These elements would then hold the balance of power in the Democratic party.[4] Here was the scenario!

Looking back to those years, the importance of the Prohibition issue in the campaign of 1932 appears unreal. That it was, in fact, of crucial importance during the economic earthquake that was shaking the world is clearly demonstrated in the president's interchanges with Senator Borah and others on the subject of Prohibition.[5]

Hoover's position on Prohibition at the time of the Republican National Convention was stated by him this way in retrospect:

> We had done our best to enforce the Prohibition law. We enormously increased the jail population. We multiplied the fines, padlockings, and confiscations. Yet the illicit traffic increased. Even the original fanatically dry states of Ohio, Kansas, Iowa, and Alabama would not cooperate with the Federal administration in enforcement as the law anticipated. As we approached the 1932 Presidential election the whole Prohibition question took on a new aspect. I, as party leader, had to abandon the Elihu Root formula and give advice to the party convention.[6]

As early as May 10, 1932, the president told Senator Borah as "the leader of the drys" that it was impossible to enforce the Eighteenth Amendment and the Volstead Act and stated "the whole liquor question should be returned to the states." Borah appeared to agree with this basic position. Hoover, attempting to embody Borah's ideas, then suggested the following as the platform plank on Prohibition:

> An amendment should be promptly submitted that shall allow the states to deal with Prohibition as their citizens may determine but subject to the retained power of the Federal government to protect those states where Prohibition may exist. There should be a safeguard against the return of the saloon and its attendant abuses.[7]

Postmaster General Brown reported on a subsequent conference on this matter in which Borah participated:

The purpose of the conference was to discuss the formula of a platform plank for the Republican party favoring the resubmission of the problem of the liquor traffic. Senator Borah stated that he was working on a plan for such resubmission, giving to the States the right to determine for themselves whether they would be wet or dry, but that he had not yet found a satisfactory method to make certain that the saloon would not return; that he hoped to complete his plan shortly and present it to the Senate before the Republican convention.[8]

It was this evasiveness of Borah which Hoover was aware of when he wrote later: "I considered witnesses to Borah's attitude highly important."[9]

In California, the president's own state, the problem of "politics in the Prohibition plank" was vividly apparent. California had been a "wet" state prior to 1920. Despite considerable "dry" sentiment among Republican voters, the majority of Republican leaders were not pleased with Prohibition, and not at all satisfied with the president's policy.[10] This prejudiced support that would otherwise have come to him from such elements. Party conflict over Prohibition was interwoven with the long-standing disagreement between Hoover's supporters and those of Hiram Johnson. Johnson stated that his "intense desire" to attend the Republican National Convention must yield to his "stern sense of duty as Senator."[11]

But out of California had come as well the reassurance of Hoover's friends. One of them, writing to Lawrence Richey, said:

Reconstruction legislation calms tense public nerves; splendidly conceived and received; leaders of group well selected; publicity satisfactory, with prospects of success. The threatened Pacific Coast financial storm is temporarily at least dispelled—thanks to pulmoter . . . reaction. . . . The February 22nd broadcast was splendid; the Cardozo appointment satisfies everyone. The President avoids the manifest trap set for his feet, confounds his enemies, gratifies the genuine demand for a worthy successor to the retired Justice, pleases the lovers of good government, and meets every requirement of the situation. Sound public policy, law, and politics for once are united. This appointment and the outstanding constructive statesmanship of the Chief Justice place the President in an unassailable position, and add to the strength and dignity of the court. The criminal law reform message is sound. It meets and deserves unqualified approval. It does not quite get the required publicity. . . .[12]

Friends of Hoover were, assuredly, troubled by the necessity of formulating a Prohibition plank in the forthcoming platform that would deal fairly with this problematical issue. Frank E. Gannett and William Allen White had corresponded in an effort to formulate a statement that would conciliate the liberal drys. Gannett felt that a moist plank in the platform would mean disaster, and that the Republican party should stand firmly against the liquor business in order to protect both home and society.[13]

William Allen White, whose article on the matter had been circulated all over the United States by the various press associations, had declared for an informal referendum in each state on the Eighteenth Amendment, although he was well aware that "without Constitutional backing we are setting a precedent which some day might rise to mock us on some other issue."[14]

The president of the Southern Pacific Company thought that despite "a lot of people who have very strong views about maintaining the country absolutely dry," an informal referendum of the American voters would guide Congress in submitting the question back to the states, and that "none of the growth of temperance which came with local option should be lost as a result of any modification of the Eighteenth Amendment."[15]

The president was reminded that the Eighteenth Amendment and the Volstead Act were both enacted during the Democratic administration of Woodrow Wilson. Neither the Republican party nor the Democratic party had ever had a Prohibition platform plank prior to ratification of the Eighteenth Amendment. The difficult problem of enforcing Prohibition was inherited by the Republican party. The Democrats had talked so much about its repeal that even Republicans had come to believe it was a Republican measure. A real referendum upon the wisdom of the amendment could be accomplished only in one way under the Constitution, namely, by an amendment to be passed by Congress providing for the repeal of the Eighteenth Amendment and referred for ratification to conventions in the several states as provided in the Constitution.[16]

A "personal and confidential" letter from newspaper publisher Frank E. Gannett to Secretary Newton at this time warned of the limitless political complications of the Prohibition issue:

> . . . plank #12 which the President submitted to me, does not entirely satisfy the conservative drys with whom I have communicated. They believe that while they might support it, the radical drys would not be satisfied. I have submitted it in confidence to one or two radical drys and, frankly, they don't like it.
>
> . . . It is going to be quite impossible to draft a plank that will please both the wets and the drys. . . .
>
> . . . I must admit that it seems hopeless to put into the platform any expression of a plan to submit the question without carrying the inference that the party is going wet.
>
> I told the President that we can win this election if there is not too much

moisture in the platform. We can't outwet the wets and no wet declaration in the platform will gain for the Republicans any wet support.

The President has grown much stronger during the past few weeks. He could be elected today against Roosevelt or any one else the Democrats might name, but he can't be elected if you alienate the dry vote.

My advice, therefore, is to be very cautious about putting something in the platform that will *do more harm than good.*[17]

Senator Simeon Fess, a dry leader who had earlier been called into consultation upon the Prohibition issue, wrote the president late in June:

I had hoped that we could avoid a controversy in our party over the 18th Amendment in the belief that if the emphasis could have been placed on the economic situation and your leadership in relief, our talking points would have been so strong that the radicals could not have made much headway. It is a subject in which a compromise is very dangerous. The radicals on either side cannot be appeased. Any suggestion that the 18th Amendment should be modified is seized upon by the wets as a confession of a break-down, which is sorely offensive to the drys. Any attempt at Federal regulation to prevent the return of the saloon is offensive to the extreme wets, and is somewhat compromising to the drys who have experienced difficulty in the past in attempting to regulate this evil.

Our plank is constructive in that it puts the power of the Federal Government back of the dry state that wants to remain dry, and the regulatory power in the wet state that desires to be wet. It concedes the traffic to be an evil, and opens the way for constructive steps to eliminate it as rapidly as the conscience of the people will demand.

On the other hand, our opponents will declare for repeal and attack the Republican candidate in the wet states as a dry, and in the dry states as a wet. Of course there is not a scintilla of fact as a basis for such a statement, but they will use it indiscriminately. The enemies in our own ranks, who would like to use the dry disaffection as a means to break down the party, will be most active in that campaign. I very deeply regret the situation, which will be difficult to handle, but I am constrained to believe that the solution proposed is constructive and the best that could be adopted, first, for the country at large, and secondly, on behalf of those of us who are uncompromising opponents of the liquor traffic.[18]

As the prospective Republican party platform statement was circulated among leaders for comment, the limitless political complications of the Prohibition issue were revealed. The *conservative* drys would not be satisfied. The impossibility of drafting a plank that would please both the wets and the drys was obvious. It appeared hopeless to put into the platform any plan to submit the question without carrying the implication that the party was going wet. It would be impossible, furthermore, to outwet the wets. No wet declaration in the platform would gain for the Republicans any wet support anyway. In this paradoxical situation, despite the president's apparent growth in political strength during the late spring, it was clear that he could not be elected if the dry vote were to be alienated.

In looking back at the political situation that existed in the summer of 1932, one might wonder why the controversy in the Republican party over the Eighteenth Amendment was allowed to develop. If the emphasis could have been placed on the apparently improved economic situation and Hoover's efforts at leadership in relief, the talking points of the Republicans would have been so strong that the radicals could not have made much headway.

The final Republican plank was constructive in that it put the power of the federal government back of the dry state that wanted to remain dry, and the regulatory power in the wet state that desired to be wet. It conceded the liquor traffic to be an evil, while opening the way for constructive steps to eliminate it as rapidly as the conscience of the people should demand.

Hoover's enemies, who wished to use the dry disaffection as a means to break down the party, were to be most active in the campaign.

Even before the convention it was already too late to avoid disaster, for a fatal compromise had been made in the preparation of the Prohibition plank; even so, Senator Borah denounced the plank the next day and withdrew his support from Hoover's candidacy. Years later Hoover explained what happened:

When the Convention met on June 14, 1932, the Resolutions Committee, as expected, was divided—wet and dry. To get our idea accepted Mr. Garfield (chairman) finally allowed the drys to write a long preamble to our central idea and the wets to write a final paragraph to attach on the end. I was greatly distressed, as I was sure that this would be interpreted as a straddle; but nothing could be done about it, as it already had been sent to the floor of the Convention. Secretary Mills called me up to say that it was the best they could do, that passage of the body of the resolution without the head and tail would hopelessly split the Convention. There followed a long debate on the floor between the opposing factions. I was listening to it over the radio when my private telephone rang and Mark Sullivan told me that Senator Borah wished to speak with me: Would I call him up? I did so at once. Borah said that he was listening to the debate and expressed great anxiety lest the plank might be defeated. I told him not to worry, that in the end it would be put through. Twenty-four hours later, Senator Borah made a public statement, denounced the platform plank, and declared that he would support no candidate on that basis. Certainly I had no support from him in the Campaign.[19]

It is notable that in the debate upon the Prohibition plank, the crowd of some fifteen thousand attending the convention was obviously in favor of the minority report, that is, favoring repeal of the Eighteenth Amendment. The final vote was 690–460 against the minority report. In the vote on adoption of the Prohibition plank submitted by the president, however, the vote was 681–472. Without the support of the southern delegations, the president's proposal would have been defeated. Although adopted by the convention, it was severely criticized.[20]

Although the convention had to straddle Prohibition, the expected nominee of the convention, namely, President Hoover, felt that the position of the party on Prohibition was of far less importance in 1932 than it had been in 1928. The major problems before the country, both domestic and international, were, in Hoover's view, economic. His basic approach, which had led to the appointment of the Wickersham Commission, was that any decision on Prohibition should be postponed until such time as the electorate as a whole could deal with it on the basis of fact. It was perhaps too much to expect that the zealots for Prohibition or the advocates of repeal would acquiesce in such a view. But it had to be the view—as it was—of the president of the United States.

But the president was also a candidate. One must respect (but not necessarily agree with) the retrospective judgment of a partisan expert of the day, Fred G. Clark, founder of the Crusaders, the important group then pushing repeal but favoring temperance. "I think if he had sponsored repeal he would have been elected overwhelmingly. Oh yes."[21] It is said that it was Secretary of War Pat Hurley who persuaded Hoover to hold the line for Prohibition, for he kept repeating that his surveys of the Bible Belt showed this to be the people's view.[22] This must be weighed against the judgment two years earlier that Hoover was "sincerely wholeheartedly for dry and the Dry Cause."[23]

Months later Clark went in confidence to the White House to exert pressure for repeal. He proposed to send Hoover a telegram that would ask his "opinion" on the idea of a beer bill; he hoped the president would then reply, "I cannot answer your questions until I see in what form the bill is presented, and [if] it represents the sentiment of the country as expressed to Congress, I will not oppose it." Then Clark tells us what happened, saying, "what could be simpler than that?" Hoover "just thought and thought—I don't know what was on his mind—but he stood up and he looked out of that bay window in the back behind his desk, and jingled coins in his pocket, and said, 'Well, Mr. Clark, I can't agree to your proposal. If I have to resort to such tactics, I do not want to be in public life.' "[24]

Earlier, Jeremiah Milbank and Lewis L. Strauss, close friends of Hoover, had urged political expediency—personal dissociation from the Eighteenth Amendment. But Hoover in reply was unbending:

> The President of the United States takes an oath to preserve, protect and defend the Constitution. If he comes into office with the intention of changing that great instrument, it is a mental reservation which makes hypocrisy of his oath; and if, as President, he acts to advocate a change in the Constitution, it would set the most dangerous precedent I can think of. There is a constitutional procedure for changing the Constitution, but the President has no part in it, and should not have. Regardless of what you believe will be the effect upon my political fortunes, and however right you may be, that is of no consequence compared with the great principle of our form of government which properly proscribes the Chief Executive from tampering with the Constitution under any circumstances.[25]

The Republican National Convention, meeting in Chicago, found its traditional reason for existence in the words of the temporary chairman, L. J. Dickinson of Iowa, who reviewed what the leader of the party, the president, had attempted to do in holding together the economic fabric of the nation. He referred in particular to the establishment of the Farm Board and the creation of the Reconstruction Finance Corporation.

The platform may be summarized briefly: endorsement of Hoover's leadership in economic crisis; the president's program for protection of the budget was noted, as were emergency loans to states for unemployment relief; banking loans were to be revised to give great protection to depositors and to regulate banking facilities; and the establishment of a home loan discount system and the encouragement of cooperative marketing through the Federal Farm Board were praised. Included as well was approval of the idea of United States participation in the World Court.

Dickinson excoriated the Democrats:

> For two long years they hampered the President at every turn. Through a highly subsidized press bureau, Democratic leaders, Democratic Senators, and Democratic Congressmen sought to distort his every word, to belittle his every effort at human and economic relief, to impugn his every motive, to frustrate his every move. Their orders were to smear Hoover.[26]

Equally realistic would have been a summary of the frustrations imposed upon the president's program by the Republican minority in the Congress. This unfortunately had to be ignored at that critical moment, for the standardbearer was about to be selected. Not one of the president's opponents, however heroic in the eyes of the people, could be nominated or elected to the presidency. This was well known to all the party representatives. An editorial in the *St. Louis Globe Democrat* on June 17, 1932, stated: "... there have been few Presidents of the United States who have been criticized as severely, have been disliked as cordially, and by leaders of his own party, as Mr. Hoover has been in the last three years. Yet they are all now with him and for him. ... Mr. Hoover has simply absorbed the leadership of the Republican party and left no competition."

In fact, the strongest plank in the platform was the endorsement of Hoover's leadership in the economic crisis. The convention debated only one plank of the proposed platform: Prohibition.

Hoover's name was presented to the convention on June 16 by Joseph L. Scott, a Catholic and orator from California. The demonstration that followed lasted thirty-two minutes. Ogden Mills represented Hoover at the convention. On the first ballot, Hoover received 1,126 ½ votes from 1,154 delegates. To a message of congratulation from the convention, President Hoover immediately replied, "If the American people shall again commit to me the high trust of this great office, I shall pledge them the full measure of my devotion to their service." In acknowledging renomination for the presidency, Hoover promised that he would labor "as I have labored to meet the effects of the world-wide storm which has devastated us with trials and suffering unequalled in but few periods of our history."[27] This promise was to be the keynote of his campaign.

Thus, in the presidential campaign of 1932, Hoover's economic program for the distressed nation was to be the issue. The Republican party was not fully disposed to admit that fact, nor were the Democrats disposed to do more than use it as a point of attack. Nevertheless, the president's program was the only affirmative proposal before the people.[28] Why was this? The Republican party record (as earlier chapters have shown) was hopelessly confused, and Democratic proposals on every one of the issues presented to the people were lamed by the record of the Democrats in the Congress. Consequently, the one certainty was President Hoover's program, and he was quite right in going to the country and making a personal canvass for a second term in the presidency.

In 1928, Hoover had stood upon the Republican platform; although his individual program then was perfectly clear, he was not personally the outstanding issue. In 1932 he himself was the issue. As Secretary Stimson, for example, clearly foresaw, "the basic issue of the campaign was not the depression but the principles of President Hoover. ... The

President had labored with great skill and energy to meet the depression with sound and constructive remedies and he had shown both courage and wisdom in resisting the Treasury raids projected by Democratic leaders in Congress."[29]

Hoover's formal acceptance of the nomination came before 4,000 on August 11, 1932 in Constitution Hall in Washington. Possibly the paragraphs that cost him the most personal trauma were those on Prohibition. Clearly, something was going to have to be done about the Eighteenth Amendment, but to Hoover, "the first duty of the President of the United States is to enforce the laws as they exist. That I shall continue to do to the utmost of my ability. Any other course would be the abrogation of the very guarantees of liberty itself." The Constitution, he pointed out, gives the president neither power nor authority with respect to changing that document. Then the president managed to say,

> It is my belief that in order to remedy present evils a change is necessary by which we resummon a proper share of initiative and responsibility which the very essence of our government demands shall rest upon the states and local authorities. That change must avoid the return of the saloon.

Hence, "each state shall be given the right to deal with the problem as it may determine, but subject to absolute guarantees in the Constitution of the United States to protect each state from interference and invasion by its neighbors. . . ." (Hoover was finally admitting that in an "increasing number of communities there is a majority sentiment unfavorable to 'the eighteenth amendment.'")[30]

While wets would not be impressed with Hoover's concessions, they were for him massive and unnerving. When the acceptance speech was over, the president confided to Secretary of State Stimson,

> I feel more depressed and troubled than I ever have been in my whole life. All my life I have been connected with the God-fearing people of this country. I believe that they represent all that is best in this country, and I feel now that I have made a decision that will affront them and make them feel that I have betrayed them.[31]

But the people knew nothing of such a deep emotion held by their president on the day after his fifty-eighth birthday. The Democratic party's contrasting declaration that they favored the repeal of the Eighteenth Amendment and the immediate modification of the Volstead Act was predictable. It probably was scant comfort to Hoover when the *New York Times* judged, "It is an honest and manly thing that the President has done in thus making his attitude clearly known,"[32] for the lead sentence in the *Literary Digest* proved to be all he had feared: "Hoover goes wet!"[33]

Hoover was silent on his campaign plans until early in September, and did not decide upon the nature of his campaign until Governor Roosevelt's campaign was well started. From the moment of his nomination by the Democratic National Convention, Franklin Delano Roosevelt took the position of vigorous attack on the Hoover administration. Hoover sensed this at once, and thus he changed a plan to refrain from active campaigning except for a few major addresses.[34] Roosevelt was saying repeatedly that the president should "aid the starving" and "prevent revolution." He announced at once his own plans for relief, recovery, and reform, which had to be met in the Republican campaign.

Stimson wrote in his diary on August 11, 1932:

> The contrast between . . . tangible evidence of a faithful president who had worked to the limit for the people during this depression on the one side, and the untried, rather flippant young man who was trying to take his place on the other . . . became so evident to me that it seemed as if really the American people and their power of choice were on trial rather than the two candidates.[35]

It was apparent at once that President Hoover intended to make an appeal for support of United States policy in the world. "We are part of a world," he said in his acceptance speech, "the disturbance of whose remotest populations affects our financial system, our employment, our markets, and prices of our farm products." In saying "I have projected a new doctrine into international affairs," he referred to the nonrecognition doctrine that had been hammered out between the secretary of state and himself.

Hoover referred in his address to the "retribution" that had struck a war-poisoned world three years before with the "inevitable world-wide slump in consumption of goods, in prices, and employment." Then, eighteen months later, in the spring of 1931, came a new calamity in the financial failures of central Europe. "If we look back over the disasters of these three years," said Hoover on August 11, 1932, "we find that three-quarters of the population of the globe has suffered from the flames of revolution." In describing the effect of this world-wide calamity upon the financial structure of the United States, the president said:

> Foreign countries, in the fact of their own failures, not believing that we had the courage or ability to meet this crisis, withdrew from the United States over $2,400,000,000, including a billion in gold. Our own alarmed

citizens withdrew over $1,600,000,000 of currency from our banks into hoarding. These actions, combined with the fears they generated, caused a shrinkage of credit available for conduct of industry and commerce by several times even these vast sums. Its visible expression was bank and business failures, demoralization of security and real property values, commodity prices, and employment.[36]

Little of this had been fully understood in the spring and summer of 1931, and little more was it grasped at the time of the president's acceptance address.

In late July 1932 the White House formulated a statement of program that was to be followed by the president in his campaign. It was the closest presentation of the president's thinking on what had been done and what could be done in the crisis that continued to confront the nation.

Perhaps a clue to why this program was formulated at this time may be found in a contemporary article by Walter Lippmann entitled "Post-Mortem on Congress," in which Lippmann asserted that "on no vital subject did the administration provide Congress or public opinion with prompt and decisive leadership."[37] This clearly fallacious criticism was shared by that part of the public who believed that the depression had been all of one piece, with its development charted, predictable, and inevitable, say, after 1930.

Here, in summary form, is the case the White House would offer the electorate. Presidential addresses would be built on this structure. The first phase of the depression, it said, was promptly and vigorously met with presidential leadership. After November 1929 leaders of business and labor were called to Washington for consultation. There were assurances of industrial peace, with maintenance of wage scales and the spreading of employment. By setting up the president's Unemployment Relief Organization and demanding that the states and local communities meet their responsibilities for relief of the unemployed, there was action to meet the two most serious needs in a depression: relief of distress and maintenance of social order.

Thus by February and March 1931, American business was well on its way out of the depression, it was said. Now events in Europe, however, produced disastrous repercussion in the United States. Europe staggered under arms and war debts and was on the brink of collapse. Bankruptcy of the Kredit-Anstalt started a train of reaction throughout the German financial system, endangering the government itself.

Here the depression entered its second phase. President Hoover anti-

cipated the course of events and tried to forestall catastrophe by setting
up a year's postponement of intergovernmental debts among all the principal nations. The world saw this as an action "saving the world from
economic chaos."

However, delay in accepting the moratorium caused by the reluctance
of France to accede promptly to the postponement of reparations payments for one year, together with European weakness, so far infected
British finance that the gold standard was abandoned by the British in
September 1931 and a genuine financial panic ensued in the United
States. Banks sought to protect themselves by calling their loans, and the
public sought to protect itself by drawing deposits from the banks in
currency, and in many cases in gold, and hoarding it. Bank failures and
hoarding rose with paralyzing effect upon the national credit system and
grave threat to gold reserves heavily drained by the demands of European nations.

Now, as the White House summarized it, President Hoover set up the
National Credit Corporation with a half billion dollars raised by banks.
It rediscounted banking assets not then eligible for rediscount at the
Federal Reserve Banks, so the banking system of the nation could extend
credit to business, industry, and agriculture until Congress could meet.
Seven hundred banks on the verge of collapse were thus saved.

Next, the president recommended creation of the Reconstruction
Finance Corporation to make loans to banks, trust companies, building
and loan associations, insurance companies, mortgage loan companies,
federal land banks, credit unions, agricultural and livestock credit corporations, and, with the approval of the Interstate Commerce Commission, railroads. It could use funds to relieve banks closed or in process of
liquidation and could place funds at the disposal of the secretary of
agriculture for making loans to farmers. The RFC by mid-summer of
1932 had saved five thousand banks, besides hundreds of agricultural
credit companies, life insurance companies, and other financial institutions. So, in one direction or another, seventy million people had benefited directly.

Other measures the president placed before Congress in December
1931 were designed to fortify economic security, broaden the credit
structure and stimulate the revival of business and agriculture. These
measures were eventually passed by Congress, most of them substantially
in the form recommended by the president. Here, in summary form, was
the case for Hoover as he faced the campaign ahead.[38]

The president was well aware that his "leadership" *as portrayed by
the Democratic opposition* would be the issue. Furthermore, President

Hoover was not certain that he could count on the Republican organization to defend him. Some Republicans wished to make the party, rather than the president, the issue, on the assumption that, after all, there were more Republicans than Democrats in the country.

Representatives of eastern state political organizations that had been loyal to the Republican party in the preceding quarter century were not pleased with what had taken place at the convention, despite the overwhelming vote for the president on the first ballot. (There had been no such support of Hoover in the convention four years earlier, they recalled.)

The party soon revealed that it was still definitely divided into the units and blocs that had been evident in the preceding twenty-five years. A number of the more extreme representatives of the party did not participate in the 1932 convention. Other representatives of blocs— particularly in the West—were not disposed to accept the platform which emerged from the committee.

Conspicuous among those who did not support President Hoover for reelection was Senator George W. Norris of Nebraska. Early in the spring he stated that he did not support Hoover in the 1928 campaign because of Hoover's views on agriculture and on the conservation of natural resources. "President Hoover has opposed every method of farm relief for which the West has fought," stated Norris.[39] He felt that if the Democrats did not nominate a man like Governor Roosevelt, whom he could support, there should be a third party.[40] This view was shared by other western progressives.

Yet, if the Republican party were to win, it must meet the Democratic attack. The president would defend his record, and he would ask—in accepted party practice—that there be Republican control of the government to carry forward his plans for the future.[41]

Hoover's defense of his record was vigorous. His acceptance speech described the administration's response on behalf of the domestic economy to the repercussions of economic disaster abroad in the preceding year:

> Two courses were open. We might have done nothing. That would have been utter ruin. Instead, we met the situation with proposals to private business and the Congress in the most gigantic program of economic defense and counter-attack ever evolved in the history of the Republic. . . .
>
> Our measures have repelled these attacks of fear and panic. We have maintained the financial integrity of our government. We have cooperated to restore and stabilize the situation abroad. As a nation we have paid every dollar demanded of us. We have used the credit of the Government to aid and protect our institutions, public and private. We have provided methods

and assurances that there shall be none to suffer from hunger and cold. We
have instituted measures to assist farmers and home owners. We have
created vast agencies for employment. . . .

In a large sense the test of success of our program is simple. Our people,
while suffering great hardships, have been and will be cared for. In the long
view our institutions have been sustained intact and are now functioning
with increasing confidence in the future. As a nation we are undefeated and
unafraid. Government by the people has not been defiled.[42]

Neither the convention nor the platform it listlessly adopted were to
prove important in the ensuing campaign. The pressing economic issue
was to be personalized—vividly, repeatedly, and in imaginative rhetoric
by opposition politicians and publicists—focusing this attack on the figure
of Herbert Hoover.

Hoover's Program for the Future

We have known all along that, owing to the ravages of the world depression, our fight is a hard one; but we have a strong case and a right cause. Our task is to acquaint every man and woman in the country with the facts and issues which confront the nation.

In periods of emergency and stress, steadfast adherence to sound principles of government is indispensable to national security and a prerequisite to recovery in business, agriculture and employment. Adherence to these principles has saved the country during the last twelve months from all manner of destructive panaceas. This adherence and the measures and policies we have adopted have preserved these principles and laid the foundation for recovery.

My chief concern now is that the work of reconstruction shall go forward steadily and that the forces we have mobilized to that end, and which are beginning to prove effective, shall continue. This transcends all personal and partisan considerations.

Herbert Hoover to Everett Saunders,
September 13, 1932 (telegram), Hoover Library

President Hoover knew that the administration would have a hard fight in the presidential election of 1932 because of the economic situation. He felt that the Republican party had "a strong case and a right cause" and must proceed to acquaint every man and woman in the country with the facts and issues confronting the nation.

His chief concern, however, was that the work of reconstruction should go forward steadily, and that the forces mobilized to that end— which, he sensed, were beginning to prove effective—should continue. He felt that this transcended all personal and partisan considerations.

The challenge facing the president in his autumn campaign was expressed by Anne O'Hare McCormick when she wrote: "Campaign slogans, campaign issues, campaign promises interest us little. . . . Never were we more aware of America. Out of this anomaly grows the consciousness, still hardly more than a sub-consciousness, that we have in our hands the magnificent making of a new society, a really new economic era."[1]

In his formal acceptance of the nomination on August 11, 1932, President Hoover began by making what seemed a startling admission: "The past three years have been a time of unparalleled economic calamity. They have been years of greater suffering and hardship than any which have come to the American people since the aftermath of the Civil War."[2]

He reviewed the events of three years and gave clear meaning, as he saw it, to every move made by his administration—both emergency moves and those that had been most criticized. He outlined a program for future action which was, in truth, partaking of a "war" message. It was also a recital of the causes of the calamity and an enunciation of a program to insure victory in the continuing struggle to remove such causes.

The electorate, and particularly that portion representing finance and industry, appeared to give a favorable response, for the president could say at his press conference on August 12 that there had been the greatest flood of telegrams that had ever come into the White House. Election day, however, was months away.

On August 14, announcement was made of a business and industrial conference that would concentrate on measures for recovery. This conference met in Washington on August 26. A speeding up of federal construction proposals was announced on September 9. It was announced the following day that the budget estimates for government departments would be somewhat reduced. On September 15 a Relief Mobilization Conference was held at the White House. All of this was indicative of the measures taken by the executive at his own initiative to further the plans he had repeatedly discussed. He would meet crises primarily by the cooperative use of the economic units that constituted the economic structure of the nation.

Friends of the president had long urged upon him that his personal canvass for the presidency was a necessity in the critical situation he was facing. To them he had said early in the year that he needed all the help he could get,[3] and he had pointed out repeatedly that members of his cabinet, and in particular Secretary Stimson, might well present to the country their knowledge of the situation facing the administration. But only the president could speak with the necessary authority of both the economic situation of the nation and measures that had been taken to meet it. Indicative of the urgency of his duties, governmental and political, is the lack of any press conference record between September 13, 1932 and January 3, 1933.[4] Characteristic of the optimism with which he habitually addressed the press was the president's statement on September 13 of the prospect that the nation would have for the first time in some thirty years of agitation a complete plan for effective reorganization of the entire structure of the federal government.

That he was a candidate-in-office determined his position. The record of his administration, his declared policies, and his recommended measures, however sound, had to be defended. As James Truslow Adams reflected: "In 1928 we had been told we were within sight of perpetual prosperity and the abolition of poverty. By 1932 we seemed to see nothing but poverty and to be faced by stark ruin on every side. Few nations, if any, have ever had to drop with such appalling swiftness from superhuman hopes to blank despair."[5]

Hoover continued to point out that the financial crisis had brought upon him, as president, the need to formulate a program which would meet the "emergencies," domestic and foreign. It was commonly asserted that, had anyone else been president, Hoover would have been the one man who would have been summoned to handle the situation when the cycle of economic breakdown, an inevitable result of war inflation, reached our own country. A great number held this view, and their number was to increase with the passage of years.

Senator Fess, ever a party stalwart, provided a setting for the campaign with a speech on September 19. He then reported back to Hoover with a summary of his points:

> Had anyone else been President, Mr. Hoover would have been the one man who would have been summoned to handle the situation (when the cycle of the economic breakdown, an inevitable result of war inflation, reached our own country . . .). . . . The President outlined a twelve-point program of rehabilitation . . . more comprehensive . . . than all the proposals enacted since the Civil War up to 1931. It is the composite judgment of the best thought of America touching each major subject. While it is properly the handiwork of the President, it is the result of the widest consultation of what in English Parliamentary language would be known as 'front bench' ability.[6]

By late September it was clear that the presidential campaign was to be in its final stages one of emotional intensity. Never before had so vast an electorate been asked to reconsider so emphatic a decision as they had made in 1928.[7]

Political campaigns are always characterized by extreme charges and extreme promises. Organization workers stress parochial appeals and emphasize personal deficiencies and weaknesses. The greatest deterrent to the hope of President Hoover for a discussion and consideration of the great issues facing the nation was the ready response of people to familiar propaganda by Democratic and insurgent Republican campaigners.

The Democrats were filled with eager hope built upon the economic struggle in all of its aspects, and they also recalled the campaign of 1912 (with its disastrous Republican division) and of twenty years before that. Their mood was exultant. All the national distresses and uncertainties could not change that fact. There would not, indeed, be a separate party effort led by a former Republican president, as in 1912, but they knew very well the depths of insurgent disaffection in the early 1930s. And they remembered full well their own party dismemberment in 1924.

President Hoover believed members of the cabinet should answer charges made against the administration by the Democratic candidate. They were asked to do so.

Secretary Stimson felt that it would be wise for him to give a major address in the East on foreign relations. This address, delivered in Philadelphia on October 1, was a survey of the foreign policy of the administration and included, as well, a glowing tribute to President Hoover as Stimson had come to know him during his term as Secretary of State:

> His is a keen and ever-ready power of analysis. His is a well poised and balanced intelligence. Behind those qualities is the most unceasing mental energy with which I have ever come in contact. And again behind that, although they are shy and never paraded in official discussions, lies the guidance of the human sympathies of one of the most sensitive and tender natures which has ever wielded such official power.[8]

In early October the President began a series of speeches that ended only with his final appeal read from his train crossing the Nevada desert on his way to his home in Palo Alto, where he was to cast his vote on election day.

At first, Hoover was inclined to make his first campaign speech at West Branch, Iowa, where he was born. He decided to speak instead at Des Moines on October 4 because of the better facilities there for accommodating large crowds as well as for national radio broadcast of his address.[9] His welcome at Des Moines surpassed all expectations of his associates.

The president was outspoken about his belief that the electorate could understand the situation of the administration only in part, for the day-to-day pressures of office could not be known to them. He sought to lead his fellow citizens to lift their eyes beyond the *immediate* situation in any case. In his Des Moines address he said:

Something infinitely deeper and of greater portent has happened to the world than any reaction from our own reckless speculation and exploitation. We are contending today with forces at home and abroad which still threaten the safety of civilization. . . . The shocks of this earthquake ran from Vienna to Berlin, from Berlin to London, from London to Asia and South America. From all those countries they came to this country, to every city and farm in the United States.[10]

The dangers, as he saw them, lurked in (*a*) a steady strangulation of credit, the lifeblood of business; (*b*) a falling off of government revenue; and (*c*) the threat to the gold standard that protected alike those with savings and those who were in debt.

Going off the gold standard is no academic matter. . . . A considerable part of farm mortgages, most of our industrial [bonds] and all of our Government, most of our state and municipal bonds, and most other long-term obligations are written as payable in gold. This is not the case in foreign countries. They have no such practice, their obligations are written in currency. When they abandon the gold standard . . . the relations of their domestic debtors and creditors are unchanged, because both he who pays and he who receives use the same medium.[11]

Of the financial policy of his administration, he said:

We determined we would stand up like men and render the credit of the United States Government impregnable through the drastic reduction of Government expenditures and increased revenues until we balanced our budget. We determined that if necessary we should lend the full credit of the Government thus made impregnable, to aid private institutions to protect the debtor and the savings of our people.

Of the Democratic attempt in Congress to create a "rubber dollar" at one point and to make the government "the most gigantic pawnbroker of history," Hoover said, "Had their program passed, it would have been the end of recovery," and he added:

These measures were not simply gestures of vote-catching. These ideas and measures represented the true sentiments and doctrines of the majority of the control of the Democratic party. A small minority of Democratic members disapproved these measures, but these men obviously have no voice today.

The president reminded his hearers that in all of the efforts of the administration to meet succeeding crises, there had been "the constant difficulty of translating the daily action into terms of public understanding," for:

The forces in motion have been so gigantic, so complex in their character, the instrumentalities and actions we must undertake to deal with them are so involved, the figures we must use are so astronomical as to seem to have but little relation to the family in the apartment, the cottage, or on the farm.

He added that of necessity many of "these battles" had to be fought in silence "because the very disclosure of the forces opposed to us would have undermined the courage of the weak and induced panic in the timid, which would have destroyed the very basis of success."[12]

Of course, there had been "hideous misrepresentation and unjustified complaint" which had to be borne in silence. "It was as if a great battle in war should be fought," said the president, "without public knowledge of any incident except the stream of dead and wounded from the front."

He included a twelve-point program for the relief of agriculture:[13]

1. Protective tariff
2. Farm Board
3. Diversion of unprofitable lands to profitable use
4. Completion of the inland waterway system
5. Credit provisions for drought-afflicted farmers
6. Readjustment of land taxes
7. Facilitation of credit for short-term loans, through the Reconstruction Finance Corporation, Intermediate Credit Banks, and ten new Agricultural Credit Institutions, for planting, harvesting, and feeding livestock.
8. Credit through the Reconstruction Finance Corporation for agricultural processors to carry their stocks and to sell farm products abroad
9. Easing of farm mortgages through extension of capital of Federal Land Banks
10. Aid to the credit structure of other nations
11. Use of foreign debt payments for the purpose of securing expansion of foreign markets for American agriculture
12. Advancement of agricultural prices through the halting and reversal of the process of deflation

In short, the president talked basic economics under cover of the format of partisan politics. Much of this program anticipated measures subsequently carried through by the Congresses of the late 1930s and by Hoover's successor in office.

There were to be six major speeches in a very brief time. The president recognized that he had to meet the extreme charges of the opposing candidate, Governor Roosevelt.[14] On the whole, Hoover dealt with economics and not with politics. He continued to deal with economic beliefs, economic proposals of both sides, and economic fallacies of the Democratic program as he saw it. It was here that the president displayed more faith in the intelligence of the American people than shrewdness in appraising their limitations. His educational program in economics was beyond their understanding at the time. Furthermore, the majority of the electorate, if not Democratic by persuasion in October of 1932, was certainly disposed to feel and think in terms of politics rather than economics, with consequent advantage to the Democratic cause.

Yet, especially in his address in Cleveland on October 15, 1932, the president relied upon the desire of his audience to understand. He attempted to reach them by dealing directly with *economic* problems as he spoke on the subject of "Unemployment and Wage and Salary Earners." He consistently felt that the Democratic explanation of the economic situation, as well as the proposed Democratic solution, was *political*. It was. And this was, to say the least, a political campaign.

In the course of his journey to Detroit, which was felt by party leaders to be the crucial tour of the campaign, the president's train stopped many times en route to permit him to speak to cheering crowds. When he arrived at the Union Station in Detroit, however, several hundred apparently unemployed persons carrying banners booed and chanted, "We want bonus. Down with Hoover." Nevertheless, Hoover was welcomed shortly in an arena by a crowd of 25,000 persons who gave him a prolonged ovation.

It was in his speech in Detroit, on October 22, that he devoted much time to answering the allegations of Governor Roosevelt with reference to federal budgeting and economy. He challenged Roosevelt on his "promise" to reduce federal expenditures by $1 billion a year, for, said Hoover, "His promised saving of a billion dollars has already been accomplished, even though we are still struggling with expenditures forced upon us by the Democratic House. . . . If we are supported by the American people and if the Democratic House will cooperate, I will make for the next fiscal year a reduction from the totals of 1932, not of a billion but of $1,500,000,000."

After his trip to Detroit, the president decided upon a whirlwind finish for his campaign that would carry him to New York, New Jersey, and finally to San Francisco. The most important of these addresses was to be given at Madison Square Garden, New York City.

Constantly the emotional currents on Prohibition appeared in public meetings in the East and in the Middle West. Particularly was it true of the New York audience! The president had been urged to discuss the issue. He refused, saying that he had nothing to add to his statement in his campaign acceptance speech. He wanted to deal with issues that transcended all other issues that had appeared four years earlier. Yet many felt that the New York address failed of its objective.

Hoover there characterized the campaign as "a contest between two philosophies of government." He reminded his audiences that during a series of "abnormal shocks during the past three years . . . our system of government has enabled us to take such strong action as to prevent the disaster which would otherwise have come to our Nation."

He feared that the changes proposed by the opposing party would destroy "the very foundations of our American system." He described his own conception of this American system of government, of social and economic life. (It was, perhaps, one of the best of his expositions of his basic point of view.)

> It is a system peculiar to the American people. It differs essentially from all others in the world. . . .
>
> It is by the maintenance of opportunity and therefore of a society absolutely fluid in freedom of the movement of its human particles that our individualism departs from the individualism of Europe. . . .
>
> This freedom of the individual creates of itself the necessity and the cheerful willingness of men to act cooperatively in a thousand ways and for every purpose as occasion arisies; and it permits such voluntary cooperations to be dissolved as soon as they have served their purpose, to be replaced by new voluntary associations for new purposes.
>
> There has thus grown within us, to gigantic importance, a new conception. That is, this voluntary cooperation within the community. Cooperation to perfect the social organization; cooperation for the care of those in distress; cooperation for the advancement of knowledge, of scientific research, of education; for cooperative action in the advancement of many phases of economic life. This is self-government by the people outside of Government. . . .[15]

It was in his address in New York that the president took up in detail one of Governor Roosevelt's proposals, public works, only to emphasize how this device had been effectively used by his own administration. But of Roosevelt's proposal to "provide employment for all surplus labor at all times" through public works, President Hoover said bluntly: "I protest against such frivolous promises being held out to a suffering people. It is easily demonstrable that no such employment can be found."[16]

Of Roosevelt's statement that "after March 4, 1929, the Republican Party was in complete control of all the instrumentalities of the Government—Executive, Senate, and House, and, I may add for good measure, in order to make it complete, the Supreme Court as well," Hoover inquired, "But is the Democratic candidate really proposing his conception of the relation of the Executive and the Supreme Court? If this is his idea, he is proposing the most revolutionary new deal, the most stupendous breaking of precedent, the most destructive undermining of the very safeguard of our form of government yet proposed by a presidential candidate."[17]

It was the Democratic candidate's apparent concept of the position in history reached by the American people that shocked the president as much as anything his opponent had said. Governor Roosevelt, in referring to the disappearance of the frontier of free land, had conceived of the American industrial plant as already built and said: "Our task now is not discovery or exploitation of natural resources, or necessarily producing more goods. It is the somberer, less dramatic business of administering resources and plants already in hand, . . . of distributing wealth and products more equitably, of adapting existing economic organizations to the service of the people."[18] To this Hoover replied:

> . . . I do challenge the whole idea that we have ended the advance of America, that this country has reached the zenith of its power, the height of its development. . . . I deny that the promise of American life has been fulfilled, for that means we have begun the decline and fall. No nation can cease to move forward without degeneration of spirit.[19]

Here was an historic clash of ideas indeed!

Hoover's attack was directed at the Democratic program when he elaborated his criticism:

> What Governor Roosevelt has overlooked is the fact that we are yet but on the frontiers of development of science, and of invention. I have only to remind you that discoveries in electricity, the internal-combustion engine, the radio—all of which have sprung into being since our land was settled—have in themselves represented the greatest advances in America. This philosophy upon which the Governor of New York proposes to conduct the Presidency of the United States is the philosophy of stagnation, of despair.[20]

The president, in the closing week of the campaign, also referred to

Senators Norris, LaFollette, Cutting, Wheeler, and Huey Long as exponents "of a social philosophy different from the traditional American
one." And, said Hoover, "Unless these men feel assurance of support to
their ideas they certainly would not be supporting . . . the Democratic
party.[21]

Refraining, as usual, from revealing unnecessarily any fear-provoking
news, the president warned in an address delivered in St. Paul, Minnesota on November 5 that "a change at this election must mean four whole
months in which there can be no definition of national policy."[22] Hoover
knew that, despite recent indications of an upward movement in industry,
economic recovery would be set back by a change of administrations. He
could scarcely have foreseen the whole tragic story of the forthcoming
"interregnum," although he said, "We have seen the very measures we
have taken for defense of our people and reconstruction of recovery subjected to the cheapest political misrepresentation." At St. Paul, as happens
sooner or later to all who labor too hard and too long, Hoover was "out
on his feet." Joslin found the radio delivery halting and without emphasis,
while the voice was tired.[23]

Small wonder. At the time, en route to Peoria and St. Louis on
November 4, the president had heard from Henry M. Robinson that the
British had warned that unless financial aid came from the United States
to England as the "financial clearing house of Europe . . . there would be
chaos and the whole world would suffer." Robinson reminded the president that he had stated "that this country is nearing the time when it
must cease to carry the economic burden of Europe except through
charity and the ordinary business process set up under proper security."[24]
At St. Paul, the President emphasized favorable news:

> Hoarded currency continues to return; imports of gold withdrawn by
> frightened European holders have continued to increase; deposits of banks
> continue to show steady expansion. In four months they have increased by
> nearly a billion dollars. This is money being put to work and an evidence
> of renewed confidence. A further indication of the upward movement of
> industry lies in the increased demand for electrical power, which has in-
> creased by over 8 per cent in the last four months. Every business index
> shows some progress somewhere in the Nation.[25]

It was at Elko, Nevada, that Hoover made his last-minute radio
appeal. The telephone connection was bad, the lighting poor, the podium
too small, and the manuscript fell on the floor and became scrambled.[26]
But the ideas were strong:

> In the longer view our problems are the questions that the world should

have peace; that the prosperity of the Nation shall be diffused to all; that we shall build more strongly the ideal of equal opportunity for all our people.[27]

As the campaign closed, it was clear that the dominant question had become a simple, personal one: Shall Herbert Hoover be returned to the White House for a second term? As if meeting this challenge, Hoover had prescribed his program for the American people: what he, as president, had done and what he as a leader—if chosen again—would do. Yet this sharpening of the issue, and Hoover's acceptance of it, was unfair to him. It was not the whole story.

The chief executive had made clear by his performance that his leadership could not be associated with the leadership of his immediate predecessors, nor with the overall leadership of the Republican party in the previous thirty years, that is to say, in the twentieth century.[28] His leadership, he had insisted from the moment he took office, was to provide a "New Day," because, unlike his immediate predecessors, Hoover had planned and urged a program to meet the needs of the American people in the new age in which they found themselves in this century.

Thus, in the end in 1932, despite all of his partisan defense of Republicans and much of their party's record, he had essentially an independent *personal* program as he sought reelection. Alert Americans—realists in politics—knew that no president could succeed without an extensive and like-minded party. The logic of this proposition led to the inevitable conclusion that Hoover must be displaced. Many, nevertheless, particularly women and those deeply devoted to voluntary methods, still retained their faith in Hoover as person and symbol. The decision would be made at the polls, however, without reliance on subtleties, for stereotypes were common.

Had the American people as a whole ever suffered invasion by foreign armies or experienced the privations of war in their midst (as the people of the southern states had), it would have been easier for them to realize why their view of the humanitarian Hoover of the war years was not their present view of Hoover. As one who had looked into the faces of starving millions in Europe, Hoover had insisted that extreme conditions of such a nature did not obtain in the United States of 1929–1933; and that in a peaceful country, unoccupied by alien forces, there was still ample opportunity for the slow working out of salvation with the full help of the people themselves. It was a question of degree.

The president saw the implications of the international economic situation at the time. He felt that the possible implications of it, that is, peace or war, were too ominous for the people to debate in the political arena during the fall of 1932. It is doubtful that they would have responded to any more vivid description of the plight of the economic world abroad—in Great Britain, or in Germany—than he chose to give them. For they did not understand their own economic crisis that was all around them.

Accordingly, the people's response to the campaign was born of more than a century of self-government conducted in the traditional American way. They insisted upon a political routine that bore faint resemblance to the needs of the day. Republicans of various persuasions ran helter-skelter before the storm. The Democrats were out to win. (The Socialists cried out but were given little attention.) Domestic Communists were vocal but impotent. The revolution abroad, meanwhile, was shaping around the forces of violence. In the United States, another kind of momentous change was shaping around the election of 1932.

— 19 —

Revolution by Election

I am a believer in party government. It is only through party organization that our people can give coherent expression to their views on great issues. There is no other way except by revolution, and we in America have ordained that the ballot shall be used for peaceful determination, not violence.

Herbert Hoover, Address at Elko, Nevada,
November 7, 1932

As late as mid-October, the *Literary Digest*, as a result of its preelection poll, found it possible to announce in a headline that "Roosevelt Leads, But It's Anybody's Race Yet."[1] A careful analyst of "straw polls" declared that an examination of all important polls led to the conclusion that the Democrats were remaining within their party; that Republicans were deserting "in droves"; and that political precedents were everywhere upset.[2]

For its part, the Republican National Committee was torn by dissension throughout the campaign. That its New York office was in a state of complete disorganization appears clearly in the committee files for the campaign. Evidence of despondency, of dependence upon volunteers rather than upon paid workers, and over-reliance upon the president's campaign speeches is unmistakable. Some stalwart workers of 1928, especially William H. Hill of New York State, were sorely missed.[3] Insuperable difficulties arose as the campaign neared the end. Evidence of failure to present a fighting front could not in any way be kept from the president.

His most ardent admirers acted valiantly to bring some order out of the chaos of conflicting views expressed by representatives from different parts of the country.

Within the Republican organization, Silas Strawn, a Chicago banker, was the western campaign manager and worked with Jeremiah Milbank, a Wall Street financier, and an eastern manager. An executive committee of fifteen elected at the meeting of the national committee in June had the power to represent the committee in the campaign.[4] But an inner group working closely with the president included Ogden Mills, Walter Brown, and Everett Saunders.

Despite all of Hoover's campaigning, he was unable to change greatly the picture that had been gradually developing in the minds of masses of Americans. He not only had signed the Tariff Bill passed by a Republican congress, but he had defended it. The Republican National Committee, which presumably thought it was acting at least in sympathy with Hoover's desires, fell to denouncing liberals as Socialists. Former President Coolidge, who by this time had become in some quarters the symbol of reaction, praised President Hoover in magazine article and speech, but this was not helpful. And on the troublesome question of the repeal of Prohibition, the president's position was not understood. An opportunity to make it better understood through insertion of carefully worded material into the Madison Square Garden speech was lost when those with the paragraphs were delayed in traffic on their way to the speech. In capsulized form, the president said to Joslin privately and no doubt grimly, "I'll tell you what the trouble is. We are opposed by 6,000,000 unemployed, 10,000 bonus marchers, and ten-cent corn. Is it any wonder that the prospects are dark? Is there any cause for surprise that we must give every ounce of strength, every one of us, to win?"[5]

In these circumstances, many of the great number of independents who supported him in 1928 could not be expected to continue their support in 1932. Despite anything the president might say or do, he was to be identified with "reaction." Roosevelt's carefully planned campaign of criticism weakened Hoover's presentation of himself as the liberal-minded, forward-looking, progressive candidate he seemed to be in 1928. Furthermore, the Hoover tactic of pointing out the fatal economic consequences of direct relief policies which millions dearly desired to try, was, to say the least, unpersuasive politics.

The greatest weakness of the incumbent's campaign, irrespective of the merit it had in theory and in courage, lay in the fact that the country was now predisposed to change. In retrospect it was thought significant that millions of voters who were radically inclined voted for Franklin Roosevelt rather than for the Socialist candidate, Norman Thomas; yet the latter was able to poll over three-fourths of a million votes (certainly a major disappointment to him). A National Progressive League formed on September 26, 1932 to aid Roosevelt won widespread support among Progressives of long standing.

In estimating the weakness of Hoover's appeal to the electorate at the time, attention must be given to the attitude of three members of the president's own party who did not support him: Borah, Johnson, and Norris. Their periodic opposition to policies identified with the president had become familiar to everyone. Johnson's clearly was a personal antagonism, because he was on the whole "regular" in his voting in the Senate. Norris's opposition rested on differences in policy exemplified by the issue of public versus private electric power development. Borah's opposition seems to have been more complex. To a considerable extent, in the minds of many, he had been useful in the election majorities of candidate Hoover in 1928, and yet he later opposed the president on almost every major issue: on methods of enforcement of Prohibition, on modification of the tariff, on measures for farm relief, and on conduct of foreign relations.

Millions of Americans had come to believe that each of these men possessed deep interest in the welfare of the people. Each in his own way—this was especially true of Norris—appealed strongly to a great element in the population who (in 1912, 1924, and later) were convinced that, on the whole, the government in Washington under either Democrats or Republicans had become dominated by private financial interests. Thus, the growing opposition of Borah, Johnson, and Norris to the president prepared many of their fellow Republicans—and of course many independents—to believe that the insurgents were right and that Hoover was wrong.

Yet careful distinctions may be made. Norris's opposition was that of the habitual breaker of party traditions. He had long been satisfactory to the voters of Nebraska. That to him was sufficient. Borah had found much in Hoover's early career and programs that appealed to him, and throughout the administration (until near the end) Borah endeavored in his own way to cooperate with the president. In turn, the president, whereas he had no reason and certainly no inclination to bring Johnson or Norris to his point of view, tried by every means known to work with Borah on each question that arose. This was true of Prohibition, farm relief, legislation on the tariff, and foreign relations, especially the issues of naval limitations, the World Court, and Far Eastern policy.

In historical perspective, it appears that, in terms of uncertainty and doubt, the political activities of Senator Johnson during this period were least important and the activities of Senator Borah most productive. But in bringing American political development to the point of revolutionary change, the activities of Senator Norris were doubtless the most influential. Norris came to represent a widely diffused attitude of Americans toward leaders in political as well as economic life.[6]

Had there not been increasing reason to substantiate this attitude throughout the period of the Hoover administration, it is extremely doubtful that the political situation would have appeared to most "independent" Americans as it did in November 1932. Johnson easily could have been disregarded as one who had been a rival in California politics; indeed, late in the campaign, twelve of the original leaders of the Lincoln-Roosevelt (Republican) League, which spearheaded the Progressive movement in California in 1912, issued a statement urging the reelection of President Hoover. This was a reply to Senator Johnson's attack upon Hoover.[7] Again, Borah's frequent disagreements could have been disregarded as those of one who had tried unsuccessfully to agree with the president, although it was not generally known how vigorous were the president's efforts to bring Borah to support the ticket. But Norris represented an opposition that was positive, continuous, and most effective in reaching masses of Americans who were deeply concerned about the charges made in the past quarter of a century against the Republican party.

The pressure on Senator Borah continued not only in the national headquarters but in Idaho. In late October it was again suggested that a personal representative of the president be sent to see Borah at his western home. Hundreds of letters poured in to Borah, including those of many "dry" organizations. To an appeal from Chairman Saunders of the Republican National Committee, Borah wired from Walla Walla, Washington, on November 4, 1932: "After consultation and reflection feel it impracticable to comply with your suggestion."[8]

Borah's refusal to campaign for Hoover was symbolic of the breakdown of party government at this time, because both had believed in the victory of 1928 and had conferred repeatedly in the course of the administration.

Other outstanding Republican leaders of national reputation and experience did not support the president. Frank Lowden was especially conspicuous. He was a personal friend of Franklin D. Roosevelt, and his disagreement with Hoover on farm policy was well known. Lowden declined to address the delegates at the opening session of the Republican National Convention in Chicago on June 14, although he finally consented to sit on the platform. At the close of the Democratic National Convention, Lowden wired his congratulations to Roosevelt. During the summer and autumn, the Republicans tried repeatedly to persuade him to come out publicly for Hoover, but he even refused to sit on the same platform with Hoover at the rally at Des Moines.[9]

In his campaigning, President Hoover made his record the outstanding issue. He refused to back away from the tariff issue.[10] He felt—and many of his closest friends and advisers agreed with him—that only in this way was there a chance of bringing a majority of voters to the Republican ticket. But this personal campaigning was precisely what the Democratic candidate and his closest advisers felt was the surest way of insuring a Democratic victory. Their argument was simple. There were in the nation more traditional Republican voters than Democratic voters, but in this campaign few Democratic votes would be lost because of their party's nominee or the nature of his record or his campaign. A great number of progressive Republican votes could be won. On the whole, liberals of independent view would vote the Democratic ticket. A protest vote was certain to be a vote for the Democratic party because the Socialist appeal—in pragmatic terms—did not fit their mood. There could be no true "victory" there. Inasmuch as driving power in an aggressive Republican organization was lacking, Hoover as *the issue* could not but result in his repudiation.

The dreary story of the continuing determination of some elements in the Democratic party to smear Hoover need not be recounted here. A specialist has concluded, ". . . he was politically destroyed in the campaign of 1932, when the Democrats made his name a synonym for depression, misery, and blind reaction. Indeed, political smear in the 1932 campaign was largely defamation of Hoover as callous, indifferent, heedlessly helpless against the ravages of the great Depression."[11] And the memory was made to linger on: "The long-memoried Democrats were never tired of invoking the bogeyman of another Hooverian depression if the Republicans should return to power."[12]

Nor need one linger over the question of who was to be benefited by the Michelson campaign. One reads in oral history memoirs the firm conjectures that John J. Raskob paid a million dollars for such purposes, with the goal the eventual renomination of Al Smith. And it is alleged that many years later Raskob sought to mend fences with the former president. In any case, it is recalled that Hoover later enjoyed referring to a dragon face on one of his famous blue-and-white China vases as Charlie Michelson.[13]

The vote cast for the presidential ticket, compared with that cast for congressional candidates,[14] would seem to indicate that the president's personal campaign had won votes, and that a portion of the public did recognize that the administration had made an impressive record during the depression. (Subsequent elections were to reinforce this view.)

The size of the voting shift in the period of four years, 1928–1932, was significant. Herbert Hoover, who had won in 1928 with 58.12 percent of the total vote of the nation had in 1932 only 39.66 percent, and Franklin D. Roosevelt won with 57.4 percent of the total vote. Moreover, the Democratic candidate won majorities in every one of the nine sections of the country. He carried 2,721 counties; Hoover carried only 372. The greatest shift was revealed in this county vote. Four years earlier Hoover had carried 2,172 counties; 912 were carried by the Democratic candidate, Alfred E. Smith.[15]

The great vote cast for Hoover and the fact that in only one section of the nation (west South Central) did the president have less than a half million votes, and in only three states outside of the South less than 50,000 votes, made it clear that the nation remained a two-party electorate, and that everywhere, despite the triumph of the Democrats, a party membership existed which was devoted neither to the incoming administration nor to the Socialists or other third parties. This must be noted and stressed, for it has been all too customary in classrooms and general accounts to refer dramatically to the repudiation by "the people" of Hoover and his party.[16]

Hoover had finished strong with his autumn campaign, and some partisans could not believe the results. Frank Kellogg wrote the following to William R. Castle: "I have been so stunned by the election that I haven't had any disposition to write to anybody. The President made a splendid speech in St. Paul, had a wonderful reception, the Auditorium was packed for a couple of hours before he spoke and thousands were turned away. However, it was of no use. Nobody could have been elected on the Republican ticket this year. Depression and beer swamped us absolutely."[17]

The "other" vote, cast for various parties, was a smaller percentage of the total (2.9 percent) than it had been in any election in the twentieth century except in 1902 and 1928. The leading candidate, Norman Thomas, had only 872,840 votes.

The Communist Party considered the election "historic" because of the inroads made in public support from "intellectuals." "The League of Professional Groups for Foster and Ford" numbered such persons as Sherwood Anderson, Malcolm Cowley, John Dos Passos, Edmund Wilson, Lincoln Steffens, Theodore Dreiser, and Waldo Frank. These saw culture in a "crisis." William Z. Foster delivered seventy addresses in the campaign before falling ill.[18]

As for various divisions of support in the campaign, it is estimated that from 60 to 65 percent of the nation's newspapers supported Hoover.[19] The Republicans were broke well before the end of the campaign, but they spent $2,952,000, while the Democrats spent $2,245,975. The use of the radio was more extensive than ever before, and the Republicans reported that their expenses for air time were double those of 1928. It was also the first presidential campaign in which "talking moving pictures" were extensively used.

Although the president came from the West, it was the West, that is, the Mountain and Pacific states, that provided the insurgent Republicans who contributed so much to Hoover's election failure. The West did not by any means determine the winner of the election. It possessed a total of 88 electoral votes; had they all gone to Hoover, he would have received 147 electoral votes—far short of the 266 required to win. The West, however, went Democratic at the level of the county vote as it had never done before. Of 664 counties in the West in 1932, Roosevelt carried all but 18. Hoover did not carry a single county in Texas (west South Central), Arizona, Nevada, or Washington. He carried only one county each in Montana, Idaho, Wyoming, Oregon, and his own state of California.

In the outcome of the election of 1932 appears ample evidence of the results of the factional fight within the ranks of the Republican party which began in May 1929. There was no such split in the Republican party as had led to Theodore Roosevelt's candidacy in 1912, nor was there an independent candidacy like that of LaFollette in 1924. Yet, by deserting Hoover, the insurgent Republicans helped to produce the same *result* in 1932 as was achieved in 1912, that is, the decisive election of the Democratic candidate.

The dominant factor in the election was the loss of popular morale caused by the long, continuing depression. Furthermore, in seeing the causes of the depression as world-wide, Hoover was not winning friends from the isolationists, but losing them to Roosevelt. It was far easier to think with Roosevelt that the depression was "national" and could be met by national means. This fit the prevailing mood of fear of outside forces in American life.

The American people were not in a mood for a great decision. They wished to keep their American dream and to eliminate from office those who failed to realize it. Secretary Wilbur had explained the situation that bothered commentators who perhaps yearned for quieter days, now gone, when he said to the Young Republicans of New Jersey at Atlantic City on January 16, 1932: "We are attempting to operate the greatest economic and social mechanism in the history of man with machinery devised largely for an agricultural civilization in which most of our citizens were assured of food. Now we have more people living on the payroll than on the land."[20]

In the election of 1932 certain elements were brought to judgment in the vote. The first issue was, of course, the president himself—there was no doubt about that. Alert people knew perfectly well that the Republican party organization had failed. At the same time, it was generally believed that the Democratic party organization was at best a very ineffective instrument for dealing with the problems that pressed upon the country.

It certainly was true that great numbers of voters were led to cast their ballots with their eyes upon not only the Democratic candidate and the Democratic platform, but also those declarations of the Democrats during the previous twenty years that symbolized the "good of the masses." This was an excellent context in which to argue for change.

On October 31 Hoover spoke directly to voters about this point of view in one major address of the campaign, when he said:

> My countrymen, the proposals of our opponents represent a profound change in American life . . . a radical departure from the foundations of 150 years which have made this the greatest nation in the world. This election means . . . deciding the direction our Nation will take over a century to come.[21]

In this election, as in no other for a generation, the voters had been asked by their president to deal directly with the problem of economics in government. Yet it cannot be said that a considerable number of the voters who went to the polls dealt with the problem of economics as it had been presented to them in campaign utterance as well as in legislative enactment and in party proposal.

The voters decided that the Democratic candidates for office, backed in most cases by the Democratic organization, should be placed in office. What the Democratic president and his Democratic majorities would do with the vote of the people was unknown. It was realized that the Democratic president, supported by party majorities in the Congress, would have a program unlike the program proposed by the Republican president and not supported by all of that party. The Democratic program would be "different." But a Democratic program with the definiteness of the Socialist program, for example, did not exist.

One certainty appeared. The program of the Democratic party would be a program on "behalf of the people" and this, when further interpreted, meant that it would not be favorable to big business. It would be favorable to those factions in the population—industry, labor, and farming—who represented the smaller units or the smaller operators: the "little men" all over the country.

There was, obviously, a feeling of "revolution" in this American election of 1932: the people were said to have voted to take control of the government out of the hands of those who seemed to represent the privileged few. This was the interpretation generally given by political figures at the time. But it was *a revolution by election*, and the American people were merely embarking on a new course of action in government as they often had since 1800.

Yet it must be emphasized that in the period 1929–1933 Hoover had presented himself as a leader with a program for a new day. Although there was ample expression by him to the effect that what had been done in the past by Americans was good, nevertheless he would offer a program that embodied powerful and fundamental new steps toward a new age.

This Hoover leadership had not won the support of a majority of the members of Congress, and it had not won the support of a majority of the leaders of his own party. Consequently, it perhaps was not to be expected that his leadership would at the time win the support of a majority of the people of the United States in a general national election. "One doesn't need further perspective upon the election to realize how inevitably the American people would misunderstand their president," reminded William Allen White, "and how easy it would be for a well-oiled partisan strafing machine to spread poison against him in the hearts and minds of the multitude."

Hoover himself had foreseen the possible consequences of the astonishing admiration the people had for him in times of prosperity. While sitting before the fire in a Miami, Florida residence he told a newsman in early 1929:

> I have no dread of the ordinary work of the Presidency. What I do fear is the result of the exaggerated idea the people have conceived of me. They have a conviction that I am a sort of superman, that no problem is beyond my capacity. Now, of course, that is not true of me, or of any other man. If some unprecedented calamity should come upon the nation, something with which no one could successfully cope, I would be sacrificed to the unreasoning disappointment of a people who had expected too much.[22]

The prediction was uncanny, for the people were in no way interested in rewarding faithful or even exceptional performance; they wanted an end to the depression—nothing less.

Hoover arrived in San Francisco on November 8, and proceeded by motor to his home on the Stanford University campus, which he had not visited since his departure for South America following the election of 1928. A friend who knew him well recalls, "I never saw a man look so shaken and so white and so overwhelmed as he did when he got out of the automobile down here on the campus."[23] He and Mrs. Hoover voted in the late morning and in the evening awaited the election returns with a group of friends at their home.

It was there that he received the news of his overwhelming defeat. He walked from group to group, thanking them. Then he put his arms about two of the faculty wives and said, "Well, life is still worth living with friends like this."[24] Mrs. Hoover simply said, "Well, it's all over and we'll go to bed."[25]

At 9:17 P.M. (Pacific time) Herbert Hoover sent his victorious opponent the following telegram: "I congratulate you on the opportunity that has come to you to be of service to the country and I wish for you a most successful administration. In the common purpose of all of us I shall dedicate myself to every possible helpful effort." To his message, he received the following reply: "I appreciate your generous telegram for the immediate as well as for the more distant future. I join in your gracious expression of a common purpose in helpful effort for our country."[26] The amenities in a democratic society had been fulfilled. Privately, Hoover's thoughts must have been on his repudiation by the electorate, for he said ruefully at one point, "Democracy is not a polite employer."[27] In retrospect, he told his niece to stick to her principles, and she would accomplish a lot—but don't expect any appreciation.[28] Also in retrospect, he said that as early as April he knew he would lose: "I couldn't be a coward and run out and throw the burden onto someone else. There is just nothing you can do under such circumstances, except to run again."[29]

That Hoover failed in the election of 1932 simply because of the depression is not necessarily true. But it is common gospel. Had he had a party that supported him in his program, or if he had been willing to modify that program in substantial ways (favoring outright repeal of Prohibition and supporting a "dole" in some form), he might have weathered the storm. Whether or not any president or party, meeting such an overthrow of hopes as did this party and president, could have won the sustained support of the people is very doubtful, of course, but this certainly must be said: Hoover did not lose the election of 1932 because he had been without a program or because he had failed to be constructive in those portions of his program that managed to be enacted into law.

The general mood of the two parties at the end of the campaign reflected, on one hand, the conservative policy that had governed America for the most part throughout a half-century. On the other hand, there was the emotional fervor of those who, during the same period, had protested over much that was done in Washington. Facing the most serious defeat that had come to them in their history and having feared for months that it was coming, the Republican organization was disillusioned and without hope to an extent unknown in national party circles since the defeat of the Democratic party in 1904. The president, however, had no time for disillusionment, and he found it difficult to understand the full reality of his defeat when it finally came.

The general conclusion of the day was that Herbert Hoover and his leadership had been repudiated. In the longer view, the vote of 1932 was also a repudiation of many of the practices associated with Republican administration of the government. To millions of citizens it was a repudiation of the view that the country was best governed by those who constituted the financial and industrial power of the nation.

"Herbert Hoover ought to be remembered for his abilities, his successes as well as his failures," was the editorial comment of the *New York Times*. *"Through all the great crisis he certainly displayed great qualities. No President ever worked harder in the hope of helping the people to escape from their troubles. Into his coming retirement the American people will follow him with respect. They will regret that he fell upon evil days wherein his usual powers could not be rightfully appreciated or made completely effective."*[30] But the *Nation* rejoiced at the retirement of Hoover, whom they saw as a "complete failure." The vote had been *against* Hoover; not *for* Roosevelt.[31] The *New Republic* concurred: "All informed observers agree that the country did not vote for Roosevelt; it voted against Hoover."[32] Yet the incoming president would be dodging issues just as the old one had, thought the *New Republic*.[33] Here, then, was the view of liberals of that day.

William Allen White commented in *The Emporia Gazette* on November 17, 1932 in a reflective mood:

> It is hard to write history in the shadow of an event but the personal qualities which made the President's defeat inevitable . . . were the qualities that saved the nation from a financial debacle: his sullen courage, his tough fibered, chilled steel brain that habitually chopped, sorted and recast facts into logical syllogisms, his taciturn habit of speech, his high boiling point which sublimated anger into grumbling . . . his tendency to push buttons and call spirits from the vasty deep to do his errands and therefore his delight in messengers rather than councillors. Each of these splendid attributes of an executive was available in a crisis to save a democracy but liable to wreck the man who used them in the service of his country.

President Hoover was desirous of preparing the way for the new executive, placing at his disposal knowledge of the situation in which the government stood in its relations with foreign powers. He wished as well to offer information, known only to him, of the economic situation of the nation.

It was now clear to Hoover, as it only gradually became clear to those who were to succeed him, how clearly defined was the position of isolation he had occupied in his long fight to provide executive leadership. He had been a powerful executive in one of the most critical periods in the history of the United States. He was not to relinquish this power easily; yet such power was still a national need.

The United States at the Crossroads

*Only a few rare souls in a century, to whose class I
make no pretension, count much in the great flow of
this Republic. The life stream of this Nation is the
generations of millions of human particles acting under
impulses of advancing ideas and national ideals gathered from a thousand springs. These springs and rills
have gathered into great streams which have nurtured
and fertilized this great land over these centuries. Its
dikes against dangerous flood are cemented with the
blood of our fathers. Our children will strengthen these
dikes, will create new channels, and the land will grow
greater and richer with their lives.*

*. . . What is said in this or in that political campaign
counts no more than the sound of the cheerful ripples
or the angry whirls of the stream. What matters is—
that God help the man or the group who breaks down
these dikes, who diverts these channels to selfish ends.
These waters will drown him or them in a tragedy that
will spread over a thousand years.*

Herbert Hoover, Address at the Gridiron Club,
Washington, D. C., December 10, 1932

Herbert Hoover, as president, was to bear the responsibility of that office
for the period of four months between November 8, 1932, and March 4,
1933.[1] His was as well the burden of the nation's uncertain immediate
future. He must work with the Congress that had been elected in 1930
and with which he had worked from December, 1931, to July, 1932.
Together, they had dealt with pressing problems. They must do so now.[2]

Along with continuing widespread unemployment, the threat of starvation in the fourth winter of unemployment, and the shaking financial
structure went lack of confidence—that sleeping monster of "fear" that

the president had dreaded arousing. He had sensed this fear as the greatest of all dangers as early as October 1929. Out of his experience in the preceding fifteen years, he knew to the depths of his soul how destructive a force could be let loose upon the world. Noticeable everywhere, however, was a relaxation of tension, because the outcome of the election could not be questioned; it was the verdict of a great majority of the voters in every section of the country.[3]

There was speculation about the future executive. Beyond the determination of change in personnel, there was little indication about the general policy that was to be adopted, the program of legislation to be proposed, or the immediate steps that would be taken in the national economic emergency.

Triumph of a political party that had been out of power for a dozen years did not in itself disperse uncertainty. The divisions in the Democratic party that had continued throughout its period of exile were now brought into sharper focus. Some in the party were to lose their influence on the new administration. It was certain that in intraparty fighting the cleavages would become even deeper and even preclude the possibility of a united party in Congress at the beginning of the new administration on March 4. Yet uncertainty came from the thought that the president-elect, Franklin D. Roosevelt, had promised an administration that would realize upon thirty years of agitation for a variety of changes. Senators Norris and Nye were interested in the activities of a Progressive League in support of the forthcoming administration as early as February 1933.[4] It was known that Senators LaFollette and Costigan also would support the new president.[5]

Meanwhile, President Hoover must proceed in this climate of uncertainty. Fortunately, he had no illusions about what the public would believe of any move that he might make and any opportunity that he might take to meet the needs of every passing hour. His mood can be assessed in a personal letter of the moment. A Minneapolis minister sent him a sermon entitled "Winning and Losing." Hoover replied:

> I am wondering if it occurred to you that this battle was not in the nature of a game or sport in which there was a question of personal winning or losing, that so far as the personal side is concerned the loss is to him who won and the gain to him who lost. By that I mean that I deserve no sympathy, but rather personal congratulations. I have not for fifteen years slept so soundly, nor had such elevation of spirit in expectant freedom, as since this election. My only feeling of anxiety is for what may come from a change of policies in our country.[6]

But March 4 lay months away.

Hoover soon realized that one of his fundamental beliefs was to be put to a new test. All along he had accepted open competition over policy as normal—to the point of political decision—but then he had asked that all come together for cooperative action. This led him to believe that he should cooperate with his designated successor. President-elect Roosevelt, however, had already come to a different decision at the moment he responded to the defeated president's telegram of congratulations.[7] Time after time Roosevelt, by adroit limitation upon what he said he would do, and legalistic reasoning for what he could not do, defeated the first purpose in Hoover's mind. There would be no assurance to the nation that there would be continuity in procedures that would appear to maintain financial stability and give economic reassurance.

Beneath the surface civilities of the four occasions on which Hoover and Roosevelt would meet seethed the basic antagonism of the two men, accentuated by a difference of attitude toward government. Hoover believed profoundly in the importance of protecting the economic interests of the nation as a whole and in confining government action to aid, information, suggestion and, if necessary, careful supervision and legislative regulation. Roosevelt believed in the basic maxim that all measures of government should be rooted in the care of the individual citizen, his freedom, his livelihood, and his faith. Despite his concern for the individual, Hoover saw the necessity of keeping alive the institutions of economic life and of government not only in the nation but in the world.

The problems of the interregnum from President Hoover's point of view were the problems of effective *government*. This meant, in Washington and elsewhere, the maintenance of freedom from disorder and of the economic and social system. These problems to the president-elect were problems of *politics*, that is, how to assure the public that the new government would deal effectively with unemployment, with personal security, and with individual freedom. Roosevelt implied that the government belonged to the citizens by their own declaration and the declarations of himself and his party.

Some observers found it difficult to understand why the American people accepted this four-month period of waiting; they urged that Hoover step aside.[8] Long nurtured in constitutional procedures, the great majority of Americans took waiting for granted. Yet it was remarkable that they did so during the winter of 1932–1933, filled as it was with unusual uncertainty about the immediate future. In a sense, it is perhaps fortunate, in view of what was to happen in the succeeding administration, that there could be a period of preparation.

President Hoover did not for a moment entertain the possibility that, having suffered an overwhelming repudiation, he should immediately hand over to his successor the duties and powers of the government. It was entirely in character for him to maintain that as long as the law said he should remain in office and be responsible for the actions of the government, he would do so. Sophisticated criticism was levied against him at the time for his position, but as the years have passed it has become evident that this, probably, was one of the more important decisions that he made.

Hoover continued to hope for cooperation from his successor. He offered to him avenues of information about domestic and foreign problems. Yet he maintained up to the end the responsibility he had previously taken for problems of finance and foreign relations; particularly did he maintain to the end his responsibility for enforcement of the law.

Throughout these trying months the Hoover administration followed this pattern. In his view of what had happened on election day, Hoover did not share either the pessimism of the more extreme conservatives of his party, nor the optimism of those Republicans who felt that the new administration would make considerable use of measures already taken by the Hoover administration.

The president looked upon the period of "interregnum" as one of education for the people. First, the incoming administration would now be faced with the necessity of formulating a program which they had not yet constructed.[9] Second, the statement of this program, Hoover felt, would warn the American people that steps were being proposed which they would not be willing to take. In brief, in this period following his repudiation, he felt as strongly as ever that the philosophy of government which underlay his own program for the New Day was rooted in American experience. It followed that it was a philosophy of government that (in due time) would again appeal to Americans as one they would wish to follow.

All through their history, Americans had by habit—and often by conviction—associated their presidential leaders with programs that symbolized something "new." The New Freedom of Woodrow Wilson and the New Nationalalism of Theodore Roosevelt had been preceded by still earlier programs that grew out of the struggle over slavery, and before that, by programs involved in the constitutional problems of the first decades of the Republic.

As a matter of fact, the leadership of Franklin D. Roosevelt was to be identified very soon with the term "New Deal" in all of its implications about the kind of program he was to advance. It was a term roughly expressive of a level of activity hitherto familiar to Americans—but not yet idealized by them.[10] Hoover's use of New Day was his own hope in this regard. Many years later when in private conversation with president-elect John F. Kennedy he was asked for advice, Hoover replied that the younger man should not be a follower of any previous president; that he should have his own program; that it should be identified with him; and that he should name it specifically and thereafter have it as *his* program.[11]

Through his experience in office, Mr. Hoover was well aware of the pressure of problems upon the government and he was certain that many problems could not be postponed. Notable among these, of course, was the increasing strain upon the banks of the nation; the increasing unemployment and distress; and the increasing uncertainty of the relationship of the United States government to foreign governments, several of which were in very unstable condition.

The president, as his first moves toward the president-elect made clear, was especially anxious that he and his successor cooperate in the area of foreign relations. Hoover's first concern was that Roosevelt be informed as far as possible of the status of foreign relations as they were known only to the officials of the government in these critical months. (This was Secretary Stimson's view also.)

President Hoover was insistent that the basic principles underlying currently existing foreign policies be maintained. This was the position from which all of his moves in this period must be viewed. And as Secretary of State Stimson made plain in his diary entry for November 9, 1932, it was his purpose to inform his successor of the actual situation in the world as viewed by him as secretary of state. In the months that followed, the differences in point of view between Hoover and Stimson were amply shown in their dealings with the president-elect.[12] The president had a less tolerant view of the capacities and intentions of the incoming president than had Secretary Stimson.

Moreover, Hoover was well aware that he and his secretary of state did not agree about various aspects of foreign policy, including the problem of the war debts. In the period between the election in November 1932 and the inauguration in March 1933, the relationship between these two powerful individuals, Hoover and Stimson, was often marred by the strain of their disagreement on questions that came definitely within the province of the secretary of state.

On March 2, Stimson stopped at the White House to have a word or two of goodbye. "I was getting the jitters whenever I thought of how I should feel when I saw the last of him disappearing out of sight on his way to California," Stimson recalled later. "I told him that I hoped that in spite of the fact that we had scrapped a great deal on some points, he did not feel that I did not thoroughly trust him and have confidence in him. He smiled and said that he had been a pretty hard man to deal with these last two years, that he had had the jitters himself. We had a nice frank confidential talk. I came away feeling as I always do when I have such a talk with him."[13]

Following the election on November 10, the British ambassador, Sir Ronald Lindsay, called on Secretary Stimson concerning a possible reconsideration of the December 15 payment on the war debt. The secretary said that he could see reason for postponing announcement until president-elect Roosevelt's views could be sounded out, and Secretary Mills, who had been called in, concurred.[14]

The next day the French ambassador, Paul Claudel, presented to Secretary Stimson a note asking for a review of the obligation owed by France. The ambassador urged that the president endeavor to settle the question of debts within the remainder of his term. Inasmuch as congressional action was necessary, the ambassador realized that President-elect Roosevelt's influence and cooperation would be required.[15]

President Hoover telegraphed Governor Roosevelt saying that, whereas he did not favor "cancellation in any form," he felt that the United States should be "receptive to proposals from our debtors of tangible compensation in other forms than direct payment in expansion of markets for the products of our labor and our farms." The president stated further that he was reluctant to proceed "with recommendations to the Congress" until he had opportunity to confer with the president-elect.[16]

The conference between Hoover and Roosevelt, attended as well by Secretary Mills and Roosevelt's adviser, Raymond Moley, was not a success.[17] Nor was Hoover's attempt of December 17 to approach Roosevelt on this matter successful.

Early in January, United States Ambassador to France Walter Edge sent a "strictly personal" communication to Hoover through Secretary Stimson, stating:

> I returned to my post after the elections with the hope that during the three months preceding the change of administration the cooperation which you offered the President-elect might be used to ease the world's tension and in particular to contribute to the solution of our financial and commercial problems with France.
>
> The recent exchange of correspondence between yourself and the President-elect especially in its effect on those in authority here convinces me that my hope is unrealizable. . . .
>
> While a desire to find a solution is evinced in official circles here there is no indication of any definite effort to bring about a reversal of that action of the French Parliament in refusing to make the December payment.
>
> The Government seems to be seeking a way out of the impasse only by some representation on our part which would be unwise or impossible to make or

some assurance as to the future from those who must assume responsibility in a few weeks.

Furthermore, though the negotiations for a Franco-American commercial treaty have reached an agreement under which over 95 percent of the average American exports to France would be guaranteed the minimum tariff treatment, nevertheless, the actual conclusion of the accord should in' my opinion be held over for the consideration of the incoming administration.

Matters as a consequence are brought virtually to a stalemate where no useful purpose can be served by my endeavoring to pursue my mission. . . .[18]

Secretary Stimson and British Ambassador Sir Ronald Lindsay had a conference on January 19. Prior to this, on January 9, Mr. Stimson had conferred with President-elect Roosevelt, and this had prepared the way for another conference between Hoover and Roosevelt on the twentieth.[19]

An extract from a presidential memorandum dated January 21 reveals the next step in negotiations with the French:

I asked Stimson and Mills to come to a meeting at the White House at 6 o'clock and I again raised the question of the note to the French, stating that it was vital from the point of view of the American people that such a note should be sent, that I regretted the delays that had taken place and that the matter must be taken in hand at once.

Secretary Stimson said that Governor Roosevelt was opposed to sending such a note; I said that he could not take the position that we should not defend the interests of Americans. It was assumed that the French would pay the money immediately on Governor Roosevelt's inauguration as a compliment to him and as a slap at the present administration. I stated I was not going to be a party to such things as that. The French were trying to avoid responsibility to the people in this matter and I proposed to go straight down the road with it. A long discussion ensued. Mr. Mills suggested that a courteous reminder should be sent to the French but that it should be submitted to Governor Roosevelt for his approval and that he should be asked to discuss it on the telephone. If the Governor's statements were correctly quoted that he regarded the French on a parity with the British despite their default, it could be pointed out to him in a covering letter that this was doing harm to the American people and that the way to straighten it out was to send a note and indicate that it had his approval. The form of the note was settled and the matter was agreed upon.[20]

This, however, by no means ended the matter. On Sunday night the president irritably recalled the day's events. Stimson had called him and Hoover asked if the French note had been sent. Stimson said that he did not propose to send it. Wrote Hoover:

A long discussion took place as to the matter and it finally resulted in my giving him positive directions to submit the note to Governor Roosevelt, that if the Governor disapproved of sending the note it at least relieved this administration from responsibility; if he approved, we would certainly collect the money. I stated that even if he disapproved of the note, I still felt we would need to go ahead with the matter. I told him if the note was sent to the French they would undoubtedly come back with some argument and give us an opportunity to set out clearly and precisely their outrageous conduct in the whole matter and leave a record that would be indelible for all time on the situation.

About six o'clock, recorded the president, "Mr. Bundy came to see me with the covering letter and the note stating that the Secretary of State had told him to sign it at my request. He again wanted to know if I still was of the opinion that it should be sent and I told him it should be sent at once and that I was irritated at the delay that had taken place, that the fog of propaganda coming out from Roosevelt's supporters was hourly undermining our situation with the French."[21] So passed another day in the life of the nation's chief executive.

To his press conference the president said off the record on January 25:

These countries that went off the gold standard fourteen months ago—the expectation would have been that the depreciation of their currency would have increased their shipment of goods to the United States. It has only begun to be enlarged in its volume during the last four or five months, and it is gradually accelerating in intensity until it has now produced definitely a very considerable unemployment and is doing further damage to agriculture.

We either have to be faced with an increase in tariffs or, alternatively, there will have to be stability in foreign currencies. . . . That means if tariffs are increased that this country joins in the same mad race of competition, of lifting tariff walls, that has been going on in Europe for the last 18 months and that has resulted in a great reduction in the consumption of world goods and has brought about constantly depreciating price levels. . . . The real remedy lies in stabilization of foreign currencies. . . .

"Of course, the World Economic Conference was originally discussed between ourselves and the British . . . a year ago next April . . . but first one incident in the world after another has prevented convocation of that conference," added the president.

In his meetings with Roosevelt in November and December, President Hoover had sought cooperation on postponement of war debts, on instructions to the forthcoming Geneva conference on disarmament, and on plans for the world economic conference to meet in London. These conversations had failed because of the political impasse between the two men. A subsequent meeting on January 20, even though preceded by important talks between Secretary Stimson and President-elect Roosevelt at Hyde Park, brought no success. Stimson, who was present at the conference on January 20, felt that "the discussion showed Mr. Roosevelt's continued belief in his own powers of personal negotiations," and that "the outgoing administration had far more understanding of the problem than Mr. Roosevelt. . . ."[22]

On December 6, 1932 the president again faced the Seventy-second Congress. In this final session of the Congress elected in 1930 were 158 members who had been retired by the outcome of the November 1932 elections. In the House now were 219 Democrats and 209 Republicans, and in the Senate, 47 Democrats and 48 Republicans. It was said, in review of this body, that "here was a Congress divided in control, weakened by the presence of repudiated representatives and under the discredited leadership of a defeated president, but nevertheless facing perplexing problems of national and world import. The necessities of the times called for cooperative planning and swift united action, but the exigency of politics suggested procrastination and obstruction."[23] This proved to be the case. The Democratic leaders were suspicious of the president's request for cooperation on the part of the president-elect.[24]

The response of this Congress to the president's call for immediate action in the deepening crisis during the "interregnum" was naturally hostile. But the president did succeed throughout this period in maintaining his position that financial stability must be maintained above everything else. He also succeeded in emphasizing the need for extending credit to the great economic units of the nation ("states and municipalities for purposes of assistance to distress") through the Reconstruction Finance Corporation. He insisted that scheduled public works should go forward to ameliorate the prevalent unemployment.[25] He urged extension of "so-called excise or sales taxes." Capital expenditures, said Hoover, "are a very important item in our economic life."[26] The St. Lawrence Seaway would extend employment, if built.[27]

The lack of party control in the Senate appeared when action was delayed on the Glass Banking Bill, although the two parties were in substantial agreement upon this measure, as the final vote demonstrated. Democratic Senator Huey Long of Louisiana launched an obstructionist fight against the Glass Bill and presented one of the most persistent filibusters in many years. His difficulties with the Democratic floor leader demonstrated the divided leadership of that party. Republican leaders maintained a policy of noninterference, implying that the problem belonged to the Democrats.

When on the first day of the session the Democrats in the House attempted to secure passage of a measure proposing repeal of the Eighteenth Amendment, the measure failed by six votes to secure the necessary two-thirds majority. An analysis of the balloting showed that 150 "lame ducks" voted on this resolution, 81 opposing and 69 supporting it. A majority of those in opposition had been defeated by wet candidates in the November elections. The wets met with success in the House when on December 21 the "Beer Bill" was passed. Senator Bingham of Connecticut sought to bring the Senate to consider the modification of the Volstead Act, but was voted down. By the middle of February, however, Congressional opinion had altered. With adoption of a resolution providing for repeal, the Democratic party promise was redeemed.[28]

A Philippine Independence Bill was passed over the president's veto.[29] That Hoover was fully aware of his political weakness in the Congress was reflected in his comment at this time: "We are in a pitiful position. Whatever the subject, there are not thirty senators we can depend upon."[30]

No new remedies for the nation's economic distress had been provided by Congress.[31] At the same time, the forces leading to further crisis gathered day by day. Perhaps the record of the session is to be judged fairly in terms of what it refrained from doing, not what it did. No revenue program was embarked upon, for Roosevelt and the Democrats had no tax program;[32] no inflationary measures were put through; the question of farm relief was left unanswered; the House declined to act on the Wagner Relief Bill passed by the Senate;[33] and the Senate took no action on the World Court.

President Hoover felt that the nullification, by the House of Representatives, of his executive orders for the consolidation of fifty-eight bureaus and commissions into a few divisions was not only a strike against economy but a repudiation of a long-considered bipartisan plan.[34] He had been working on this project for more than ten years, for the Joint Committee on Reorganization of the Government, which comprised representatives of the executive and members of both parties in the House and Senate, was created in December 1920. The Senate, on the other hand, gave him cause to be "enthusiastic" in their passage of the bill for reorganization, so that the president could tell his press conference on February 8, 1933, "After 20 years of agitation we will certainly accomplish something that will be a continuing benefit for generations to come."[35]

An opportunity to talk directly to the people was presented by the National Republican Club's Lincoln Day dinner in New York on February 13. The president had been committed for some time to address the organization. He presented a survey of the American economic way of life against the background of the political problems of the nation. Warning of the rapid degeneration into economic war "which threatens to engulf the world," Hoover said:

> The American people will soon be at the fork of three roads. The first is the highway of cooperation among nations. . . . The second road is to rely upon our high degree of national self-containment. . . . The third road is that we inflate our currency, consequently abandon the gold standard, and with our depreciated currency attempt to enter a world economic war, with the certainty that it leads to complete destruction, both at home and abroad.[36]

The next day his host at the Lincoln Day dinner, Charles D. Hilles, wrote to the president:

> I very much hope that your reaction this morning, after weeks of hostility on the Hill, and in consequence of the reception you received in New York last night, is such as usually follows a dramatic demonstration of the leadership of opinion. It may be too much to expect that the result in Congress will be a heightened activity along the lines you have advocated, but you have done your full part in making the people understand what will happen to them if the present dominant forces succeed in demolishing the limitations and the rules of the right conduct of government.
>
> We all realize that you came to us at personal inconvenience, and we are grateful to you, but "going to the country" with a just cause is at times one of the highest duties that a President of a self-governing nation is called upon to perform. We feel, therefore, that while you have done us a great honor you will appreciate the fact that our interest in your coming was not entirely selfish.
>
> The possibilities of a meeting such as last night's, the spirit of a meeting such as last night's, and the power of the associated action of a group such as last night's—with the inspiration you gave to us—should be compensation for the strain that the evening put upon you.[37]

The president's gracious response, "Mrs. Hoover and I thoroughly enjoyed the dinner and were delighted and gratified by the warmth of our reception," indicated that the meeting had been a bright spot in an otherwise grim period.

The economic situation in the new year had not been good. The process of decline had begun earlier. Secretary Stimson, whose duties lay primarily in the international arena, recorded in his diary from time to time the president's problems and struggles. Late in November he noted that Secretary Chapin had pointed out "the tremendous deterioration in business since the week before election when the success of Roosevelt became apparent. Ever since then things have been gradually slumping away until we now confront a very gloomy and serious situation in business."[38] In January, Stimson confided to his diary a serious conversation in which the president told Justice Hughes and himself of the "financial deterioration" in the country since the election. "He gave a pretty bad picture." Unemployment was increasing a half million a month, and half of the mortgages under $25,000 were in default. Hoover said he hoped to appoint a commission with Roosevelt because the country would be given the impression that "something is being done" and a panic would be averted. Hughes was shocked by the gravity of the situation.[39]

Both the president and his secretary of state early realized that the period of interregnum would be a strain. Wrote Stimson, ". . . and now the one problem that comes up in my mind is the problem of cooperation for the future in order that the nation shall not lose by the transition."[40] The situation actually embarrassed the British ambassador when at length he was asked to confer privately with Roosevelt. Stimson told him not to worry, "that this was like a big war that we were in and that we were trying to extemporize the best kind of arrangement that would work."[41] Hoover at first viewed the situation philosophically. The election, he said, gave the people a chance to "blow off" steam. But when they find that the new crowd is not going to settle matters and save them, "there is going to be real trouble, and it is coming right off." Many business orders had been placed contingent on a Hoover victory, but now business was slipping. The president felt that somehow the national psychology must be changed; to do so would play into the hands of the Democrats— but the country was more important than anything else.[42]

Throughout the crisis of these dark months the president worked as few executives ever have—without total collapse. Those about him felt the raw pressure. A week after the election, with Hoover en route from California, Stimson wrote, "I am trying to take all the spare time I can to get back in condition before the President arrives, for I know that when he does come there will be the usual pressure."[43] By mid-January Stimson was exhausted, but ahead lay more weeks of crisis, especially in the financial area.[44] Overall, the strain on the president was immense. Defeated at the polls, he must still carry the burden of responsibility. And soon, in addition to the problems of interaction with Roosevelt and the Democratic Congress, there would come threatened financial collapse.

❋ ❋ ❋ ❋ ❋ ❋

The banking crisis of February and March 1933 could be viewed as a financial crisis comparable to that, say, of the late 1920s and early 1930s. It could be viewed broadly, in terms of national and state regulation,

Federal Reserve policy-making, bank management practices, misconduct of some bankers, intervention by banks in the foreign policy arena (short-term loans to nations and overseas banks), and still other important subjects. Or, one could concentrate on the final days before Inauguration Day, 1933, to ascertain certain "true reasons" for the nationwide closing of the banks in the first hours of the Roosevelt administration.[45]

While the banking collapse is an economic and social phenomenon in its own right—a part of the overall world history of the day—it has been treated persistently in terms of the clash in point of view and personality between President Hoover and President-elect Roosevelt. Throughout, it has seemed vital to those who participated at the time and to later writers to assess motives and to affix personal blame. Sometimes great factors at work (the debt payment imbroglio, international rivalries, a future World Economic Conference, trade and currency dislocations, and the hopes and ambitions of bankers and industrialists in particular states) fail to obtain a hearing. Looking back from summer, 1933, in half year perspective, Sir Arthur Salter, a British leader whose book *Recovery, the Second Effort* had recently appeared, gave Henry Stimson clearly and tersely "the best statement of views on [it] ... that I got from anybody in London. ... He felt that in America we were pulling out of the depression a year ago in the summer of 1932 with the assistance of the open market purchases which had been instituted by the Federal Reserve Board under the pressure of Mr. Hoover." But these had been abandoned in the fall, so that the market sagged; disappointment and discouragement followed —and now for the third or fourth time. "This was the first bad blow and led to the banking crisis of March."[46]

The last two weeks of the administration were most critical. It was on February 18 that Hoover dispatched an urgent letter to the president-elect calling upon him for a gesture of cooperation in the desperate currency contraction that faced the nation as the people withdrew the largest amounts of money on record at the time.[47] Said the president of the United States, after writing and then on second thought striking out a recital of the grave events of the spring and summer of 1932, "I hope you will forgive me for even pretending to make this suggestion to you. I would not do so but for the deep anxiety I have at the grave situation of the country." His letter went unanswered for two weeks; the eventual excuse given by Roosevelt for the delay was that it had somehow been a secretarial error.[48]

Now decidedly alarmed, the president prepared a memorandum on February 21 on what he was doing and what concerns he felt. (There would be more such private statements, clear up to March 3.) He asked the attorney general about his constitutional right to ask for opinions of

Federal Reserve Board officials; his purpose was "to demand from them a formal opinion as to the present situation and what should be done." Secretary Mills was sent to the Federal Reserve Board to ask that they advise Roosevelt "of the seriousness of the situation and that nothing could steady the situation except his making the three declarations [in the Fess letter, below]." Mills guessed that the board would probably fear reprisals and would not act.

Not for publication, and to be used only "in case of a general debacle" or an attempt to blame the Republicans, Hoover now wrote a letter to Fess that stated bluntly, "Today we are on the verge of financial panic and chaos." He said that fear of the new administration was the problem. There was hoarding of gold; bank suspensions; declining prices; personal debts were not being paid; orders were being cancelled; unemployment was up; and there was a flight of capital abroad. The real problem? Delay in Roosevelt's cooperation in foreign economic relations; Democratic congressmen were proposing currency tampering; RFC loans were being published; and there were still other considerations. Wrote Hoover, "The President-elect is the only man who has the power to give assurances which will stabilize [the] public mind as he alone can execute them." What could the incoming president say to the country? "I do not refer to action on all the causes of alarm but it would steady the country greatly if there could be prompt assurances that there will be no tampering or inflation of the currency; that the budget will unquestionably be balanced even if further taxation will be necessary; that the government credit will be maintained by refusal to exhaust it in issue of securities. Not publicizing RFC business would be helpful."[49] The administration, said the hard-working president, was devoting days and nights to putting out the fires and localizing them. Hoover offered his best judgment:

> What is needed, if the country is not to drift into great grief, is the immediate and emphatic restoration of confidence in the future. The resources of the country are incalculable, and the available credit is ample but the lenders will not lend, the men will not borrow unless they have confidence. Instead they are withdrawing their resources and their energies. The courage and enterprise of the people still exist and only await release from fears and apprehensions.[50]

Meanwhile the distraught president relied on newspaperman Mark Sullivan to contact Bernard Baruch. A memo from Sullivan explains his failure to persuade the financier to contact Roosevelt. Baruch, guessed Sullivan, hoped for the treasury appointment; he disliked some of Roosevelt's advisors; disliked giving unasked advice; and was certain to be needed later, when the advisors lost out—as he thought they surely would.

"The net of it is that Bernie will not make this suggestion [that Roosevelt make a statement] to Roosevelt although Bernie thinks it is a thing which should be done."[51]

The next day, Hoover wrote to Mills to ask him to go over fundamentals with William Woodin (who had just been named incoming secretary of the treasury). "I trust Mr. Woodin will realize that because a Republican Administration has stood staunchly for those principles and policies, it is no reason for their abandonment, for they are fundamental."[52] Indeed, the president had devoted his Lincoln Day dinner speech almost entirely to an analysis of the depression and fundamentals on international finance. He referred then to "waves of fear and apprehension" and to "unreasoning panic."[53]

Newspaper readers in mid-February were jarred by the news from Michigan, where an eight day banking moratorium had been declared.[54] The president had simply been unable to save that situation, although he did relieve weak spots in four major cities elsewhere. Stimson recorded that he had been "working like a Turk of late" and hoped to prevent a collapse while in office.[55] The secretary's diary, which for some time had been quiet on economic matters, now took on an air of urgency. Soon Herbert Feis of the State Department would tell Stimson what the president, Mills, and Stimson had long believed, that there ought to be an early arrangement on the debts if at all possible.[56]

A correct picture of the deteriorating banking situation during the Michigan crisis would include reference to the front page news made by the hearings of the Senate Banking and Currency Committee, where revelations of the extraordinary stock market operations of Charles E. Mitchell, president of National City Bank, shook confidence in the nation's bankers.[57] Wrote Stimson of the situation inside the administration,

> The news as a whole at Cabinet Meeting today was bad. The President is very gloomy over the condition of affairs in this country, and the general slump that is going on and the fact that the new President-elect has said nothing to help the occasion. Everything in Detroit hangs upon his intervention. Congress will not pass the necessary legislation unless he speaks, and he has not spoken. The President has been sending people to see him, to try to urge him to help in the situation, and he has even written him, but he gives no indication of realizing the emergency of it.[58]

Next day he talked with Hoover on the telephone and was told that the indifference of Roosevelt was "the act really of a madman. Things are very gloomy."[59] As for Congress, Senator Borah was very pessimistic, Stimson noted, for he said nobody had any plans, "that they were running around like so many sheep."[60]

Now came a blockbuster. James Rand, the industrialist, dictated very slowly to Joslin over the telephone a startling piece of intelligence after lunching with Rexford Tugwell (one of Roosevelt's inner circle of advisors). He [Tugwell] said they were fully aware of the bank situation and that it undoubtedly would collapse within a few days, which would then place responsibility in the lap of President Hoover."[61] Soon, the irate chief executive wrote to Rand that Tugwell "breathes with infamous politics devoid of every atom of patriotism. Mr. Tugwell would project millions of people into hideous losses for a Roman holiday."[62] Wrote Stimson privately, "I have direct evidence that this wretched little man Tugwell . . . has said that the country was bound to have a smash and that it better come right off. By saying this, there have incidentally been alarmed a lot of people who wouldn't otherwise be alarmed."[63]

Mark Sullivan, now moving into the White House, was investigating the feasibility of a bank deposit guarantee. The estimate was that there were fifty million savings accounts, averaging just under $500 each—perhaps $25 billion in all—thus comprising more than half of all deposits. He wondered whether accounts of under a thousand dollars should be guaranteed.[64] Again Hoover wrote Roosevelt, for "the financial situation has become even more grave." Even now, he was confident, a declaration by the president-elect would "contribute to confidence and would save losses and hardship to millions of people." If the new Congress, of the same party control as the executive, could be in session instantly on March 4, it would be capable of expeditious action and would make for stability. Again, said Hoover, he had a deep desire to cooperate in every way.[65]

Many historians have been critical of what they call "the tone" of the presidential letters to the president-elect, and they have been protective of Roosevelt for not desiring to take action not in acordance with his campaign utterances. Hoover and his supporters have stressed the reality of the crisis and the possibility, in retrospect, that the banks need not have been closed across the nation but only in certain states and for limited periods. Admittedly, the president had just concluded a political campaign and was fully aware that President Cleveland had made a comeback after a loss at the polls; Secretary Stimson had reminded Hoover of this the week after election day. Hoover was indeed conscious that a "record" was being made in the interregnum, and his conversation, papers, and speeches in these four months naturally show this.

Yet Roosevelt, too, was necessarily involved in playing a role. The publicity-conscious president-elect managed to be portrayed in the press on March 1 as "giving close attention to the banking situation" for he was "in receipt of complete information on developments." Still, his inaugural address was not expected to touch on banking except "in general terms." Somehow he looked to the public like a man of "action"—not "words."[66] It was a skillful posture and certainly noticed and resented by the increasingly angry and exhausted incumbent in the White House.

The final week of the Hoover Administration was one of world uncertainty as well as confusion about Roosevelt's policies on gold, inflation, banking regulation, and related matters. World news on March 1, for example, was pessimistic. In addition to the usual page one stories of bank misconduct emanating from Washington, there was news of Japanese advances in China and of the Reichstag fire and Hitler's expected repressions because of it. There was news that a British debt mission would be unlikely to be received in Washington in the early Roosevelt days. On this Arthur Krock noted that "the entire procedure of the conferences is as nebulous as it ever was, although the new administration will take office in four days."[67]

Although the president tried, as usual, to reassure the public, pointing out, for example, that compared with twenty years earlier there had developed "both the spirit and the method of cooperation in the prevention of war which gives profound hope of the future,"[68] he was too knowledgeable to ignore the potential threat of a Hitler. To Stimson he called the new regime monarchical and reactionary in flavor, anti-Communist, of course, but curiously committed to "a very radical governmental program."[69]

In a lead editorial, "Craving Assurances," the *New York Times* noted the failure of Roosevelt to give assurances on sound currency and inflation. Grover Cleveland had not hesitated to do this, and Alfred E. Smith had just done so in his Washington testimony. Merely pointing to the Democratic platform was not enough, for the Democratic party was clearly infected with inflation poison; if Roosevelt "temporizes and compromises with it, the ruin of his Administration will be certain." If he felt that waiting until the inauguration was necessary (to "avoid admission that the situation is acutely dangerous"), he would certainly want to face the inflation issue squarely thereafter, "opposing it with the courage and directness of ex-Governor Smith." Only in such a way "can he hope to relieve the national anxiety and assure the country that the currency is to be kept uncontaminated and unchallenged."[70]

In Washington, hope continued that the president-elect would speak out on the nature of his economic program. As the head of the New York Curb Exchange warned of coming inflation,[71] Arthur Krock reported that "many Democrats" were joining with the administration in the belief that "hysterical moves" against sound institutions could be thwarted by statements or moves by Roosevelt. In any case, his "political advisers" doubted he could make good on a pledge to control inflation.[72] Meanwhile, the *New York Times* urged "the balancing of the national budget, the maintenance of a sound currency and an international effort to reduce tariffs."[73]

Hoover repeatedly stood during the banking crisis for a program of controlled withdrawal from the banks and, as late as March 2, for a possible guarantee of bank deposits. He also corresponded with the Federal Reserve Board regarding emergency powers under the Enemy Trading Act, section 5 (left over from World War I).[74]

In the meantime, in state after state, action was being taken by the governors, the legislatures, or both: three and four day holidays were declared; withdrawals were restricted; and certain kinds of bank funds were segregated. A complete list by state lay before Hoover as he worked. The press carried stories on the state holidays in late February and early March, and the Associated Press noted in a summary article on March 1 that "banks in several commonwealths functioned yesterday under the protective hands of their state governments, which exerted stabilizing influence through legislative and administrative acts."[75] Some states had full holidays, others were content with limited withdrawals. On March 2, the loans to banks by the RFC in January were given national publicity, so that additional institutions were focused upon by a nervous public.[76]

The next day it was revealed by newsmen that the conference between Hoover and Roosevelt on March 2 had been without result. Whereas the president might have considered "radical legislation" to deal with the banking situation, "Congress would not follow Mr. Hoover's recommendations." Roosevelt had "flatly rejected" a Hoover proposal that they join in recommending legislation to guarantee a percentage of time deposits in banks.[77] The mood in Washington was such, Arthur Krock reported, that "anything" Roosevelt should come to do would be appreciated.[78] (Some weeks later Stimson would be told by Roosevelt that he had "the good fortune" to come into office just when the crisis was so bad that the people and their representatives in Congress threw up their hands and said, "Please lead us—tell us what to do!")[79]

By "leadership" the public of that day clearly meant a president and a Congress working together—going the same way, whatever way that might be. It seems quite incorrect to imply, as some textbooks do, that simply through loss of the election Hoover had lost public confidence and even the affection of his own party.[80] This will not do. For example, the *New York Times* was an ardent supporter of Governor Roosevelt in 1932, so that a reader noted in late February the "widely known unfavorable attitude of the *New York Times* toward Hoover."[81] Shortly, however, a *Times* lead editorial on the outgoing president judged that he had borne himself "with remarkable fortitude and almost incredible energy. No

President ever worked so hard or lived such laborious days as Herbert Hoover. With unsparing application he gave himself night and day to the discharge of the duties of his office. The wonder is that he did not break under the strain. What bore him up was apparently a high resolve to omit nothing which might contribute to better the morale of the people and help to bring on brighter days." Who could blame him if his motives were sometimes colored by the desire to further personal ambition? The administration had been "free of scandals," said the *Times,* and "the President was his own man. No clique or group or interest claimed the rights of ownership over him." If the country had been prosperous, Hoover would have been hailed as one of the greatest of presidents. "His undoing came from the outside." Here was a figure of Greek tragedy, for an "inexorable fate had beaten down his best efforts." Readers were told that time would probably deal kindly with his reputation and memory. "With extraordinary ability, and almost unequaled grasp of facts and tendencies and developments, and with an iron industry which amazed all observers, he gave his utmost to his country with indomitable purpose through four anxious and baffling years." And the *Times* concluded its judgment (written in the very midst of the bank crisis) by recalling that the country came to appreciate Cleveland; "it may yet do as much for Herbert Hoover."[82] In an extravagant vein, a partisan wrote, "History will prove what Herbert Hoover has done and it will mock us for what he might have done had we the intelligence to give him a chance."[83]

On March 3, the Federal Reserve Board belatedly wrote Hoover that the gold reserves in Chicago were being dangerously depleted. (Some time earlier, their contention had been that there was no gold problem.) In this letter from Eugene Meyer the Board was finally forced to conclude, "the situation has reached a point where immediate action is necessary to prevent a banking collapse."[84] The tired president opened the letter pushed under his door by the secret service at 1:30 A.M. and replied with spirit, for a few hours before (at 11:00 P.M.) Roosevelt had told him that no proclamation should be issued; that both administrations would have to do it; and that in the two key states (including New York) the governors had acted. Under these circumstances, the outgoing president was at a loss to understand why such a communication should have been sent to him in the last few hours of his administration: "I believe the Board must now admit [this] was neither justified nor necessary."[85]

Among those staying in the White House at the time was Hoover's friend Henry M. Robinson. In a contemporary manuscript of fourteen pages, "The History that Will Do Justice to President Hoover," Robinson stressed the failure of the opposition to cooperate and quoted Hoover as then saying, "I do not know that we can save the country from a general conflagration before these gentlemen have a chance to take over the government and put their policies into force, whatever they may be. But one thing is sure. It would be a great help if they would not pour gasoline on it every hour. Perhaps they want a breakdown. That is always the technique of revolution."[86] (Roosevelt had even said, "Let them bust; then we'll get things on a sound basis.")[87]

One can scarcely blame Hoover for his angry outburst, for he was exhausted—but nevertheless in a fighting mood. On March 2 at 7:00 A.M., Mark Sullivan remarked to him that the battle was over, that he had done everything humanly possible and it would have to go at that. Hoover looked Sullivan in the eye and said, "We will fight until 10:49 A.M. March 4th when I go to the Capitol—then I am going to the nearest town where I can get a room on the 30th floor of a hotel—I am going to sleep for 36 hours."[88]

The morning before Inauguration Day President Hoover attempted, for the last time, to get joint action from the incoming president-elect. Seated in the White House that would be his home for the next twelve years, Roosevelt "declined to give any assurance that he would join in any action at that time."[89] Later in the day, Thomas W. Lamont of the J. P. Morgan Company called the Roosevelt group to recommend that no action closing the banks be taken because "the leading New York bankers had told him that the banks could pull through and reopen on Monday if Roosevelt's inaugural speech were to provide sufficient stimulus to public confidence. (Roosevelt was not much interested in what the bankers thought," records Raymond Moley.)[90]

The national bank holiday was proclaimed at 10:30 P.M., Sunday, March 5. Throughout the banking crisis the team of Ogden Mills, Arthur Ballentine, and James Douglas worked effectively to keep both Hoover, Roosevelt, and the incoming treasury secretary, William Woodin, informed. The Hoover team would stay on in Washington for some time, facilitating much of the action to come.[91] The president cancelled plans to leave at once for California and instead arranged for a one week stay in New York City where he could be reached if necessary. It would ultimately be his view that "it was the most political and the most unnecessary bank panic in all our history. It could have been prevented. It could have been cured by simple cooperation. . . ."[92] Nevertheless, the retiring president stood ready to serve, as was his lifelong custom.

Herbert Hoover had done what he thought best throughout the difficult four-month interregnum. Those around him saw him as a tower of strength. They regarded Franklin Roosevelt as ill-informed, lacking in a coherent program, and exerting his personality and energies to some form of dramatic action on the world scene after March 4 (a personalized summit conference with the French and British?). That Roosevelt saw himself inevitably as the elected representative of "the people" there can be no doubt. But this can be overemphasized. That Hoover had every reason to believe that the financial and business community and a large part of the public continued to view his leadership with approval seems evident. After all, almost forty percent of the electorate had voted to keep him in office only a few months earlier! The conduct of Roosevelt was unnerving to the leaders of the departing administration; this feeling was by no means limited to the president.[93]

It is not now possible to reach a judicial decision on the correctness or appropriateness of the courses pursued by the president and the president-elect in connection with the economic crisis of November 1932– March 1933. Some who have passed judgment on Roosevelt have not, perhaps, made sufficient allowances for his expressed need for full freedom of action after March 4.[94] Some of the very large number who have passed judgment on Hoover do not seem to have realized that his interaction with Roosevelt was thoroughly discussed with cabinet members like Mills and Stimson; that Roosevelt's readiness to use leaks to the press was ultimately a reason for Hoover's formality and eventual coldness in correspondence; and that contemporary Roosevelt problems and delays in putting together an administrative team placed a great burden on the capacity of the outgoing administration for action that might help national survival after March 4.[95] The interregnum was indeed a period when Americans were presented with a choice at the crossroads. That truth may be clearer now than it was for most people in 1932–33.

Epilogue

To some of those who watched the train pull out of the station, he was a most tragic figure. But to those of us who truly knew him through close association behind the wall of silence he had erected for the public good, he was the man who had served his country devotedly through unparalleled disaster and under unexampled handicaps, and who could await unafraid and with a clear conscience the evaluation of his acts by history.

Theodore Joslin, *Hoover off the Record* (1934)

Less than a week before he retired from government office, President Hoover wrote to Everett Saunders, Chairman of the Republican National Committee, in response to his request for a statement on "party organization." Expressing his appreciation of the loyal and effective work of Saunder's committee and the thousands of party workers, Hoover praised the work of party organization as a public duty that was often thankless to a degree, yet in the highest sense a public service. Judged Hoover:

> A party deserves to exist only as it embodies the thought and conviction of earnest men and women who have the welfare of the nation at heart. It must be a party of ideals since only exalted purpose can bring great numbers of people together in united action. But the consummation of ideals must be organized.

The party chairman was told that organized political parties had become an absolute necessity in the proper functioning of popular government in the United States. Only through such organization was it possible for the people to express their will. The nation would be a bedlam of wholly discordant voices without such organization, and without loyalty to it. What could parties do for the country?

Political parties have great obligations of service whether the party be in

300

power or not. In these times cooperation and not partisanship is the need of the country, but it is no less an obligation of the party to subject all proposals to the scrutiny of constructive debate and to oppose those which will hurt the progress and welfare of the country.

As he contemplated the role of parties in the American system, the departing president found certain "fundamentals and safeguards" that were by no means the property of any of the parties. Rather, they were held in common by all.

They embrace rigid adherence to the Constitution; enforcement of the laws without respect to persons; assurance of the credit of the Government through restraint of spending and provision of adequate revenue; preservation of the honor, and integrity of the Government in respect to its obligations, its securities and its sound currency; insistence upon the responsibilities of local government; advancement of world peace; adequate preparedness for defense; the cure of abuses which have crept into our economic and political systems; development of security to homes and living; persistence in the initiative, equal opportunity and responsibilities of individuals and institutions; and finally every encouragement to the development of our intellectual, moral and spiritual life.

Moreover, the basic role of government in time of crisis was seen to be affirmative and protective:

In great emergencies humanity in government requires the utilization of the reserve strength of all branches of the government, whether local or national, to protect our institutions and our people from forces beyond their control. This must and can be accomplished without violation of these fundamentals and safeguards.

Upon these foundations lies the freedom, the welfare and the future of every citizen in the country. By them we will march forward. We do not claim them as the exclusive property of the Republican Party. They are the inheritance of all parties. This is a program which can command the respect and support of all who would maintain the United States in the high position amongst nations it now holds, and one from which we should not deviate in fidelity.[1]

Here was a profound statement forged in four years of incredible experience.

The final hours of the administration were a mixture of strict formality and unbearable tension. The transfer of "first place" in the American system then had three phases: on March 4, 1933 the president-elect called upon the president; the president accompanied the president-elect to the Capitol building where, in the Senate chamber, they together witnessed the inauguration of the vice-president-elect; and finally the president sat on the platform erected outside of the Capitol and witnessed the taking of the oath of office and heard the inaugural address of the new president.

But up to the last moment on March 3 there had been conferences at the White House and by telephone between the president and the president-elect about the pressing banking crisis. Despite his preoccupation with that crisis, Hoover had found time that day to express his appreciation to his press conference members for their "cooperation in the last four years. . . ." He added, "I have had a pleasant association with you through a troublesome time. I want you to know that I appreciate it. We have all had difficulties but nevertheless I have only recollections of a pleasant association with you all. I am in hopes if any of you come out to the Pacific Coast you will come and see me, and we will be able to discuss matters at more length in terms of objectivity than when we are in the midst of the battle. . . ."[2] Soon, however, the plain fact would be that the press would revel in the carefully cultivated intimacy of the next president's press conferences.[3]

It was noted by many commentators at the time that there was unrest in Washington. The police had therefore taken unusual precautions. They remembered that only four weeks earlier Franklin Roosevelt had narrowly escaped assassination at Miami, Florida. Thus the new administration would come into office in an atmosphere of drama, tension, and crisis.

Following the inauguration, Mr. and Mrs. Hoover went by car to the Union Station and, instead of going to Florida or to California, they went to New York. The enthusiasm of Hoover supporters gathered at the Washington train station was a dramatic testimony that there were many who had retained their faith in Hoover leadership. "I shall never forget," the Justice Stone's widow recalled many years later, "the expression on Mr. Hoover's face."[4] Indeed, the ex-president in his first moments out of office seemed deeply touched and his entire being struck an observant reporter as rejuvenated.[5]

Thus ended a four-year service to the nation.[6] Herbert Hoover, "the depression's political victim No. 1,"[7] gave way to a victorious rival of opposing views. There was precedent for this situation in American history. Like defeated presidents John Adams and William Howard Taft, Hoover was in later years to serve his country again, not as president—as millions hoped he might—but (after twelve years of political exile) in new and important capacities.[8] He was to serve two presidents in work, at home and abroad, not only on relief of suffering—the great mission that had interested him earlier—but in plans for reorganization of the federal government in the better interest of the citizens who supported it. In vast numbers of speeches ("addresses on the American road" as he would call them in volume after volume), in memoirs, and in radio addresses the Hoover voice would still be heard. The past would not fade, for him. "Of course, as you know, Mr. Hoover's memory was absolutely fabulous. I never ran into anything like it," recalls a newsman.[9]

Publicly, after leaving office, the nation's former leader was silent for a time on national issues. In private, he did speak candidly, as is natural. To Stimson he unburdened himself in the summer of 1933:

> My hunch is that after making a long series of specious yet impossible proposals on disarmament and economics, and securing the necessary refusals from Europe, that we will have laid the foundation for a plunge into a period of wild nationalism. That has, in my view, been the intention from the beginning. —Economic war with still higher tariffs, depreciated currencies, quotas, embargoes, militaristic appeals with bigger navies, etc., etc.
>
> It is the natural fruit of demagoguery both at home and abroad.
>
> However, the sun still shines and the rich get richer and the thrifty, saving back-bone of the country will get poorer.[10]

Meanwhile, there had been no retirement from public notice when he left the house. "I envy," he told Stimson, "your ability to go where you please without being plagued to death with suspicions and people."[11] The events of the week before the Bank Holiday continued to gall—as they would for years. Said Hoover, ". . . the final debacle in the United States was the break-down of confidence out of fear of what the new Administration would do, as had it not been for this the country would have marched ahead."[12] Nor did it help that there was so much discussion of a new public morale. "The eulogies on the better spirit of the country do not take into account the revived antagonisms of employees and employers which we had so greatly mitigated, the terrorization of small business men, nor the motivation of all big business and investment by fear instead of confidence."[13] He meant, of course, fear of the federal government (a factor discounted by many then and later by focusing on fear of prolonged depression). Hoover's devotion to a system in which there would be cooperation between government and business, as in his cabinet days, had not died. The absence of personal references is to be noted, for, as James A. Farley judged after years of acquaintance with Hoover, "Very, very rarely did I hear him say an unkind thing about anybody."[14]

Six months had passed. To Edward Eyre Hunt who, more than most of his associates, had understood fully for years his basic viewpoint on such matters, he wrote:

> The impending battle in this country obviously will be between a properly regulated individualism (which I have always expounded as American Individualism) and sheer socialism. That, directly or indirectly, will be the great political battle for some years to come.
>
> In the meantime I see a consistent effort on the part of our opponents to entirely misrepresent my position as being the advocate of 19th century *laissez-faire* and other long forgotten social theses.

His position would have to be clarified! Perhaps a book of "extracts" from speeches would be a possibility.[15] A month later he wrote Christian Herter that there had been no invasion of personal freedoms in his administration, nor had news been manipulated or controlled by public outcry against the press. Reflecting on his own record, Hoover found the new pattern repugnant.

> The thing that troubles me most of the whole situation is the total stifling of criticism. The cry that even constructive suggestion is unpatriotic has been so generally adopted by the newspapers as to practically stamp out free speech. And yet the very continuance of democracy is wholly dependent upon unrestricted constructive criticism. Many times I have thought I could not bear to keep still, but up to date I think it has been the right thing to do.

But when it came to inflation of the currency he would make an exception; he was "taking steps."[16]

As Thanksgiving neared, and he reflected on the many conversations of past months with fishing guides, neighbors, old friends, and well-wishers, the Hoover spirits began to rise.

> The people themselves, down at the grass roots, are beginning to realize the gross violation of such primary things as the Bill of Rights. I do not suppose one person out of a thousand on the street knows the existence of those provisions in the Constitution. But they have an inheritance from the suffering and struggling by which our race attained those protections. Sometime later on . . . it might be worth presenting this novel idea and perhaps emphasizing that the whole framework of our Government and the Constitution itself was erected for the guardianship and development of these rights, and that they are being violated in spirit in every town and village every hour of the day.[17]

William Allen White, writing in the *Saturday Evening Post* of March 4, 1933, stated that in his opinion only history would show whether or not

"Hoover was the last of the old Presidents or the first of the new." Much would depend, it would turn out, on the portrayal of the years 1929–1933 by historians in the decades to come.

The Hoover administration ended in a contrast of political principle that must be emphasized by the historian; certainly there was a sharp contrast. There had been the definite program of the New Day based on the economic and political life that Americans had lived for a century and a half; and there were the indefinite possibilities of the unfolding New Deal that was to alter the structure of American society for many years to come.

President Hoover was a chief executive with a program and high hopes for his countrymen and their country. He offered leadership but was not always followed. He attempted to use tools available within the American political system, but many chose to follow other political figures instead. He can be seen in the role of statesman, repeatedly. Certainly, he served his country first and his own interests second.[18] What was the touchstone that Hoover used both as president and in his long career? While there is ample evidence in speeches and correspondence of the day, we may look instead to what may have been one of his very last letters. In 1964 he wrote to an old friend:

> All my public life I have had four tests as to whether things are well with the American people:
>
> 1. Is representative government maintained in working order?
> 2. Are our defenses sufficient?
> 3. Is the Bill of Rights enforced in the country?
> 4. Are the doors of the churches and schools open, and are they contributing moral leadership in the country?
>
> I don't expect perfection. All I need to sleep well, is to know that they are moving in the right direction.[19]

Only a few presidents have carried such heavy burdens of decision and execution as Hoover did. Some presidents were helped by their political party; Hoover had a divided party, headed in several different directions. Party organization, functioning in its familiar way, was a hindrance to effective action more often than not in the period 1929–1933. The reason for this lay primarily in the parochial nature of traditional American politics. The special interests of sections and of states, and the demands of local constituencies on their congressional representatives in the nation's capital made action in the national interest exceedingly difficult.

In a review of the presidency of Herbert Hoover familiar themes appear: the coming of the depression and the efforts of the president to bring economic forces to a place where they could resume the normal course of expansion in the United States; the impact of events abroad upon the American nation; and the formulation of new foreign policies to aid in solving world economic problems. Desire grew among an increasing number of American citizens, however, for drastic change in the economic, social, and political life of the United States.

The answer to why the people rejected President Hoover's program for the new scientific era, a program rooted in voluntarism and cooperation rather than federal domination, is to be found in certain characteristics of American democracy that were a century in the making. The faith of the Founding Fathers that experts would be chosen by the people to carry on government within the limits set by the Constitution had been challenged during and after the Jacksonian era by many leaders in American political life. The so-called revolt of the masses that took place in America drew its strength from a growing acceptance of the slogan, "restore the government to the people." The successful leader, according to the proponents of this widely accepted philosophy of government, need not be an expert, for his guide would be what "the people" thought they wanted. This concept of leadership was at the root of the conflict between the progressive Republicans and the president throughout the Hoover administration, and it would be paramount in the New Deal era to come.

Hoover's own judgment in perspective on his most important single contribution as president was several times presented in conversations with Edgar Eugene Robinson. What he had done, the former president said reflectively, was "to protect and defend constitutional government." At a time of crisis when in office Hoover had told the press, "The first obligation of my office is to uphold and defend the Constitution and the authority of the law."[20]

Herbert Hoover, as president of the United States, conducted himself as an enemy of war and its armaments; as a friend of constitutional government; as a supporter of voluntary methods; and as a preserver of a partially regulated capitalist system that could hold its own in the face of such rival ideologies of the day as fascism, socialism, and communism. There would be for America no collapse or revolution; on the contrary, despite the economic emergency, there was a real record of accomplishment. President Hoover in the White House years was, above all, a determined spokesman for the traditional American virtues, hopes, and ideals of individual opportunity, personal freedom, and love of country.

The Historical Record

The Historical Record

*He is not the man to underestimate either the historic
crisis he has lived through or the momentous part he
has played in it. He has a strong sense of history. The
truck load of papers he recently removed from the
White House will be filed away with others in his personal archives to complete the record of a thoroughly
documented career. This record has high historic
value, and it is significant of Mr. Hoover's love of order
and sequence, of the importance he attaches to his
administration and of his desire to clarify and justify
his official acts.*
Anne O'Hare McCormick, February 5, 1933

The historian, seeking facts and meanings amid the spectacular events
of these years of crisis, 1929–1933, is impressed by certain problems.
There is an incompleteness in all contemporary accounts. Participants in
an event, who were once well informed on aspects of what took place,
were usually unable, because of the necessity for silence, to present the
facts publicly at the time. Their later explanations cannot substitute fully
for the contemporary record.

On the other hand, outside observers of an event are lamed by incomplete knowledge in telling about it. Yet what passes then for historical
narrative—and for a considerable period after an event—must be composed from the limited materials made available by certain participants
and the incomplete accounts of observers. All too often, these may be
entirely from one side of the disputed questions. With the Roosevelt
archives open for two decades while the Hoover archives were still
closed, a generation of historians has received perspectives on Hoover
(directly in the case of researchers; indirectly in the case of book readers)
from, of all places, the archives of Roosevelt and his associates.

The "first-hand account" acquires authenticity by repetition and often
takes on semblance of truth through lack of competition and critical
examination. Indeed, it may not be possible to be critical. Contemporary

history is written, therefore, in the light of the interests and intentions of the generation of writers that immediately follows the events described. It is inevitably filled with bias as well as inaccuracies. Worse, certain pre-suppositions absolutely prevent entertaining drastically alternative inter-pretations.

To revise that early story and to replace it with a verified account appropriate to the day of readership is the work of the historical scholar. He proceeds with knowledge of the outcome of the events he describes. He has great strength in the documentary record of the participants and may discard or at least modify the accounts of contemporary observers. These are advantages. But hazards remain.

Documents remain supreme in importance to the historian seeking an enduring interpretation. Not to rely on the speech, letter, diary or chron-ology, recorded spoken word, and memorandum is to lead to develop-ments in scholarship that are fraught with grave consequences to truth. The high place given to the accounts of some participants written long after the event and to the interviews of willing participants (oral history) conducted long after the event, cannot minimize the supreme importance of documentary history.

Yet documents by themselves cannot and certainly do not tell the story in a way to be understood by succeeding generations. A structural framework for documentary evidence must be formed. This framework must include not only the points of view and the knowledge of the con-temporary observers, but also the materials known at the time of the event.

The contemporary observer who is a participant in the flow of events and who himself keeps a record at the time makes an invaluable contribu-tion to the work of the later historian. Hoover, in writing a foreword for Dawes's *Journal as Ambassador to Great Britain,* emphasized this truth:

> He is giving the invaluable guidance of experience to this generation. He is making the accurate backgrounds of written history when the distant time comes that this period can be truly appraised. The history of the gigantic forces which dominate national and international life can never be written from the current newspapers, magazines, or even the *Congres-sional Record.* They record such public knowledge as there may be of these incidents at the time, but what lies behind those incidents will be appraised from such contributions as this book. General Dawes has seen as few Ameri-cans have seen the struggles of men in these vital years, and he has seen as few men have seen the forces which make the destiny of nations.

The antithesis of the participant who *preserves* the record is the par-ticipant who *presents* the record as he *recalls* it (or wants to recall it for present advantage). The first states the facts as nearly as can be done. The second furnishes an explanation from memory. Both contributions are highly important, but they should not be confused. Occasionally, of course, they are combined in a memoir based on contemporary records; the results are variable.

It is a matter for astonishment that the Hoover Presidential Library Association was so successful in getting 327 reminiscences on tape recorder and then in typescript. Raymond Henle exclaimed after four years at the interviewing task: "I sometimes marvel when I think of all the men of attainment that I have seen who have been willing to devote one or two hours to this without any complaint at all. I just think to myself: 'My word, if that could be put down in dollars and cents, this would be a billion-dollar program. But it has been very heartwarming. . . .' "[1]

The achievements of the Hoover administration shed much light on the subsequent history of the American people. Yet the stirring events of those years of crisis, which were all-absorbing at the time, are now seen as less important than the pattern of executive action shown in times of crisis in the United States—action taken in the years 1929–1933 without discarding institutions, vital patterns, and key values. In particular does the record reveal the weaknesses at the time of congressional government and of political party domination.

Most of all, perhaps, the record reveals the development in those years of presidential power, for it may be contrasted with twelve years of Franklin Roosevelt at the center of the stage and with the extension of that power by many of his successors in office. The real test in a judgment of President Hoover is the manner in which he applied presidential power to the health of the Constitution and to the continuing right of the people of the United States to self-government.

How Hoover Preserved and Protected the Record

Herbert Hoover's view of the importance of history is revealed in an often repeated story of the incident that led to his decision to collect materials on World War I. "The initial inspiration of this Library," he said at the dedication of the Hoover Library on War, Revolution and Peace at Stanford University on June 20, 1941, "was Andrew D. White. It was while reading his works one day when crossing the North Sea in 1914 that I was greatly impressed by his complaint that there was so little of the contemporaneous literature and documentation of great events ever preserved."[2]

Hoover thought that the record in document, in personal memoir, and in newspaper—everything in writing—should be preserved "safe and unharmed" so that it might be used by later generations to formulate the story of the past.

The presidential files for the period 1929–1933 were sent from the White House to Stanford University. There, supplemented by documentary materials from many sources, they became an important part of the Hoover Archives which formed a small section of the vast collections of the Hoover Institution. Subsequently, the presidential papers were transferred to the National Archives and Records Service, Herbert Hoover Presidential Library, West Branch, Iowa. They were opened to general use by scholars in 1966, subject to restrictions on literary property rights.

Mr. Hoover's view of the importance of such preservation was stated in these words:

> I have never delivered a ghost-written public statement of importance. The proof lies in the preserved handwritten manuscripts of almost every draft. I did submit such drafts to my colleagues and did accept suggestions, but I entered them with my own hand.[3]

Hoover (like many and perhaps most public figures) did, however, distinguish between preserving the record and making it available, that is, permitting its publication by scholars or members of the public. Repeatedly, he made clear his distaste for personal publicity that was likely to result in an invasion of his own privacy or that of his family or associates. (His distaste for unfavorable publicity was, of course, typical of those who lead, but in his case the calumny of the Michelson years, 1931–1932, and the unjustified charges of later years doubtless accentuated this feeling.)

The reader of the postpresidential papers at the Presidential Library immediately senses Hoover's unwillingness to make his private record public. Two examples suffice. When Henry Stimson sought to place some of his personal diary entries in the published *Foreign Relations* series of the Department of State in 1943, Hoover gave him a blunt opinion: "My experience with the utter dishonesty and malice of this Administration in the use of documents and otherwise causes me naturally not to wish to subject myself or my family to any more of it than I can help. There seems to be no urgency as history will not be honestly documented or written until this Administration passes from the earth anyway."[4]

When the correspondence of E. T. Clark, secretary to President Coolidge, was up for public sale, Hoover wrote to Grace Coolidge, ". . . I think you have a legal right to stop any letter from or to yourself or the President or disclosing confidential matters being sold. At least I think you should stop their publication. If you feel as I do these should not be disclosed, I would suggest that you consult some legal friend concerning the matter."[5]

As for Hoover's own papers, these were severely restricted from strangers (but were available to some intimates on occasion) for years. Although this restrictive situation infuriated historians (and may have contributed to sending innumerable researchers instead to Hyde Park for a generation), the ex-president's reasoning was plain enough. He told Mrs. H. V. Kaltenborn, wife of the famous radio commentator, "No, it is too soon. I can't hurt people who are still alive." In any case, the present project was the first to gain unrestricted access to the presidential papers.[6]

Herbert Hoover knew, of course, that styles in historical interpretation change over time. It may have been one of his goals to delay detailed and penetrating consideration of his administration until the New Deal generation largely passed from the scene—but this is not certain.

THE HOOVER PRESIDENTIAL PAPERS

The indispensable source for study of the presidency of Herbert Hoover is of course to be found in the extensive collection of manuscripts now in the Herbert Hoover Presidential Library at West Branch, Iowa with a selection of major files reproduced at the Hoover Institution. These papers are rich beyond belief in documentary materials. The process through which the president moved to a decision to act is revealed in the manuscript materials that recorded the steps in his decision. Innumerable subjects that were of deep interest to Mr. Hoover, especially those of economic and social concerns, were accumulated—as no single governmental unit or group of units would gather them.

No man has read his way through the Presidential Papers and it seems very unlikely that anyone ever will. Part of the problem is bulk: 570 linear feet of files, neatly arranged in grey boxes. The present project rests in part on about a year of reading through these papers. Permission was given by Herbert Hoover to E. E. Robinson to see what he wished in these papers in 1952 and again in 1955. Years later, V. Bornet retraced some of the earlier work, used many files not then readily available, and profited from the archival functions performed in the meantime by a staff of trained archivists, especially Thomas Thalken, who was for some years in charge of the manuscripts. Publication of a *Public Papers* set also began in the interval (see below).

Today the Hoover Presidential Library has prepared numerous finding aids, guides, and descriptive materials to help point the researcher's way through the official and personal papers of a man who lived ninety years. In November 1971 a master handbook entitled *Historical Materials in the Herbert Hoover Presidential Library* (West Branch, Iowa: National Archives and Record Service) was published that described the manuscript materials. Consideration was also given to oral history reminiscences, microfilm and picture collections, and procedural matters.

There is little point in duplicating here the detailed guidance offered in print (and in personal letter, on request) by the archival staffs in Stanford and West Branch; however, a simple indication of the categories of the Presidential Papers—not as they were in the White House years, necessarily, or in the 1950s, but as they emerged in professional hands—is instructive.

A start can be made in the vast files of Hoover as secretary of commerce, 1921–1928; and this can be continued in the papers entitled "The Pre-Presidential Interim, 1928–29." Two small collections bracket the era, "The Colorado River Commission, 1921–1954" and "The American Child Health Association, 1921–1935."

The presidential papers themselves consist of file boxes arranged by subject, by addressee ("individuals"), by states, and by departments. There are also files on foreign affairs, certain commissions and organizations, and matters of personal interest to the president. Press clippings are carefully filed, and a comprehensive compilation of public papers and statements is available. (Thus the habitual user of the *New York Times Index* or the *State Papers and Other Public Writings, 1929–1933* has much more useful tools at hand). A secretary's file offers innumerable cross-references. Files on certain crises and countries, and a calendar of appointments, phone calls, and meetings (social and otherwise) are available. Xerox copies of records from other depositories (for example, the Harding papers, Unemployment Relief papers, Strong-Norman correspondence, etc.) help the busy researcher.

All in all, the Hoover Presidential Library, through its possession of valuable records, its finding aids, its adjacent museum exhibits, and its specialized staff, makes possible the most exhaustive kinds of research projects on Hoover, the offices he held, the organizations of which he was a member and the great events of his era.

The Hoover Institution also possesses very valuable Hoover materials. It houses the papers of Ray Lyman Wilbur, Mark Sullivan, Will Irwin, and other Hoover associates. Until the opening of the Hoover Library in West Branch, Iowa, the Hoover papers were located in the Hoover Institution. In the 1960s the secretary of commerce papers (1921–1929), presidential papers, and postpresidential papers were transferred to Iowa; the papers of Hoover on the Commission for Relief in Belgium, 1914–1919, the U.S. Food Administration, 1917–1919, and the American Relief Administration, 1919–1924, and the papers of a very large number of Hoover friends, associates, and coworkers remained at the Hoover Institution on the Stanford campus. The Hoover Institution has some 298 boxes of Hoover papers, many of which are not duplicated at West Branch. The oral history reminiscences, 327 of them, are in both depositories. The book collections of both are outstanding, and both have finding aids that are extremely helpful. The Hoover Institution collection of books, periodicals, and manuscripts on socialism and communism are unsurpassed. Among the most useful manuscript collections at Hoover Institution for this project are those of Ray Lyman Wilbur, Edward Eyre Hunt, and Raymond Moley. The Hunt papers in particular show Hoover's faith in voluntary association as a method in achieving important goals.

OTHER MANUSCRIPT COLLECTIONS

During the course of this study, search was made in other manuscript collections, especially in the Library of Congress; permission to quote was generously given in the cases of the papers of Charles Evans Hughes, William E. Borah, George W. Norris, Thomas J. Walsh, Bronson R. Cutting, Charles L. McNary, Ogden Mills, Andrew W. Mellon, and others.

The Borah papers are voluminous. Most helpful for this study was the general correspondence dealing with the campaigns during the period 1912–1936. The Cutting papers were of value in this work for the years 1905–1935; the Hughes papers, however, were of little value in this study. The McNary papers contain important additions to our knowledge of the "workings" of the Senate and its relationship with the president.

The Ogden Mills papers are rich in the categories labeled "Agriculture," "Russia," "General Correspondence," "The Letter-Press volumes for 1929," and "Tariff volume for 1929–30." Mills's views on the depth of the depression and its causes are revealed, especially in the speeches.

In the Norris papers the most valuable sections for this study were those on the campaign of 1930, the Hughes Supreme Court appointment, and the work of the Progressives.

The Thomas J. Walsh papers were not particularly useful for this study. The papers include materials dealing with the Democratic opposition and the correspondence between Walsh and Governor Franklin D. Roosevelt. The Walsh-Emson papers, although unsorted when they were consulted for this study, contain some material on the period 1929–1933. The Roosevelt papers at Hyde Park were used extensively for the campaign of 1932 and the interregnum, 1932–1933 (see Robinson, *The Roose-*

velt Leadership) and in connection with the campaign of 1928 (see Bornet, *Labor Politics*). They were heavily used as source material for the studies of Roosevelt's governorship by Bellush and by Freidel.

A large collection of the William Allen White papers in the Library of Congress was examined for the Hoover presidential years. These were supplemented with a separate collection of letters from William Allen White to Helen Sutliffe, formerly in the possession of E. E. Robinson and now in the Manuscript Collections of Stanford University.

Other manuscript collections of interest to the student of this period include:

Edward Price Bell, personal emissary of President Hoover. Papers in the Newberry Library of the University of Chicago include 100 documents pertaining to the period 1929–1930. *William R. Castle.* His *Diary* is on deposit at Harvard University and his papers are at the Hoover Presidential Library. *Calvin Coolidge.* Papers are in the Forbes Library at Northampton, Masachusetts and the Library of Congress. A portion of these materials has been opened to the public. *Charles G. Dawes.* Papers, including the *Diary,* are deposited in the Northwestern University Library. This diary was used in the preparation of Dawes's *Journal as Ambassador to Great Britain.*

Hiram W. Johnson. An extensive collection is now in the Bancroft Library, University of California, Berkeley, California. The collection includes not only the correspondence files of Senator Johnson, but also what may be termed a "diary," comprising a weekly letter that Senator Johnson wrote from Washington, D.C. to his son, Hiram Johnson, Jr. during the Senate years. These present a picture of the Washington scene from the viewpoint of an independent member of the Republican party. Excerpts from the diary appeared in *American Heritage* (August 1969).

Frank Lowden. The large collection of Lowden papers in the Regenstein Library of the University of Chicago were used by William T. Hutchinson in the preparation of his biography of Lowden. These papers were not especially helpful for the period 1927–1934. Chapter 28 of Hutchinson's biography, "No Help to Hoover, 1929–1933" is an important contribution based upon the Lowden papers. It deals with Lowden's political activities, his friendship with Franklin Roosevelt, his relations with midwestern farm leaders, his friendship with leaders of the Republican party personally opposed to Hoover, and his relations with scholars.

Dwight W. Morrow. These papers are deposited at Amherst College.

Frank B. Kellogg. The papers of President Coolidge's secretary of state are in the Minnesota Historical Society Collections, St. Paul, Minnesota.

Henry L. Stimson. Stimson's papers, including the invaluable *Diary* deposited at Yale University, were the basis of a carefully prepared book by himself and McGeorge Bundy entitled *On Active Service in Peace and War.* Diary entries were usually made on the same day or early the following morning. The average daily entry is two or three pages or more in length; thus Stimson's views can be seen in superabundant detail, whereas those of others can only be seen through Stimson's eyes and on his terms. Elting Morrison's *Turmoil and Tradition* (Houghton Mifflin, 1960), is based upon the Stimson papers. The *Diary* and papers became available for purchase on microfilm late in 1973. Southern Oregon State College Library purchased large sections of the microfilm as a service.

A number of other collections were used, either through on-site research by V. Bornet or through purchase of Xerox copies. Among such collections were the papers of Will Irwin, Mark Sullivan, and Dare Stark McMullen at the Hoover Institution, and the papers of George Hastings, French Strother, Taylor-Gates, and Strong-Norman at Hoover Library. Earlier research by both authors was carried out at the Roosevelt Library, Hyde Park, New York. Collections used by E. E. Robinson in connection with *The Roosevelt Leadership, 1933–1945* and *The Memoirs of Ray Lyman Wilbur,* and by V. Bornet when working on "Labor and Politics in 1928" are related to the overall perspectives in the present volume.

Specially Prepared Manuscripts

In response to a request, Deets Picket, Research Secretary of the Board of Temperance, Prohibition and Public Morals of the Methodist Episcopal Church, prepared a list of the religious affiliations of the individual members of the Seventieth Congress, which was transmitted to E. E. Robinson with a letter of August 21, 1929.

A summary from George C. Robinson's unpublished study of the *Presidential Veto* was made available by him to the authors.

Photographs

Both the Hoover Library and the Hoover Institution have collections of photographs of Hoover, his family, and his associates. These files and certain others were exhaustively explored to provide a fresh look at President Hoover and some of his associates as they were in the years 1929–1933. Acknowledgment of copyright has been made, where known, in each case. It is hoped that this visual introduction to the presidential years, prepared at some expense and much effort, will help acquaint readers with the man as he appeared to leaders and the public at the time.

ORAL HISTORY REMINISCENCES

Oral history reminiscences, over three hundred (327) of them (1975), are at the Hoover Presidential Library, West Branch and the Hoover Institution. These were gathered to show the infinite variety of Hoover's long and complex life and career. Part of these reminiscences are by contemporaries who focus on the presidency. As Allan Nevins showed in the first volume of his biography of Henry Ford, oral history interviews can fill in gaps in the record and provide tiny details (for example, of boyhood and schooldays) to carry the story. Great care is required in their use; indeed, a thorough knowledge of related printed materials is almost a prerequisite to their intelligent use.

Such reminiscences can do no more than supplement and help confirm the major account of problems faced and action taken by a chief executive of the United States. Nevertheless, when the multi-volume biographer of Hoover some day tackles his staggering job, the interviews will have to be pored over and drained of their every nuance. They were read in their entirety by V. Bornet during the course of the present research and proved well worth the arduous work of Raymond Henle and his associates who carried forward the project.

The oral history reminiscences are naturally highly variable. Some of the most casual are of great value; some of the longer ones tend to restate what was read in secondary literature about great events. In using them one must constantly be on guard to make sure that what one is reading is a first hand account. Imagination and initiative went into the program; the extent of cooperation achieved is in itself a tribute to the extent of individual dedication to Hoover's memory shared by almost everyone interviewed.[7] The entire set of reminiscences is deposited at both Hoover Institution and Hoover Library. An index has been prepared (too late for general use in this project). The chief value of the hundreds of bound volumes lies, however, not in their use for reference purposes but in the opinions, sentiments, and sincere emotions that emerge out of the memories of those who knew Herbert Hoover at various stages in his career.[8]

DOCUMENTARY AND OTHER PRINTED SOURCES

The *Congressional Record* for the period 1929–1933 provides sometimes startling revelations of the stages of the political struggles during the Hoover years. Speeches in Congress—extracts from which have been occasionally quoted—were given much attention by the American people at the time. The *Congressional Record* also reveals the atmosphere of politics that actually existed in Washington, and adequate attention has not normally been given to the quick and open daily reaction of members of the Congress to questions that arose and proposals made by the president (a very important exception would be Schwarz, *The Interregnum of Despair*). The votes taken in the Congress have been examined. Exhaustive summaries of these votes were made by E. E. Robinson in an attempt to trace the exact course of party irregularity. The summaries of presidential and congressional action in the yearly reports published in the *American Political Science Review*, as well as several series of yearbooks, especially the *American Year Books,* were also quite useful.

Certain vital documentary collections were published after the close of the Hoover administration. These include:

William Starr Myers, ed., *The State Papers of Herbert Hoover and Other Public Writings, March 4, 1929 to March 4, 1933* Vols. 1 and 2 (Garden City: Doubleday, Doran & Co., 1934). Extensive typescript volumes located in the Hoover Library and Hoover Institution may be used to supplement this set. The first volume of *Public Papers of the Presidents of the United States: Herbert Hoover. Vol. 1, March 4, 1929 to December 31, 1929,* compiled by Dwight Miller (Washington, D.C.: National Archives, 1974) made a contribution to future Hoover scholarship, especially by including press conferences. Documents for this set were compiled by Dwight Miller, senior archivist of the Hoover Library, who also assisted in their selection and annotation; Ellis W. Hawley, professor of history at the University of Iowa, served as consultant to the project.

The careful researcher will want to rely on the texts in the *Public Papers* set in preference to the *State Papers* volumes when there is a difference in wording. Another set very late in appearing under government sponsorship was *The Proclamations and Executive Orders of Herbert Hoover, 1929–1933,* 2 vols. (Washington, D.C.: National Archives, 1974). This set is chiefly notable for its information on additions to the public domain, especially to national parks, forests, and monuments during the administration.

W. S. Myers and W. H. Newton, eds., *The Hoover Administration: A Documented Narrative* (New York: Charles Scribner's Sons, 1936) is a documentary source of great general value. *The Hoover Policies,* Ray Lyman Wilbur and Arthur M. Hyde, eds. (New York: Charles Scribner's Sons, 1937) is a detailed offering by contemporaries. Many of Hoover's later speeches appear as *Addresses on the American Road* (8 volumes, various publishers, 1938–1960). Some Hoover and Coolidge speeches of 1932 appeared as *Campaign Speeches of 1932* (Garden City: Doubleday, Doran & Co., 1933). In 1973 an experienced archivist at the Hoover Library expressed surprise at the number of large libraries that have neither the Newton and Myers nor the Wilbur and Hyde books; young scholars are sometimes unaware, on arrival at West Branch, how much information on the presidency (from the administration's viewpoint) is close at hand.

Copies of the publicity releases of the Democratic National Committee are filed in the Hoover Library. Much of this material is otherwise not easily available.

Particular attention should be given by Hoover researchers to a volume edited by Theodore G. Joslin, entitled *Hoover After Dinner* (New York: Charles Scribner's Sons, 1933). It contains the addresses Hoover gave to newsmen who were members of the Gridiron Club in Washington, and their guests. These addresses were not made public at the time, but were subsequently published in Myers, *State Papers*. In an introduction to the Gridiron addresses, Joslin writes: "A true estimate of a public official can be made only by what he says and does himself, not by what others say about him or attribute to him." The addresses may well be read in conjunction with the Hoover *Memoirs*.

Another contribution to posterity by Joslin was his book *Hoover Off the Record* (Garden City: Doubleday, Doran & Co., 1934). In this extremely important book the secretary to the president for the years 1931–1933 provides a running account of his personal observations of President Hoover's actions and words during the period of his services at the White House. The book seems to be less well known to scholars than the Archie Butt volumes of the Roosevelt and Taft years, for example, and Hoover, in a sense, predicted this. The ex-president thought its publication premature. Ten months out of office he wrote: "I have been greatly troubled over Joslin's activities. Whatever the book may be, he will not have an audience for a long time yet—and you know my feelings about publicity. Some day you can do a good historical job, and I will help you at it."[9]

THE HOOVER MEMOIRS AND OTHER WRITINGS

The *Memoirs of Herbert Hoover*, as published, appear in three volumes, *Years of Adventure 1874–1920* (New York: Macmillan Co., 1951); *The Cabinet and the Presidency 1920–1933* (New York: Macmillan Co., 1952); and *The Great Depression 1929–1941* (New York: Macmillan Co., 1952). (They do not bear volume numbers.) The style of these *Memoirs* is of the early years of the twentieth century: adventure, the presentation of problems, and their solutions. A list of addresses made by Hoover prior to 1929 is given in the Appendix of the second volume, *The Cabinet and the*

Presidency, but the resources of both the Hoover Library and the Hoover Institution will be found more comprehensive. Viewed in the light of certain assumptions about Hoover's character made in the present volume, the *Memoirs* have been treated and used here as a valuable record not only of events as seen by Hoover from the inside, but also of the constraints Hoover felt in presenting his beliefs in later years.

When Hoover wrote his own analysis of the New Deal in the third volume of his memoirs, published only after the passage of two decades and aided by research assistants, he did not, and in the nature of things probably could not, satisfy all of his scholarly reviewers or his critics as he gave his version of the past, but his goal remained much as he expressed it in 1928 to a biographer. Then he wrote, "I am afraid we have to make some changes in order to get accuracy, and to avoid certain things which it is useless to put in writing." Again, "I have reconstructed the incident and put it in its true form."[10]

Proper consideration of Hoover as writer is beyond the present scope of this work. Some sidelights may be noted, however. He took great pride in *American Individualism* (Garden City: Doubleday, Page & Co., 1922), often referring to it at appropriate moments (when asked about his fundamental views). He had firm ideas about the effect he wanted to achieve and loved to number in sequence each point he made. On one occasion, he and Castle, Morrow, and Mills together drafted a memorandum for the French. Noted Hoover, "I did not like the dispatch very much as it was too lawyerlike, too technical, and befuddled people's minds on the big issues." The next day he wrote "Published our dispatch anyway."[11]

Eugene Lyons is one of many who remembered that Hoover had his own ideas on words, style, and arrangement, for ". . . he wouldn't permit anything he wrote to be changed by any editor, and the very minor changes that I had made, even unto punctuation, he simply removed— went right back to his original text."[12]

Hoover seemed to know exactly what effect he was trying to create with his major books. In writing the four volume *American Epic* (Chicago: Henry Regnery Co., 1959–1964) he said he wanted to make sure "that America's part in this is remembered" and that everyone associated with the nation's famine relief would be given credit for it. "Americans don't get much credit abroad these days for what they do," he said.[13] The two books in which "the real Hoover" is most noticeable, probably, are *The Ordeal of Woodrow Wilson* and the first volume of the *Memoirs, Years of Adventure*.[14]

False conclusions about Hoover's personality can be reached by the too-casual reader of such "late" volumes as Hoover's *Fishing for Fun and to Wash Your Soul* (New York: Random House, 1963) edited by William

Nichols. Far too many readers of such pleasant, chatty works have concluded that only in later years did Hoover develop a sense of humor or a
certain "humanness." Actually, the well-known pages 76–77 appeared
first in a Hoover address at Madison Courthouse, Virginia in 1929,[15] and
include such widely admired phrases as "the forces of nature discriminate
for no man" and "all men are equal before fishes." The subtle Hoover
humor, so much commented upon by all who knew him *personally*, was a
lifetime possession.

We cannot leave the subject of Hoover as writer without brief mention of his planned magnum opus, the unpublished fourth volume of the
Memoirs—variously entitled "The War Book," or "Freedom Betrayed."
Despite herculean efforts, Hoover never seems to have produced a draft
fully satisfactory to him, especially in terms of total accuracy. A brief
summary of its contents and meaning is that of FBI agent Vincent K.
Antle, for years assigned to the ex-president when he was in Florida.
On the basis of daily notes of many conversations, Antle says Hoover
described the volume as "a documentation of how the United States
became involved in the cold war, and the progress the Communists made
in the federal government, particularly during the Roosevelt and Truman
administrations."[16]

Hoover's method in research while at the Waldorf Astoria Hotel in
New York City was to use the library of the University Club and its
service for interlibrary loans. A cab brought items to him since he never
went there himself. He used bound rag paper volumes of the *New York
Times*.[17] Research assistants worked for Hoover, sometimes while employed full time elsewhere. As with his speeches, he placed his early
drafts in both galley and page proof. Thus there was repeated revision
while in printed form. Throughout the years historians have been strikingly unkind to the *Memoirs*, making much of even minor errors and
especially attacking their allegedly defensive tone. This is especially true
of volume 3, which is in part memoir and in part an attack on the New
Deal. In this connection, it needs to be said, perhaps, that most memoirs
are self-justifying almost by their very nature. A survey would probably
show that the Hoover *Memoirs* long have been among the least read of
major presidential volumes, as students of history have demonstrated
disinterest in both their content and their message. (This is conjecture,
to be sure, but not entirely.) Related to the published *Memoirs* is the
unpublished oral history reminiscence by Hoover on the subject of the
development of American radio regulations, which was prepared by the
Columbia University Project in 1950 and is part of their collection.

In view of the extensive bibliographical work undertaken at the
Hoover Library and the Hoover Institution, it is scarcely necessary to

more than indicate that the *Addresses on the American Road* volumes contain many but by no means all of the postpresidential speeches. *The New Day* (Stanford: Stanford University Press, 1928) presents the formal 1928 speeches, while the speeches in Latin America appeared as *Addresses Delivered During the Visit of Herbert Hoover to Central and South America* (Washington, D.C.: Pan American Union, 1929). There is a large bound "bible" of Hoover speeches and statements made throughout his career to be found at both the Hoover Library and the Hoover Institution. The sheer bulk of such material will distinctly overwhelm or at least overawe the observer, be he scholar, man of public affairs, or student.[18]

Hoover was certainly in demand as a speaker after 1933. In the first six months of 1950, for example, he turned down fifteen hundred invitations. Said he:

> I no longer care to speak (except a few minutes of pleasant extemporaneous remarks to help out some occasion) unless it is a major opportunity to say something that can be a contribution to public questions. That requires weeks of thought and research, it requires at least twenty minutes of clear radio time, and it requires that I do not come on the platform when the audience is all worn out with previous speakers.[19]

In 1928 the presidential candidate said the following to a key publicity figure: "I can make only so many speeches. I have just so much to say. I write a speech as I build a bridge, step by step, and that takes time."[20] The Hoover archives are filled with handwritten drafts. Even at private clubs among the most personal of friends, Herbert Hoover stuck to his principles on the matter. "If I talk from memory or extemporaneously," he said, "I might leave out something that I want to say that's very important."[21]

MEMOIRS OF CONTEMPORARIES

Of much value is the memoir of Henry L. Stimson written with McGeorge Bundy, *On Active Service in Peace and War* (New York: Harper, 1948), based on Stimson's diary. Another outstanding but less noted memoir based on day-by-day accounts is the Charles G. Dawes, *Journal as Ambassador to Great Britain* (New York: Macmillan Co., 1939). The autobiography of George W. Norris, *Fighting Liberal* (New York: Macmillan Co., 1945), and William Allen White's *Autobiography* (New York: Macmillan Co., 1946) have enjoyed a considerable readership over the years.

Leland Cutler, *America is Good to a Country Boy* (Stanford: Stanford

University Press, 1950), an autobiography, contains considerable material
dealing with President Hoover. Particularly valuable is the account of
relations between Hoover and Wilbur. The description of the Gridiron
Club Dinner of 1929 is especially important because it throws light upon
the relationship between Hoover and Donovan.

*The Moffat Papers, Selections from the Diplomatic Journals of Jay
Pierrepont Moffat 1919–1943*, edited by Nancy H. Hooker (Cambridge,
Mass.: Harvard University Press, 1956), furnishes observations of foreign
policy in process of formation (see Chapter 2, "Washington 1931–1933").

The Memoirs of Ray Lyman Wilbur, edited by Edgar E. Robinson
and Paul C. Edwards (Stanford: Stanford University Press, 1960), a
lengthy volume, is revealing on a variety of political and social matters
(see especially Chapters 22–31). The book by Edgar Eugene Robinson,
The Roosevelt Leadership, 1933 to 1945 (Philadelphia: Lippincott, 1955)
was commissioned as "a contemporary appraisement." V. Bornet was
research associate on this volume for a year (see p. 20).

CONTEMPORARY COMMENT

For fifteen years the *New Republic*, a weekly magazine founded in 1914,
exercised great influence upon the thinking of scholars and editors
throughout the nation. Although without a large circulation, the editorial
pages of this "journal of opinion" nevertheless reached many persons
with the repeated message that a new avenue to the development of
sound leadership might be found in the critical study of governmental
processes.

Unlike many nationally circulated magazines, this journal retained its
character as an opinion-moulding agency by insisting that it considered
each question of personnel, program, or policy as it might be considered
in a town meeting or around the council table or among a small group of
friends discussing events of the moment.

It was this *approach* to public affairs (not as yet shared by a great
number of people) that was to have a profound influence in later years
upon the action that the United States government would take. Critical
the *New Republic* was; but on the whole its criticism was intended to be
constructive. This distinguished the *New Republic* from those journals
that saw government as an appropriate target for continuous criticism.
The column contributed weekly by TRB is extremely valuable for the
period of the Hoover administration. (The style, intent, and format of
the present book preclude constant citations of innumerable periodical
sources such as this one.)

Examination of the comments appearing in weekly periodicals reveals that under "The National Scene," *Time* magazine could be a useful guide. The files of the *New York Times* for those years were indispensable, in particular, the special dispatches to that paper from the Washington bureau, and the summaries prepared by skilled observers at periodic intervals. These reporters gave their views of what had been accomplished in certain three, six, or twelve month periods. The *New York Times Index* has independent value; it was read and studied much like a textbook. The pages of *Survey Graphic* are useful for opinions and for factual data on efforts to give relief. *Literary Digest* and *Fortune* were read as a matter of course.

A list of all important discussions of the Hoover presidency that appeared in periodicals of the time was prepared, but it is not feasible to present this list here. The following need to be mentioned, however:

Anne O'Hare McCormick, *The World at Home* (New York: Alfred A. Knopf, 1956) gives selections from her writings, chiefly from her column in the *New York Times*. Editing was by M. T. Sheehan. Allan Nevins, "President Hoover's Record," *Current History* (July 1932) was an early and premature attempt at full appraisal by this distinguished historian. William Allen White, "Herbert Hoover—the Last of the Old Presidents or the First of the New?" *Saturday Evening Post* (March 4, 1933) was another contemporary effort by one whose view of party and party leaders must be weighed in the balance of time. A pamphlet, J. W. H. de Belleville, "The Man Who Does Not Forget" (Country Editor Publishing Service, August 6, 1932), may be found in the file Presidential Papers, Accomplishments, Hoover Library; it is a favorable treatment of its subject. Particularly valuable is Ray Lyman Wilbur, "President-Elect Hoover: An Intimate Study," *Current History* (December 1928), pp. 359–67, an account by one who knew Hoover extremely well. Beginning students of the Hoover character should read this very closely and be prepared to document thoroughly major departures from its intimate portrayal of Hoover *as he was*. Very large numbers of articles may be viewed at both the Hoover Library and the Hoover Institution, where an arrangement in chronological order facilitates their use. Clipping files, press releases, and analyses of editorial comment are also available.

Biographies, Interpretations, Special Studies

The following have been used by the authors, but they are by no means a complete listing of valuable and pertinent books and studies. The periodical literature, in particular, is immense for aspects of the administrations of all modern presidents, and for Hoover there is a continuing stream (see especially *Mid-America* and such state journals as *Annals of Iowa*). Masters theses and doctoral dissertations continue to be produced from work of various intensity at archives in various parts of the country. The availability of new bibliographical finding tools, of lists in the *American Historical Review* and in the footnotes to books such as those listed here, makes a list of articles unwieldy. Hoover Presidential Library tries to obtain copies of all such articles, and these may be reproduced for a small fee.

Moreover, the general historical literature on social, political, economic, diplomatic and other aspects of the United States in the Hoover years is repeatedly listed in textbook publications and is not offered here. Inclusion of an item below is by no means an endorsement of the quality or the point of view of the particular title, nor on the other hand is omission to be construed as anything but an oversight. Nevertheless, it is true that works in the following list will be found most helpful in understanding various aspects of the presidency of Herbert Hoover.

Allen, Frederick Lewis. *Only Yesterday*. New York: Harper, 1931.

———. *Since Yesterday*. New York: Harper, 1940.

Allen, Robert S. *Why Hoover Faces Defeat*. New York: Bohn, 1932.

Bailey, Thomas A. *A Diplomatic History of the American People*. New York: Meredith Corp., 1940, 1969.

Barber, James David. *The Presidential Character*. Englewood Cliffs. Prentice-Hall, 1972.

Bernstein, Irving. *The Lean Years*. Boston: Houghton Mifflin, 1960.

Bornet, Vaughn Davis. "Labor and Politics in 1928." Ph.D. dissertation, Stanford University, 1951.

————. *Labor Politics in a Democratic Republic: Moderation, Division, and Disruption in the Election of 1928.* Washington, D.C.: Spartan Press, 1964. (Reissued, Ashland, Ore.: Ashland Letter Shop, 1975.)

Brandes, Joseph. *Herbert Hoover and Economic Diplomacy: Department of Commerce Policy, 1921–1928.* Pittsburgh: University of Pittsburgh Press, 1962.

Burner, David. *The Politics of Provincialism.* New York: Knopf, 1968.

Chambers, Clarke. *Paul U. Kellogg and the Survey.* Minneapolis: University of Minnesota Press, 1971.

————. *Seedtime of Reform.* Ann Arbor: University of Michigan Press, 1967.

Corey, Herbert. *The Truth About Hoover.* Boston: Houghton Mifflin, 1932.

Crowther, Samuel. *The Presidency vs. Hoover.* Garden City: Doubleday, 1928.

Current, Richard N. *Secretary Stimson: A Study in Statecraft.* New Brunswick: Rutgers University Press, 1954.

Davis, Joseph S. "Herbert Hoover, 1874–1964: Another Analysis," *South Atlantic Quarterly* 68 (1969): 295–318.

DeConde, Alexander. *Herbert Hoover's Latin-American Policy.* Stanford: Stanford University Press, 1949.

Degler, Carl N. "The Ordeal of Herbert Hoover," *Yale Review,* June 1963, pp. 565–83.

Dexter, Walter P. *Herbert Hoover and American Individualism.* New York: Macmillan Co., 1932.

Fansold, Martin L. and George T. Mazuzan, eds. *The Hoover Presidency: A Reappraisal.* Albany: State University of New York Press, 1974.

Ferrell, Robert H. *American Diplomacy in the Great Depression: Hoover–Stimson Foreign Policy, 1929–1933.* New Haven: Yale University Press, 1957.

Freidel, Frank. *Franklin D. Roosevelt: The Triumph.* Boston: Little, Brown & Co., 1956.

————. *Franklin D. Roosevelt: Launching the New Deal.* Boston: Little, Brown & Co., 1973.

Fusfeld, Daniel R. *The Economic Thought of Franklin D. Roosevelt and the Origins of the New Deal.* New York: Columbia University Press, 1956.

Galbraith, John K. *The Great Crash, 1929.* New York: Houghton Mifflin, 1955.

Hamill, John. *The Strange Career of Mr. Herbert Hoover under Two Flags.* New York: W. Faro, 1931.

Handlin, Oscar. *Al Smith and His America.* Boston: Little, Brown & Co., 1958.

Hard, William. *Who's Hoover?* New York: Dodd, Mead & Co., 1928.

Hicks, John D. *The Republican Ascendency, 1921–1933.* New York: Harper, 1960.

Hinshaw, David. *Herbert Hoover: American Quaker.* New York: Farrar, Strauss, 1950.

Hofstadter, Richard. *The American Political Tradition and the Men Who Made It.* New York: Alfred A. Knopf, 1948.

Hutchinson, William T. *Lowden of Illinois.* Chicago: University of Chicago Press, 1957.

Huthmacher, J. Joseph and Warren I. Susman, eds. *Herbert Hoover and the Crisis of American Capitalism.* Cambridge: Schenkman, 1973.

Irwin, Will. *Herbert Hoover: A Reminiscent Biography.* New York: Grosset & Dunlap, 1928.

Johnson, Walter, ed. *The Selected Letters of William Allen White, 1899–1943.* New York: Henry Holt, 1947.

Joslin, Theodore G. *Hoover Off the Record.* Garden City: Doubleday, Doran & Co., 1934.

Kennedy, H. A. S. *Hoover in 1932.* San Francisco: Farallon, 1931.

Kennedy, Susan Estabrook. *The Banking Crisis of 1933.* Lexington, Kentucky: University of Kentucky Press, 1973.

Krock, Arthur. *Memoirs.* New York: Funk & Wagnalls, 1968.

Liggett, Walter W. *The Rise of Herbert Hoover.* New York: H. K. Fly Co., 1932.

Lisio, Donald J. *The President and Protest: Hoover, Conspiracy, and the Bonus Riot.* Columbia: University of Missouri Press, 1974.

Lloyd, Craig. *Aggressive Introvert: A Study of Herbert Hoover and Public Relations Management, 1912–1932.* Columbus: Ohio University Press, 1972.

Lohbeck, Donald. *Patrick J. Hurley.* Chicago: Henry Regnery Co., 1956.

Lyons, Eugene. *Herbert Hoover: A Biography.* Garden City: Doubleday & Co., 1964.

————. *Our Unknown Ex-President.* Garden City: Doubleday & Co., 1948.

McGee, Dorothy Horton. *Herbert Hoover: Engineer, Humanitarian, Statesman.* New York: Dodd, Mead & Co., 1959.

Mason, Alpheus T. *Harlan Fiske Stone: Pillar of the Law.* New York: Viking Press, 1956.

May, Henry F. *The End of American Innocence.* New York: Alfred A. Knopf, 1959.

Meltzer, Milton. *Brother, Can You Spare a Dime?* New York: Alfred A. Knopf, 1969.

Michelson, Charles. *The Ghost Talks.* New York: G. P. Putnam's Sons, 1944.

Mitchell, Broadus. *Depression Decade, 1929–1941.* New York: Rinehart & Co., 1947.

Moeller, Beverley Bowen. *Phil Swing and Boulder Dam.* Berkeley and Los Angeles: University of California Press, 1971.

Moley, Raymond. *After Seven Years.* New York: Harper, 1939.

————. *The First New Deal.* New York: Harcourt Brace, 1966.

————. *27 Masters of Politics.* New York: Funk & Wagnalls Company, 1949.

Mowry, George E. *The California Progressives*. Berkeley and Los Angeles: University of California Press, 1951.

―――. *The Urban Nation, 1920–1960*. New York: Hill & Wang, 1965.

Myers, William Starr. *The Foreign Policies of Herbert Hoover, 1929–1933*. New York: Charles Scribner's Sons, 1940.

Nelson, Claire E. "The Image of Herbert Hoover as Reflected in the American Press." Ph.D. dissertation, Stanford University, 1956.

Olson, James S. "From Depression to Defense: The Reconstruction Finance Corporation: 1932–1940." Ph.D. dissertation, State University of New York, Stony Brook, 1972.

Peel, R. V., and Donnelly, T. C. *The 1928 Campaign*. New York: R. R. Smith, Inc., 1931.

―――. *The 1932 Campaign*. New York: Farrar & Rinehart, 1935.

Pryor, Helen B. *Lou Henry Hoover: Gallant First Lady*. New York: Dodd, Mead & Co., 1969.

Pusey, Merlo J. *Charles Evans Hughes*. 2 vols. New York: Columbia University Press, 1963.

―――. *Eugene Meyer*. New York: Alfred A. Knopf, 1974.

Radosh, Ronald. *American Labor and United States Foreign Policy*. New York: Random House, 1969.

Rappaport, Armin. *Henry L. Stimson and Japan, 1931–1933*. Chicago: University of Chicago Press, 1963.

Robinson, Edgar Eugene. *The Roosevelt Leadership, 1933–1945*. Philadelphia: J. B. Lippincott, 1955.

―――. *They Voted For Roosevelt*. Stanford: Stanford University Press, 1947.

―――. *The New United States*. Stanford: Stanford University Press, 1946.

Romasco, A. U. *The Poverty of Abundance*. New York: Oxford University Press, 1965.

Roosevelt, Nicholas. *A Front Row Seat*. Norman: University of Oklahoma Press, 1953.

Rothbard, Murray N. *America's Great Depression*. Los Angeles: Nash Publishing Co., 1963.

Runkel, William. "Hoover's Speeches During His Presidency." Ph.D. dissertation, Stanford University, 1950.

Saloutos, T., and Hicks, J. D. *Agricultural Discontent in the Middle West, 1900–1939*. Madison: University of Wisconsin Press, 1951.

Schattschneider, E. E. *Politics, Pressures, and the Tariff*. New York: Prentice-Hall, 1935.

Schlesinger, Arthur M., Jr. *The Coming of the New Deal*. Boston: Houghton Mifflin, 1959.

―――. *The Crisis of the Old Order, 1919–1933*. Boston: Houghton Mifflin, 1957.

————. *History of American Presidential Elections, 1789–1968.* 4 vols. New York: Chelsea, 1971. Vol. 3. Contains Lawrence H. Fuchs' essay on 1928.

Schofield, Kent M. "The Figure of Herbert Hoover in the 1928 Campaign." Ph.D. dissertation, University of California, Riverside, 1966.

Schwarz, Jordan. *The Interregnum of Despair: Hoover, Congress, and the Depression.* Urbana: University of Illinois Press, 1970.

Seldes, Gilbert V. *The Years of the Locust: America, 1929–1933.* Boston: Little, Brown & Co., 1933.

Slossen, Preston W. *The Great Crusade and After, 1914–1928.* New York: Macmillan Co., 1937.

Smith, Gene. *The Shattered Dream: Herbert Hoover and the Great Depression.* New York: Morrow, 1970.

Stein, Herbert. *The Fiscal Revolution in America.* Chicago: University of Chicago Press, 1969.

Strauss, Lewis L. *Men and Decisions.* Garden City: Doubleday & Co., 1962.

Sullivan, Lawrence. *Prelude to Panic: The Story of the Bank Holiday.* Washington, D.C.: Statesman Press, 1936.

Sullivan, Mark. *The Education of an American.* New York: Doubleday, Doran & Co., 1962.

Swain, Donald C. *Wilderness Defender: Horace M. Albright and Conservation.* Chicago: University of Chicago Press, 1970.

————. *Federal Conservation Policy, 1921–1933.* Berkeley and Los Angeles: University of California Press, 1963.

[Tucker, Ray T.] *The Mirrors of 1932.* New York: Brewer, Warran & Putnam, 1931.

Timmons, Bascomb N. *Portrait of an American: Charles G. Dawes.* New York: Henry Holt, 1953.

Train, Arthur. *The Strange Attacks on Herbert Hoover.* New York: The John Day Co., 1932.

Warren, Harris. *Herbert Hoover and the Great Depression.* New York: Oxford University Press, 1959.

Wecter, Dixon. *The Age of the Great Depression, 1929–1941.* New York: Macmillan Co., 1948.

Wehle, Louis B. *Hidden Threads of History.* New York: Macmillan Co., 1953.

White, William Allen. *The Autobiography of William Allen White.* New York: Macmillan Co., 1946.

Williams, William Appleman. *The Contours of American History.* New York: Watts, 1966.

————. *Some Presidents: Wilson to Nixon.* New York: Random House, 1972.

Wilson, Carol Green. *Herbert Hoover: A Challenge for Today.* New York: Evans, 1968.

Wilson, Joan Hoff. *American Business and Foreign Policy, 1920–1933*. Lexington: University of Kentucky Press, 1971.

————. *Ideology and Economics: United States Relations with the Soviet Union, 1918–1933*. Columbia: University of Missouri Press, 1974.

Wolfe, Harold. *Herbert Hoover: Public Servant and Leader of the Loyal Opposition*. New York: Exposition Press, 1956.

Wood, Clement. *Herbert Clark Hoover: An American Tragedy*. New York: Swain, 1932.

Zieger, Robert. *Republicans and Labor, 1919–1929*. Lexington: University of Kentucky Press, 1969.

Zucker, Norman L. *George W. Norris: Gentle Knight of American Democracy*. Urbana: University of Illinois Press, 1966.

Notes

1: A Crisis in American Politics

1. See Thomas A. Bailey, *Presidential Greatness* (New York: Appleton, 1966) for analysis, incisive comment, and full criticism.

2. A new look at the Harding and Coolidge administrations has been provided in such works as Robert K. Murray, *The Harding Era* (Minneapolis, 1969); Francis Russell, *The Shadow of Blooming Grove* (New York, 1968); Donald Mc-Coy, *Calvin Coolidge* (New York: Macmillan Co., 1967); and Andrew Sinclair, *The Available Man* (New York: Macmillan Co., 1965).

2: Why Hoover Was Chosen

1. See Merle Curti, *American Philanthropy Abroad: A History* (New Brunswick; Rutgers University Press, 1963) for the full story.

2. The most penetrating view of Hoover's appeal as a volunteer is that of Ray Lyman Wilbur in "President-Elect Hoover," *Current History* 29 (December 1928); pp. 359–67. See also Benjamin M. Weissman, *Herbert Hoover and Famine Relief to Soviet Russia, 1921 to 1923* (Stanford: Hoover Institution Press, 1974).

3. Roosevelt to Hugh Gibson, January 2, 1920. Quoted by Frank Freidel, *Franklin D. Roosevelt: The Ordeal* (Boston: Little, Brown & Co., 1954), p. 57.

4. Harding to Oscar Bigler, February 18, 1920, copied into Bigler to Richey, January 6, 1931, PPI Box 13, Hoover Library.

5. Joseph Brandes, *Herbert Hoover and Economic Diplomacy: Department of Commerce Policy, 1921–1928* (Pittsburgh, 1962), p. x. A decade later that judgment was too harsh. Thus: "Hoover to a remarkable extent made Commerce the most spectacular of the departments . . . ;" and ". . . Hoover performed innumerable scientific services for industry . . . ." Frank Freidel, *America in the Twentieth Century*, 3d ed. (New York: Alfred A. Knopf, 1970), p. 251.

6. Ellis W. Hawley and others have been concentrating on the elements of the Hoover program in the years 1921–1929. See his fully researched essay in *Herbert Hoover and the Crisis of American Capitalism* (Cambridge, Mass.: Schenkman Publishing Co., 1973), pp. 3–34. He concludes that "the Hoover of the 1920's has been difficult to label . . . ; yet he did have a coherent system of thought . . . ; and if he must be labeled, the term 'associational progressive' would seem to fit

better than any other" (p. 27). Gerald D. Nash prefers "cooperative capitalism" (Ibid., p. 101). Murray N. Rothbard uses the term "corporate liberal" (Ibid., p. 115). All contributors to that book agree that Hoover was neither "an advocate of laissez-faire" nor "a slavish servant of big business" (Ibid., p. 115).

David Burner and Thomas R. West call Hoover "a Progressive and later a Conservative" by American terminology. See "A Technocrat's Morality: Conservatism and Hoover the Engineer," in Stanley Elkins and Eric McKitrick, eds., *The Hofstadter Aegis* (New York: Alfred A. Knopf, 1974), pp. 235–56.

7. Craig Lloyd, *Aggressive Introvert: A Study of Herbert Hoover and Public Relations Management, 1912–1932*, pp. 140–141. Says Lloyd, "Given great publicity, the letter had alarmed Gary, and the latter, with the concurrence of the directors of the American Iron and Steel Institute, had finally notified the president that steps were being taken for the 'total abolition of the twelve-hour day.'" Not legal repression, but public opinion, was the Hoover method, it is stated (p. 141).

8. See the Hunt papers, Hoover Institution.

9. Edward Anthony reminiscence, July 12, 1970, Hoover Institution. A repetition, using *Who's Who in America,* after the nomination, covering the whole country, gave Hoover 8,762, Smith 1,270. Ibid., p. 78.

10. The successes of the Democratic party since 1932 have overshadowed its earlier weaknesses. See K. C. MacKay, *The Progressive Movement of 1924* (New York: 1947); or, on the record of Democratic support at the polls, see E. E. Robinson, *The Presidential Vote, 1896–1932* (Stanford University Press, 1934) and idem, *The Evolution of American Political Parties: A Sketch of Party Development* (New York: Harcourt, 1924).

11. Herbert Hoover, *American Individualism* (Garden City: Doubleday, Page & Co., 1922), available in reprint form from Herbert Hoover Presidential Library Association, West Branch, Iowa.

12. See bibliography for examples of books written for young people to provide guidance in right conduct.

13. Edward Anthony reminiscence, July 12, 1970. Hoover Institution, p. 45. Without Hill, Mr. Anthony guessed, Hoover would not have been nominated (Ibid., pp. 47–48). The absence of Hill from the 1932 effort was a serious loss, Anthony said.

14. Christian A. Herter, editorial in *The Independent,* June 30, 1928.

15. For details on the election, see Roy V. Peel and Thomas C. Donnelly, *The 1928 Campaign, an Analysis* (New York, 1931).

16. Editorial, *Commercial and Financial Chronicle,* June 23, 1928.

17. Vaughn D. Bornet. *Labor Politics in a Democratic Republic: Moderation, Division, and Disruption in the Election of 1928* (Washington, D.C., Spartan Books, 1964).

18. For the acceptance speech, see Herbert Hoover, *The New Day* (Stanford: Stanford University Press, 1928), pp. 9–44.

19. Edward Anthony reminiscence, p. 75.

20. Acceptance address. August 11, 1928. For a statistically based analysis of prosperity in 1928, see Bornet, *Labor Politics,* chapter 1, passim.

21. *New York Times,* June 19, 1920.

22. See, on this theme, *Seedtime of Reform: American Social Service and Social Action, 1918–1933* (Minneapolis: University of Minnesota Press, 1963).

23. These matters are treated minutely in Bornet, *Labor Politics,* chapters 9, 10, and 11. See also Mark O. Hatfield's pioneering study, "Herbert Hoover and Labor: Politics and Attitudes, 1897–1928" (M.A. thesis. Stanford University, 1948).

24. The Republican candidate specified to his publicity staff three areas about which nothing should be spoken without prior approval: prohibition, religion, and Mrs. Smith. A restriction on the latter was imposed because "some zealots already had compared her unfavorably with previous first ladies." Alfred H. Kirchofer Reminiscence, April 4, 1969, p. 8, Hoover Institution.

25. When Hoover was shown the speech twenty years later, he remarked, "I reread it. I wouldn't change a word of it today. It's still a great speech . . . ." Walter Trohan Reminiscence, November 15, 1966, p, 15, Hoover Institution. The speech was reported in the *New York Times,* November 6, 1928, but see Hoover, *The New Day,* pp. 211–15, for the above version.

26. *New York Times,* November 8, 1928.

27. Alpheus T. Mason, *Harlan Fiske Stone: Pillar of the Law,* p. 264.

28. Alan J. Gould reminiscence, October 27, 1970, p. 3, Hoover Institution. (Gould was the executive editor of Associated Press for 21 years and knew Hoover and Roosevelt well.)

29. A useful volume of essays which (because of its distribution problems) became available only when this book was in the proof stage is Martin L. Fansold, ed., and George T. Mazuzan, assoc. ed., *The Hoover Presidency: A Reappraisal* (Albany, N.Y., 1974). It contains addresses delivered at a conference in April, 1973. The account of the campaign by Donald McCoy concludes that "Herbert Hoover ran a remarkably able campaign for president in 1928." (p. 45).

30. Confidential source.

3: A New Kind of President

1. From notes made at the time by E. E. Robinson. A minor annoyance was the posting of the Smith concession telegram on the bulletin board before Hoover got to see it. Adaline W. Fuller reminiscence, September 29, 1967, p. 22, Hoover Institution.

2. Hoover reports that he "had only a single failure, that being Senator Norris of Nebraska," in the effort to secure "unity in action from all groups in the Republican party" after the nomination [*The Memoirs of Herbert Hoover:*

The Cabinet and the Presidency (New York: Macmillan Co., 1951)], p. 197.

On Michelson's peculiar talents, Arthur Krock judged that he was "one of the ablest political propagandists since the days of Andrew Jackson's pamphleteers..." (*Memoirs*. p. 123). He ghost-wrote many Democratic spokesmen's speeches.

3. *New York Tribune*, February 27, 1929.

4. According to Frank Freidel (*Franklin D. Roosevelt: The Triumph*, p. 33), Roosevelt received about a thousand replies.

5. For Governor-elect Roosevelt's defense of such a position, see his letter of January 28, 1929 to Nicholas Roosevelt in *FDR His Personal Letters 1928–1945* (New York: Duell, Sloan & Pearce, 1950), 1:26–32. Based upon a reading of these replies in 1952 by V. Bornet, it should be said that the Roosevelt summary was grossly overdrawn.

6. Walsh Papers, Manuscript Division, Library of Congress.

7. Senator Borah was not offered the secretaryship of state, as stated in Claudius O. Johnson, *Borah of Idaho* (Seattle: University of Washington Press, 1969) and repeated by writers of various textbooks. Herbert Hoover to Edgar E. Robinson, November 17, 1955. In the author's possession.

8. Hon. Joseph C. Green reminiscence (called "verbatim"), November 22, 1967, p. 37, Hoover Institution.

9. Letter of clerk of Supreme Court to Akerson, secretary to the president, President's personal file, box 10, Hoover Library. In a wire by F. Strother to Richard W. Hale of Boston appears the statement that Herbert Hoover "is on the rolls of an Orthodox Meeting (of Quakers) by birthright. At Inauguration did swear did not affirm. Has repeatedly stated he would fight." In the Presidential Library.

10. Roosevelt to Hoover, March 4, 1929, Presidential Papers, Roosevelt, Hoover Library. The Roosevelt margin was a scant 25,564.

11. Hoover, *Memoirs: The Cabinet and the Presidency*, p. 222.

12. On the day preceding Hoover's departure from Washington to Florida the Senate had voted $250,000 for a proposed fact-finding study on law enforcement. This had been agreed upon in a conference with Hoover. It had been accompanied, as well, by a proposal close to his heart: to coordinate the administrative activities of the various branches of the government.

13. William Starr Myers, ed., *The State Papers and Other Public Writings of Herbert Hoover* (Garden City, N.Y.: Doubleday, Doran, 1934), 1: 5–6. The address may also be found conveniently in Dwight Miller, comp., *Public Papers of the Presidents: Herbert Hoover, vol. 1, March 4, 1929 to December 31, 1929* (Washington, D. C.: National Archives, 1974), pp. 1–12. Hereafter cited as *Public Papers*. It has been thought best not to change footnote references in the present volume from manuscript sources to this set, especially since items in the new *Public Papers* series are given chronologically and are therefore easily located. (Only the 1929 volume was available by our press time.)

14. Myers, *State Papers,* p. 7. It will be recalled that Mrs. Hoover took a particularly active role with one voluntary agency, the Girl Scouts of America.

15. T.R.B., *New Republic,* April 10, 1929, pp. 224–25.

16. Krock, *Memoirs,* p. 133.

17. Robert R. Updegraff, "What Will Hoover Do?" *Magazine of Business,* December 1928, p. 653.

18. *Henry Lewis Stimson Diaries,* microfilm edition, Manuscripts and Archives, Yale University Library, retrospective account dictated August 28, 1930, p. 2.

19. Carbon copy of a Castle memorandum on an article by Benjamin B. Wallace, "How the U.S. Led the League in 1931," May 16, 1945, Castle Papers, "Hoover," Hoover Library.

20. "Almost any Hoover fan could tell you," wrote a correspondent in the *New York World* (January 22, 1929), "that Mr. Hoover both collects books and reads them. That after reading reports and papers that would send a columnist and his readers into headaches, he reads till late at night all sorts of books and has done so all his life; travel, biography, adventure, history, occasional detective stories; anything with value to it, . . . That his personal library is enormous, that he is a collector of scientific books in the original editions, that his gift of war documents to the Stanford Library is one of its prized possessions, and world-known. And that the only reason the busy youths of the press haven't ferreted out and broadcast this particular private taste is that its owner is too busy, during the time that other people are awake to work with him, to exhibit its indulgence."

21. Generalizations based on long contact by Edgar E. Robinson with Hoover on the Stanford campus and in later years.

22. Edward Eyre Hunt to Hoover, April 21, 1938, PPI 907, Hoover Library. Hunt observed that he had had a good deal to do with developing the methods of study and research, but "the impulse was yours."

4: The Politics of the New Day

1. Hoover, *American Individualism,* pp. 7–90.

2. Ibid., pp. 54–55.

3. Ibid., p. 68.

4. Ibid., pp. 70–71.

5. Mason, *Harlan Fiske Stone,* p. 270. When aged usher Ike Hoover wrote of these daily events, the White House physician commented, "He certainly erred when he said you did not exercise at those early morning periods. I do not see how anyone could classify them as a joke from the standpoint of exercise. Ike was never present at that time of day and his observations are blind on that score." Adm. (Dr.) Joel T. Boone to Hoover, January 26, 1934, PPI, Hoover

Library. Ike Hoover was also unqualified to comment on the nature and value of the Hoover lunch and dinner sessions, and was not capable of understanding the lifestyle of the complex president. The time has come for history books to see the president's lifestyle for what it was—not what this usher said it was.

The oral history reminiscences contradict Ike Hoover repeatedly. Alonzo Fields was in charge of the medicine ball breakfast and he kept a diary (Oral History reminiscence, July 24, 1970, Hoover Institution). The views of all other subordinates on President and Mrs. Hoover border on the worshipful. (Observation based on reading all of the oral histories.)

6. Press conference, March 22, 1929. These unpublished documents are in the Hoover Library. There has been vastly too much concentration on comparing Roosevelt and Hoover "style" in press conference behavior rather than consideration of reliable factual content and genuine effort to use the conference to educate both newsmen and, through them, the public. See the *Public Papers* series as it appears.

7. T.R.B., *New Republic*, March 27, 1929. Craig Lloyd, *Aggressive Introvert*, treats such matters with full archival research.

8. Not until Hoover left office was this address printed, in 1934. T. G. Joslin, ed. *Hoover After Dinner* (Garden City, N.Y.: Doubleday, Doran, 1934), pp. 3–12. Or see Myers, *State Papers*; see also *Public Papers*, 1: 67–72.

9. Hoover was not a spokesman for the "New Era." In Arthur M. Schlesinger, Jr., *The Age of Roosevelt: The Crisis of the Old Order, 1919–1933* (Boston, 1957) the words "New Era" are repeatedly and persistently applied to the years 1919 to 1933. Thus, ca. 1932, "And so the New Era faded away" (p. 255). Yet Hoover's official title for the campaign addresses in book form was *The New Day*, and Hoover in his *Memoirs: The Great Depression* was repeatedly caustic. On pages 5, 7, 15, 17, 19, and 125 he condemned "New Era" or "New Economic Era" economics and adherents. It was "a foolish idea" (p. 5), an "illusion" (p. 7), and "due for a jolt" (p. 15). The Joseph Davis argument that "New Era" as a proper noun was used by Hoover in a personal sense is unpersuasive. "Herbert Hoover, 1874–1964: Another Analysis," *South Atlantic Quarterly* (1969); p. 313.

10. A large five-volume set of documents published in the 1970's, *Conservation in the United States* (New York, 1972), gave scant attention to the Hoover administration. In an address on October 18, 1952, Hoover said bluntly, "Republicans originated practically the whole idea of Federal conservation of natural resources," establishing the first national forests, the Forest Service, the first national park, the Oil Conservation Board, federal reclamation of arid lands (1902), and the first gigantic multi purpose dam. Quoted in Franklin L. Burdette, ed., *Readings for Republicans* (New York: Oceana, 1960), pp. 176–77. A reading of the Taylor Gates Collection at the Hoover Library and the Wilbur Papers at Hoover Institution should change many minds on Hoover as conservationist. See chapter 5 below.

11. See Burke correspondence in the Hoover Library (Presidential Papers, Republican National Committee, Burke).

12. Burke correspondence.

13. Huston to Richey, April 17, 1929, Presidential Papers, Republican National Committee, Hoover Library.

14. See Huston file, Hoover Library. Hoover told E. E. Robinson on June 26, 1956 that Huston was his choice.

15. Telegram, Hoover to Millbank, October 24, 1929, Hoover Library.

16. Quoted in Jordan A. Schwarz. *The Interregnum of Despair: Hoover, Congress, and the Depression*, p. 47. Schwarz suggests that "most of the Old Guard never forgave Hoover for not rising to prominence through party ranks." (Ibid., p. 46).

17. Hoover to Horace A. Mann, June 19, 1929, Presidential Papers, Mann, Hoover Library.

18. Hoover to Walter H. Newton, April 15, 1929, President's Secretary's File, Hoover Library.

19. Mark L. Requa to Lawrence Richey, June 6, 1929, Presidential Papers, Requa, Hoover Library.

20. See, for example, Requa file, Hoover Library.

21. An Iowa lawyer particularly urged Hoover not to forget the existence of thousands of Democrats who so far had favored Hoover's policies and position. I. T. Jones to L. Richey, July 30, 1929, Presidential Papers, Huston, Hoover Library.

22. The White House staff could hardly help; at the time it consisted of three secretaries, a military and naval aide, and three dozen clerks. The mail load averaged 400 letters daily. See Louis W. Koenig, *The Invisible Presidency* (New York: 1960), p. 16.

23. "Never in any other activity did he encounter such difficulty in finding the right man for the job." David Hinshaw, *Herbert Hoover: American Quaker*, p. 173.

24. Borah to Hoover, December 28, 1929, President's Personal File 543, Hoover Library.

25. Details supportive of this paragraph will appear in appropriate chapters below.

26. David B. Burner, "Before the Crash: Hoover's First Eight Months in the Presidency," in *The Hoover Presidency*, p. 54.

27. Ibid., p. 54.

5: Plans for the National Estate

1. An interesting sidelight: Looking over membership lists in 1930, the secretary of the Royal Geographical Society in London hit upon a familiar name. Forthwith, he cabled the president: "It was only about a fortnight ago that I realized . . . that Mr. H. C. Hoover, who for 20 years had been a Fellow of our

Society . . . was the President of the United States" (Letter of July 23, 1930, Hoover Library).

2. Press conference, March 12, 1929. *Public Papers*, 1:21.

3. Press conference, March 15, 1929. Ibid., p. 26.

4. See, on these matters, Burl Noggle, *Teapot Dome* (Baton Rouge, 1962), especially p. 127.

5. Ibid., p. 209.

6. Ibid., p. 210.

7. Press conference, April 2, 1929.

8. Wilbur to Hoover, May 22, 1929, Hoover Library. See also Requa to Richey, May 15, 1929 and Wilbur to George Akerson, May 21, 1929, Presidential Papers, Oil Matters, Colorado Springs, Hoover Library.

9. Hoover to Dan Moody, May 23, 1929, same file, Hoover Library.

10. Requa to Richey, June 12 and June 13, 1929, same file, Hoover Library.

11. U.S., Congress, Senate, *Congressional Record*, 71, pt. 3:2641.

12. Requa to Richey, June 12 and June 13, 1929, Presidential Papers, Oil Matters, Colorado Springs, Hoover Library.

13. Requa, "The Trend of the Petroleum Industry, from the Armistice to 1934" (privately printed), p. 24.

14. Hoover to Requa, June 17, 1929, Presidential Papers, Oil Matters, Colorado Springs, Hoover Library.

15. Press conference statement, June 25, 1929. *Public Papers* 1:197–99.

16. William Starr Myers and Walter H. Newton, *The Hoover Administration: A Documented Narrative* (New York, 1936), p. 481.

17. Press conference, September 17, 1929, Hoover Library.

18. Press conference, October 8, 1929, Hoover Library.

19. Press conference, October 18, 1929, Hoover Library.

20. June 25, 1929. *Public Papers*, 1:197. See also Hoover, *Memoirs: The Cabinet and the Presidency*, pp. 226–29, and Edgar E. Robinson and Paul C. Edwards, eds., *The Memoirs of Ray Lyman Wilbur* (Stanford: Stanford University Press, 1960), pp. 441–65, for detailed discussion of the steps taken in construction of the Hoover Dam during the Hoover administration. Chap. 23–29 of the Wilbur memoir are useful on the conservation policies of the administration.

21. Myers, *State Papers*, 1:521–29.

22. Quoted in Norman L. Zucker, *George W. Norris: Gentle Knight of American Democracy*, p. 123.

23. Concluding sentence in ibid., p. 163.

24. Mellon to Hoover, March 9, 1929, Ogden Mills Papers, Library of Congress.

25. *Public Papers*, 1:121–23, 416–17. A film, "The City of Washington," was presented to Mrs. Hoover later. Mellon to Mrs. Hoover, May 22, 1929, Ogden Mills Papers, Library of Congress.

26. Press conference, July 5, 1929, Hoover Library.

27. There is an Albright oral history reminiscence in the Oral History Project, Columbia University.

28. Albright reminiscence, September 22, 1967, p. 82, Hoover Institution.

29. Ibid., p. 85. For a time, however, against Albright's strong wishes, cemeteries and some office buildings were also included.

30. Ibid., p. 53.

31. Hoover to W. E. Carson, August 7, 1929, donating the camp to Shenandoah National Park at the end of his term of office. Myers, *State Papers*, 1:246–47.

32. Ibid., 2:107–8.

33. In R. L. Wilbur and A. M. Hyde, *The Hoover Policies* (New York, 1937), p. 243.

34. Address of April 9, 1927 to Izaak Walton League, in Joslin, ed., *Hoover After Dinner*, p. 91. See also Herbert Hoover, *Fishing for Fun—And to Wash Your Soul* (New York, 1963).

35. Presidential Papers, National Timber Conservation Board, Hoover Library.

36. Bureau of Fisheries Report, February 1933, Taylor-Gates Collection, Commerce (A-II-9), Hoover Library.

37. See Herbert Hoover, *The Challenge to Liberty* (New York: Charles Scribner's Sons, 1934) and the *Addresses on the American Road* volumes. Judges a historian who has studied Hoover as one who "began to fire up the engines of Progressive reform" as Secretary of Commerce and continued in the presidency, "Yet any judgment of Hoover's term in the White House must first acknowledge that he organized the beginnings of 'many reforms that were needed'. Some of these reforms came about during his term, some—delayed by the depression—came later, a few remain as points of discussion more than a generation later." David B. Burner, "Before the Crash: Hoover's First Eight Months in the Presidency," in *The Hoover Presidency*, p. 54.

6:   Hoover and the Farmer

1. See David Potter, *People of Plenty: Economic Abundance and the American Character* (Chicago, 1954).

2. See the chapters "Agrarians and American Foreign Policy" and "The Decline of Agrarian Isolationism" in Wayne Cole, *Senator Gerald P. Nye and American Foreign Relations* (Minneapolis, 1962).

3. For a summary of Hoover's view of the agricultural problem, see Wilbur and Hyde, *The Hoover Policies*, pp. 146–52; T. Saloutos and J. D. Hicks, *Agricultural Discontent in the Middle West, 1900–1939* (Madison, Wis., 1951), is useful.

4. Hoover, *The New Day*, p. 53.

5. Hoover, *Memoirs: The Cabinet and the Presidency*, p. 255.

55555555555

6. *Congressional Record,* 71, pt. 1:440.

7. Ibid., p. 735.

8. *Public Papers,* 1:77–78.

9. Ibid., p. 78.

10. Ibid.

11. See William T. Hutchinson, *Lowden of Illinois,* 2:648n.

12. *Public Papers,* 1:87–88.

13. *Congressional Record,* 71, pt. 1:301–5.

14. The Hoover archives amply reveal these points. See the White House "Appointment Book" for daily activities related to the farm problem.

15. Press conference, April 19, 1929, Hoover Library.

16. *Public Papers,* 1:84 gives the president's views.

17. The vote was seventy-four (forty-seven Republicans and twenty-seven Democrats) for the bill, and eight (three Republicans and five Democrats) opposed. Thirteen senators did not vote, eleven of whom were absent.

18. *Public Papers,* 1:88.

19. *Congressional Record,* 71, pt. 3:2729.

20. Presidential Papers, Farm Matters files, Hoover Library.

21. Wilbur and Hyde, *The Hoover Policies,* p. 152.

22. Press conference, July 2, 1929, Hoover Library.

23. *Public Papers,* 1:221.

24. Hutchinson, *Lowden of Illinois,* p. 647.

25. Hoover, *Memoirs: The Great Depression,* p. 51.

26. Ibid., p. 52.

27. Press conference, July 10, 1930, Hoover Library.

28. Comment on this change may be found in Hutchinson's chapter, "No Help to Hoover": "The Farm Board fiasco, moreover, apparently made many farmers apathetic toward any new scheme of governmental aid. The imminence of the presidential election year inclined leading politicians to devote more attention to their personal fortunes than to devising a farm program upon which they could all unite. . . . Effective agricultural aid is the key to nation wide recovery. If farm commodity prices do not rise; then all other prices must fall" (*Lowden of Illinois,* 2:653).

29. Press conference, September 4, 1931, Hoover Library.

30. U.S., Department of Agriculture, *Third Annual Report of Federal Farm Board* (Washington, D.C.: Government Printing Office, 1932).

31. Myers, *State Papers,* 1:577.

7: The Palsied Hand of Prohibition

1. The statement first appeared in a letter: Hoover to Borah, February 23, 1928, President's Personal File 37, Hoover Library.

2. Hoover, *Memoirs: The Cabinet and the Presidency,* pp. 200–201.

3. Ibid., p. 276.

4. *Public Papers,* 1:101–2.

5. Myers, *State Papers,* 1:6.

6. *Public Papers,* 1:17.

7. Hoover Library.

8. Mason, *Harlan Fiske Stone,* p. 273.

9. *Public Papers,* 1:159–60.

10. Donovan to Hoover letters in Presidential Papers, Donovan, Hoover Library.

11. Mellon to Hoover, April 10, 1929, Ogden Mills Papers, Library of Congress.

12. Mellon to Hoover, May 31, 1929, Ogden Mills Papers.

13. *Public Papers,* 1:178.

14. Ibid., 1:404–36.

15. Press conference, December 27, 1929, Hoover Library.

16. Hoover, *Memoirs: The Cabinet and the Presidency,* p. 283.

17. Myers, *State Papers,* 1:493.

18. Hoover, *Memoirs: The Cabinet and the Presidency,* p. 278.

19. Harvey O. Higgins, "The Great Prohibition Mystery," *The Outlook,* December 12, 1928. Also condensed in *Readers Digest,* February 1929.

20. Katherine Fullerton Gerould, "This Hard-Boiled Era," *Harper's Magazine,* February 1929. The entire mood of Charles Merz, *The Dry Decade* (Garden City, N.Y., 1930, 1931) was gloomy about possibilities for enforcement.

21. Books on Borah shed much light on his relationship with Hoover. For example, see Johnson, *Borah of Idaho;* Robert James Maddox, *William E. Borah and American Foreign Policy* (Baton Rouge, 1969); and Marian C. McKenna, *Borah* (Ann Arbor: University of Michigan Press, 1961).

22. Johnson, *Borah of Idaho,* pp. 259–60.

23. Hoover to Borah, December 30, 1929, Presidential Papers, Borah, Hoover Library.

24. Ibid.

25. Borah to Hoover, December 31, 1929, Presidential Papers, Borah. Hoover Library.

26. Ibid.

27. Colonel Raymond Robins to Borah. Quoted without exact date in Johnson, *Borah of Idaho,* p. 462.

28. Hoover to Borah, January 2, 1930, Presidential Papers, Borah, Hoover Library.

29. Borah to Hoover, January 3, 1930, same file, Hoover Library.

30. Johnson, *Borah of Idaho,* p. 466. Borah supported disarmament, resistance to "big navy" advocates, the Latin American policy, and many treaties.

31. Senator Norris, who supported Smith in 1928, was already a lost cause.

8:   Legacy in Foreign Relations

1. Hoover, *Memoirs: The Cabinet and The Presidency,* p. 378.

2. Address on the League of Nations, Stanford University, October 2, 1919, unpublished manuscript, Hoover Library.

3. Hoover to Woodrow Wilson, April 11, 1919. In William Starr Myers, *The Foreign Policies of Herbert Hoover, 1929–1933,* pp. 16–17.

4. Hoover, *Memoirs: The Cabinet and the Presidency,* p. 182. Joan Hoff Wilson, *Ideology and Economics: U.S. Relations With the Soviet Union, 1918–1933* (Columbia, Mo., 1974) contains references to Hoover's attitude toward the USSR in the 1920s.

5. Hoover, *Memoirs: The Cabinet and the Presidency,* pp. 177–78.

6. Address on the League of Nations, October 2. 1919.

7. Address before the Gridiron Club, Washington, D.C., April 13, 1929, *Public Papers,* 1:70.

8. Hoover, *Memoirs: The Cabinet and the Presidency,* p. 210.

9. Alexander DeConde, *Herbert Hoover's Latin-American Policy,* pp. 48–49.

10. *Public Papers,* 1:406.

11. DeConde, *Hoover's Latin-American Policy,* pp. 185–86 and 440.

12. Hoover, *Memoirs: The Cabinet and the Presidency,* p. 214.

13. DeConde, *Hoover's Latin-American Policy,* pp. 25–31.

14. "Hoover even before he was inaugurated applied the good-neighbor ideal specifically to Latin America, whereas Roosevelt appropriated the same concept and gave it world-wide application" (Ibid., p. 127). Hoover did not invent the term. Textbook historians are well aware of the Hoover role, due to the DeConde book, but the general public seems completely unaware of the Hoover contribution.

15. Stimson, "Bases of American Foreign Policy During the Past Four Years," *Foreign Affairs,* April 1933, pp. 383–96, as quoted in DeConde, *Hoover's Latin-American Policy,* p. 123.

16. U.S., Department of State, Press Release, no. 92, July 4, 1931, p. 31, quoted in DeConde, *Hoover's Latin-American Policy.* p. 51.

17. Press Release, no. 92, p. 32, quoted in ibid., p. 125.

18. President Hoover signed the tariff act for reasons discussed before, chap. 9.

19. DeConde, *Hoover's Latin-American Policy*, p. 77.

20. Allan Nevins, "President Hoover's Record," *Current History*, 36 (1932): pp. 385–94, as quoted in ibid., p. 127. The *New York World* found the first eight months of Hoover foreign policy "dazzling." Quoted in Burner, *op. cit.*, p. 63.

21. For Hoover's early interest, see particularly the references to the manuscripts of Edward Price Bell in George V. Fagan, "Anglo-American Naval Relations 1927–1937" (Ph.D. diss., University of Pennsylvania, 1954) noted in Robert H. Ferrell, *American Diplomacy in the Great Depression: Hoover-Stimson Foreign Policy, 1929–1933*, pp. 75–76. R. G. O'Connor, *Perilous Equilibrium: The United States and The London Naval Conference of 1930* (1962; reprinted, Westport, Conn.: Greenwood, 1969), is a thorough study from sources other than the Hoover Archives.

22. Hoover, *Memoirs: The Cabinet and the Presidency*, p. 340.

23. The Dawes *Journal*, under date of May 19, 1929, displays the care with which President Hoover prepared his statements and the way in which he worked with those in whom he had confidence. Dawes recounts how the statement on naval disarmament was prepared in Washington. The President went over the matter with Dawes, using as a basis a formula prepared for him by Gibson. This statement was then taken up with Stimson and, as agreed upon, was then submitted to State Department experts for rewording. Stimson and Dawes conferred again, and then Dawes reviewed the discussion with the President. The following day, there was still another discussion between Dawes and the President (Charles G. Dawes, *Journal as Ambassador to Great Britain*, pp. 1–4).

24. Presidential Papers, Foreign Affairs, Disarmament, Hoover Library.

25. Ibid.

26. Ibid.

27. Ibid. Hoover's unsatisfactory correspondence with Secretary of State Cordell Hull, December 20, 1940 to June 28, 1941, when Hoover was struggling to get the Roosevelt administration to facilitate American feeding of civilians in the occupied countries, contained the Hoover outburst. "Not only am I deeply shocked at the present attitude of our Government, but I know tens of millions of Americans would also be shocked. History will never justify the Government of the United States siding with the starvation of these millions." Hoover to Hull, June 3, 1941, Postpresidential Papers, Hull box 902, Hoover Library.

28. Dawes, *Journal*. p. 100.

29. MacDonald to Hoover, October 12, 1929. Typed copy in Presidential Papers, Foreign Affairs, Disarmament, Hoover Library.

30. Hoover, *Memoirs: The Cabinet and the Presidency*, p. 346.

31. Press conference, July 23, 1929. Hoover Library.

32. Hoover, *Memoirs: The Cabinet and the Presidency*, pp. 345–46.

33. Dawes. *Journal*, p. 95.

34. Borah to Hoover, October 19, 1929. Presidential Papers, Borah, Hoover Library.

35. See Maddox, *William E. Borah*. Undersecretary of the Treasury Ogden L. Mills had written to Senator Borah on December 13, 1928: "You will remember that about a year ago I called on you and explained to you, in a general way, the basis of the agreement which had been reached with Greece for the settlement of their indebtedness to the United States Government, and of the differences arising from the so-called Tripartite Loan Agreement of February 10, 1918. The bill authorizing the Secretary of the Treasury to execute such an agreement of settlement with Greece has passed the House of Representatives and is now pending in the Senate. I do not want to take up your time again, but I am taking the liberty of writing you because of the very strong feeling which I have that the good faith of the United States is involved and that in view of the fact that we are very rightly requesting other nations to live up to their obligations to the extent of their capacity to do so, there should be no question as to the United States living up to its obligations" (Ogden Mills Papers, Library of Congress).

36. *Congressional Record*, 1929, 71, pt. 1:120.

37. Maddox, *William E. Borah*, p. 214.

38. Press Conference, June 13, 1930, Hoover Library. Myers, *State Papers*, 1:311.

39. Dawes, *Journal*, June 30, 1930, p. 219.

40. Robinson to Hoover, July 17, 1930, Presidential Papers, Robinson, Hoover Library.

41. Hoover, *Memoirs: The Cabinet and the Presidency*, p. 350.

42. Myers, *State Papers*, 1:357–58. Confidential documents were sent June 2. Files on the matter are in Hoover Library. O'Connor says the President showed great firmness (*Perilous Equilibrium*, pp. 223–24).

43. O'Connor, *Perilous Equilibrium*, pp. 223–24.

44. *Congressional Record*, 1930. 73, pt. 0:378.

45. Dawes, *Journal*, p. 22.

46. O'Connor, *Perilous Equilibrium*, pp. 247 and 261.

47. Dawes, *Journal*, p. 247.

48. *New York Times*, April 30, 1930; July 7, 1930; August 30, 1930.

49. The *Times* reporter saw the return of the American delegation as the "second most important event of its kind" since Wilson's from Versailles and Kellogg's after the Kellogg-Briand Pact. *New York Times*, April 30, 1930, p. 1.

50. Richard Leopold, *The Growth of American Foreign Policy* (New York, 1962), pp. 448–49; O'Connor, *Perilous Equilibrium*, p. 247.

51. O'Connor, *Perilous Equilibrium*, p. 265.

52. Hoover, *Memoirs: The Cabinet and the Presidency*, p. 330.

53. Myers, *State Papers*, 2:81.

54. Hoover, *Memoirs: The Cabinet and the Presidency*, p. 337.

55. The military crisis in the Far East is discussed in chap. 14.

56. Hoover, *Memoirs: The Cabinet and the Presidency*, p. 335.

57. Nicholas Roosevelt, *A Front Row Seat*, pp. 186–88. See also Roosevelt to Hoover, September 27, 1930, Presidential Papers, Foreign Affairs, Diplomatic, N. Roosevelt, Hoover Library.

58. But the time for entry into the League was evidently past by the 1930s; neither Hoover nor Franklin D. Roosevelt would move in that direction.

9:   A Hostile Senate: The Tariff

1. This chapter was intact prior to reading Jordan A. Schwarz, *The Interregnum of Despair: Hoover, Congress, and the Depression,* which contains interesting material drawn from manuscript collections. States Schwarz: "The president becomes a somewhat secondary figure in this narrative; Congressional attitudes and actions are the focus" (p. 7). An earlier title of this work was "The Politics of Fear: Congress and the Depression during the Hoover Administration." See also his "Hoover and Congress: Politics, Personality, and Perspective in the Presidency," in *The Hoover Presidency*, pp. 87–100.

2. *Congressional Record,* 71st Cong., 1929, 71, pt. 4:3800. Watson was a thwarted candidate for the Republican presidential nomination in 1928 (Schwarz, *The Interregnum of Despair*, p. 47).

3. Schwarz, *The Interregnum of Despair*, has vigorously critical sketches of the conservative senators: Watson, "the nadir of Republicanism"; Moses, the "paradigm" of the Old Guard senator; "Faithful Fess" is humorless and pedantic; Jones is wedded to the Columbia River basin.

4. *Congressional Record,* 71st Cong., 1929, 4:4121.

5. Brookhart, 64; Frazier, 61; Nye, 58; LaFollette, 54; Norris, 53; McMaster, 47; Blaine, 46; Borah, 46; Howell, 45; Norbeck, 43; Cutting, 42; Pine, 35; Schall, 35; Couzens, 33; Johnson, 28; Dale, 28; Capper, 26. Five voted against their party more than one-half of the time; fourteen, more than one-third of the time. On the Democratic side, six voted against their party majority one-third of the time: Ransdell, 36; Broussard, 32; Trammell, 32; Copeland, 31; Walsh (Massachusetts), 30; Fletcher, 30; Kendrick, 28; Dill, 28.

6. *Congressional Record,* 71st Cong., 1929, 71, pt. 3:3287–88.

7. Ibid.

8. Ibid., p. 3288.

9. Ibid.

10. Marvin to Hoover, April 16, 1929, Presidential Papers, old file 60, Hoover Library.

11. *Congressional Record,* 71st Cong., 1929, 71, pt. 4:3972.

12. Marvin to Hoover, September 30, 1929, Presidential Papers, old file 60, Hoover Library.

13. See Thomas S. Barclay, "The Publicity Division of the Democratic Party, 1929–1930," *American Political Science Review* 25 (1931) :68; also his "The Bureau of Publicity of the Democratic National Committee, *American Political Science Review,* 27 (1933) :63–66.

14. *Public Papers,* 1:221.

15. This incident is described by David Hinshaw in *Herbert Hoover: American Quaker,* pp. 179–81. It is based upon the author's personal files.

16. Hoover developed this theme some years later in "The Crisis and the Political Parties," *Atlantic Monthly,* September 1937, pp. 257–68.

17. *Congressional Record,* 71st Cong., 1929, 71, pt. 5:5131–32.

10:   Financial Catastrophe: 1929–

1. Hoover, *Memoirs: The Cabinet and the Presidency,* p. 175.

2. Hoover, *Memoirs: The Great Depression,* p. 13.

3. Ibid., p. 14.

4. Hoover, *Memoirs: The Great Depression,* pp. 5, 7, 15, 17, 19, and 125.

5. Ibid., pp. 3–20 passim.

6. John Kenneth Galbraith, *The Great Crash, 1929* (New York, 1954). The book was written in a Vermont summer and autumn on the urging of Schlesinger. See revised edition of 1961, p. ix.

7. John Kenneth Galbraith, "The Days of Boom and Bust," *American Heritage* (August, 1958) :28 ff.

8. Ibid., p. 32.

9. Ibid. "In the full perspective of history, American businessmen never had enemies as damaging as the men who grouped themselves around Calvin Coolidge and supported him in what William Allen White called 'that masterly inactivity for which he was so spendidly equipped' " (p. 102).

10. Ellis W. Hawley in *Herbert Hoover and the Crisis of American Capitalism,* p. 115.

11. Hoover, *Memoirs: The Great Depression,* p. 16.

12. Ibid., p. 21.

13. Hoover Library materials reveal the awesome extent of the president's activities and concern.

14. Coolidge had been assured by William Z. Ripley of Harvard that regulation of corporate machinations was a state—not federal—responsibility—"as was then the case" (Galbraith, "Days of Boom," p. 33).

15. Ogden Mills Papers, Library of Congress.

16. Hoover, *Memoirs: The Great Depression,* pp. 16–17.

17. Irving Fisher, "Has Wall Street Gone Wild?" *Liberty,* February 1929, condensed in *Readers Digest,* March 1929, p. 664.

18. Dawes, *Journal,* pp. 94–98.

19. Krock, *Memoirs,* p. 122. Under the circumstances the Hoover inaugural address jarred Mr. Krock.

20. A day-by-day account with merit is in Robert T. Patterson, *The Great Boom and Panic, 1921–1929* (Chicago, 1965), chap. 6–7.

21. Wilbur and Hyde, *The Hoover Policies,* pp. 152–53.

22. Text in Hoover Library.

23. Patterson, *The Great Boom,* p. 134.

24. It is well to remember throughout that statistical reporting and the flow of orderly information then—and decades later—were two quite different things.

25. Such a view was shared even in such journals as the *Nation* and *New Republic.* "Fortunately, the present breakdown is not likely to be serious in any case," was the editorial view of the latter in late November. Quoted in Arthur A. Ekirch, Jr., *Ideologies and Utopias: The Impact of the New Deal on American Thought* (Chicago, 1969), p. 26.

26. Press conference, November 5, 1929, Hoover Library. At the time, it is said, Hoover simply *refused* to intimate that the low priced stocks had become a good buy. Galbraith, *The Great Crash,* p. 111 and 111n.

27. *Public Papers,* 1:383, 388.

28. Press conference, November 19, 1929, Hoover Library.

29. For a succinct summary of the steps taken by President Hoover, the personnel of the groups called into conference, and the announcements made and steps taken as a result of these conferences, see Myers and Newton, *The Hoover Administration,* pp. 23–31. How far many were from accepting the Hoover method of consultation and conference as a productive method in a democracy has never been more clearly stated than by Galbraith, who gives a hostile disquisition on "no business" business meetings (*The Great Crash,* pp. 143–46).

30. Telegram, Hoover to Barnes, November 15, 1929, Presidential Papers, Hoover Library.

31. *New York Times,* December 7, 1929.

32. Ibid., November 25, 1929.

33. Ibid., November 28, 1929.

34. Ibid., December 30, 1929.

35. Ibid., January 24, 1930.

36. Ibid., December 20, 1929.

37. Walsh Papers, Library of Congress.

38. Lincoln Steffens, *The Autobiography of Lincoln Steffens* (New York, 1931), pp. 856–57.

39. The recriminations of later years against Hoover seem wide of the mark.

40. *New York Evening Post,* November 21, 1928.

41. Hoover, *Memoirs: The Great Depression,* p. 29. Harvard professor

A. B. Hart, in commenting on commissions as part of the Hoover idea, wrote in 1929: "It is idle to criticize the President for having no nostrum to cure our ills. The very idea of ready-made and final solutions is itself a survival of the conception of society as simple and static. Hoover's mind is essentially a twentieth century mind" (*American Year Book 1929*, p. 10).

42. A mature account is Albert U. Romasco, "Herbert Hoover's Policies for Dealing with the Great Depression: The End of the Old Order or the Beginning of the New?" in *The Hoover Presidency*, pp. 69–86.

43. Charles A. and Mary R. Beard, *America in Midpassage* (New York: Macmillan, 1939), p. 90.

44. Hoover to White, October 28, 1929, Hoover Library.

45. Hoover to Dr. W. O. Thompson, December 30, 1929. In Myers, *State Papers*, 1:198.

46. *New York Herald Tribune*, March 8, 1930.

11: The President's Party Abdicates

1. The precise figures follow: of 257 votes taken, the following votes against the party were cast by the eleven senators who were most irregular: Norris, 202; Blaine, 197; LaFollette, 193; McMaster, 174; Nye, 168; Borah, 164; Brookhart, 160; Norbeck, 155; Frazier, 146; Schall, 137; and Howell, 136.

2. T. J. Walsh to D. P. Dayton, December 24, 1929, Walsh Papers, Library of Congress.

3. *Congressional Record*, 71st Cong., 1929, 71, pt. 4:5872.

4. Ibid.

5. Shaw to Fess, August 6, 1930. Copy to Lawrence Richey, Presidential Papers, President's personal file 659, Hoover Library.

6. Shaw to Hoover, October 8, 1930, same file, Hoover Library.

7. *Congressional Record*, 71st Cong., 1929, 71, pt. 4:3971–73.

8. Ibid.

9. Ibid., p. 4119.

10. Ibid., p. 4121.

11. Ibid.

12. Ibid., p. 5872.

13. Ibid.

14. Ibid, pp. 3799–3800.

15. The members of the Finance Committee were: Reed Smoot, Utah (Chairman); James E. Watson, Indiana; David A. Reed, Pennsylvania; Samuel A. Shortridge, California; Walter E. Edge, New Jersey; James Couzens, Michigan; Frank L. Greene, Vermont; Charles S. Deneen, Illinois; Henry W. Keyes, New Hampshire; Pat Harrison, Mississippi; Frederick M. Sackett, Kentucky; F. M. Simmons,

North Carolina; Hiram Bingham, Connecticut; William H. King, Utah; Walter F. George, Georgia; David I. Walsh, Massachusetts; Alben W. Barkley, Kentucky; Elmer Thomas, Oklahoma; and Tom Connally, Texas.

16. Myers, *The Foreign Policies of Herbert Hoover*, p. 127. The vote against the flexible tariff was forty-seven to forty-two.

17. Burke to Hoover, May 14, 1930, President's personal file 300, Hoover Library.

18. Full text of the economists in *New York Times*, May 5, 1930. (The original is missing from Hoover Library.)

19. Based on a searching examination of some twenty textbooks in common use.

20. The first signatory, and the author, was Paul H. Douglas, supporter of Norman Thomas at the time and vocal advocate of a New Party. It was an unpersuasive beginning that could scarcely have escaped the president's notice. Many prominent economists signed. The statement was sent to economics departments at colleges and universities throughout the country, was signed by those who agreed with it, and was then mailed to the originator. Vernon A. Murd's marginal notes on V. Bornet letter to him of February 6, 1973; Paul H. Douglas to Bornet, March 22, 1973. Claire Wilcox revised the text. Letters in possession of V. Bornet. Douglas and Wilcox financed the mailing, which also went to "every member" of the American Economic Association.

21. Hoover, *Memoirs: The Cabinet and the Presidency*, p. 296.

22. *New York Times*, May 29, 1931. Paul H. Douglas, *In the Fullness of Time* (New York, 1971) argues again against protective tariffs per se.

23. For the pattern of labor partisanship see Bornet, *Labor Politics*, chapter 11.

24. *New York Times*, May 29, 1931.

25. Ibid. All of this will be familiar to any who have watched the discomfort of American textile, television, automobile, and other producers at keen Japanese competition in the 1960s and 1970s, and the efforts to avoid tariff increases by obtaining quota allocations from the Japanese.

26. Myers, *State Papers*, 1:316.

27. Ibid., p. 314.

28. Hoover to Richard Lloyd Jones, June 16, 1930, Presidential Papers, President's personal file 501, Hoover Library. In retrospect, Professor Douglas remained unclear on the Hoover approach: "I think poor Hoover wanted to take our advice." He only signed, he said, because the party was committed to protection (Douglas, *In the Fullness of Time*, p. 71).

29. Myers, *The Foreign Policies of Herbert Hoover*, p. 127.

30. Hoover's subsequent explanation of his action during the debate and at the time of signing the bill is found in his *Memoirs: The Cabinet and the Presidency*, pp. 291–99. The information given here on the joint addressees (The President, the Congress) of the economists and their timing (while the bill still lay before the Congress) seems to have escaped his notice when writing his memoirs.

31. The President's Research Committee on Social Trends, *Recent Social Trends in the United States*, 2 vols. (New York: McGraw-Hill, 1933). Reissued in one volume, this was a textbook used in countless classes for two decades; it went out of print only in 1950.

32. Chambers, *Seedtime of Reform*, p. 245.

33. The 1937 Hughes–Hoover correspondence in the Hoover Library bears retrospectively on this appointment.

34. *Congressional Record*, 72d Cong., 1930, 72, pt. 4:3450.

35. *Congressional Record*, 72d Cong., 1930, 72, pt. 8:8341–42. Since there were three Democrats on the Court, the addition of another Republican seemed appropriate, he added.

36. Richard L. Watson, Jr.. in "The Defeat of Judge Parker: A Study in Pressure Groups and Politics," *Mississippi Valley Historical Review*, September, 1963, p. 214, stresses how uncontroversial the appointment seemed.

37. When asked who had last served from the Fourth Circuit Mr. Hoover replied that it was Daniel, who retired in 1860. The Seventh Circuit (Indiana, Illinois and Wisconsin) had been twenty years without a justice. The Fifth Circuit (Georgia, Florida, Alabama and Mississippi) had been without one since Justice White died in 1921. The Third Circuit (Pennsylvania, Delaware, New Jersey) had been eight years without a justice.

38. *Congressional Record*, 72d Cong., 1930, 72, pt. 8:8488.

39. The Republican senators who opposed Parker's confirmation were: Blaine, Borah, Capper, Couzens, Cutting, Deneen, Frazier, Howell, Johnson, Norris, Nye, Pine, Robinson (Indiana), Schall, Steiwer, and Vandenberg. They were joined by twenty-three Democrats and one Farmer-Laborite. There were twenty-nine Republicans and ten Democrats supporting Parker. Counting pairs, the vote was forty-nine to forty-seven.

40. Watson, "The Defeat of Judge Parker," p. 234. When Parker died, *The New York Times* called him "one of the most distinguished jurists on the Federal bench" (Quoted in Ibid.).

41. Quoted in ibid., p. 234.

42. There is a mimeographed copy of a letter bearing the seal of the Office of the President of the American Federation of Labor, Washington, D. C., stating: "It is difficult indeed for me to employ language that would adequately express my deep feeling of appreciation and gratitude over the magnificent and successful fight you made against the confirmation of the appointment of Judge John J. Parker to be a Member of the Supreme Court of the United States" (President of AFL, William Green, to Borah, May 7, 1930, William E. Borah Papers. Library of Congress).

43. These can be listed as follows: The Agricultural Marketing Act, with the establishment of a Farm Board and regulation of marketing practices in agricultural perishables; Congressional reapportionment; revision of tariff, including flexible provisions and reorganization of the Tariff Commission; establishment

of a Federal Power Commission; reform of parole and probation and federal prisons; establishment of a Federal Criminal Identification Service; consolidation of prohibition enforcement activities; organization of a narcotics bureau; expansion of veterans' hospitals; establishment of disability allowances to disabled veterans; consolidation of all veterans' services; organization of a definite plan of river and harbor improvement; increase in federal highways; enlargement of government building construction; ratification of the London Naval Treaty; and reform of the airmail service.

44. Julius H. Barnes to Hoover, July 7, 1930, Presidential Papers, President's personal file 659, Hoover Library.

45. Cleveland and Wilson were the Democratic exceptions to Republican sovereignty since 1861.

46. Turner Catledge Reminiscence, September 15, 1969, p. 20, Hoover Institution.

47. Ibid. The memories of contemporaries in the oral history reminiscences, the Hoover speeches and press conferences, and the appraisals of the day in newspapers and magazines appear to bear out the present picture of Hoover as a chief executive operating within the Constitution, rather than as the power-seeking official portrayed in one interpretive essay. See Jordan A. Schwarz, "Hoover and Congress," *op. cit.* One quotation there, on Hoover as "dictator" in the eyes of Borah, rests on a 1921 comment (see p. 92 and the notes, p. 205). Few who really knew Hoover would grant that, as Dr. Schwarz puts it, "In a way, Hoover considered himself America's indispensable man" (p. 92). Still, the essay offers interesting judgments, among them the opinion, "Rarely had Congress been held in such low esteem as it was during the Hoover years" (p. 99).

12:   The Voters Turn Away

1. Mr. Hoover's correspondence with Julius H. Barnes, President of the United States Chamber of Commerce, and with Chairman Alexander Legge of the Farm Board at the end of March, reveals the concern of both Barnes and Legge with the "grain situation." Legge felt that Barnes entirely ignored "the seriousness of the business calamity brought upon us by speculation and the crash in the Stock Exchange" (President's personal files 711 and 227, Miscellaneous, Hoover Library).

2. The vast costs of the New Deal, World War II, Korea, Vietnam, social programs, thermonuclear preparedness, and the space race have diminished our capacity to comprehend governmental finance in the Hoover presidential years, no doubt.

3. The Pensions Bureau had been a part of the Department of the Interior, and the Soldiers' Homes had been administered by the Department of War.

4. Donald J. Lisio, *The President and Protest: Hoover, Conspiracy, and the Bonus Riot* (Columbia, Mo.: University of Missouri Press, 1974), p. 21.

5. The reader will bear in mind that the federal budget increased from $4 billion in the 1930s to approximately $300 billion in the early 1970s and inflation changed the value of the dollar. Population grew from, say, 130 million to over 200 million.

6. Press conference, October 17, 1930. In Myers, *State Papers*, 1:401–2. For a discussion of unemployment and unemployment estimates in 1928, see Bornet. *Labor Politics*, chap. 1.

7. Press conference, October 21, 1930, Hoover Library.

8. Revealing the popular attitude, perhaps, was a letter from H. G. Gay, Chairman, Order of Railroad Telegraphers, Southern Railway System, to Senator Gerald P. Nye (copy to Senator Norris), December 23, 1930: "I have just finished reading newspaper accounts of your untiring activity in uncovering the dirty work, and rotten policies, undermining methods used by the National Republican Committee to defeat our beloved friend Senator George W. Norris of Nebraska, and could not resist writing you a few lines to congratulate you on your efforts in his behalf. . . . If the entire membership of your house of representatives were composed of such men as yourself, and Senator Norris, the United States would not be in the fix it is today with millions of men out of work, starving to death because of their inability to get jobs to support themselves and families, and living in the richest country in the world whose president is unwilling to allow an appropriation to come from the federal treasury to feed the starving human beings that are helpless, for fear that a small increase in taxes on the very rich would be necessary" (George W. Norris Papers, Library of Congress).

9. John W. Hill reminiscence, December 2. 1971, pp. 9, 17.

10. Ibid.

11. In Henry L. Stimson and McGeorge Bundy, *On Active Service in Peace and War*, p. 196.

12. See Craig Lloyd, *Aggressive Introvert*, on public information policies.

13. Republican National Committee, *The Hoover Administration: The Policies and the Achievements in the First Sixteen Months* (Washington, D. C., 1930).

14. J. F. Lucey to W. H. Newton, August 15, 1930, Hoover Library.

15. See Farm Board Counsel G. E. Farrard to Henry M. Robinson, August 25, 1930, Hoover Library.

16. A. S. Dale to the White House, September 15, 1930, Presidential Papers, Accomplishments of the Administration, Hoover Library.

17. French Strother to A. S. Dale, October 3, 1930, same file, Hoover Library.

18. H. M. Robinson to Hoover, November 6, 1930, same file, Hoover Library.

19. This matter is discussed at length in Robinson and Edwards, *The Memoirs of Ray Lyman Wilbur*, pp. 415–19. See also the press conference of October 28, 1930, Hoover Library.

20. Recalled in H. M. Robinson to Hoover, July 17, 1930, Hoover Library.

21. Myers, *State Papers*, 1:375–84. The president wrote Henry M. Robinson

on September 13, 1930, enclosing "the first draft of my proposed address to the bankers," and stating: "There are many changes I want to make but I would be glad if you could scribble all over it and even delete the whole thing if you think it desirable" (Hoover Library).

22. Thomas S. Barclay reminiscence, July 23, 1968, p. 16, Hoover Institution.

23. See, for example, the correspondence of Thomas J. Walsh of Montana, Walsh Papers, Library of Congress.

24. An article by Frank R. Kent in *Scribners Magazine,* quoted in Myers and Newton, *The Hoover Administration,* p. 46, describes fully this elaborate effort at smear tactics.

25. White to Norris, November 5, 1930, Norris Papers, Library of Congress.

26. *Congressional Record,* 1931, 74, pt. 2:1258–60.

27. Myers, *State Papers,* 1:467–68.

28. Stimson *Diary,* November 5, 1930, p. 126.

13:   A Political Impasse

1. Stimson to Hoover, December 24, 1930, President's personal file 1140, Hoover Library.

2. An authoritative discussion is in William Meulemans, "The Presidential Majority; Presidential Campaigning in Congressional Elections" (Ph.D. Diss., University of Idaho, 1969).

3. Press conference, December 5, 1930, Hoover Library.

4. Leland W. Cutler to Secretary George E. Akerson, November 5, 1930, Hoover Library.

5. *Chicago Daily Tribune,* January 7, 1931.

6. A *New Republic* unsigned article of January 14, 1931, quoted in Edmund Wilson, *The Shores of Light: A Literary Chronicle of the Twenties and Thirties* (New York, 1952), p. 530.

7. See Bornet, *Labor Politics,* chaps. 4, 5, 9, 10, on the actions of the Socialist and Communist parties on the eve of the depression.

8. See the biographical volumes by Frank Freidel; see also Bernard Bellush, *Roosevelt as Governor of New York* (New York, 1955).

9. Politics-Campaign Material 1912–1936, Borah Papers, Library of Congress.

10. *Congressional Record,* 74, pt. 6:5468.

11. Ibid., p. 5696. Washington's thoughts at that time in fact showed great caution. He observed to the secretary of state on May 24, 1793: "In the present posture of French Affairs, I thought we ought to consider very deliberately on all these measures before we acted; for it was impossible to decide with precision what would be the final issue of the contest, consequently, that this Governmt [sic], ought not go faster than it was obliged; but to walk on cautious ground."

John C. Fitzpatrick, ed., *The Writings of George Washington*, 39 vols. (Washington, D. C.: U.S. Government Printing Office, 1931–34), 32:468n.

12. Cleveland A. Dunn to Borah, December 23 and 26, 1930, Borah Papers, Library of Congress.

13. Norris Papers, Library of Congress.

14. See *Wanted: A New Alignment in American Politics* (New York: League for Independent Action, 1930).

15. Myers, *State Papers*, 1:496–99.

16. Editorial in the *New Republic*, 65, January 7, 1931, p. 203. Schwarz, *The Interregnum of Despair*, chap. 3.

17. Thomas J. Walsh to William E. Borah, September 20, 1930, Walsh Papers, Library of Congress.

18. John Dewey, "Policies for a New Party," *New Republic*, April 8, 1931, p. 204.

19. Clarke A. Chambers, ed., *Paul U. Kellogg and the Survey* (Minneapolis, 1971), p. 130. Kellogg almost endorsed LaFollette in 1924.

14:   Hoover's Leadership in the World of 1931

1. Myers, *State Papers*, 1:496.

2. Ibid., p. 499.

3. *Congressional Record*, 74, pt. 7:6419.

4. Hoover to Dawes, March 11, 1931, Presidential Papers, Dawes, Hoover Library.

5. Russell Gerould in the *Boston Herald*, quoted in *Literary Digest*, April 4, 1931, p. 9.

6. *New York Times*, March 27, 1931.

7. Robinson and Edwards, eds., *The Memoirs of Ray Lyman Wilbur*, p. 495.

8. One who served Hoover well was Nicholas Roosevelt, who went to Budapest as minister to Hungary in the autumn of 1930. He was asked to study economic conditions in neighboring nations and to coordinate the information in nontechnical form. Nicholas Roosevelt, *A Front Row Seat*, pp. 186, 218.

9. Newspaper accounts and yearbook articles are helpful here. A brief educated synthesis is in David Thomson, *World History, 1914–1961* (New York: Oxford University Press, 1964) and a sophisticated economic analysis appears in Charles P. Kindleberger, *The World in Depression, 1929–1939* (Berkeley and Los Angeles: University of California Press, 1973). The President's Des Moines speech of October 4, 1932 is a helpful summary. See also his *Memoirs: The Great Depression*, chap. 7; Wilbur and Hyde, *The Hoover Policies*, pp. 402–419; and Myers and Newton, *The Hoover Administration*, chaps. 5–7. Overall, the serious economic and political literature on this is enormous, but as Professor Thomson

says, "experts still disagree about the precise reasons for the crisis." Professor Kindleberger has his own rationale, and finds the views of such experts as Professors Samuelson and Friedman irreconcilable. The latter's explanation is "wrong;" the former's "is perhaps no more satisfactory." The sophisticated business cycles explanations of Professor Schumpeter are noted but not endorsed. Interestingly, "the conventional wisdom of the period was not as wrong as most modern economists believe in its concern with the dangers of speculation, the necessity to raise prices, the desirability of lowering tariffs, and the need to stabilize exchange rates" (Kindleberger, *The World in Depression*, pp. 19–28). Few or no words of admiration are given Hoover for his herculean efforts of 1931 by the economists cited here. An article showing no interest in President Hoover's views then or since is Harold van B. Cleveland and W. H. Bruce Brittain, "A World Depression?" *Foreign Affairs* 53 (January 1975) :223–41, which tries to "combine historical and analytical approaches." The Depression was caused "by a prolonged contraction of the money supply" (p. 223).

10. Thomson, *World History*, p. 71.

11. Bismarck is reported to have said, "the next time we win a war against France, we'll demand that we pay her an indemnity;" this, because of the resulting inflation! (Kindleberger, *The World in Depression.* p. 34n).

12. Myers and Newton, *The Hoover Administration*, p. 73.

13. Speech delivered at Des Moines, Iowa, October 4, 1932, in Myers, *State Papers*, 2:298–99.

14. Hindenburg to Hoover (June 1931), quoted in Hoover, *Memoirs: The Great Depression*, p. 69. As the German situation deteriorated, Hoover wrote, "The political disturbances are so extensive, the misery of the people is so great, unemployment has been rising steadily; that the pressure of reparations is so great that he [Ambassador Sackett] does not believe the present form of government will stand in Germany, and that we must face the possibilities of a debacle or revolution unless something can be done." Hoover Memorandum, May 6, 1931, Presidential Papers, "Financial, Moratorium," Hoover Library.

15. Stimson *Diary*, June 15, 1931, p. 178.

16. Milton Friedman and Anna Jacobson Schwartz, *A Monetary History of the United States, 1867–1960* (Princeton, N.J.: Princeton University Press, 1963), p. 314.

17. Hoover, *Memoirs: The Great Depression*, p. 81.

18. Kindleberger, *The World in Depression*, is thorough and sure-footed on the details. The chronology in Myers and Newton, *The Hoover Administration*, is indispensable.

19. From April to September, the fall in American industrial production was 18 percent, in factory payrolls 20 percent, construction contracts 30 percent, and common stock prices 40 per cent (Hoover, *Memoirs: The Great Depression*, p. 83). Friedman and Schwartz note that this banking crisis (February to August 1931) saw commercial bank deposits fall $2.7 billion, or more than in the whole period August 1929 to February 1931 (*A Monetary History*, p. 315).

20. Hoover Memorandum, June 5, 1931, Presidential Papers, "Financial, Moratorium," Hoover Library.

21. Ibid.

22. Hillis to Hoover, October 16, 1930, Hoover to Hillis, October 21, 1930, President's personal file 882, Hoover Library. Hillis was chairman of the Republican National Committee in World War I, and in the 1930s was a director of many corporations.

23. Joslin, *Hoover Off the Record*, p. 108.

24. Stimson and Bundy, *On Active Service in Peace and War*, p. 204.

25. Myers, *State Papers*, 1:565. The president also said, "Such a session would through the fears and apprehensions it would create, undoubtedly increase unemployment." These words were omitted from both the mimeographed copy sent out at the time and from the published statement in *State Papers*. Press conference, May 22, 1931, Hoover Library.

26. Dawes to Hoover, April 2, 1931, President's personal file 149, Hoover Library.

27. Hoover to Dawes, April 15, 1931, same file, Hoover Library.

28. Hoover to Dawes, April 15, 1931, same file, Hoover Library. Dawes, on his return home from London, wrote in his journal at sea on May 26, 1931: "I hear much criticism of President Hoover for his unquestionably useful efforts to mitigate the evils of the situation. It is to his great credit that he is being criticized for doing too much instead of too little" (Dawes, *Journal*, p. 347). The criticism was most common in *financial* circles, then and later. And see Murray N. Rothbard's essay in *Herbert Hoover and the Crisis of American Capitalism* (Cambridge, Mass., 1973) which condemns "massive intervention."

29. Robinson to Newton, June 2, 1931, Presidential Papers, Robinson, Hoover Library. A note to Hoover from Ray Lyman Wilbur on August 12, 1931. included: "The Bohemian Grove [California] group were more friendly than last year. Do wish you could get to Jackson Hole in September." This note included some important observations, including Wilbur's opinion that "labor troubles at Hoover Dam were due to heat" (Hoover Library).

30. Myers, *State Papers*, 1:572–75.

31. Ibid., pp. 572–77.

32. Secretary of the Interior Ray Lyman Wilbur, in his memoirs, describes the circumstances attending the illness and death of President Harding, for Dr. Wilbur was summoned to San Francisco as a consulting physician when President and Mrs. Harding, accompanied by the Hoovers, reached that city on Harding's fatal tour. There was no "strange death of President Harding" (Robinson and Edwards, eds., The Memoirs of Ray Lyman Wilbur, pp. 378–85).

33. Dawes, *Journal*, pp. 350–51.

34. Myers, *State Papers*, 1:588.

35. Ibid., p. 590.

36. Myers and Newton, *The Hoover Administration*, p. 92.

37. Dawes memorandum, June 24, 1931, President's personal file 149, Hoover Library. France had received only $1.5 billion in reparations while paying $10 billion plus 6 percent on the debts. The United States would end up paying two-thirds of the battlefield expenses, Dawes predicted.

38. McCormick, *The World at Home*, p. 76.

39. But see Myers and Newton, *The Hoover Administration*, pp. 95–105, for a day-to-day account of the resistance of the French to the terms of the moratorium and the complications that ensued in the European situation. See also Joslin, *Hoover Off the Record*, pp. 102–5.

40. See Ferrell, *American Diplomacy in the Great Depression*, based on the Castle diary. At this time was the first true diplomatic use of the transatlantic telephone, notes Professor Ferrell.

41. Telegram, Dawes to Hoover, July 23, 1931, President's personal file 149, Hoover Library.

42. Telegram, Hoover to Henry Robinson, July 27, 1931, President's personal file 149, Hoover Library.

43. Hoover to Mills, July 8, 1931, President's personal file 1506, Hoover Library.

44. Borah to Hoover, July 23, 1931 and Hoover reply. Borah to Hoover, September 2, 1931. Hoover to Borah, September 8, 1931, President's personal file 543, Hoover Library.

45. See Clair E. Nelson, "The Image of Herbert Hoover as Reflected in the American Press" (Ph.D. diss., Stanford University, 1956), pp. 110–14.

46. Joslin, *Hoover Off the Record*, p. 114.

47. Gold flows became a familiar phenomenon to newspaper readers of the 1960s and may be better understood than in the early 1930s.

48. See Herbert Hoover, *Memoirs: Years of Adventure, 1874–1920*, chap. 6. The account in Will Irwin, *Herbert Hoover: A Reminiscent Biography*, was carefully edited by Hoover. See Irwin Papers, Hoover Institution.

49. Hoover, *Memoirs: Years of Adventure*, p. 47 and Irwin, *Herbert Hoover*, p. 104.

50. Castle memorandum, May 16, 1945, Castle Papers, Hoover Library.

51. Tony Shao-yi, former premier of China, quoted in "Hoover's Fine Record in China," *Outlook*, May 2, 1928, p. 11.

52. Henry L. Stimson, *The Far Eastern Crisis*, pp. 32–37.

53. Hoover, *Memoirs: The Cabinet and the Presidency*. p. 365. There came to the White House during the ensuing crisis a helpful sixty-eight page pamphlet: Roy Hidemichi Akagi, *Understanding Manchuria: A Handbook of Facts* (1931); in Presidential Papers, "Manchuria, Correspondence, 1932," Hoover Library.

54. Hoover, *Memoirs: The Cabinet and the Presidency*, p. 365.

55. See Bailey, *Diplomatic History of the American People*, 8th ed. (New York, 1968), on American public opinion. The earlier editions of the book, (for

example. 1946), contain judgments based on examination of Hoover Library press clippings. Charles Tansill, *Back Door to War* (Chicago, 1952) is rich in quotations from clipping files.

56. Richard N. Current has shown there were two doctrines of "nonrecognition," and the Hoover doctrine rather than the Stimson doctrine prevailed in 1932–33, meaning no sanctions of any sort other than moral ["The Stimson Doctrine and the Hoover Doctrine," *American Historical Review* (April 1954): 513–42]. Hoover credited William Jennings Bryan with originating the nonrecognition doctrine (See *Memoirs: The Cabinet and the Presidency*, p. 373). See also Elting E. Morison, *Turmoil and Tradition: A Study of the Life and Times of Henry L. Stimson* (Boston, 1960), p. 386.

57. Stimson *Diary*, September 24, 1930, p. 27.

58. Quoted in Stimson and Bundy, *On Active Service in Peace and War*, p. 285.

59. Castle memorandum (carbon copy), May 16, 1945, Castle Papers, "Hoover," Hoover Library.

60. Hoover to Stimson, June 3, 1936, Postpresidential Papers, Individual, Stimson, Hoover Library.

61. Enclosure with the Hoover to Stimson letter, June 3, 1936.

62. Stimson to Hoover, June 6, 1936, Hoover Library.

63. *Memoirs: The Cabinet and the Presidency*, pp. 370–72.

64. Once, when confronted by Stimson, Hoover seems to have conceded that in the remote case of the Nine-Power Countries joining in a boycott, the United States might join in. This concession led Stimson to record, "To my surprise I found he was not absolutely and to the last resort against a boycott . . ." (*Diary*, December 6, 1931, p. 132).

65. Hoover, *Memoirs: The Cabinet and the Presidency*, p. 370. It is to be noted that within the State Department Castle vigorously opposed sanctions, while Stanley Hornbeck, James G. Rogers, and Allen Klots favored them (Stimson *Diary*, December 6, 1931, p. 131). It is interesting that the Secretary was engaging in such quiet discussions in his Department.

66. Elting Morison states that "as the situation deteriorated, the President believed that anything beyond a stand on moral forces would endanger the immediate peace while Stimson, as time passed, believed something more substantive was needed to restrain the Japanese and, perhaps, to preserve a peace in the future" (*Turmoil and Tradition,* p. 383).

67. Hoover, *Memoirs: The Cabinet and the Presidency*, p. 376.

68. Ferrell, *American Diplomacy in the Great Depression*, p. 589. For the dispute about the origin of the doctrine (Hoover or Stimson) see ibid., p. 590 and letters from Hurley and Wilbur, January, 1933, reproduced in Myers, *The Foreign Policies of Herbert Hoover*, pp. 164–68. The origins were Hoover's; the phrasing Stimson's.

69. Text in U.S., Department of State, *Foreign Relations of the United States: Japan, 1931–1941,* 2 vols. (Washington, D. C., 1943), 1:83–87.

70. Nor, it might be added, because his views on the Constitution in 1932 were probably little changed in 1940–41, would he have waged war without declaration by Congress. See the vigor of his repeated insistence on this in *Addresses on the American Road, 1940–1941* (New York, 1941), pp. 51, 56, 64, 66, 71, 85, 87, 88, 101, 103, 106, 110, 114. For example, "Failure of Congress to assert its responsibilities or for the Executive to take warlike steps without the approval of the Congress is a direct destruction of the safeguards of freedom itself" [Speech, "The Crisis," September 16, 1941 (ibid., p. 110)].

71. Hoover, *Memoirs: The Cabinet and the Presidency*, p. 369, and in full in Myers, *The Foreign Policies of Herbert Hoover*, pp. 156–60.

72. Hoover, *Memoirs: The Cabinet and the Presidency*, p. 370.

73. Castle memorandum (carbon copy), May 16, 1945, Castle Papers, Hoover Library.

74. Hoover to Beard, December 17, 1945, Postpresidential Papers, Hoover Library.

75. Beard to Hoover, December 23, 1945, Postpresidential Papers, Hoover Library.

76. Stimson to Major General William Lassiter, November 12, 1931, Stimson Papers, microfilm roll 82.

77. Stimson to Elihu Root, December 14, 1931, Stimson Papers, microfilm roll 82, in reply to Root to Stimson, November 20, 1931, same place.

78. Stimson to Lippmann, November 14, 1931, Stimson Papers, microfilm roll 82.

79. Various letters show this. See Stimson to Lippmann, January 2, 1932, Stimson Papers, microfilm roll 82.

80. Hoover, *Memoirs: The Cabinet and the Presidency*, p. 370.

81. A reconciliation of the Hoover, Myers, Stimson, Beard, and various textbook accounts is not appropriate here. Richard N. Current, *Secretary Stimson: A Study in Statecraft*, is an unflattering portrayal of Stimson. On the other hand, Armin Rappaport, *Henry L. Stimson and Japan, 1931–33*, stresses the role of Stimson throughout at the expense of President Hoover as the policymaker of last resort (see especially p. 140n). This is not surprising in the light of the book's title, however.

82. Quoted in Current, "The Stimson Doctrine and the Hoover Doctrine," p. 526.

83. Ibid., p. 527.

84. Stimson *Diary*, January 26, 29, 1932. Quoted in ibid.

85. Stimson *Diary*, February 25, 1932. Quoted in ibid. Stimson was beginning to envision the prospect of inevitable war someday between Japan and America. They were "different civilizations based on different theories" (Stimson *Diary*, March 9, 1932. Quoted in ibid.). Hoover called such talk "phantasmagorias" (Stimson *Diary* entry for April 5, 1932, quoted in ibid.).

86. Quoted in ibid., p. 536. Stimson on January 9, 1933 urged a strong American stance toward Japan on President-elect Roosevelt and found a warmer reception (Roosevelt said why not withdraw our ambassador?). As his relationship with Roosevelt warmed, Stimson commented once in a Hoover cabinet meeting, "I am Roosevelt's acting Secretary of State" (Castle *Diary,* January 24, 1933. Quoted in ibid., p. 539). Stimson's appointment by Roosevelt as secretary of war in the late 1930s seems to have had both personal and policy roots!

87. For an able recital of how the subsequent administration did not build on this structure, until bypassing it in favor of economic sanctions in 1941, see Cohen, *America's Response to China,* pp. 135–53. That account is strongly contradictory of the Stimson and Bundy conclusion that in the decade after Hoover, "the basic American stand for treaty rights and a strong China was never deserted" (*On Active Service in Peace and War,* pp. 255–56). (The American silver policy of those later years wrecked the Chinese currency, for example.) There is no straight line from Hoover's nonrecognition policy to Pearl Harbor, whether Stimson thought he could see the coming of inevitable war or not. A careful reading by V. Bornet of the Hoover correspondence with Charles A. Beard, William Castle, Walter Trohan, and Charles Tansill strongly supports these views. It is unfortunate that the Department of State chose to imply the link by issuing the *Foreign Relations of the United States: Japan, 1931–1941,* since the turn to sanctions in the summer of 1941 marked a sharp break in American policy. Even worse in this respect was the Department of State publication (with a statement from Cordell Hull), *Peace and War: United States Foreign Policy, 1931–1941* (Washington, D.C., 1942).

88. Hoover to Dawes, October 8, 1931. Presidential Papers, Dawes, Hoover Library.

89. Joslin, *Hoover Off the Record,* p. 146.

90. *Literary Digest,* November 7, 1931, p. 7.

91. *New York American.* Quoted in *Literary Digest,* November 7, 1931. For an account of Borah's interviews with the President and with the press the day before Laval's arrival, see Johnson, *Borah of Idaho,* p. 320.

92. Quoted in *Literary Digest,* November 7, 1931. French reaction was duly noted by American diplomats in France. See Cable 690 from Howell to Secretary of State Stimson, October 27, 1931, Presidential Papers, Borah, Hoover Library.

93. Myers and Newton, *The Hoover Administration,* pp. 138–39.

94. Press reaction followed partisan lines, to some extent.

95. Nancy H. Hooker, ed., *The Moffat Papers: Selections from the Diplomatic Journals of Jay Pierrepont Moffat, 1919–1943* (Cambridge, Mass.: Harvard University Press, 1956), p. 47.

96. Joslin, *Hoover Off the Record,* pp. 136–41; Myers and Newton, *The Hoover Administration,* pp. 124–35.

97. Myers and Newton, *The Hoover Administration,* pp. 125–27.

98. Ibid., p. 135. See also, Joslin, *Hoover Off the Record,* pp. 136–41.

99. *Literary Digest,* October 17, 1931.

100. Ibid. See chap. 15 for full discussion.

101. Quoted in Robinson to Richey, October 10, 1931, Presidential Papers, Robinson, Hoover Library.

102. Press conference, October 30, 1931, Hoover Library.

15:    A Program for a New Congress

1. McCormick, *The World at Home,* pp. 65, 100.

2. Secretary Wilbur, in a conversation with E. E. Robinson in Washington, D. C., December 23, 1931.

3. Press conference, September 1, 1931, Hoover Library.

4. Myers and Newton, *The Hoover Administration,* devote 100 pages to "Remedies for the Drain upon Gold and the Contraction of Credit," "The Struggle Over Taxation and Economy," and "The Struggle to Balance the Budget," covering the period January–July 1932.

5. Myers, *State Papers,* 2:7–8.

6. White to David Hinshaw, August 10, 1931. Hoover to White, August 14, 1931. Hoover's rapid response to correspondents with ideas is to be noted here, as elsewhere.

7. Press conference, September 1, 1931, Hoover Library.

8. See E. Pendleton Herring, "Second Session of the Seventy-second Congress, December 5, 1932, to March 4, 1933," *American Political Science Review* 27 (1933): 846–74.

9. Here was a foretaste of the provisions of the National Recovery Act of the New Deal period. See Ellis Hawley's essay in *Herbert Hoover and the Crisis of American Capitalism,* p. 24. He did not want to "open wide the door to price fixing, monopoly, and destruction of healthy competition." Quoted in Robert F. Himmelberg's admirable essay in ibid., p. 68.

10. Walter Lippmann, *Interpretations 1931–1932* (New York: Macmillan Co., 1932), p. 92.

11. An unnamed "business journal," quoted as the lead sentence in an article entitled "The Congressional Battle-Royal," (*Literary Digest,* December 12, 1931, p. 5).

12. *Cincinnati Times-Star.* Quoted in ibid.

13. *New York Times.* Quoted in ibid.

14. From his *Emporia Gazette.* Quoted in ibid., December 19, 1931, p. 5.

15. Summary in *Literary Digest,* December 19, 1931, pp. 5–6.

16. This was not published at the time. Text in Myers, *State Papers,* 2:87. See also Joslin, ed., *Hoover After Dinner,* pp. 65–72.

364 HERBERT HOOVER

17. Paraphrased from press conference of December 11, 1931, Myers, *State Papers*, 2:83–84.

18. Ibid., pp. 84–85. General readers have had little opportunity to review the Hoover analysis in his own words. Typical of college readers is a "Problems of American Civilization" volume of source extracts, *The Great Depression and American Capitalism*, edited by Robert F. Himmelberg (Boston: D. C. Heath, 1968), which carries two extracts from Franklin Roosevelt and one from an economist, but nothing from President Hoover (1929–1933), even though Hoover's 1224-page public papers set has been available since 1934. Perhaps the National Archives publication of Hoover speeches, proclamations, statements, and press conferences beginning in late 1974 may stimulate a new interest among those who prepare books of readings.

19. Myers and Newton, *The Hoover Administration*, p. 174.

20. Joslin, *Hoover Off the Record*, pp. 157, 158.

21. Ibid., p. 164.

22. Ibid., p. 164.

23. Ibid., pp. 168–70. He did go, ultimately, but stayed up working until 3 A.M. as a result.

24. *New York Times*, December 9, 17, 23, 27, 1931.

25. The narrative here will to some extent be at variance with certain previous accounts, including one relied upon by textbooks: Gerald D. Nash, "Herbert Hoover and the Origins of the Reconstruction Finance Corporation," *Mississippi Valley Historical Review*, December 1959, pp. 455–68. Nash concludes that the "impetus" for RFC came from Eugene Meyer, not Hoover; that the latter opposed it for four months in 1931; and that he gave in only when the pressure became too great. Thus Hoover deserves little credit for RFC. His chief source is a few remarks from a speech given by Meyer in 1954, "From Laissez Faire with William Graham Sumner to the R.F.C.," in *Public Policy Yearbook of the Graduate School of Public Admistration* (Cambridge, Mass., 1954). In chatty fashion, Meyer assumed most of the credit for RFC. A competent article by James S. Olson, "The End of Voluntarism: Herbert Hoover and the National Credit Corporation," *Annals of Iowa*, Fall, 1972, 1104–13 is skeptical of the Meyer version and shows well the progression of events from NCC to RFC. The Merlo J. Pusey biography, *Eugene Meyer* (New York, 1974), makes no new contribution on the events of September to December 1931, but it is full on the career as publisher.

26. Olson, "The End of Voluntarism," pp. 1108–9.

27. Ibid. See also Pusey, *Eugene Meyer*, pp. 216–17, 241.

28. Stimson *Diary*, October 29, 1931, p. 199. Also Mark Sullivan, Jr. reminiscence, November 30, 1968, p. 9, Hoover Institution. Confronted in the spring of 1932 with a letter defending the merits of speculation that drove stock prices down to prices based only on current earnings, Hoover exploded in reply, "men are not justified in deliberately making a profit from the losses of other people" (Hoover to Thomas W. Lamont, April 2, 1932, Presidential Papers, Lamont, Hoover Library).

29. See *New York Times Index* entries under "United States—Banks and Banking," 1931.

30. *New York Times,* December 18 and 31, 1931.

31. Charles A. and Mary R. Beard duly noted, "Hoover had few ardent friends in Wall Street. . ." [*America in Mid-Passage* (New York, 1939), p. 144].

32. Turner Catledge reminiscence, September 15, 1969, p. 20, Hoover Institution. David Hinshaw says that Hoover told him in late August 1931 of an RFC plan "then in the making" (*Herbert Hoover: American Quaker*, p. 255), so it appears possible that Hoover had no illusions that NCC would suffice indefinitely. As usual, the president planned for contingencies.

33. Schwarz, *The Interregnum of Despair,* contains an able account of the overall campaign to pass the RFC bill.

34. Quotation from Olson, "The End of Voluntarism," p. 1110.

35. See the NCC records in the Hoover Library that were used and cited in ibid., pp. 1110–11.

36. Especially to be noted is Hoover's distaste for the publicity given RFC loans and his inability to get the Democratic Congress to delete this devastating provision of the law. The National Credit Corporation went out of business in the summer of 1934 after "more than 1,200 advances had been made to banks in 31 states." *New York Times,* July 28, 1934. The peak had come in February, 1932, when commitments reached $188 million. While 4,182 banks subscribed $425 million in all, only 39 percent of this sum was to be needed because of the creation of the RFC. Hoover, incidentally, felt the need initially to ask Congress for only $500 million for the RFC.

37. Jesse H. Jones (with Edward Angly, who spent three years on the research), *Fifty Billion Dollars: My Thirteen Years with the R.F.C.* (New York, 1951), p. 4. The quote continues: ". . . but I insisted on its being operated on a business basis with proper accounting methods, and that when Congress gave the R.F.C.'s money away the Federal Treasury should replace it."

38. This paragraph follows the Olson account, in general, and the quote is his. The bankers, for their part, hoped in vain that some change in Federal Reserve procedures (rediscounting of NCC frozen collateral) would give them security. Olson, "The End of Voluntarism," p. 1112.

39. Lamont to Hoover, April 1, 1932, Presidential Papers, Lamont, Hoover Library. Note closely that "relief to the banking situation" is not necessarily dependent on sizable loan totals—a point argued here (but not by Professor Olson in his article that focuses on loans as meaningful *results*). NCC was clearly a success for a time in terms of psychological improvement, both in banking and journalistic circles.

40. "Should the Reconstruction Finance Corporation be Abolished?" *Congressional Digest,* April 1953, pp. 106 ff.

41. Hoover to Lawrence Richey, August 9, 1933, Presidential Papers, Richey, Hoover Library.

42. *New York Times*, June 15, 1932. See also ibid., July 28, 1932.

43. Press conference, January 8, 1931, Hoover Library.

44. Myers and Newton, *The Hoover Administration*, pp. 168–71.

45. Myers, *State Papers*, 2:134.

46. Henry F. Misselwitz, a United Press reporter, filed his notes on this exclusive interview with his bureau chief. It was found in 1975 in the files of United Press International and was quoted at length in a newspaper feature article [*Oregon Journal*, January 6, 1975, p. A7, as modified by comparison with a copy of Misselwitz to Morris D. Tracy, February 29, 1932 (obtained by Hoover Library on request)].

47. Stimson apparently told Edward A. Clark who told Coolidge. Schwarz, *The Interregnum of Despair*, p. 159. Herring, "Second Session of the Seventy-second Congress," pp. 552–54.

48. Myers and Newton, *The Hoover Administration*, pp. 179–80.

49. Garner, however, went so far as to term the president's address on the 200th anniversary of Washington's birth a "partisan" document. John Nance Garner received at least one vigorous protest. J. F. Burke to Garner, February 24, 1932 (carbon copy), Presidential Papers, Republican National Committee, Hoover Library.

50. Robinson and Edwards, eds., *The Memoirs of Ray Lyman Wilbur*, pp. 556–57.

51. Ibid., pp. 557–58.

52. Press conference, May 27, 1932, Hoover Library.

53. Myers, *State Papers*, 2:197. Henry M. Robinson, through Lawrence Richey, had transmitted a telegram to the president urging that "the Chief find some way to send another message to Congress . . . to emphasize what he has already said and to the effect that our credit must be held sacred and that propaganda in opposition to us is being circulated throughout this and many other countries, in some instances through misunderstanding, in others opposition to a republic in a deliberate attempt to undermine and destroy it; that envy and malice are the basis of an organized campaign against us and the enemy are at our gates. . . . It is of supreme importance to have Senate and House agree to frame a bill that will cover any possible deficit and serve notice on the world that we are a patriotic and united people" (Robinson to Richey, May 9, 1932, Hoover Library).

54. Myers, *State Papers*, 2:197–98.

55. Ballot of bank presidents by a Recording and Statistical Department, June 1932, forwarded to Hoover. Presidential Papers Box 26, "Rand," Hoover Library. Herbert Stein, *The Fiscal Revolution in America*, draws distinctions between attitudes toward budget balancing then and decades later.

56. *Literary Digest*, June 11, 1932, p. 5.

57. Herring, "Second Session of the Seventy-second Congress," p. 874. A useful account of the period appears in Schwarz, *The Interregnum of Despair*.

58. Schwarz, *The Interregnum of Despair*, pp. 104–5.

59. Ibid., p. 65. Schwarz is especially knowledgeable on matters concerned with the legislative career of Senator Wagner.

60. Myers, *State Papers*, 2:232–33.

61. Ibid., p. 141.

62. Robinson and Edwards, eds., *The Memoirs of Ray Lyman Wilbur.* p. 555.

63. McCormick, *The World at Home*, p. 114.

64. Quoted in Schwarz, *The Interregnum of Despair*, p. 104.

65. Ibid., p. 103.

66. Ibid.

67. Ibid., p. 185, as quoted in *Literary Digest*, June 25, 1932, p. 5. Newspaper opinion was sharply divided along party lines, however.

68. "I believe we have reached the turning point in the depression" (*Literary Digest*, July 9, 1932, p. 37). All comments on Dawes's views were favorable. Ibid.

69. Myers and Newton, *The Hoover Administration*, pp. 236–37.

16: The Politics of Distress: Bonus Marchers

1. A summary account may be found in Bornet, "Labor and Politics in 1928" (Ph.D. diss., Stanford University, 1951), pp. 256–364.

2. Ibid., p. 455.

3. U.S., Congress, House, Committee to Investigate Communist Activities in the United States, *Investigation of Communist Propaganda*, 71st Cong., 2d sess., 1930, 2, pt. 3.

4. A point made in a farewell editorial in the *New York Times*, March 3, 1933.

5. Hoover, *Memoirs: The Cabinet and the Presidency*, p. 283.

6. Donald J. Lisio, *The President and Protest*, pp. 6–14.

7. Ibid., p. 18.

8. Ibid., pp. 19–22. "Hoover's approval of large expenditures for veterans' benefits and his efforts on their behalf have never been adequately recognized" (p. 23). He was "not an obstructionist," but had "encouraged, signed, and even sponsored legislation to assist the country's veterans" (p. 24).

9. Ibid., p. 25. Hoover "should have been among the veterans' favorite Presidents" (p. 27).

10. Myers, *State Papers*, 1:508.

11. Legislative reasoning was divided. Fiorello La Guardia, for example, saw the bonus as unnecessarily favoring one group of the unemployed. LaFollette saw it as a rival to his public works bill. Schwarz, *The Interregnum of Despair*, p. 174.

12. McCormick, *The World at Home*, p. 110.

13. See the exhaustively researched book by Lisio, *The President and Protest,* and Lisio's summary article, "A Blunder Becomes a Catastrophe: Hoover, the Legion, and the Bonus Army," *Wisconsin Magazine of History* (August 1967), which conveys certain of his most important research findings. Helpful are James F. and Jean H. Vivian, "The Bonus March of 1932: The Role of General George Van Horn Moseley," in the same issue; John W. Killigrew, "The Army and the Bonus Incident," *Military Affairs,* (Summer, 1962); a master's thesis that used some Hoover Papers, Stuart G. Cross, "The Bonus Army in Washington, May 27–July 29, 1932" (M.A. thesis, Stanford University, 1948); and Bennett Milton Rich, *The Presidents and Civil Disorder* (Washington, D.C.: Brookings, 1941). A book by Roger Daniels, *The Bonus March: An Episode of the Great Depression* (Westport, Conn.: Greenwood, 1971) devotes eighty-seven useful pages to what it terms the "siege" and "battle," and offers a critical bibliography. Throughout, though very detailed, it is anti-Hoover and anti-military; it is contradicted on some major matters by the Lisio book, although in other areas it is judged by Lisio to be reliable. The writing in Hoover's *Memoirs: The Great Depression,* is evidence of the apprehensions of Cold War years and the hurt produced by years of calumny.

14. Lisio, *The President and Protest,* p. 77.

15. Joslin, *Hoover Off the Record,* p. 264.

16. Lisio, *The President and Protest,* pp. 2, 123.

17. Manuscript, Charles Cochran, "George Washington Sent Artillery to Evict Bonus Marchers," to Newton, October 30, 1932, Presidential Papers, Bonus, Box 373, Hoover Library.

18. A brief sketch of his career is in Lisio, *The President and Protest,* pp. 51–54.

19. Phillips P. Brooks reminiscence, September 1, 1970, p. 12, Hoover Institution.

20. A letter, forwarded by Benjamin F. Castle to Edgar Rickard, September 12, 1932, Presidential Papers, Bonus, Box 373, Hoover Library.

21. Lisio, *The President and Protest,* pp. 59, 74, 80. "Hoover's supportive actions have been overlooked by historians" (p. 74).

22. The Pullman strike, Chicago, 1895; also in Nevada, 1907, Colorado, 1914. and West Virginia, 1921. Killigrew, "The Army and the Bonus Incident," p. 59.

23. Rich, *Presidents and Civil Disorder,* p. 216.

24. Ibid., pp. 217–19. Writing in 1941, Rich concluded that the use of troops in America to that year had "met with complete success" (p. 219). The *Washington Post* thought Hoover too gentle with Communist elements among the Bonus Army! Quoted by Lisio, *The President and Protest,* p. 61.

25. Cross, "The Bonus Army in Washington," pp. 30–31. A number of booklets and pamphlets then and later celebrated the Communist effort, and extravagant claims by Communist leaders well after the event helped confuse government leaders and the public about their power and leadership.

26. Lisio, *The President and Protest,* pp. 83–84.

27. Lisio, *The President and Protest*, pp. 55–57. See also Wilson, *Ideology and Economics*, chap. 1.

28. Daniels, *The Bonus March*, p. 155.

29. There would be a misunderstanding then and later about the concurrence, if any, of Chief of Police Glassford in this step.

30. Because Hoover had wanted to mechanize the army. He liked MacArthur's confidence that he would carry this through. Michael J. Le Pore, M.D. reminiscence, December 5, 1966, p. 18, Hoover Institution.

31. Killigrew, *The Army and the Bonus Incident*, p. 62.

32. Lisio, *The President and Protest*, p. 105.

33. Sociologist Whiting Williams to reporters, *New York Times*, July 31, 1932, p. 3. (The three full pages of coverage of events are to be noted.)

34. Hoover to Commissioners, July 29, 1932, Presidential Papers, Bonus. Box 373, Hoover Library.

35. Lisio, *The President and Protest*, p. 200.

36. Ibid., p. 197. ". . . Hoover would not sign any document that would give the army sweeping latitude." Personal pressure on Hoover by both Hurley and MacArthur was without effect (ibid., pp. 197–99).

37. Maj. Gen. H. W. Blakeley, "The Day the Army Was Smeared," *Combat Forces Journal* 2 (February 1952): 26. Captain Eisenhower and Major Patton were among those present.

38. Hurley order to MacArthur cited in Lisio, *The President and Protest*, p. 200.

39. Lisio is decidedly authoritative on this matter; the Daniels account is inadequate. Contemporaries knew nothing of it at all. See Dwight Eisenhower reminiscence, July 13, 1967, pp. 2–3, Hoover Institution, which claims MacArthur did not permit formal presentation of the orders to him; F. Trubee Davison (assistant secretary of war for air) reminiscence. September 14, 1969, p. 2, Hoover Institution, says the order was "intercepted"; and General Moseley's typed document, "The Bonus March: 1932," says Hurley directed him to, so he personally told MacArthur in private ("he was very much annoyed"). Photostat from Moseley Papers, Library of Congress, pp. 8–10. See also Hoover, *Memoirs: The Great Depression*, and Lisio, *The President and Protest*, chap. 10, especially pp. 210–12. Moseley says he sent Col. Clement H. Wright, secretary of the general staff, to tell MacArthur the second time. Reminiscences in Hoover Institution.

40. Lisio, *The President and Protest*, p. 192.

41. Overheard by Major Dwight Eisenhower at the time. Ibid., p. 193.

42. The odd story of how it happened is in Vivian, "The Bonus March of 1932," pp. 34–35. In one instance an army reserve private was merely helping the police burn some unsanitary areas but was photographed doing that routine task. An army investigation later determined that no officer issued instructions to burn dwellings.

43. Davison at lunch with Hoover years later talked with him about this episode, and quotes Hoover as saying, "The next morning when I talked to Mac-Arthur he was obviously ill at ease about it. I upbraided him." F. Trubee Davison reminiscence, September 14, 1969, p. 5, Hoover Institution.

44. See, for example, the first *New York Times* survey of national press opinion, which indicated that adverse comment was rare; however, the Hearst and Scripps-Howard chains were hostile to the action taken and naturally laid blame at the president's door.

45. Irrefutable evidence of the disobedience of orders appears in Lisio, *The President and Protest*, pp. 233–34. In 1934 the ex-president, in a fit of irritation, nearly told the story; he only hinted at it in his memoirs (a too delicate narrative of this particular matter which historians have totally—and we now know mistakenly—disbelieved). A close reader of the Joslin quote at the beginning of this chapter (written in 1934) is a giveaway to those who read it now.

46. Lisio judges that this was a major Hoover error—a blunder that "plagued him for the rest of his life" (ibid., p. 215). MacArthur may have offered his resignation (see ibid., p. 228; the later memory of a member of Hoover's inner circle is cited as evidence). It may be well to refer back to the quotation from Secretary Joslin for a rationale for Hoover's acceptance of responsibility.

47. Stimson *Diary*, July 28, 1932, p. 112.

48. Pasadena resident to Hoover, July 29, 1932, Presidential Papers, Individuals, Roosevelt, Hoover Library.

49. No infants died from use of tear gas (Daniels, *The Bonus March*, p. 179), although in 1973 a new text could still say that two were [Walter T. K. Nugent, *Modern America* (Boston, 1973), p. 218].

50. Press statement, vol. 63, item 2150, Hoover Library. A grossly incorrect account by Eleanor Roosevelt in *McCall's* magazine years later (July, 1949) was replied to (not entirely accurately) by Hurley (*McCall's*, November 1949).

51. See for example, Lisio, *The President and Protest*, p. 230. Mitchell's definition of "criminal" included many minor violations.

52. Joslin, *Hoover Off the Record*, p. 276.

53. Lisio, *The President and Protest*, p. 252.

54. Ibid., p. 253.

55. See Louis Lochner, *Herbert Hoover and Germany* (New York: Macmillan Co., 1960).

56. Quoted from the issue of July 23, 1932 by Cross, "The Bonus Army in Washington," pp. 61–62.

57. Lisio, *The President and Protest*, has this as his major unifying theme, following charge and countercharge through later decades. Later claims by Communist leaders that they started and led the riot of July 28 are disallowed convincingly. Some will have important reservations on Lisio's treatment of Hoover in the post-presidential period.

58. E. E. Robinson, *The Presidential Vote, 1896–1932*, pp. 390–93.

17: Hoover in the Campaign of 1932

1. Mark Requa, in a letter to Secretary Newton on January 7, 1932, expressed his disgust with the meeting and methods of the Republican National Committee, and remarked, "It will not save the country" (President's secretary's file, Hoover Library).

2. T.R.B., "Washington Notes," *New Republic,* April 20, 1932, p. 270.

3. Hilles to Hoover, March 26, 1932, President's personal file 882, Hoover Library.

4. T. N. Carver to Hoover, March 28, 1932, File 46A, Hoover Library. Carver urged further that the candidate and the platform be as one in viewpoint. Carver to Walter H. Newton, March 29, 1932, Presidential Papers, Republican Party correspondence, Hoover Library.

5. Indeed, the marijuana issue became years later a political divider among citizens puzzled over appropriate legislation.

6. Hoover, *Memoirs: The Great Depression,* p. 318.

7. Ibid., p. 319.

8. *New York Times,* June 21, 1932.

9. Hoover, *Memoirs: The Great Depression,* p. 319.

10. Mark L. Requa had sent Walter H. Newton a memorandum from San Francisco to the effect that William Haas of Levi, Strauss & Company, when asked for a contribution to finance the Hoover campaign, had replied "nothing doing now unless there is to be a wet platform—and no straddling," and that Haas was "just one of many." Newton replied to Requa on April 21, 1932: "Admitting the force of that argument, under present circumstances and conditions I think this thought must always be borne in mind: a great deal of our support came from a certain group, who were enthusiastic and tireless. They have been the President's mainstay ever since then. Whatever is agreed upon must be acceptable to such an extent to them that their continued support is assured." Both letters in Presidential Papers, Republican party correspondence, Hoover Library.

11. The hatred and jealousy of Johnson toward Hoover can best be seen in a private communication Johnson sent to his son in 1928: "Some of our political wiseacres here claim that Hoover has been stopped in his mad career to the Presidency. I do not believe it. Every rogue, every unconvicted thief, every scoundrel, politically, gravitate naturally to his banner. . . . Wherever there is a delegate to be bought, we find that delegate for Hoover. Wherever there is a crook to be placated by a promise of future preferment, or office, there is a Hoover shouter. Wherever there is a big business enterprise, that seeks to despoil the people and rob the government, there you find a 'business man' for Hoover. The sum total of all this is the control of the Republican Party" (Johnson Diary, March 17, 1928). Quoted in *American Heritage,* August 1969, p. 71. (Such accusations

were common with that frustrated senator.) Such gross overstatement would in a few years characterize his private comments about Roosevelt.

12. George E. Farrand to Richey, March 3, 1932, Presidential Papers, Robinson, Hoover Library.

13. Gannett to Hoover, April 13, 1932, Presidential Papers, Republican party correspondence, Hoover Library.

14. White to Hoover, May 10, 1932, President's personal file 455, Hoover Library.

15. Paul Shoup to Frank A. Miller, May 23, 1932, Presidential Papers, Republican party correspondence, Hoover Library.

16. Richard H. Templeton to Walter H. Newton, May 27, 1932, same file, Hoover Library.

17. Gannett to Newton, June 6, 1932, same file, Hoover Library.

18. Fess to Hoover, June 25, 1932, President's personal file 632, Hoover Library.

19. Hoover, *Memoirs: The Great Depression,* pp. 319–20.

20. *New York Times,* June 17, 1932.

21. Fred G. Clark reminiscence, October 29, 1969, p. 28, Hoover Institution. This observation was twice repeated.

22. Ibid., p. 10. "It's now no secret." Clark became general chairman of the American Economic Foundation.

23. Stimson *Diary,* November 4, 1930, p. 37. See also entry for September 30, 1930.

24. Clark reminiscence, p. 7.

25. Memorandum made within twenty-four hours by Lewis Strauss; quoted in his *Men and Decisions,* p. 59.

26. *Proceedings,* Republican National Convention, p. 101.

27. Telegram, Hoover to Bertrand H. Snell, chairman, Republican National Convention, June 16, 1932. In Myers, *State Papers,* 2:209–10.

28. Governor Dan W. Turner of Iowa gave the president a candid criticism of the National Republican Platform from the point of view of the midwestern states. He thought the president could correct this in his speech of acceptance and suggested specifically: "a policy on the part of the Federal Reserve System in addition to their present open market transactions, that will increase the circulating medium and directly improve commodity prices; a Federal Farm Loan Corporation that will reestablish farm credits at a low rate of interest; and finally, a stronger statement with regard to the stabilization of prices on the farm." Memorandum, file 46A, July 8, 1932, Hoover Library.

29. Stimson and Bundy, *On Active Service in Peace and War,* p. 283.

30. Myers, *State Papers,* 2:261–62.

31. Stimson *Diary,* August 11, 1932, pp. 137–38.

32. Quoted in *Literary Digest,* August 20, 1932, p. 3.

33. "Hoover Rallies the Republican Hosts" (ibid.).

34. Joslin, *Hoover Off the Record*, p. 246. It is unclear just when Hoover first saw a copy of a Roosevelt campaign letter of 1928 which decried "the materialistic and self-seeking advisers who surround [Hoover]; men whose influence has already made it manifest that high ideals and a forward-looking policy—not only for this country, but for the world—would stand as little chance under Mr. Hoover as they have stood under President Harding, President Coolidge, and Mr. Mellon." Roosevelt to Mr. and Mrs. Arthur M. Baldwin [and others], October 15, 1928. (Copied into a Hoover manuscript.) Roosevelt Collection, Box 934, Hoover Library.

35. Stimson and Bundy, *On Active Service in Peace and War*, pp. 283–84.

36. Myers, *State Papers*, 2:247–49.

37. *New York Herald Tribune*, July 19, 1932.

38. This outline summary fits the facts now known. It is based on a formal document prepared at the time by French Strother and sent to William Allen White, July 27, 1932, President's secretary's file, Hoover Library.

39. Norris to Clarence W. Westbrook, April 30, 1932, and Norris to E. E. Good, May 21, 1932, Norris Papers, Library of Congress.

40. "I have great faith in Governor Roosevelt," wrote Norris to a constituent on July 20, 1932, "and I am going to do everything I possibly can to bring about his election. As long as Mr. Hoover stays in the White House I have no hopes whatever of any relief for stricken agriculture" (Norris Papers, Library of Congress).

41. Republican National Committee, *The Republican Administration: Its Tasks and its Accomplishments*, (Washington, D. C.: The Republican National Committee).

42. Myers, *State Papers*, 2:249–50.

18:   Hoover's Program for the Future

1. *New York Times*, September 4, 1932; McCormick, *The World At Home*, p. 126.

2. Myers, *State Papers*, 2:247.

3. Castle wrote in his diary on February 18, 1932: "The President said a couple of days ago that for the coming election he must have all the support he can get." Quoted by Ferrell, *American Diplomacy in the Great Depression*, pp. 168–69.

4. Still, campaign speeches made news.

5. James Truslow Adams, *History of the United States* (New York, 1933), 4:338.

6. Fess to Hoover, September 21, 1932, President's personal file 632, Hoover Library.

7. Still, one thinks of Cleveland's second effort in 1892, Lincoln's in 1864, and Taft's in 1912—among others. Neither Coolidge nor Lyndon Johnson chose to seek such a test.

8. In Stimson and Bundy, *On Active Service in Peace and War,* p. 285.

9. Joslin, *Hoover Off the Record,* p. 299.

10. Myers, *State Papers,* 2:295–99.

11. Ibid., pp. 301–2.

12. Ibid., pp. 303, 307, 297.

13. Ibid., pp. 309–17.

14. On October 25, 1932, in Baltimore, Roosevelt said according to the *New York Times* text: "The crash came in October, 1929. The President had at his disposal all the instrumentalities of government. From that day to Dec. 31 he did absolutely nothing to remedy the situation. Not only did he do nothing, but he took the position that Congress could do nothing. The deficit in the treasury continued to increase, but never did he urge that the budget be balanced until December 1931, nearly two long years later, when the leaders of the Democratic House announced their determination to balance the budget. Then the President urged that it be done. He was right, but as usual he was right at the wrong time. He was two years too late." *New York Times,* October 26, 1932. The remark came late in the speech. The radio probably did not carry it. See *New York Times,* October 26, 1932, p. 10 for CBS's explanation. Hoover commented on this statement in his speech in Indianapolis on October 28: "It seems almost incredible that a man, a candidate for the Presidency of the United States, would broadcast such a violation of the truth. The front pages of every newspaper in the United States for the whole of the two years proclaimed the untruth of such statements" (Myers, *State Papers,* 2:390). The Myers *State Papers* inserted the first date as "December 31, 1931," and omitted the later sentences. It seems clear that Hoover was fooled by the awkward newspaper text. When the Roosevelt *Public Papers* appeared, the date "December 31, 1929" was inserted into the text (vol. I, p. 837). It was an unfortunate episode, all around, especially because the *New York Herald Tribune* got it right: "December 31." The mimeographed reading copy says, "From that day to December 31, he did . . ." (p. 14). In Moley Papers, Hoover Institution. What Roosevelt *intended* in the "did absolutely nothing" phrase remains unclear.

15. Myers, *State Papers,* 2:410.

16. Ibid., p. 421. However, he obviously was not thinking in terms of the solutions to be hit upon in the WPA at times, later.

17. Ibid., p. 422. Thus a hint of the division of 1937 was brought into view, that is, the Roosevelt Court fight. A Hoover friend at the speech wrote to the president as follows: "His copy furnished the press does not include the 'Supreme Court' reference, but he distinctly in a sneering voice made the above quotations so that all who were there or on the radio, could hear him" (M. L. Bullard to Hoover, October 26, 1932, President's personal file 1772. Hoover Library.

18. Franklin D. Roosevelt, Commonwealth Club address, San Francisco, California, September 23, 1932 (*Public Papers, 1928–1932*, pp. 751–52). The spoken words were Roosevelt's but the text was Raymond Moley's. Moley, a professor of public law at Columbia University, was later to make the authorship extremely explicit. Berle, Moley, and others worked on it, for the Commonwealth Club was "an association of extraordinarily intelligent men devoted to the nonpartisan discussion of great public issues." Raymond Moley, *After Seven Years*, p. 58n.

19. Myers, *State Papers*, 2:423.

20. Ibid. Moley wrote, "Hoover and Mills were among the few articulate outsiders who perceived the boldness and coherence of the political and economic proposals that Roosevelt had made . . ." (*After Seven Years*, p. 51).

21. Myers, *State Papers*, 2:409.

22. Ibid., p. 457.

23. Joslin, *Hoover Off the Record*, p. 324.

24. The Benjamin Strong–Montagu Norman correspondence of the 1920s illuminates this remark. Xerox copies, Hoover Library.

25. Myers, *State Papers*, 2:457.

26. Earl Behrens reminiscence, August 1, 1971, p. 8, Hoover Institution.

27. Myers, *State Papers*, 2:478.

28. Joan Hoff Wilson, *Herbert Clark Hoover, Forgotten Progressive* (Boston: Little, Brown, 1975) apparently treats this theme.

19: Revolution By Election

1. *Literary Digest*, October 15, 1932, pp. 10–11.

2. *New York Times*, October 16, 1932.

3. See a confidential letter to Henry M. Robinson September 19, 1932: "If it be organized, it is organized as a club for conversation." Presidential Papers, Robinson, Hoover Library. A reading of the committee files also supports the present view. The Republican National Committee files show the belief the election was lost before October; files 249, 257, and 920 also showed gloom. The Requa file shows financial poverty (a $200,000 deficit). Regular supporters were depression oriented. The Detroit speech could not be put on radio until Hoover personally raised the money. See also Joslin, *Hoover Off the Record*, pp. 317–18.

4. Comparison of the Democratic and the Republican National Committee membership during the period 1928–1932 reveals that the businessman's control of national party organizations was clearly illustrated "in every section of the country . . . except in the lower South." *American Political Science Review* 26 (1932): 360–61.

5. Joslin, *Hoover Off the Record*, p. 315.

6. The "independent" in registration and/or voting in the late 1930s had

Norris as godfather; unfortunately, independence of party often became equated with nonparticipation in political affairs.

7. *San Francisco Chronicle*, November 2, 1932.

8. Borah Papers, Library of Congress. Mrs. Mabel Walker Willebrandt had had a long conference with Senator Borah on July 27. He saw no way "at the present time that it would be possible for him to take any active part in the campaign or make any public speeches." Copy of Willebrandt to Mark L. Requa, July 27, 1932, referred to in Requa to Newton, August 4, 1932. Requa then undertook to see Borah and transmitted Borah's response to Secretary Newton that "so long as the issues remain as they are in this campaign, the matter of my changing my position is foreclosed." Borah said further that "it is not a matter of personal feeling, it is a difference of view upon what I conceive to be the most fundamental proposition before the American people." Requa to Newton, August 16, 1932, President's secretary's file, Hoover Library.

9. William T. Hutchinson, *Lowden of Illinois*, 2:660–62.

10. Hoover wrote to the editor of the *Florida Beacon* (Jacksonville) that Roosevelt's possible reduction of tariffs would bring "poverty and despair" to the state, for it needed the tariff to compete with peon labor that produced its very same commodities elsewhere. Hoover letter of October 24, 1932, President's personal file 664, Hoover Library.

11. Bruce L. Felknor, *Dirty Politics* (New York: Norton, 1966), p. 33.

12. Thomas A. Bailey, *Democrats and Republicans* (New York: Meredith Press, 1968), p. 108.

13. Assembled from a number of oral history reminiscences at the Hoover Institution. Walter Trohan of the *Chicago Tribune* recalled the vase incident.

14. "The 1932 election stands apart from the other twelve in the modern period. It was the only one in which neither major party's congressional total was within ten percent of its presidential vote. The figure for the Republicans was 88.8 in the trough of a deep depression. Congress was low in public esteem. Members seeking reelection faced difficulty in framing convincing arguments in favor of their return to the House of Representatives. For once, interest of the country was very definitely shifted to the presidential candidates. This phenomenon is not peculiar to the United States. The deep crisis in capitalistic countries produced a more than disquieting lack of appreciation for the legislators' ability to discover the blueprints of escape from economic breakdown." Cortez A. M. Ewing, *Congressional Elections, 1896–1944* (Norman, Oklahoma; University of Oklahoma Press, 1947), p. 37.

15. Edgar E. Robinson, *The Presidential Vote*, pp. 24–30. See also his *They Voted For Roosevelt* and *The Roosevelt Leadership, 1933–1945*, pp. 59–80.

16. It is all too easy to lose sight of the voter who does not vote for the winner. Thus multiple millions voted with determination for such figures as Adlai Stevenson, Barry Goldwater, and George McGovern. Such language as *"the country turned its face away"* fails to convey this simple reality.

17. Kellogg to Castle, November 18, 1932, Castle Papers, Hoover Library.

18. *Literary Digest*, November 5, 1932, p. 46.

19. H. C. Byle, "The Editor Votes," *American Political Science Review*, August 1933, pp. 597–611.

20. Robinson and Edwards, eds., *The Memoirs of Ray Lyman Wilbur*, p. 554.

21. Myers, *State Papers*, 2:428.

22. Willis J. Abbot in the *Christian Science Monitor*, as quoted in the *New Orleans States*, November 26, 1932. Copy in Jahncke to Richey, November 29, 1932, Presidential Papers, Navy Department, Hoover Library.

23. E. E. Robinson reminiscence, September 13, 1967, p. 7, Hoover Institution.

24. Marjorie Test Loomis reminiscence, January 20, 1970, p. 9. See also Birge M. Clark reminiscence, March 1969 (mimeographed), p. 32, Hoover Institution.

25. Phillips P. Brooks reminiscence, September 1, 1970, p. 21, Hoover Institution. (Brooks was the Hoover's butler.)

26. For the full story, see Robinson, *The Roosevelt Leadership*, p. 82. Roosevelt's first draft contained the words "in readiness to cooperate," but these were struck out.

27. Quoted in Victor L. Albjerg, "Hoover, the Presidency in Transition," *Current History*, October, 1960, p. 219.

28. Hulda Hoover McLean reminiscence, September 25, 1967, p. 17, Hoover Institution. Of her father and his famous brother she had said: "Of course, both Uncle Bert and Tad had a moral code of 'black is black and white is white, and there aren't any grays' " (ibid., p. 30).

29. In General Leslie R. Groves reminiscence, August 9, 1968, p. 5, Hoover Institution.

30. *New York Times*, November 9, 1932. Italics added. One who emerges from a close reading of most latter-day judgments on Hoover can scarcely believe that contemporaries could have read such an opinion in their morning paper *at the time*.

31. "The End of Herbert Hoover," *Nation*, November 16, 1932, p. 470.

32. *New Republic*, November 16, 1932, p. 1.

33. Ibid., November 9, 1932, p. 341.

20:   The United States at the Crossroads

1. The so-called lame-duck amendment had on January 6, 1932, passed the Senate, and on February 16 it had passed the House, in the form of a resolution proposing to the states an amendment to the Constitution providing that the terms of the president and the vice-president should end on January 20, and the terms of senators and representatives on January 3 of the years in which their terms would normally have ended. The secretary of state proclaimed the

Twentieth Amendment in effect on February 6, 1933; thirty-nine of the forty-eight states ratified it.

2. On this period, see the detailed treatment in Robinson, *The Roosevelt Leadership,* chap. 4, "Interregnum."

3. The liberal magazines of the day thought that "Republican orators" should bear some responsibility for evoking "fear" of the consequences of Democratic victory. The Democrats, however, portraying the president as callous, also could bear some of this responsibility.

4. Norris Papers, Library of Congress. In the same file is a list of 3,000 progressives.

5. See editorial, "A Snare Set for Mr. Roosevelt," in the *Chicago Tribune,* March 6, 1933.

6. Hoover to Harry P. Dewey, November 22, 1932, Hoover Library.

7. See Robinson, *The Roosevelt Leadership,* p. 82.

8. Among the letters suggesting that President Hoover not only invite President-elect Roosevelt to conference but "resign" or "abdicate" or "merge" are the following from Presidential Papers, Roosevelt, Hoover Library.

"The suggestion made by Mr. Joseph P. Tumulty, who was Secretary to President Wilson, that Mr. Hoover resign as president of the United States and surrender this high office to you immediately after your election is assured, is very pertinent, and as I see it, should, for our country's good, be complied with" (a banker from McKinney, Texas to Roosevelt, November 5, 1932).

"It was a revolution, in our orderly American way. An immediate abdication is fully justified. The precedent may be useful during the trying years ahead" (E. S. Kochersperger to Hoover, November 9, 1932).

"On election night it occurred to me that . . . you . . . would do all in your power to effect a merger of your administration and the next, so that, as far as possible, the forces set in motion by you, as well as those of your successor, could be marshalled with irresistible effectiveness. Since that night, I have seen indications that all this was in the minds of many, in all sections of the country, irrespective of party . . ." (Charles H. Strong, Secretary of Committee of the Bar for Hoover in the State of New York, to Hoover, November 13, 1932).

"By nominating the Hon. Franklin D. Roosevelt your Secretary of State, and subsequently you and your successor resigning your offices, you would, by one stroke not only fulfill the wishes of the American people, but incidentally by this same stroke regain some of that confidence that you have lost among your people during your administration" (C. G. Bittel to Hoover, November 9, 1932).

9. As Anne O'Hare McCormick observed on February 5, 1933. "Mr. Hoover always had a program. He is responsible for bringing the point program into practical politics . . ." (*The World at Home,* p. 164).

10. The term was by no means new. Hoover had said in his address at Madison Square Garden on October 31, 1932: "We are told by the opposition that we must have a change, that we must have a new deal." As is well known, Roosevelt as presidential candidate had called for a "New Deal." John D. Hicks, in *The*

Republican Ascendancy, 1921–1933, has pointed out that in 1924 a "Committee of One Hundred," supporting LaFollette for the presidency, had declared, "We believe that the time has come for a new deal" (p. 105).

11. Noted at the time by Vincent K. Antle, local FBI agent routinely assigned to Hoover when in Florida. Reminiscence (based on notes), July 8, 1972, Hoover Institution. Kennedy, of course, utilized "New Frontiers," as all know.

12. J. P. Moffat, writing of the conference of Hoover and Roosevelt on November 22, 1932, commented: "A good many people here expect Roosevelt to recognize Russia, as being something he can do at once and on his own, in foreign affairs, and which will have little repercussion or real meaning. Other than that, the general impression is that he will carry on the Stimson policies almost unchanged" (Hooker, ed., *The Moffat Papers*, pp. 77–78). Interpretive essays on foreign policy by Selig Adler and Joan Hoff Wilson appear in *The Hoover Presidency*, pp. 153–188.

13. Stimson and Bundy, *On Active Service in Peace and War*, p. 296.

14. In Presidential Papers, Roosevelt, Hoover Library (1932 and 1933) appeared a memorandum of discussion with president-elect Roosevelt on debts and a full interchange with Stimson as well, including a long preliminary letter by the president. President's personal file 1506 contains the material gathered by Secretary Mills during the last days of the administration and labeled "Mills Notes."

15. Memorandum of conversation between Secretary Stimson and French Ambassador Paul Claudel, November 11, 1932, Presidential Papers, Roosevelt, Hoover Library.

16. Myers, *State Papers*, 2:485–86. A memorandum "for departmental use only" of a State Department press conference on November 14 reveals that there was "no change in our viewpoint that discussion must be direct negotiations with each country." No conference was anticipated, and there were no conversations with envoys pending the Hoover–Roosevelt consultation (Presidential Papers, Roosevelt, Hoover Library).

17. See Robinson, *The Roosevelt Leadership*, pp. 87–89.

18. In President's personal file 230 B, Hoover Library.

19. These meetings are described in Robinson, *The Roosevelt Leadership*, pp. 89–91.

20. In Presidential Papers, Roosevelt, Hoover Library.

21. Hoover memorandum, January 22, 1933, Presidential Papers, Foreign Affairs, "Financial, Moratorium," Hoover Library.

22. Stimson and Bundy, *On Active Service in Peace and War*, p. 293.

23. E. Pendleton Herring, "Second Session of the Seventy-second Congress," pp. 404 ff.

24. The famous confidential memorandum written by Hoover to Senator David A. Reed on February 20, 1933 has been gleefully seized upon as evidence of Hoover's insincerity, for it contains the observation that "abandonment of 90

percent of the so-called new deal" would be required if Roosevelt cooperated fully with Hoover in economic matters. On a close reading, however, this clearly was an incidental aspect for Hoover; what he thought and repeatedly said was *vital* was to avoid a "debacle," and he fervently hoped that a debacle was not a part of the new deal. Quoted in Myers and Newton, *The Hoover Administration*, p. 341.

25. For the coming fiscal year proposed expenditures would be: interest on public debt $725 million; trust funds, refunds, District of Columbia, etc. $310.9 million; public works (nonmilitary) $305 million; military, $612.7 million; veterans, $818.4 million; all other, $461 million. Total, $3,233 million. Myers, *State Papers*, 2:579.

26. Ibid., p. 580.

27. Ibid., p. 597.

28. As a sidelight, it was confidently stated in one magazine that newspapermen were "wet" through and through and that this party sponsorship was of great meaning in getting them off on the right foot with the new administration! The thirsty newsmen were sick of the Hoover dry period.

29. For a president who was thought of as remote from the Congress and without party control, Hoover's veto record is startling. Only three bills were passed over his veto. He vetoed outright twenty-one bills and pocketed sixteen more. In the first session of the Seventy-first Congress there was no veto; in the second, there were four, and four pocket vetoes, and one passed over his veto; in the third session there were seven vetoes, seven pocket vetoes, and one passed over his veto; in the Seventy-second Congress, in the first session, there were seven vetoes and one pocket veto; in the second session, three vetoes, seven pocket vetoes, and one passed over his veto. (These figures, based on the record of the Journals of House and Senate, are taken from the manuscript copy of the *Presidential Veto* prepared by G. C. Robinson.) Hoover was on unassailable grounds with his veto on the Philippines. See *Memoirs: The Cabinet and the Presidency*, pp. 359–61. Premature independence without guarantees would bring economic and political ruin, he said.

30. Joslin, *Hoover Off the Record*, p. 339.

31. President Hoover sent an urgent message to Congress on January 17, stressing the necessity of balancing the budget by a reduction in expenditures and an increase in revenues to be gained partly through a sales tax. The next day he commented ruefully to his press conference, "The Appropriations Committee seems to insist upon using the preliminary figures set up and not including the supplemental reductions. . . . If those figures were used—the final figures. . . .[for] appropriations would show a saving of $43,000,000 in the five bills already dealt with in the House Committee . . ." (Press Conference, January 18, 1933, Hoover Library).

32. Professor Schwarz is surefooted in discussing these matters; see *The Interregnum of Despair*, p. 216.

33. Ibid., pp. 208–12.

34. Press Conference, January 20, 1933 (Myers, *State Papers*, 2:582–83). The president had already told his press conference on January 3 that "the proposals of Democratic leaders in Congress to stop the reorganization of Government functions which I have made is a backward step. The same opposition has now arisen which has defeated every effort at reorganization for twenty-five years" (Myers, *State Papers*, 2:561). At the time he referred to Congress as "that bear garden up there on the hill" (Joseph C. Green reminiscence, November 22, 1967, p. 29, Hoover Institution.

35. Press Conference, Hoover Library.

36. Myers, *State Papers*, 2:592–93.

37. Hillis to Hoover, February 14, 1933, President's personal file 882, Hoover Library.

38. Stimson *Diary*, November 30, 1932.

39. Ibid., January 7, 1933. Soon the Secretary reported precisely to Roosevelt what he had heard from Hoover. He explained that Hoover's motive for "prompt and dramatic action" on the debts was to stop the deterioration. "Roosevelt seemed to accept this" (Memorandum of a conversation with Roosevelt on January 9, 1933, Stimson *Diary*).

40. Ibid., November 8, 1932.

41. Ibid., January 30, 1933.

42. Ibid., November 30, 1932. Such an attitude gratified Stimson, who prided himself in standing aside from the political arena. He sometimes recorded his wish that the president could somehow ignore all "political" considerations.

43. Ibid., November 14, 1932.

44. At one point, when asked by Joslin to come to the White House to discuss the French note, he simply refused, saying he wouldn't come! It was "the last straw." Off he went to play a few holes of golf (Ibid., January 21, 1933). In mid-February the president showed the strain. After a Cabinet meeting Stimson tried to discuss with him the subject of Canada and the gold standard. "His only response was that he had only two weeks more and was glad of it" (Ibid., February 17, 1933).

45. Accounts of the crisis, variously delimited, appear in the Hoover memoirs, in Myers and Newton, *The Hoover Administration*, in Wilbur and Hyde, *The Hoover Policies*, and in Hoover biographies. There are accounts in the literature on Roosevelt. See Robinson, *The Roosevelt Leadership*, Chap. 4, and Frank Freidel, *Franklin D. Roosevelt: Launching the New Deal*, Chap. 11. An early account based on close contact with participants is the too little noted 1936 volume by Lawrence Sullivan, *Prelude to Panic: The Story of the Bank Holiday*. The extensive bibliography in the very detailed Susan Estabrook Kennedy, *The Banking Crisis of 1933*, makes other listings obsolete, except that additional accounts by economists are conveniently mentioned in Kindleberger, *The World in Depression*. Books by Raymond Moley and by Theodore Joslin, and the insights of the Stimson *Diary* bring one closer to the tense psychology of the crisis.

46. Stimson *Diary,* July 20, 1933.

47. In the last fourteen banking days of the Hoover administration, hoardings totaled $1,212,000,000. This was an average of $86 million taken out of circulation every day and put in vaults, shipped abroad, or tucked away. "On only one of the fourteen days was any money returned to circulation, showing that the people had any confidence at all and that confidence was limited to a million dollars or less than one percent" (Joslin, *Hoover Off the Record,* p. 395).

48. The correspondence is in Myers and Newton, *The Hoover Administration,* pp. 344–45. For a later account of this interchange, see Robinson, *The Roosevelt Leadership,* pp. 95–99, which is based on Roosevelt archival materials. See also the early chapters in Moley, *The First New Deal.* Professor Freidel, in his *Franklin D. Roosevelt: Launching the New Deal* (p. 189), agrees with Moley (p. 144) that when Roosevelt finally replied on March 1, with a short cover letter enclosing another allegedly written earlier, *both* were together in the stenographic notebook of March 1, but the "enclosure" was back dated to February 20. See also Kennedy, *The Banking Crisis,* p. 142. The president-elect is not directly charged with duplicity, nor need we affix blame; but that his failure to answer deeply disturbed President Hoover has long been minimized by historians. Members of the Cabinet were also incensed. Wrote Stimson, ". . . I don't see how he can avoid paying some attention to it. The condition of mind that the new administration has of the situation is beyond belief. . . . I cannot believe nor ever could believe that such a situation could exist in the face of such a threatening catastrophe" (*Diary,* February 28, 1933).

49. These three, really four, suggested courses of action are normally described as a bald, political, attempt by a "partisan" Republican who lost to inflict his party's policies on the Democrat who won. To agree with such a view requires an interpretation of Hoover as primarily "political," together with disregard for the plain wording of the Democratic platform and of most Roosevelt speeches of the 1932 campaign.

50. Hoover to Fess, February 21, 1933, Presidential Papers, Roosevelt, Hoover Library.

51. Sullivan to Hoover, February 21, 1933, ibid.

52. Hoover to Mills, February 22, 1933, ibid.

53. Myers, *State Papers,* 2:591. To Stimson, the final speech draft was on "the cause of the depression, both inside and out, . . . clear and strong" (*Diary,* February 7, 1933).

54. See Kennedy, *The Banking Crisis,* chap. 4.

55. Stimson, *Diary,* February 14, 1933.

56. Ibid., February 19, 1933. Stimson fully agreed (Ibid., February 20, 1933).

57. It was front page news in the *New York Times* on February 22–25, 27, and 28, 1933. Mitchell resigned on the twenty-eighth.

58. Stimson, *Diary,* February 21, 1933.

59. Ibid., February 22, 1933. A visit to the president on the twenty-fifth found

the White House still concerned with the banking crisis, for it was "still overhanging us with its shadow." Moley found Roosevelt practically silent on the bank crisis through the nineteenth, for example, while Louis Howe thought "all this fuss about the banks [in Detroit] silly" (Moley, *The First New Deal*, p. 138n).

60. Stimson *Diary*, January 29, 1933.

61. Joslin to Hoover, February 25, 1933 (with enclosure), Presidential Papers, Roosevelt Box 29, Hoover Library.

62. Hoover to Rand, February 28, 1933, ibid.

63. Stimson *Diary*, February 28, 1933. The unfortunate Tugwell remark has proven impossible to explain away, even by his biographer. See Kennedy, *The Banking Crisis*, p. 143.

64. Sullivan to Hoover, February 28, 1933, Presidential Papers, Roosevelt Box 29, Hoover Library.

65. Hoover to Roosevelt, February 28, 1933. Delivered in person by a secret service agent and read by various Roosevelt advisers on the scene. See Robinson, *The Roosevelt Leadership*.

66. *New York Times*, March 1, 1933.

67. Ibid., March 1, 1933.

68. Speech of February 13, 1933. Myers, *State Papers*, 2:594.

69. Stimson *Diary*, January 31, 1933. (The *Diary* is strangely silent on Hitler.)

70. *New York Times*, March 1, 1933.

71. Ibid., March 1, 1933.

72. Ibid., March 2, 1933.

73. Editorial, ibid. In his February 13 address, Hoover said that the best way to lower tariffs would be to restore the gold standard and hold a World Economic Conference.

74. Hoover to Governors of the FRB, March 2, 1933, Hoover Library.

75. *New York Times*, March 1, 1933. Three-column itemized lists were public knowledge (Ibid., March 2, 1933).

76. Ibid. "The final verdict about the loan publicity must be that Garner's insistence upon it was an act of irresponsible demagoguery" (Moley, *The First New Deal* p. 134).

77. *New York Times*, March 3, 1933.

78. Ibid.

79. Stimson *Diary*, March 28, 1933. The conversation at the time was about the banking bill.

80. See the Freidel and Kennedy volumes for the lack of leadership theme. A more recent essay is Frank Freidel, "The Interregnum Struggle Between Hoover and Roosevelt," in *The Hoover Presidency*, pp. 134–149, who is "more sympathetic toward Roosevelt and his advisers." (p. 149).

81. W. F. Miller, dated February 27, 1933, to the *New York Times*, March 2, 1933.

82. Editorial, *New York Times*, March 3, 1933. Stimson wrote, "the President . . . has been pretty near the most sensible one in all the confusion . . ." (*Diary*, December 15, 1932). As for Roosevelt, Stimson wrote, "It is time that we here feel that this fear about Roosevelt and his untrustworthiness seems to be pretty well founded from information which has come from every side and from people who have known him intimately . . ." (Ibid., November 22, 1932). Hoover had "shown up very well indeed in all of this negotiation with Roosevelt. His letters have been dignified and on a high plane of unselfishness. They made Roosevelt look like a peanut" (Ibid., December 21, 1932). "Roosevelt is rather slapdash" (Ibid., January 16, 1933). Owen D. Young found Roosevelt lacking in "grasp on the debt matter" and commented on "his ignorance about it" (Ibid., January 20, 1933).

83. Lilian M. Wheeler to the *New York Times*, March 2, 1933.

84. Meyer to Hoover, March 3, 1933, same file, Hoover Library.

85. Hoover to Meyer, March 4, 1933, same file, Hoover Library.

86. In Mark Sullivan Papers (typed manuscripts), Hoover Institution.

87. Roosevelt to Herbert Feis, quoted in Kennedy, *The Banking Crisis*, p. 143.

88. Anecdote in Robinson, "The History that Will Do Justice to President Hoover," p. 12. An anti-Hoover bias in Kennedy, *The Banking Crisis*, is maintained throughout. Nowhere is it more thinly based than in the comment, "A sleeping President could not help New York and Chicago" (p. 149). Words like "petulantly" are inserted as descriptive of serious presidential motives in that time of dire emergency (p. 151).

89. Moley, *The First New Deal*, p. 149.

90. Ibid. It is interesting that Roosevelt could have told Stimson later that "most of the bankers were conscientious and were doing their duties fully." Memorandum of March 28, 1933 in Stimson *Diary*, p. 141.

91. Little note has been taken by historians of this service.

92. Speech of December 16, 1935. Quoted in *Memoirs*, p. 395. Stimson wrote that there was fear in New York "that there will be a bad inflation which will upset values and destroy national credit. That is what everybody is afraid of and nobody has been able to get Roosevelt to take a strong position against it" (Stimson *Diary*, March 3, 1933). See also L. Sullivan, *Prelude to Panic*, p. 116 on the "authoritative word passed in the New York financial community" of a forthcoming "asset currency" and fear that gold would be abandoned. Thus, Sullivan says (writing in 1936), was swept away instantly "the last support of monetary confidence." This anecdote is seldom noted and its exact source (apparently interviews with some bank executives and financial leaders) is uncertain.

93. Wrote Stimson, "The President doesn't want to see him alone. He has been warned by so many people that Roosevelt will shift his words, that he wants some witnesses" (*Diary*, November 16, 1932). In the area of foreign affairs, Constantine Brown reported that Roosevelt had no interest in Manchuria at all (ibid., November 11, 1932). The public relations consciousness of the Hyde Park group was

offensive (ibid., December 23, 1932). Roosevelt's posture on the debts was "a highly foolish position to take" (ibid., January 20, 1933). Roosevelt was called by Hoover "a very dangerous and contrary man" (ibid., January 3, 1933). Roosevelt's telegram of December 20 struck Stimson as "terribly wrong," and he didn't blame the president for "trying to show him up." Clearly, there were "temperamental differences" (ibid., December 21, 1932). As for Mills, he and Roosevelt "didn't like and didn't trust each other" (ibid.). The fact that Hoover had been "very cordial and friendly" at the very first meeting and not at all "stiff," had not really helped (ibid., December 31, 1932), for Hoover would come to say that he would never talk to Roosevelt *alone* again (ibid., January 3, 1933).

94. The vigor of the indictment of Roosevelt and his advisers in the third volume of the Hoover *Memoirs* derived in part from the harshness of two decades of Democratic Party campaigning against the Hoover "record." The emotionalism of the Myers and Newton and the Lawrence Sullivan volumes is partially related to their 1936 publication dates, no doubt. Roosevelt wrote later, "No participation by me as a private citizen would have prevented the crisis; such participation in details would have hampered thorogoing action under my own responsibility as President" (Quoted in E. E. Robinson, *The Roosevelt Leadership*, pp. 101–2). Since Roosevelt's noncooperation was thus *deliberate,* one s at a loss to see the pertinence of the current overemphasis by those who dwell on Hoover's "politics," or on his "tone" in letters of the day. See, for example, Kennedy, *The Banking Crisis,* pp. 137–38.

95. Based in part on a thorough reading of the Stimson *Diary,* October 1932–September 1933. Stimson was incredulous over the fact that Roosevelt seems to have thought his Cabinet appointments could be delayed or concealed until as late as March 2 (*Diary,* February 3, 1933). Stimson had firmly resolved, however, to give Roosevelt "a fair chance" and not be swayed by the "unfavorable" impressions that were filtering in (*Diary,* December 24, 1932). In "The View from the State House: FDR," (in *The Hoover Presidency,* pp. 123–33), Alfred B. Rollins offers incisive comparisons of Hoover and Roosevelt, chiefly at the latter's expense. Rollins thinks historians "no longer feel compelled to destroy or defend Herbert Hoover." (p. 133).

Epilogue

1. Hoover to Saunders, February 27, 1933, Presidential Papers, Republican National Committee, Hoover Library. The Committee reply was both courteous and warm and was signed by all present at the meeting (text in *New York Herald Tribune,* February 28, 1933). The committee indecisively debated, excluding insurgents from the Republican caucuses (ibid., dispatch by Theodore C. Wallen).

2. Press conference, March 3, 1933, Hoover Library.

3. *Literary Digest,* March 25, 1933, p. 10.

4. Mason, *Harlan Fiske Stone,* p. 289.

6. Charles G. Dawes wrote the following to the President on January 28: "Not to have been able to fight with you in the field, engaged as you were almost single-handed—when not only your own interests but that of our country were vitally at stake—was a grief to me which I cannot express. . . . It is due to you and the successive steps in legislation achieved during your administration only through your initiative and leadership, that complete demoralization was averted, and a sound currency and governmental credit was saved. Roosevelt from the very nature of things must carry out your most important policies if he is to succeed. His success or failure will be determined largely by his ability to prevent degenerative changes by Congress in existing legislation for the passage of which in its present form you were responsible. The difficulties which beset you in office, and the opportunity for service to which you rose, have come but to three of our former Presidents—and you will be remembered with them. It involved you in untold anxiety and strain, and demanded unceasing work night and day, but you conquered, and you leave office decorated with universal public respect" (Presidential Papers, Dawes, Hoover Library).

7. Jesse Jones, *Fifty Billion Dollars*, p. 7. Said Hoover later, "Well, I can lay claim to only one thing: that credit has been given to me by Republicans and Democrats alike as being the only man in the world with enough economic knowledge to create a worldwide Depression" (Walter R. Livingston reminiscence, November 13, 1969, p. 54, Hoover Institution).

8. Said Charles H. Halleck, "I have always thought that the Republican Party would have maintained a lot more stature if we had gone right back and nominated Mr. Hoover again. . . . And I have talked with a great many people in our party, of preeminence and integrity and understanding, and I've heard many, many people express that" (reminiscence, March 6, 1966, p. 11, Hoover Institution).

9. Walter Trohan reminiscence, November 18, 1966, p. 3, Hoover Institution.

10. Hoover to Stimson, June 26, 1933, Postpresidential papers, Stimson, Hoover Library.

11. Hoover to Stimson, July 9, 1934, Postpresidential papers, Stimson, Hoover Library.

12. Hoover to Stimson, August 22, 1933, Postpresidential papers, Stimson, Hoover Library.

13. Hoover to Akerson, September 9, 1933, Postpresidential papers, Akerson, Hoover Library.

14. He continued, "I think I can truthfully state that I never met a more dedicated American patriot than Mr. Hoover. He was a gentleman . . ." (James A. Farley reminiscence, December 7, 1966, p. 2, Hoover Institution). Said Charles A. Edison, "He was never vindictive. I've never known him to be vindictive, but he was obviously hurt by some past events, but he would pass them off" (Charles A. Edison reminiscence, December 6, 1966, p. 8, Hoover Institution).

15. Hoover to Hunt, September 14, 1933, Postpresidential papers, Hunt, Hoover Library. For an emerging dispute about certain William Appleman

Williams interpretations (see bibliography), consult Robert F. Himmelberg essay in *Herbert Hoover and American Capitalism*, pp. 62–64.

16. Hoover to Christian Herter, October 4, 1933, Postpresidential papers, Herter, Hoover Library. A writer in 1974 said, "Hoover's tolerance and restraint toward protest have not yet been recognized . . ." (Lisio, *The President and Protest*, p. 50n).

17. Hoover to Franklin W. Fort, November 14, 1933, Postpresidential papers, Fort, Hoover Library.

18. A point stressed by an Iowa community leader. Ralph Evans reminiscence, March 8, 1970, p. 13, Hoover Institution.

19. Hoover to Walter Trohan, January 22, 1964, Postpresidential papers, Trohan, Hoover Library. Hoover added, "But being almost ninety, I am not certain but that these ideas are old stuff and banal at that." (Somehow, the reality of Herbert Hoover as a man utterly devoted to liberty and therefore to the Bill of Rights and personal freedom seems to have totally escaped our children's textbooks. In any case, space devoted to Hoover is decidedly minimum in grade and secondary school texts. Perhaps this will change.)

20. Press statement, July 28, 1932 (*State Papers*, 2:245).

The Historical Record

1. Henle to George Killion in the latter's reminiscence, January 25, 1970, p. 14, Hoover Institution.

2. Speech on "Dedication of the Hoover Library on War, Revolution, and Peace," June 20, 1941 (*Addresses on the American Road, 1940–1941*, p. 196).

3. Hoover, *Memoirs: The Great Depression*, p. 233.

4. Hoover to Stimson, October 9, 1943, Postpresidential papers, Stimson, Hoover Library.

5. Hoover to Mrs. Calvin Coolidge, October 15, 1942, Postpresidential papers, Coolidge, Hoover Library.

6. "As this is the first case of anyone being admitted to consult these archives, I think we must need establish certain procedures" (Hoover to Thomas Thalken, Archivist, September 1, 1955. Copy to E. E. Robinson).

7. The following or its equivalent was stated now and then: "They [the memories] don't necessarily need to be flattering or favorable. If you remember anything on the other side, I think that makes you a human being. But anything at all that you would recall of him would be greatly appreciated" (Comment of Raymond Henle in William J. Hopkins reminiscence, August 8, 1968, p. 5, Hoover Institution).

8. Many of the interviews have documents and photographs bound with them, and these have value independent of the text of the reminiscence.

9. Hoover to G. Akerson, January 9, 1934, Postpresidential papers, Individuals, Hoover Library.

10. Hoover to Will Irwin, February 13, 1928, Irwin Papers, Hoover Institution.

11. Memorandum of July 3, 1931, Presidential Papers, "Financial, Moratorium," Hoover Library.

12. Eugene Lyons reminiscence, October 4, 1968, p. 3, Hoover Institution.

13. Irene Corbally Kuhn reminiscence, November 20, 1969, p. 7, Hoover Institution. His books brought only modest income. For a detailed list of royalties, see Morton Blumenthal reminiscence, December 8, 1966, Hoover Institution.

14. Alan J. Gould reminiscence, October 27, 1970, p. 14, Hoover Institution. The present writers concur in this opinion if one excludes such nonbook materials as the John O'Laughlin correspondence with Hoover (perhaps 2,000 items) and the 400 Hoover–Wilson letters. (Gould was executive editor of the Associated Press for twenty-one years.) The letters to and from Wilson appear in Francis William O'Brien, ed., *The Hoover–Wilson Wartime Correspondence. September 24, 1914 to November 11, 1918* (Ames, Iowa: University of Iowa Press, 1974) and a second volume that will deal with the Versailles Treaty.

15. This speech may be found in typescript in the McMullen Papers, Hoover Institution.

16. Vincent K. Antle reminiscence, July 8, 1972, p. 35, Hoover Institution. According to all accounts, Truman was a great Hoover favorite.

17. Mark Kilby reminiscence, March 30, 1968, pp. 2–3, Hoover Institution.

18. A small bibliographical volume is Arnold S. Rice, ed., *Herbert Hoover, 1874–1964: Chronology–Documents–Bibliographical Aids* (Dobbs Ferry, New York: Oceana, 1971).

19. Hoover to Edwin S. Friendly, February 10, 1950. Printed as part of Friendly reminiscence, Hoover Institution.

20. Alfred H. Kirchhofer reminiscence, April 4, 1969, p. 9, Hoover Institution. Such memories were typically reinforced by contemporary notes and memoranda and, very often, had been repeated throughout a lifetime to friends and acquaintances. Direct quotes have not been used here unless there was a very high probability that the words were verbatim from Hoover. Many quotes fell by the wayside because of this self-imposed policy.

21. Stated at the Dutch Treat Club, New York City; reported in Rube Goldberg reminiscence, October 3, 1968, p. 16, Hoover Institution. The addresses delivered at the Bohemian Grove on the status of world affairs were not available at the time of the present research effort, nor were many drafts of Hoover's speeches and books. In the latter case, drafts had not yet been deposited. Galleys are available in the Hoover Institution.

Index

Adams, Charles Francis, 29, 103
Adams, James T., 257
Agricultural Credit Corporations, 154, 260
Agricultural Marketing Act, 77, 161, 352
agriculture: history of, 7–8, 68–70; and
  Republicans, 15, 72, 119, 135, 151,
  173–76; and Hoover's relief programs,
  31, 44, 74–81, 154, 214, 221, 252, 260;
  vs. industry, 69–70, 120, 273; and
  McNary–Haugen Bill, 70–71; and
  Farm Board, 71–81; and tariff, 76; and
  export debenture plan, 76, 77, 78; and
  Agricultural Marketing Act, 77, 161,
  352; and stock market crash, 80–81,
  181; and drought, 153–54; and
  prohibition, 241; and Democratic party,
  274; and Congress in 1932, 288; and
  grain situation, 353
Agriculture, Department of, 14, 29, 153,
  156
Akerson, George, 43
Albright, Horace Marden, 64
Aldrich, Nelson W., 113
Aldrich, Winthrop, 206
American Farm Bureau Federation, 141
American Federation of Labor, 22, 141,
  146, 156
American Individualism (Hoover), 39–41,
  238
American Legion, 203, 231, 235
American Petroleum Institute, 56
Anderson, Henry, 87
Anderson, Sherwood, 272
anti-trust laws, 57, 211–12
Argentina, 101
Arizona, 48
Arkansas, 153
armaments, limitations on, 98, 102–6,
  196, 345, 353
Asia, 14, 179
Australia, 52
Austria, 183–84, 190

Babson, Roger, 130
Baker, Newton D., 87

Ballentine, Arthur, 298
Baltimore Sun, 224
banking: and government, 125; and vote
  for Hoover, 151; and depression, 164,
  252, 283; and World Bank, 185; and
  National Credit Corporation, 206–7,
  218–20, 365; McCormick on, 208; and
  home loans, 212; and Hoover's twelve-
  point economic program, 214–17; and
  currency hoarding, 221–22; and
  Reconstruction Finance Corporation,
  252; and crisis of 1933, 290–99, 302,
  356–57, 381
Banking and Currency Committee, 293
bankruptcy laws, 221, 229
Barkley, Alben W., 181
Barnes, Julius, 129, 353
Baruch, Bernard, 126, 292
Beard, Charles A., 132, 201–2
Beard, Mary R., 132
"Beer Bill," 288
Belgium, 11
Bermuda, 103
Beveridge, Albert, 72
Bingham, Hiram, 106, 115, 121, 288
Black, John D., 76
Blaine, John J., 19, 74, 77, 145, 148
Bolivia, 100
bonus certificates, 230–31, 261
Bonus Expeditionary Force, 230–38
Borah, William E., and Republican party,
  8, 17, 113, 114, 115; and Hoover, 19,
  26, 48–49, 73, 92–96, 148, 165, 269–70,
  343; as Republican insurgent, 72, 77,
  135, 172–78; on naval limitation,
  104–6; and tariff, 117–18, 137, 143; on
  Supreme Court appointments, 145; and
  war debts, 194, 204–5; and National
  Credit Corporation, 206; and
  prohibition plank, 242, 245–46; and
  banking crisis, 293
Boston Transcript, 205
Boulder Canyon Project Act, 61
Boulder Dam, 154
Bourne, Jonathan, 72
Brookhart, Smith W., 26, 114, 135, 145;

389

on farm relief, 74–75, 77–78
Brown, General Lyttle, 59
Brown, Walter F., 29, 241, 268
Bruning, Heinrich, 184
Bryan, William Jennings, 6, 165, 360
Buckner, Mortimer, 206
budget: Hoover's proposals for, 154–55, 212, 220, 224, 380; and administrative reductions, 223, 256; and economic crisis, 229
building program: and rotation of construction, 63–64; and Hoover's economic plan, 131, 353; and drought relief, 154, 155; for unemployment relief, 170–71, 211, 214, 256; and bonus marchers, 232
Bundy, McGeorge, 286
Burke, James Francis, 28, 30, 44–45, 140
Burton, Theodore E., 114
business: in the early 1920s, 8; and private enterprise, 22, 55, 125, 220; and government construction, 62–64; and stock market crash, 126, 132; and economic conferences, 129–30, 251, 256; and Hoover, 160, 303; and International Chamber of Commerce, 184–85; and depression, 220, 289–90; and Roosevelt, 274, 289–90; and political enemies, 348; and political party control, 375
Business Cycles and Unemployment, Committee on, 123
Butler, Pierce, 15, 145

California: and Johnson, 2; and political parties, 12, 46–48, 169; and prohibition, 47, 85, 242; and Petroleum Conference, 57; and water supply problems, 61–62; and employment, 171
Cannon, Joseph, 6, 8
Caraway, Thaddeus, 27
Carver, Thomas Nelson, 240
Castle, William R., Jr., 101, 195–202 passim
Central Valley project, 61
Chamber of Commerce, 211
Chamber of Commerce, International, 184
Chandler, Harry, 47
Chicago Board of Trade, 80
Child Health and Protection Conference, 160
China: and mining, 52; and United States, 100, 201; and foreign intervention, 108, 196–200, 295; and Hoover, 179,

195–96, 203
Cincinnati Times-Star, 212–13
civil service, 16–17
Clapp, Moses, 72
Clark, Fred G., 246–47
Clark, J. Reuben, 100
Claudel, Paul, 284
Cleveland, Grover, 180, 294, 295, 297
Cochran, Thomas, 240
Colorado, 57
Colorado River Commission, 61
Commerce Department, 29, 76, 156, 188; Hoover and, 18, 23, 333
Communists: and Workers Party, 22; in Europe, 98; and Fish Committee, 229, 238; and bonus marchers, 233–34, 237, 370; and election of 1932, 266, 272
Comstock, Ada, 87
Congress, U.S.: and leadership, 6, 11; and Hoover, 13, 43; and farm problem, 68–69, 72–81; on prohibition, 85, 89; Seventy-first, 113–15; and tariff, 116–22, 133, 136–40; and relief programs, 131–32, 179–81, 212–16; and election of 1930, 150, 161; and war debts, 194–95; Seventy-second, 212, 287; and party division, 215, 216, 222–26; and economic issues, 216, 220, 252–54; and "interregnum," 287–89. See also Republican party; Senate, U.S.
Congressional Record, 170
conservation, 43, 47, 52–67, 131, 338
conservatives: in Republican party, 16, 112, 282; and Hoover, 120, 165; and prohibition, 244
Constitution of the United States, 3, 353; Hoover on, 247, 249, 301, 306, 361
construction, see building program
Coolidge, Calvin: and Hoover, 1, 26, 55; and tone of administration, 6–12 passim, 16, 18; and farm problem, 70–71; on Russia, 98; and economy, 124; and Republican party, 177, 240, 268
Cotton, Joseph B., 104
Couch, Harvey, 218, 220
Couzens, James, 77, 140
Cowles, Gardner, 220
Cowley, Malcolm, 272
credit: and National Credit Corporation, 206, 218–20, 252, 365; and Hoover's plans, 214, 259–60, 287, 366
Crusaders, 246
Cummins, Albert, 72
Curtis, Charles, 1, 17, 18, 26
Cutler, Leland W., 47

Davis, James J., 29, 156
Dawes, Charles G., 15, 29; and naval
limitation, 102–6, 345; on stock market,
126; and Hoover, 178, 187–88, 386;
and European financial crisis, 190–93,
204; and National Credit Corporation,
220, 221; and economic upswing, 227
Democratic party: and Hoover, 12,
118–19, 212, 225, 237, 247, 252–53;
in 1920s, 15; on defeat, 23, 27–28; and
stock market crash, 132; and election
of 1930, 143, 150, 164–68; and use of
Republican disunity, 164–65, 271; and
party division, 215, 226, 280, 287; and
campaign of 1932, 241, 252–53, 267,
272, 274; on prohibition, 243, 249; and
Roosevelt, 250, 261–63; and economy,
258–61
Democratic Republican Party, 5
depression: and economic conferences,
129–31; and Hoover's relief programs,
131–32, 154, 180–81, 189, 206–27, 260;
as viewed in 1930, 150, 164–65,
170–71; and banking, 164, 252, 283,
290–99, 356–57; and Congress, 179–81;
and business, 220, 289–90; and
campaign of 1932, 248–49, 251, 271–75
passim; and election outcome, 275, 276,
302. *See also* banking; economy;
employment
De Re Metallica (Hoover), 17
Denman, C. B., 78
Dewey, John, 130, 178
Dickinson, L. J., 247
Disarmament Conference, 107–8, 194,
286, 303
Dixon, Joseph, 72
Dodd, William E., 130
Doheny, Edward L., 54
Dolliver, Jonathan, 72
Donovan, William J., 26, 88
Dos Passos, John, 272
Douglas, James, 298
Douglas, Paul H., 351
Dreiser, Theodore, 272
Drought Bill, 154
drought of 1930, 153–54, 180, 210, 260
"dry" states, 2, 27, 85, 91, 92, 151,
241–46. *See also* Prohibition
Dunn, R. G., 130

economy: in the early 1920s, 7–8, 124;
Hoover on, 39, 55, 209, 253–59 *passim*,
277; and farming, 69, 74–81, 260; and
crisis of 1929, 123–33; and Hoover's

relief plans, 131–32, 154, 180–81, 189,
210–15; and tariff, 134–49; and
employment, 151, 155–58, 170, 180–81;
in 1930, 152, 160, 164, 170–74; in
Europe, 182–95, 209, 224, 250; and
currency hoarding, 207, 221–22, 264,
292, 382; and Reconstruction Finance
Corporation, 216–20, 225, 252; and
campaign of 1932, 241, 246, 247, 248,
252, 274; and banking crisis of 1933,
288–99, 302. *See also* private enterprise
Edge, Walter, 26, 284
Eighteenth Amendment, 19, 82–96,
241–49, 288. *See also* Prohibition
Electrical Utilities Committee, 152
Emergency Construction Bill, 154
Emergency Employment Bill, 170
employment: in 1930, 48, 133, 151, 160,
170; and Hoover's relief plans, 129–30,
155–58, 210–15; and Congressional
disagreement, 180; in 1931, 221, 229;
and veterans, 232, 261; Hoover on,
254; and Hoover vs. Roosevelt, 262–63;
in 1932, 279, 283, 290, 292
Enemy Trading Act, 296
Europe: and Hoover, 11, 207; and
League of Nations, 98; and financial
crisis, 107, 179, 182–95, 250–52; and
Federal Reserve Board, 123. *See also*
France; Great Britain
Export Bonus plan, 74
exports, *see* foreign trade

Fall, Albert B., 54–55
Farley, James A., 303
Farm Bill, 74–81 *passim*
Farm Board: and McNary–Haugen Bill,
71; establishment and purpose of,
72–79; and depression, 80–81, 260;
bankers' opinion of, 151; and election
of 1930, 161; Borah on, 174; and
Hoover, 189, 247, 352; Lowden on, 342
Farm Relief, 44
Farmers' Party, 173
Farmers' Union, 141
farming, *see* agriculture
Federal Land Banks, 206, 214, 260
Federal Oil Conservation Board, 56–57
Federal Power Commission: and water
resources, 62, 352
Federal Reserve Banks, 252
Federal Reserve Board, 123, 156, 292,
296, 297
Federal Reserve System, 125, 128, 189,
206, 222, 372

Feis, Herbert, 293
Fess, Simeon D., 17, 244, 257, 347;
    Hoover and, 45, 115, 292
Finance Committee, Senate, 139, 141, 350
financial crisis, *see* depression; economy
Fish Committee, 229, 238
Fisher, Irving, 130
Fisheries, Bureau of, 66
Fletcher, Henry P., 142
Fleur, Walter, 206
Food Administration, 11, 29, 75
Fordney–McCumber Tariff Bill, 8
foreign relations, 97–108; and war debt
    moratorium, 185–95, 205, 251–52,
    284–86; and nonrecognition policy,
    250–51, 360; and "interregnum," 282
Foreign Relations Committee, 104
foreign service, 101, 108
foreign trade, 76, 77, 78, 156
Forest Service, 338
Foster, William Z., 272
France: and Hoover, 11; and naval
    limitation, 106; and financial crisis,
    183; and war debts, 185, 191–92, 252,
    284–86, 359; and Laval, 204–5
Frank, Waldo, 272
Frazier, Lynn V., 77, 114, 135, 145

Gannett, Frank E., 242–44
Garfield, James R., 61, 245
Garfield Commission, 61
Garner, John Nance, 149, 206, 212, 218,
    227
Garner Bill, 223
Garner–Wagner Relief Bill, 225
Gary, Eugene B., 14
Georgia, 12
Germany, 183–84, 192–93, 251, 266, 357
Gibson, Harvey, 206
Gibson, Hugh, 29, 102, 108
Gillett, Frederick H., 114
Glass, Carter, 114
Glass Banking Bill, 287
Glass–Steagall Bill, 222
Glassford, Pelham D., 232, 233, 235, 236,
    237
Goff, Guy D., 17
gold standard: and Great Britain, 184,
    195, 203–7 *passim*, 252; and hoarding,
    207, 221–22, 264, 292, 382; and the
    United States, 259, 295, 297, 359; and
    Europe, 286
Good, James W., 29
government: Hoover's view of, 11, 59,
    152, 209, 262, 301; vs. politics, 15;

distrust of, 82; and dishonesty, 125;
    and economy, 209; reorganization of,
    381
Grand Coulee Dam, 61
Great Britain: Hoover's experience in, 11;
    and naval limitations, 102–6; and
    economic crisis, 183–84, 195, 203, 204,
    252, 266; and financial aid, 264; and
    World Economic Conference, 286–87;
    and debt mission, 295
Greece, 346
Green, William, 130, 176
Grubb, William, 87
Grundy, Joseph R., 114, 137–43 *passim*

Haas, Harry J., 219
Haiti, 100, 108, 201
Hanna, Mark, 5
Harding, Warren G., 5, 6, 7, 12, 18, 20,
    98, 177; scandals under, 8, 16, 54
Harrison, Pat, 221
Haugen, Gilbert N., 74
Hawks, Frank, 51
Hearst, William Randolph, 6
Herter, Christian, 304
Heywood, Scott, 58
Hill, John W., 159
Hill, William H., 18, 155, 267, 334
Hilles, Charles D., 185, 240, 289
Hitler, Adolph, 295
Hoar, George F., 72
Home Building and Home Ownership
    Conference, 155
Home Loan Discount Banks, 214, 222
Honduras, British, 103
Hoover, Herbert: inauguration of, 1, 25,
    30–31, 82; and Johnson, 2, 46–47, 74,
    269–70, 371; experience of, 10–14, 23,
    35; and Republican party, 12–25,
    31–32, 44, 134–49, 163, 169–81; and
    leadership abilities, 32–33, 44, 48,
    115–16, 160–61, 167, 207, 216, 265,
    275, 278; personal characteristics of,
    33–38, 132; and Stimson, 35, 197–200,
    258, 283–84, 289; and the "New Day,"
    39–51; and Borah, 49, 92–96, 104, 105,
    148, 173–75, 269; on conservation,
    52–67; on the farm crisis, 68–81; on
    prohibition, 82–96, 240–46; and
    League of Nations, 97–98; and foreign
    relations, 99–101, 182–205; and naval
    limitations, 102–6; and the tariff,
    110–22, 134–44; and the stock market
    crash, 123–33; and Supreme Court
    appointments, 144–47; and

Congressional election of 1930, 150–68; and emergency economic program, 209–27; and Bonus Expeditionary Force, 231–37; and campaign of 1932, 239–72; and election of 1932, 272–78; and Roosevelt, 279–99, 379; and use of conferences, 349
Hoover Dam, 63, 340
"Hoover Doctrine," 197
House of Representatives, U.S., 23, 110, 116–17, 168, 179–80, 211, 215, 226, 288. *See also* Congress, U.S.
Houston, David, 206
Hughes, Charles Evans, 46, 87, 144–45; and Hoover, 13, 26, 29, 55, 290
Hull, Cordell, 345
Hunt, Edward Eyre, 14, 37, 304
Hurley, Pat, 203, 233–35, 246
Huston, Claudius, 45
Hyde, Arthur M., 29, 78, 153

Idaho, 72
Illinois, 85, 153
Immigration Act, 90
imports, *see* foreign trade
inaugural address (Hoover): quoted, 25, 82; and law enforcement, 31, 86–87
independents, 7, 19, 113, 114, 120, 148, 222, 268
Indiana, 153
industrial society: and the farmer, 69–70, 72, 120; and coercion, 128–29; and the depression, 129, 131, 180, 256, 357; and unemployment, 157; and Democratic party, 274
insurgent Republicans: history of, 5–9, 72–73; and farmers, 72, 77; on tariff, 111–12, 116, 119–21, 134–44; and Supreme Court appointments, 144–47; and failure to control party, 148–49; and third party, 172–77 *passim*; and Seventy-second Congress, 212; and campaign of 1932, 269, 273
Interior Department, 29, 62, 163, 182, 223
"interregnum," 264, 281–99
Iowa, 72, 153, 258–59
isolationism, 22, 104, 205–6, 273
Italy, 106

Japan: and naval limitations, 106; Hoover's view of, 195–96, 199, 201–3; and South Manchurian Railway, 196;

and aggression, 108, 196–201, 206, 295; Stimson's view of, 361, 362
Jefferson, Thomas, 4, 5
John Hay Agreement, 197
Johnson, Hiram W., 8, 29, 134; as Hoover's opponent, 2, 19, 46–47, 74, 105, 269–70, 371; on farm relief, 77; on naval limitation, 105–6; as independent, 113, 114; and tariff, 137–38, 140; against Supreme Court appointments, 145; and Democrats, 226–27; and prohibition plank, 242
Johnson, Percy, 206
Jones, Jesse H., 23, 26, 218, 220
Jones, Wesley L., 114, 115
Jones Bill, 84
Jordan, David Starr, 17
Joslin, Theodore G., 184, 195, 204, 216–17, 228, 231–32, 294
Justice, Department of, 85–93 *passim*, 163, 223

Kansas, 57, 72, 153
Kellogg, Frank W., 29, 272
Kellogg, Paul U., 178
Kellogg–Briand pact, 103, 196–97, 201–2
Kentucky, 153
Kenyon, William S., 87
King, W. H., 58
Klein, Julius, 130
Kredit-Anstalt, 108, 183, 251
Krock, Arthur, 32, 126, 295, 296

labor: and Republicans, 15, 16; as national group, 120; and economic conferences, 130, 251; and Hoover's relief plans, 131, 155–56, 180; on Supreme Court appointment, 146, 147; and Progressives, 172; and Democrats, 274
Labor, Department of, 29, 151
Labor Party, 173
LaFollette, Robert M.: as Progressive candidate, 6, 8, 172; as insurgent, 72–73, 77; on naval treaty, 106; against Hughes' Supreme Court appointment, 145; Hoover's view of, 264; on the bonus, 367
La Gorce, James Oliver, 232
La Guardia, Fiorello, 367
lame-duck amendment, 377
Lamont, Robert P., 29, 129, 156
Lamont, Thomas W., 185, 206, 219, 298
Latin America, 99–101, 344

Laval, Pierre, 204–5
law enforcement: and inaugural address, 31, 82; of prohibition, 84–96, 353; and National Law Enforcement Commission, 86–87, 90–91, 144; and Hoover vs. Borah, 92–96; and "interregnum," 282
League of Nations: and Hoover, 97–98, 347; and World Court, 106–8; and problems in Far East, 196–97, 199–200, 203, 206
League of Nations Covenant, 8, 102, 111
Legge, Alexander, 78–79, 153, 353
Lemann, Monte, 87
Lincoln, Abraham, 5, 21, 24, 28, 190
Lincoln–Roosevelt League, 270
Lindbergh, Charles, 51
Lindsay, Sir Ronald, 284–85, 290
Lippmann, Walter, 202, 212, 251
Literary Digest, 206, 250, 267
Loesch, Frank J., 87
London Conference on Naval Limitation, 103–4
London Naval Treaty (1930), 105–6, 353
Long, Huey, 58, 264, 287
Longworth, Nicholas, 26
Los Angeles Times, 47
Louisiana, 85
Lowden, Frank O., as Republican presidential nominee, 9, 14–15, 70–71; and farm bill, 79–80; and Hoover, 178, 270–71

MacArthur, Douglas, 233–35, 369, 370
McCarthy, Wilson, 220
McCormick, Anne O'Hare, 150, 192, 208, 231, 256
McCormick, Paul, 87
MacDonald, Ramsay, 64, 102–3
McKellar, Kenneth D., 106, 130
McKelvie, Samuel, 78
McKinley, William, 4, 6, 7, 21
MacKintosh, Kenneth, 87
McNary, Charles L., 26, 68, 74, 76, 114
McNary–Haugen Bill, 70–71
Manchuria, 196, 200–202, 206, 384
Mann Act, 90
Marvin, Thomas, 117–18
Maryland, 84
Mason, Julian, 240
Massachusetts, 84
Mellon, Andrew: and Hoover, 13, 19, 28, 29; and building program, 63–64; and law enforcement, 88; and economics, 123, 155, 185–86

Memoirs: The Great Depression (Hoover), 233, 338
Meyer, Eugene, 217, 218, 220, 221, 297, 364
Michelson, Charles, 26, 119, 165, 271, 336
Michigan, 12, 45, 84, 293
Milbank, Jeremiah, 45, 247, 268
Mills, Ogden: and Hoover, 10, 19, 26; on war debts, 185–86, 194; and economics, 204, 218, 220, 221, 292; and campaign of 1932, 245, 248, 268; on Hoover and Roosevelt, 284, 299; and Woodin, 293; and banking crisis, 298
Minnesota, 72
Missouri, 153
Mitchell, Charles E., 125, 293
Mitchell, W. C., 130
Mitchell, William DeWitt, 29, 145, 163, 236
Moffat, J. P., 205
Moley, Raymond, 284, 298
Monroe Doctrine, 100–101
Montana, 57, 153
Morgan, J. P., 185
Morrow, Dwight, 103, 164
Moses, George H., 17, 106, 112, 114, 347
Muscle Shoals project, 8, 62–63

Narcotics Act, 89
Nation, 277
National Association for the Advancement of Colored People, 146–47
National Credit Corporation, 206, 214, 218–20, 252, 365
National Grange, 141
national parks, 64–66
National Park Service, 64
National Progressive League, 269
National Timber Conservation Board, 65
nationalism, 303
Naval Arms Conference (1922), 98
naval limitation, 102–6, 345
Naval Treaty (1930), 105–6
Navy, Department of, 29
Nebraska, 72, 153, 158
Nevada, 48
"New Day," 21, 39, 42–43, 265, 282, 305, 338
New Deal, 61, 282
New Era, 124, 338
New Mexico, 48, 57
New Republic, 174, 277
New York (state), 48, 190, 222

New York City, 84, 127
New York Herald Tribune, 91, 107, 224
New York Times: on political parties, 12;
  on Hoover, 20, 32, 150, 213, 249, 277,
  296–97; on naval treaty, 106; and
  Nicholas Roosevelt, 108; on the tariff,
  141; on Parker, 147; and Stimson's
  letter on Japan, 202; and
  Reconstruction Finance Corporation
  Bill, 217; on Roosevelt, 295–96
New York World, 26, 163
Newspapers, *see* press *and individual
  newspapers by name*
Newton, Walter H., 43, 45, 116
Nicaragua, 100, 201
Nine-Power Treaty of 1922, 196, 201, 360
nonrecognition doctrine, 201–3, 250–51,
  360
Norbeck, Peter, 76–77, 114, 135, 145
Norris, George W.: background of, 6, 8,
  17, 113, 114, 115; and Hoover, 17,
  73–74, 253, 264, 269–70, 335; and
  water supply bill, 62–63; and
  conservation, 67; on farm relief, 77;
  and naval treaty, 106; and Hughes,
  145; as insurgent Republican, 148, 172,
  175–76; and election of 1930, 158, 166;
  popularity of, 354
North Dakota, 72
Nye, Gerald, 70, 77, 135, 145

Ohio, 153
oil conservation, 47, 53, 56–57, 338
Oklahoma, 57–58
Old Guard, 142
Orient, *see* China; Japan
Overman, Lee S., 113, 114

Palmer, A. Mitchell, 233
Pan-American Commercial Conference,
  209
Parker, John J., 144–47, 174, 352
Parmentier, Jean, 191
Patman, Wright, 231
patronage system, 16, 46, 115
Pearson, Paul M., 182
Pell, John, 150–51
Pennsylvania, 48, 85, 236
People's Legislative Service, 172
Perkins, Thomas N., 185
Peru, 100
Petroleum Conference (1929), 54, 57–58

Philippine Independence Bill, 288, 380
political parties: usefulness of, 3–7; and
  Hoover, 25, 31–32, 164, 300–301; and
  economic interests, 120–21. *See also*
  third parties *and individual parties by
  name*
politics, 11, 15, 23, 113, 261
Pound, Dean Roscoe, 87
Pratt, William V., 103
President's Conference on
  Unemployment, 14
presidents, U.S.: before Hoover, 4–9, 20,
  21; and third parties, 176–77
press, 6, 39, 160; Hoover's use of, 41–42,
  221, 338. *See also individual
  newspapers by name*
Principles of Mining (Hoover), 17
private enterprise: vs. government
  control, 8, 62–63, 74; Hoover's view of,
  22, 55; businessmen's view of, 220
Progressive Party, 8, 73, 137–38, 160, 269
progressives: insurgents as, 72, 73, 119,
  148; and Hoover, 165, 333; and third
  party, 172–77
Prohibition: Democrats on, 19, 26; and
  American people, 22; California on,
  47–48, 82; controversy on, 84–96; and
  Justice Department, 85–93; and Law
  Enforcement Commission, 86–88, 91;
  Hoover's view of, 89–90, 249–50, 268;
  Borah on, 92–96; and rural America,
  95; and election of 1930, 161; and
  political parties, 226, 243; and
  campaign of 1932, 240–48, 262;
  political complications of, 244–45, 276;
  and attempt at repeal, 288
public, American: characteristics of, in
  1928, 22; and distrust of government,
  82; and understanding of world affairs,
  108–9; and Senate, 111; and Hoover,
  131, 159, 216, 236–37, 261, 306; and
  currency hoarding, 207, 221–22, 264;
  and fear, 210–11, 279–80; and bonus
  marchers, 235–36; Hoover on, 259, 282
Public Domain, Commission on the
  Conservation and Administration of
  the, 59, 60
public works, 62–63, 157–58, 225,
  262–63, 287. *See also* building program
Public Works Department, 226
Puerto Rico, 182

radio, 16, 39
railroads, 8, 154, 171, 214
Railway Employees, 156

Railway Engineers, Brotherhood of, 22
Rand, James, 294
Rankin Bill, 152–53
Rapidan Camp, 44, 64, 102–3, 184
Raskob, John J., 130, 271
Recent Economic Changes, Committee on
    (1927), 123, 156
Reclamation Act, 59
Reclamation Service, 59, 61
Reconstruction Finance Corporation:
    purpose of, 216–20, 225, 252; as
    Hoover's accomplishment, 247; and
    relief for agriculture, 260; and
    "interregnum," 287, 292, 296; and
    Eugene Meyer, 364
Recovery, the Second Effort (Salter), 291
Red Cross, 154
Reed, David, 70, 103, 140
Relief Mobilization Conference, 256
Republican National Committee, 44–45,
    46, 48, 267, 268, 375
Republican National Convention: of 1928,
    17–19, 70–71; of 1932, 241–48, 270
Republican party: historical view of, 5–9,
    16; and Hoover, 12–13, 15, 44–50, 169,
    252–54; and conservatives, 16, 31–32;
    division in, 18–19, 26, 134–49, 161–64,
    179–81, 215, 226, 271; in California,
    46–48; and domestic programs, 56, 67,
    70–81, 92; insurgents in, 72–81,
    116–21, 158, 172–79, 181, 269, 270; and
    1930 election, 143, 150, 158, 161–68,
    273–77; and 1932 campaign, 239–55,
    258, 267, 272–73
Republicanism, 16, 70, 163, 176
Requa, Mark L., 47, 57–58, 375
Resolutions Committee, 17, 245
Reynolds, Jackson, 206
Richardson, Seth, 163
Richey, Lawrence, 43, 45, 206
Rickard, Edgar, 26
Robinson, Henry M., 26, 47, 188–89; on
    foreign relations, 105, 193, 264; on
    Hoover and history, 297–98
Robinson, Joseph T., 103, 106, 218
Rolph, James, 236
Roosevelt, Franklin D.: and support of
    Hoover, 12, 30; vs. Hoover, 27, 250,
    261–63, 268–69, 345, 374, 384–85;
    and national parks, 64; as governor of
    New York, 166, 173; and public works,
    262–63; popularity of, 272–73; as
    president-elect, 280–87, 292–93; and
    banking crisis, 290–92, 294–96, 298;
    Stimson on, 384
Roosevelt, Nicholas, 108, 356

Roosevelt, Theodore: as a leader, 4, 6–7,
    24; and Progressive party, 9, 16, 172,
    176; and natural resources, 53
Root, Elihu, 26, 91, 107, 198, 202
Rules Committees, 215
Russia, 52, 98, 104, 192, 196, 379

St. Louis Globe Democrat, 248
Salter, Sir Arthur, 291
Saunders, Everett, 268, 270, 300
Schilling, William F., 78
Schwab, Charles M., 130
science, 2, 53, 263
Senate, U.S.: and party division, 8–9, 16,
    134–49, 179, 215, 222–26, 287; and
    farm relief, 44; "old guards" in, 46–47,
    140; Republican insurgents in, 72–73,
    116–21, 212, 214; and naval limitations,
    104–6; and tariff bill, 111–22, 134–44;
    view of president's power, 112–13; and
    relief programs, 131–32, 179–81,
    212–16, 220; and Supreme Court
    appointments, 144–47; and European
    crisis, 194–95; and government
    reorganization, 288. *See also*
    Republican party
Shaw, Leslie M., 136
Sherman Antitrust Act, 57
Shipping Board, 158
Shortridge, Samuel, 46, 115
Shouse, Jouett, 119, 165
Simmons, Furnifold M., 113, 114, 135–36,
    138
Sinclair, Harry F., 54
Smith, Alfred E.: as presidential
    candidate, 6, 19, 22, 25, 27, 271, 272;
    on economy, 295
Smoot, Reed, 17, 27, 113, 114, 115, 138,
    139, 143
Smoot–Hawley Tariff Act, 101, 140, 141
Social Trends, Research Committee on,
    160
socialism, 55
Socialist party: and economic change, 7;
    appeal of, 15, 21, 23; and conservation,
    67; and 1924 election, 172; and
    Republican insurgents, 173; and
    Kellogg, 178; and 1932 election, 266,
    271, 272
Socialist Workers' Party, 237
South Dakota, 72
State, Department of, 23, 108
Steffens, Lincoln, 130, 272
Stephens, Hubert D., 145

Stimson, Henry L.: and Hoover, 28–29, 99, 197–200, 258, 283–84, 289; on Latin American policy, 101; and naval limitations, 103–4; and European financial crises, 184–86, 191; and Far East, 196–97, 201–3; and bonus marchers, 235; and campaign of 1932, 248–49; on Hoover and Roosevelt, 250; and economy, 256, 290, 293–94; and Roosevelt, 283–87 *passim*, 296, 299; and war debts, 284–85; and World War II, 361
stock market crash, 119, 124–26, 128–32. *See also* depression; economy
Stone, Harlan Fiske, 24, 28, 41, 87, 145
Stone, James C., 78
Strauss, Lewis L., 247
Strawn, Silas, 268
Strother, French, 43, 161–62
Sullivan, Mark, 292, 294, 298
Sullivan, P. J., 115
Supreme Court, 50, 144–47

Tacna–Arica dispute, 100
Taft, William Howard, 1–7 *passim*, 145, 177
tariff: and division in Senate, 2, 47–48, 111–22, 134–40; Fordney–McCumber, 8; and Democrats, 27; and limited revision vs. high, 31, 110–12, 116–22, 134–44; and farmers, 76, 260; and employment, 133; and commission, 135–38; economists on, 140–43; Smoot–Hawley, 140–44; as campaign issue, 271; Hoover on, 383
Tariff Bill of 1909, 72
Tariff Commission, 135, 138, 142
taxation: in early 1920s, 8; and farmers, 75; and Hoover, 131, 212, 214, 223; and tariff, 135; and 1932 campaign, 240; and sales taxes, 287
Teague, C. C., 78–79
Teapot Dome, 55
Tennessee Valley Authority, 8, 63
Texas, 57–58
third parties: and Roosevelt, 7; and farming, 69; and Republican insurgents, 172–77; and election of 1932, 272; and tariff, 351. *See also by name*
Thomas, Norman, 23, 130, 268–69, 272, 351
Transportation Act of 1920, 171
Treasury, Department of, 85–88, 125

Trinidad, 103
Tripartite Loan Agreement, 346
Tugwell, Rexford, 294
Turner, Dan W., 372

Unemployment Conference, 14
unemployment crisis, *see* employment
Unemployment Relief Organization, 214, 251
United States: East, 16, 70, 120, 262; Middle West, 16, 72, 112, 176, 187, 189, 262; West, 16, 69, 70, 72, 119, 176, 241, 273; South, 46, 69, 70, 73. *See also* Congress, U.S.; public, American
Uruguay, 101
Utah, 57

veterans: Hoover's aid to, 152, 230, 353, 367; and Rankin Bill, 153; and Bonus Expeditionary Force, 231–37
Veterans Administration, 152
vetoes, 380
Viennese Kredit-Anstalt, 108, 183, 251
Villard, Oswald Garrison, 147
Virgin Islands, 182
Virginia, 153
Volstead Act, 82–91 *passim*, 241, 243, 249, 288. *See also* Prohibition
voters, *see* public, American

Wage Earners Protective Conference, 22
Wagner, Robert, 115
Wagner Relief Bill, 288
Walsh, David I., 106
Walsh, Thomas J., 27, 106, 113, 114, 115, 130, 139, 177–78
War Debt Commission, 98
war debts: moratorium, 185–86, 189–95, 205, 251–52, 284–86, 293; and British debt mission, 295
War, Department of, 29, 62
War Finance Corporation, 212, 217
Warren, Francis E., 113, 114
Washington, George, 3, 24, 65, 175
Washington, 48
Washington Post, 212, 227
Waters, Walter W., 232, 236
waterways, 43, 60–63, 287, 353
Watson, James E., 17, 77, 112, 114, 115, 138–39, 212, 347
Ways and Means Committee, 110, 223

West Virginia, 153
"wet" states: and 1928 campaign, 27;
    and law enforcement, 48, 84, 91, 92;
    increasing sentiment for, 166; and 1932
    campaign, 240–46, 249, 250, 371; and
    "Beer Bill," 288; and newsmen, 380.
    See also Prohibition
Wheat Corporation, 75
White, William Allen: on Hoover, 24,
    213, 277, 305; on party disunity, 120;
    and Norris, 166, 176; on emergency
    relief, 210; and Prohibition plank,
    242–43
Whitney, George, 206
Whitney, Richard, 125
Wickersham, George W., 87
Wickersham Commission, 47–48, 246
Wilbur, Ray Lyman: and Interior
    Department, 29, 52–53; and Hoover,
    47; and Petroleum Conference, 58;
    and unemployment, 156; and charges
    of dishonesty, 163; on the Virgin
    Islands, 182; on war debts, 192; and
    financial problems, 223, 226, 273
Williams, Carl, 78
Williams, Ralph, 45
Wilson, Charles S., 78

Wilson, Edmund, 272
Wilson, Hugh, 205
Wilson, Woodrow, 5, 6, 7, 17, 23, 24, 36,
    177
Wisconsin, 45, 72, 84
Woll, Matthew, 22, 141
Woodin, William, 293, 298
Work, Hubert, 28, 45
Workers' Ex-Servicemen's League, 233
Workers Party of America, 22, 229
World Bank, 185
World Court of International Justice, 31,
    106–8, 151, 247, 269, 288
World Disarmament Conference (1932),
    107–8, 194
World Economic Conference, 286–87,
    291
World War I: causing dislocation, 183;
    and war debts, 185–91; and American
    Legion, 203
World War Disability Act, 230
Wyoming, 57

Young, C. C., 46, 61
Young, Owen D., 185
Young, Roy A., 125